Science Content

Student Development

Pedagogy

Science content and pedagogy are woven together using a carefully crafted developmental approach.

274 CHAPTER 10 Using Cooperative Learning with Science Instruction

Activity 10.5 Lesson Design: Using Multiple Cooperative Learning Strategies While Classifying Rocks

Overview: In this activity, you will have your students repeat the tests they just performed (hardness, luster, streak, acid) on a group of unknown rocks and classify them. At the same time, you will design individual accountability, equal participation, simultaneous interaction, and positive interdependence into the activity.

Science content notes →

Aquarium rocks, pebbles, rock salt, marble chips, and small stones are good rock samples for students to bring to school: Earth science

Wear safety goggles when classifying rocks: Safety

Materials: An empty foam egg carton, safety goggles, a streak plate, vinegar, a magnifying glass, small rock samples (aquarium rocks, pebbles, rock salt, marble chips, small stones)

Procedure: Have your students bring in their own rock samples. Remember that rocks are made of minerals, but not always in the same amount. Using the tests they performed on the minerals, students classify the rocks. Be certain that they wear their safety goggles. Structure individual accountability, equal participation, simultaneous interaction, and positive interdependence into the lesson.

Assessment: If you can, teach the lesson to your students or your college classmates. How did it go? Compare your lessons with those of your peers. You will see that there are many different ways to structure cooperative learning into a lesson. ■

Characteristics of an Equitable Classroom

Students are likely to feel accepted in a well-managed classroom

A well-managed classroom is one in which students are more likely to feel accepted. In such a classroom, students are more likely to speak out, share opinions, and take risks. This is important because girls are often socialized by parents and teachers to be more passive than boys. If a boy has an opinion and states it freely, his behavior is culturally accepted. If a girl engages in the same behavior, she is often labeled as obnoxious, pushy, or unfeminine. In order to learn, students must ask questions and often challenge things they hear in class. As a teacher, it is important to support and encourage students who feel it is inappropriate to share an idea or express an opinion. Learning and practicing social skills helps all students participate more equally in the science classroom. You will read more about this topic after you complete the next activity.

Pedagogy notes →

Activity 10.6 Reflection: Monitoring Yourself to Ensure Equity in Your Classroom

Overview: In this activity, you will check to ensure there is equity in your classroom.

Check to ensure that there is equity in your classroom; continue to monitor yourself in this area

Procedure: Once you implement cooperative learning in your classroom, there are some questions you can ask to ensure that your classroom is an equitable one. Do boys and girls receive the same amount of attention from you in class? Do members of underrepresented groups receive the same amount of attention as those who are of majority groups? Think about comfort in the classroom. Do girls and students of underrepresented groups feel comfortable raising their hands and asking questions? Is a student ever made to feel uncomfortable if she or he gives an incorrect answer? Do students ever tease or ridicule one another in your class?

Assessment: If your classroom is not an equitable one, what can you do to improve it? ■

Science and Science Teaching

Science and Science Teaching

Science is something you can do!

Sharon J. Sherman
The College of New Jersey

Houghton Mifflin Company   Boston   New York

Senior Sponsoring Editor: Loretta Wolozin
Associate Editor: Lisa A. Mafrici
Editorial Assistant: Sarah Rodriguez
Senior Project Editor: Julie Lane
Editorial Assistant: Jennifer O'Neill
Senior Production/Design Coordinator: Jennifer Waddell
Senior Manufacturing Coordinator: Marie Barnes
Senior Marketing Manager: Pamela Laskey
Associate Marketing Manager: Jean Zielinski Demayo

Cover design by Catherine Hawkes, Cat & Mouse
Cover illustration by Leslie Evans

Grateful acknowledgment is made to the following sources for permission to reprint
selections from copyrighted material:

Quotes from *Benchmarks for Science Literacy*. Copyright © 1993 by American Association
for Advancement of Science. Reprinted by permission of Oxford University Press.

Quotes from *National Science Education Standards*. Reprinted by permission of the National
Academy Press.

Printed in the U.S.A.

Library of Congress Catalog Number: 99-71933

ISBN: 0-395-88782-8

2 3 4 5 6 7 8 9–CRW–03 02 01 00

In memory of my father, Max Sapirstein—engineer, inventor, and artist—who taught me at an early age that science was something I could "do."

Brief Contents

Contents

CHAPTER 3 Introducing the Processes of Science 55

Bringing Inquiry and Discovery to Your Classroom 57

Constructing Knowledge and Communicating Scientific Thought 74

CHAPTER 4 Guiding Inquiry 80

Children Engage in Inquiry 81

Bringing Inquiry-Based Instruction to Your Classroom 84

The Elements of Inquiry-Based Instruction 91

Your Development as an Elementary Science Teacher 100

PART TWO   Instruction and Assessment in a Standards-Based Science Classroom

CHAPTER 12 Technology as Design Knowledge: Science and Technology Education United 313

CHAPTER 14   Managing Materials and Resources in Classrooms: All Those Critters   373

Preface

For elementary school teachers, teaching science is often a daunting task. Teachers frequently have preconceived notions that science is a subject that is difficult to understand and particularly challenging to teach. *Science and Science Teaching* attempts to dispel these notions. Its mission is to welcome all teachers into the world of science teaching, and especially to help novice teachers to become a part of the community of science educators. Filled with hands-on, minds-on activities that are easy to prepare and bring to students, each chapter integrates content and pedagogy in an interesting and understandable way. The text puts science into action and makes it an exciting subject. It shows teachers that science is "something they can do."

My primary goal is to lessen science anxiety and help teachers develop confidence in their ability to tackle this subject. I have thus designed this text so that it is useful for both preservice and inservice teachers studying methods of teaching science. My approach was developed from nearly three decades of experience in helping students learn and teach science. This text introduces readers to scientists, master teachers, and administrators who aim to convince them that scientists are "real" people and science is a natural part of their everyday lives. The goal is to shatter the stereotype of scientists as strange creatures who are far removed from reality and to eliminate the false notion that only geniuses can engage in science. By starting with a nonthreatening, do-able approach, teachers can enjoy teaching science from the outset.

A Developmental Approach

Written specifically to address the developmental needs of novice teachers who are gaining expertise in the field, this text distills basic science ideas, blends them with simple instructional strategies, and enables new teachers to practice as they engage in activities in elementary and middle school classrooms or in their own college classrooms. Once they have mastered the basics, beginning teachers move on to learn and teach more advanced concepts and experiment with more complex instructional strategies. This text is intended to nurture the novice teacher, build confidence, and foster development in the profession.

Broad Coverage of Content and Pedagogy

Topical coverage includes examination of the nature of science; a focus on the processes of science; and applications of life, physical, and earth and space science, as well as educational technology, technology as design and problem solving, and safety in the science classroom. These topics are suggested by the *National Science Education Standards* and *Benchmarks for Science Literacy: Project 2061*. The use of the computer as a tool for teaching and learning is threaded throughout the book and is prevalent in each chapter. Children's literature is integrated into many science activities, and each chapter includes a list of children's books that relate to the science ideas covered in the chapter. Resources for teachers, both print and electronic, accompany each chapter.

Science Content and Pedagogy Entwined

In *Science and Science Teaching,* content and pedagogy are joined, with science domains threaded throughout the book. The content domains are vehicles for discussing instructional strategies and are used for pedagogical purposes. Pedagogical coverage includes learning to deliver inquiry-based instruction; creating standards-based lesson plans; linking instruction and assessment; designing performance assessments; using a variety of teaching strategies, including cooperative learning, learning styles, and multiple intelligences; and integrating science across the curriculum. Also covered are strategies for including students with special needs in the regular classroom and ways to work with students who are gifted or talented.

Interpreting Theory Through the Lens of a Practitioner's Eye

To begin, I speak directly to the novice teacher, both as an educator and a member of the community of science educators, using an informal, conversational style. New teachers need knowledge of theory and practice, but these are often like two separate floors of a building with no staircase to join them. *Science and Science Teaching* builds that staircase. It interprets theory through the lens of a practitioner's eye, always mindful of the developmental needs of the teacher. It includes over one hundred hands-on, minds-on activities and opportunities for reflection, problem solving, scientific thinking, and use of technology in teaching. Master teachers give practical advice by sharing their expertise with those who are just beginning their careers.

Building Science Content Knowledge and Confidence

Elementary and middle school science teachers often feel more comfortable with life or earth and space science and shy away from physical science, which is sometimes perceived as being cold and impersonal. As a result, teachers often shortchange themselves and their students in this science content area. For this reason I introduce physical science early in the text, using examples that are more palatable for teachers. For example, change of state can be taught with chemicals. It can also be taught by allowing chocolate to melt and become a liquid and then solidify. Density can be taught by using cylinders made of different metals. It can also be taught by floating corks, cubes of butter, toy boats, and aluminum foil barges in water. These are some of the ways in which the text focuses on helping teachers learn to develop science concepts and, more important, to feel comfortable with and enjoy teaching science. Thus, learning to teach physical science can become a metaphor for all teachers' competence to become knowledgeable science teachers. Throughout the text, science is related to real life, building connections and making science meaningful.

Lessening Science Anxiety by Becoming a Resourceful Learner

Today there is an emphasis on enabling teachers to learn new content on their own. By engaging in discussions with colleagues, contacting experts via the Internet, and taking workshops and courses, teachers develop strategies for accessing new content knowledge. When they don't know or understand a science concept, they have avenues for learning. This healthy behavior is intended to replace feelings of fear and panic that commonly cause science anxiety and lead teachers to shy away from science teaching. Rather than attempting to teach huge amounts of science content in one text and one course, teachers learn how to *learn* science. This is like the ancient Chinese proverb that says, "If I give you a fish you eat for a day, but if I teach you to fish you eat for a lifetime." Today's teachers will encounter so much new content knowledge in their professional lives that they must be motivated to learn more science on their own. Their experiences in life, high school courses, and college science courses, as well as in workshops and graduate courses, serve as the basis for their content background. This text ties that content to pedagogy and motivates teachers to "keep on learning."

Text Organization and Key Themes

To become confident, competent science teachers, novices must develop knowledge of content, pedagogy, and developmentally appropriate practice. These three strands are carefully woven together throughout the text. The text is divided into three parts. Part One provides background knowledge for science teaching. Part Two focuses on instruction and assessment in a standards-based science classroom. Part Three concentrates on curriculum and its integration in science teaching. Each chapter focuses on several different ideas and begins with essential questions, which are addressed in the chapter.

Chapter 1 describes several inquiry-based science classrooms, discusses the importance of assessment, introduces the reader to science standards, focuses on the role of research in science teaching and learning, and discusses the importance of instructional technology and technology as design knowledge.

Helping New Teachers Develop Science Literacy

Science teachers must develop science literacy. State and national standards documents assert that teachers should understand some of the key concepts and principles of science and be familiar with the natural world. They must develop a capacity for scientific ways of thinking. *Science and Science Teaching* puts that goal into action. Beginning with Chapter 1, teachers are introduced to scientific thinking. Chapter 2 is devoted to science and scientists. Here teachers meet four scientists: a Nobel laureate, a life scientist, an earth scientist, and a physical scientist. The scientists speak directly to the reader, sharing stories about their own work and providing simple activities for the college or elementary/middle school classroom. These activities are interesting, engaging, and thought provoking. They are designed to provide motivation for learning more. Chapter 2 focuses on the meaning of science and science literacy, and provides insight into how scientists think and work.

Becoming Familiar with the Processes of Science

Chapter 3 includes more than a dozen activities to familiarize teachers with the processes of science. It builds on the ideas presented in Chapters 1 and 2 and helps students develop their understanding of scientific thinking. Later chapters focus on life, earth, space, and physical science topics with more complex ideas introduced as simple ideas are mastered. Chapter 3 introduces the science process skills and provides opportunities for practicing scientific thinking.

Delivering Inquiry-Based Instruction

Science is about inquiry. It is about asking questions and searching for answers. Inquiry teaching is an essential element of science education. It is often difficult for *new* teachers to set up inquiry-based classrooms. That is partly because the classroom in which students explore and ask questions, direct their own learning, work cooperatively with others, and discover new things often looks disorganized. What can be the issue for novices? Most administrators and many host teachers like order. They don't like noise. New teachers fear chaos in the classroom and losing control of their students. They lack established routines that work seamlessly to moderate students at work in active inquiry environments. The ability to develop inquiry-based instruction develops along a continuum. Chapter 4 introduces the elements of inquiry-based instruction and covers such topics as how to move from teacher-directed inquiry to student-directed inquiry, ways to motivate students in the science classroom, questioning skills, techniques for uncovering preconceived notions about science concepts, and how to help students make sense of their explorations.

Novice teachers can move from teacher-directed inquiry, a sort of step-by-step approach, to more student-centered methods. Starting with teacher-directed inquiry allows them to experiment with inquiry teaching while maintaining order and control in the classroom. They have control of the materials, can practice supervising distribution and collection, and can monitor students with ease. Once they have mastered this technique, they move on to practice implementing student-centered methods whereby they act as facilitators and co-inquirers, not lecturers who remain at the center of attention.

This book describes the continuum and provides many activities to enable new teachers to practice inquiry teaching. This gives them the confidence to allow their students to engage in inquiry and discovery as described in the science standards. The text also provides ways to implement inquiry-based science in schools with low budgets. My extensive experience in underfunded, inner-city elementary schools has given me years of experience with such classrooms. This is an unfortunate reality in many urban, rural, and suburban schools in the nation. Teachers need to be creative to bring inquiry-based science education to all students.

Building a Constructivist Base

In Chapter 5, students read about the theory of Jean Piaget, who emphasizes the child's personal construction of reality and actual developmental level, and the work of Lev Vygotsky, who extended Piaget's teachings to include the influence of language, interaction with adults, and the social and economic system. Chapter 5 addresses constructivist theory and its relation to science teaching, focusing on the work of cognitive psychologists. It shows teachers what a constructivist classroom looks like and puts theory into practice.

Planning, Teaching, and Assessing

Chapters 6, 7, and 8 focus on planning for instruction, linking instruction and assessment, and designing performance-based assessments. These three topics are closely linked, and mastery of the ideas presented in these chapters is essential in creating a standards-based science classroom. These chapters focus on writing lesson plans; planning units; using assessment to scaffold instruction; and developing performance tasks, response formats, and scoring systems. Readers use journals, science logs, portfolios, and observation checklists. They also learn basic information about diagnostic, formative, and summative assessment.

Including All Learners

Chapter 9 focuses on including all learners in the science classroom. This very practical chapter offers classroom-tested ways to engage students with different abilities, learning styles, and interests. The activities provide practice in designing lessons to include all learners, with a focus on students with learning disabilities as well as those who are gifted or talented.

Using Cooperative Learning

Chapter 10 is about using cooperative learning in the science classroom. It too is a very practical chapter. It discusses cooperative learning theory, but focuses predominantly on ways to plan lessons that incorporate cooperative learning strategies. Dozens of strategies are described, and the beginning teacher has many opportunities to plan science lessons that use cooperative learning.

Focus on Educational Technology

Chapter 11 focuses on using educational technology (also referred to as *instructional technology*)—the computer as a tool for teaching and learning—in the classroom. It provides basic information about the Internet, describes different types of software available for science classrooms, and suggests dozens of uses of instructional technology. Its topical coverage is quite thorough, and it lists many high-quality web sites that are essential for teaching science.

The Designed World

Chapter 12 is about technology as design and problem solving. Technology education involves teaching your students to solve problems and satisfy human needs and wants in a practical way. To determine just what these needs and wants are, a wide range of factors must be considered simultaneously, so technology brings together, or integrates, many different subject areas. This chapter introduces the design loop as a problem-solving strategy and teaches readers to use this technique in addition to the processes of science. As in the other chapters, numerous activities are available for practice.

Science Across the Curriculum

Chapter 13 deals with integrating science across the curriculum. Integrating science across the curriculum is a practical tool teachers can use to help their students see meaningful connections between science and the other subjects they study. It breaks the barriers between subjects, unifies disciplines, connects lessons to real-life experiences, and brings teachers together to collaborate in creating interdisciplinary units and lessons. Chapter 13 contains many examples of science integrated with other disciplines. It provides opportunities for hands-on practice and use of online resources to expand topical coverage.

Managing Resources

Chapter 14 focuses on managing resources in the science classroom. It's about safely handling critters of all sorts, and it provides information about many of the science kits and curriculum packages on the market today. It focuses on safety precautions to take when working with animals, plants, and chemicals, and talks about handling a variety of critters in the classroom. Hands-on activities give novice teachers experience with bringing plants and animals into the classroom. Internet resources broaden topical coverage.

Pedagogical Elements

Opening Stories

Each chapter opens with an interesting story that connects to the theme of the chapter. The stories are about real people who share important ideas with the reader. In these stories novice teachers hear from master teachers, beginning teachers, a Nobel laureate, and a student who grew up with technology. The stories lead into the focusing questions.

Focusing Questions

Each chapter begins with a set of focusing questions. These questions invite the reader to think about what is to come. They serve as objectives that will be met in the pages that follow.

Activities

Science and Science Teaching is filled with more than one hundred activities. There are *hands-on activities* that illustrate science concepts, *online activities* that integrate technology into lessons, *problem-solving opportunities* that foster thinking, and *lesson design* activities in which the teacher creates new lessons. Each activity has an overview, a materials list, a procedure, and an assessment. Most assessments are performance based. The activities can be used by the professor in the college classroom or by the novice teacher in the elementary or middle school classroom.

Standards Boxes

Each chapter shows how to put national and state standards into action. Standards boxes reference particular standards and show how the standards work when implemented in the classroom.

Standards Marginal Icons

A special icon located in the margin calls attention to places where standards are either discussed or implemented in the classroom.

Constructing Your Knowledge of Science and Science Teaching

Each chapter ends with a summary that asks the reader to reflect on the topics covered in the chapter and presents a new set of focusing questions. Through this process, the reader constructs his or her own knowledge of science and science teaching.

Key Terms

Each chapter contains a list of key terms. Each term is referenced to the page(s) on which it is discussed.

Questions, Extensions, Applications, and Explorations

At the end of each chapter are questions for further study. Sometimes there is research to do, a phone number to call for resources, a web site to check out, or something to think about. This section extends, applies, and explores further the ideas presented in the chapter.

Suggested Resources

To assist the new teacher in gathering resources to implement the content and pedagogy in each chapter, a list of resources, both print and electronic, is included. The electronic resources were verified just before this text went to press, but online resources change frequently, so if you log onto a site and it isn't there, it may have moved or been removed. In that case, carry out an Internet search on your own and locate a new site that covers the same topic.

References

The references for each citation in the text appear at the end of the text.

Tables, Figures, and Photos

Numerous tables, figures, and photos appear throughout the text to clarify the content and make it more meaningful.

Margin Notes

Science content notes and pedagogy notes appear in the margins throughout the text. These are intended to reinforce important concepts and stimulate thought and reflection. Science notes reinforce the science content. They are classified by discipline: life, physical, and earth and space science. Science and mathematics, technology, and safety are also noted. Pedagogy notes call out the pedagogical techniques covered in the text.

Glossary

A glossary defining key science content and pedagogy appears at the end of the text.

Index

A very thorough index developed by Alan Sherman, experienced scientist and author, appears at the end of the text. It is more detailed than the usual index and is designed to help the reader find activities, stories, and people.

Acknowledgments

Science and Science Teaching is a user-friendly text that will serve as a valuable tool for learning to teach science in the elementary and middle school. Many people worked with me to make this text a reality, and I would like to acknowledge their contributions.

First, I want to thank the wonderfully talented people at Houghton Mifflin. For nearly 25 years my husband, Alan, and I have been Houghton Mifflin authors, writing textbooks in the college chemistry division and working with a fine group of professionals. One of these exemplary professionals is Deborah Seme, senior sales representative. Debby visited me at The College of New Jersey and asked me to think about writing a science methods text. She was persistent, and I eventually agreed to meet Loretta Wolozin, senior sponsoring editor, who traveled to New Jersey to meet me and think through the ideas behind *Science and Science Teaching*. Our many conference calls helped me to focus my thoughts, and her suggestions and ideas strengthened my work. She assembled an outstanding team and paid careful attention to detail throughout the project. Above all, I am impressed by Loretta's total commitment to bringing the highest-quality textbooks to today's college students. Lisa Mafrici, associate editor, was a joy to work with. Her thoughtful ideas, extensive knowledge of the field, support, and superb organizational skills kept the project going. Elaine Silverstein, developmental editor, helped me analyze and synthesize the content. She took 14 rough-draft chapters and helped me turn them into finished products. Julie Lane, production editor, played a major role in the project. She organized all aspects of production, made sure the deadlines were met, paid careful attention to detail, and was a pleasure to work with. Jennifer O'Neill and Sarah Rodriguez assisted with a variety of tasks related to production and handled them well. I would also like to thank the many reviewers whose comments and suggestions were crucial in improving my work. They are William Boone, Indiana University; William Croasdale, University of Rhode Island; Daniel Dobey, SUNY Fredonia; James J. Gallagher, Michigan State University; Patricia Morrell, University of Portland; Douglas Zook, Boston University.

Next, I would like to thank the students who worked with me on this project and inspired me to keep on writing. Amari Verastegui assisted with research and offered constant motivation. Amy Burr assisted with research and shared her lessons with me. Theresa Lupo assisted with the initial organizational phase of the project and helped me get started. Kate Schmidt took charge of research in children's literature. David "Freddy" Friedrich shared his ideas and lessons, and often popped into my office to see how the project was going. Karen Schaffroth and Janel Braun shared their lesson ideas, as did Christina Campagna and Amy Davis. Lynette Catalano shared her cooperative learning strategies, and Tom Terzano and Kristen Hellmers shared their experiences in teaching with technology. Meredith Saltiel, a special learner and a very special person, enriched my classroom and enabled me to learn more about including students with disabilities.

There are many others I would like to thank, beginning with the master teachers. Linda Zalewitz shared her thoughts on an ongoing basis, critiqued my work, helped me solve problems, and contributed to the text. Norine Seiden, science supervisor, shared her expertise and supported me throughout the project. Kathy Dullea and Carol Olsen were eager to share their work with the readers. Steve Wulfson, software editor for *Science and Children*, generously donated his time, allowing me to interview him for Chapter 11. Roseann Howarth, Diane Glace, and the students at Rutgers Preparatory School were happy to share their work with me.

Next, I would like to thank the scientists who contributed to this text. My good friend Russell Hulse of Princeton University listened to my ideas, critiqued my work, and shared his thoughts with readers. After winning the Nobel Prize in Physics, Russell developed a deep interest in science education, and I applaud his devotion to making available meaningful science experiences for teachers and students. I thank my colleagues at The College of New Jersey, Marcia O'Connell and Martin Becker, for allowing me to interview them and for sharing their own stories with readers. Thanks to Jill Foley for taking the time from her graduate studies at Princeton to address our readers. I thank my colleagues Robert Weber and Ron Todd of The College of New Jersey and Gregory Camilli of Rutgers University who brainstormed ideas with me. Special thanks go to Dean Suzanne Pasch, Associate Dean Lawrence Marcus, and my colleagues at the School of Education at The College of New Jersey for their support and encouragement. Thanks to the FIRSL committee at TCNJ for sponsoring my research for this text. I would also like to thank the teachers and students in classrooms in The College of New Jersey's Professional Development School Network who hosted my student teachers and invited me into their classrooms to test my ideas. Special thanks go to my secretaries Thomasine Preston, Edilma Evans, and Carol Tamasi, who assisted me in many ways. Thanks to Trenton High School student Roy Preston III who worked with me as I checked web addresses for the Instructor's Resource Manual.

Finally, I thank my family. My husband, Alan, who shares my interest in science and love for writing, supported and encouraged me from the start of the project to the finish. He read the completed manuscript, offered comments, assisted with proofreading, and created the index, for which I am very grateful. My sons, Robert and Michael, were involved in the project as well. Rob wrote the first draft of Chapter 11 and shared his story about growing up with technology. Mike offered constant motivation as I wrote, considered my ideas from the perspective of a college student, and at the same time decided that he would write his first book, which is almost done. I would also like to thank my mother, Gertrude; my "stepfather," Bernard; my sister, Pam; my brother in-law, Howard; and my nephews, Mark and Scott, for being such an important part of my life. Thanks to Lauren Pachman for her support via e-mail. In closing I would like to remember several very special people who influenced me. They are Isidore, Gussie, and Louis; Rose and Sam; Ethel and Bernard; Norma and Joe; Florence and David; Faye and Dick; Abraham, Mickey, and Warren.

S.J.S.

Science and Science Teaching

Background Knowledge for Science Teaching

Part One provides background knowledge for science teaching. You will begin by visiting active, effective, inquiry-based elementary science classrooms. You will learn science content, methods of instruction, and developmentally appropriate practice. You will learn about life, physical, and earth and space science, meet several scientists, and think about what makes a scientifically literate person. You will build a foundation for inquiry-based teaching so that your classroom is one in which students ask questions, experiment, develop their own theories about how the world works, communicate their ideas to others, debate, discuss, reflect on the experience, and enjoy science.

CHAPTER 1

In the Elementary Science Classroom

In this chapter I invite you to join me as I observe four active elementary science classrooms led by novice teachers. In these classrooms, students have the freedom to explore and to question. This enhances their awareness of the natural world as their teachers help them develop a healthy respect and responsibility for their environment. When they encounter a new situation, students have many different avenues for learning. The novice teacher does not have all of the answers. His or her elementary science classroom is one in which everyone learns—even the teacher. As students learn, they share what they have learned with one another, and they connect that new knowledge to their existing knowledge of the world.

We'll first visit a kindergarten where students are involved in color mixing, then a sixth grade where a culminating lesson on aeronautics is taking place, a fifth grade where students are investigating the effectiveness of yeast, and a fourth grade engaged in a WebQuest on the Internet. After visiting the elementary classrooms, we'll return to the college classroom and reflect on the field experiences. Then you'll examine the factors that shape elementary science today.

As you read the chapter, think about the answers to these questions:

1. **What does an elementary science classroom look like?**
2. **What is inquiry-based science?**
3. **How does assessment support inquiry-based instruction?**
4. **What are science education standards, and why do we need them?**
5. **What is the role of research in science teaching and learning?**
6. **What does a constructivist classroom look like?**
7. **How does a teacher serve the needs of diverse learners in the elementary science classroom?**
8. **What is the role of technology in the science classroom?**

With all of these ideas in mind, let's begin our journey into elementary science.

Kindergarten Color Mixing

The first class I visit is a kindergarten where two student teachers are team teaching. As I open the classroom door, I hear the buzz of quiet chatter. Two long tables face me, and at the tables sit 24 kindergartners. The students are working in cooperative pairs, and on the table in front of each pair is a paper plate with two lumps of white shaving cream and two popsicle sticks. A sheet of newspaper covers the desk. The kindergartners have been instructed not to touch the shaving cream and certainly not to put it in their mouths. The student teachers circulate around the room; each one is holding small bottles of food coloring. There are four colors: red, green, blue, and yellow.

Integrating literature and science

They have just read and discussed with the class a book by Eric Carle called *Brown Bear, Brown Bear, What Do I See?* It is a book about colors, a topic covered in the kindergarten science curriculum. The students have learned about primary colors and secondary colors, and now they will do a hands-on activity. This will enable the teachers to assess the students' understanding of the concepts that have been introduced today.

This kindergartner is learning about color mixing. She must predict the name of the secondary color that forms when she mixes yellow and blue.

The pair of kindergartners whom I observe has a small card that reads, "YELLOW + BLUE = ?" They must predict the name of the secondary color that will result when the two primary colors, yellow and blue, are mixed. The students discuss the question, pick up a crayon, and write the word "GREEN." The teachers praise them, and then place one drop of yellow food coloring on the first lump of shaving cream and one drop of blue food coloring on the second lump. The teachers instruct the students to use the popsicle sticks to mix each lump of cream separately. Happily, the students follow the directions. Soon there are two brightly colored lumps of shaving cream on the plate, which the students eagerly merge into one large green mound. Their eyes widen as the color that they form on the plate matches the prediction they made earlier: "YELLOW + BLUE = GREEN." As a result of this assessment, the teachers now have some evidence of the children's level of understanding of mixing primary colors.

Next, the teachers present a new challenge: they ask each pair of students to create a new color. Students will have a clean paper plate, two new lumps of shaving cream, and two popsicle sticks. The teachers will provide the food coloring the students request. One group asks for a drop of green and a drop of blue, predicting that they will make purple. But the new color doesn't look like purple at all, so they try again. This time they add a drop of red, which helps. Another pair mixes red and yellow, predicting that they will make orange. Their color turns out to be a dark shade of orange. The teacher asks them to think about how they could produce a lighter shade of orange.

Kindergartners engage in problem solving: Science process

Throughout the room, kindergartners think and experiment, and by the time the lesson is over, there are many new colors on the plates and much information to share. The teachers give each pair of students a chance to share results with the class by giving an oral report. Tomorrow they'll review *Brown Bear, Brown Bear, What Do I See?* again and see how many of the colors mentioned in the book the kindergartners successfully produced.

The students have been active, engaged, and involved in their learning. No discipline problems have arisen, although some students could not resist the temptation to play with the shaving cream on their hands, which was anticipated and treated as an extension of the activity. Clean-up is easy and takes about five minutes. The teachers collect the newspaper, plates, and popsicle sticks; some students have colored shaving cream on their hands, and they wait their turn at the sink. During clean-up, the students talk animatedly about the activity they just finished. The lesson is a success, and both the cooperating teacher and I are impressed.

Sixth-Grade Aeronautics

Next, I visit a sixth-grade classroom. This group is learning about aeronautics. The student teachers had to do a great deal of research and gather many resources before teaching about this topic. They learned about Bernoulli's principle; the forces of gravity, lift, thrust, and drag; and air and pressure. They learned how airplanes fly, and spent a great deal of time researching activities that were developmentally appropriate for their students.

Children learn about
the forces of flight.

*Teachers adapt lessons
for special learners*

Since their placement is in the upper elementary grades, and this school has self-contained classes only in the primary grades, the student teachers work with 75 students each week. This particular class contains 25 students; six have learning difficulties, and two or three have behavior problems. Working with the cooperating teacher and with me, the student teachers determined ways in which individual students' needs could be met. One student had difficulty taking notes, so the teachers taught note taking using the chalkboard and the overhead projector, and repeating the content, checking often for understanding and providing extra help both in and out of class. As I observe this lesson, I notice that the teachers use a tape recorder to record instructions about the activity for a student who has trouble following directions.

*Scientists represent the
diversity of society*

This lesson teaches about individuals who have made important contributions to the field of aeronautics. As part of their research, the student teachers visited both the elementary school and local public libraries, conferenced with the librarians, and identified 30 different sources containing information about men and women of different racial and ethnic groups who made significant contributions to the field. They brought the books, journals, and other resources to class today, and each student chose a different person to research. Instead of writing a report about the person, each student uses a different form of poetry to communicate the information. The forms of poetry the students use include haiku, cinquain, and diamante (Figure 1.1 on page 6 defines a *cinquain* and provides examples). The lesson takes 42 minutes to complete: a 7-minute introduction, 25 minutes for students to research and write about the person they have chosen to study, and 10 minutes for student sharing and a general wrap-up. Once again, the lesson is successful, and the student teachers reach all learners, including those with special needs.

Cinquain

A cinquain is a five-line poem that follows a grammatical pattern:

First line – a noun
Second line – two adjectives describing the noun
Third line – three verbs telling what the noun does
Fourth line – a statement about the noun (a phrase or clause)
Fifth line – repeats the noun or gives synonym

Harriet Quimby
independent, brave
exploring, breaking-ground, moving ahead
first American woman to earn a pilot's license
Role Model

Bernoulli
brilliant, creative
inventing, experimenting, thinking
as the speed of a fluid increases, the pressure decreases
Originator of Bernoulli's Principle

Colonel Guion S. Bluford Jr.
courageous, confident
discovering, thinking, charting new territory
first African-American astronaut in space
Guion S. Bluford Jr.

Figure 1.1
Students use poetry to communicate what they have learned in science class

Fifth-Grade Yeast Investigation

Students engage in performance-based assessment

The third class I visit is a fifth grade. Here students are carrying out a **performance task** so their teacher can assess their understanding of concepts of science, ability to apply scientific thinking in new situations, and ability to work together in groups. A performance task asks students to solve a problem. It gives them practice in applying concepts and thinking critically while allowing the teacher to gain insight into students' thinking. It also gives students experience with real-life problems and situations.

The teacher presents the fifth-graders with this problem: You are a food scientist who has been hired by the owners of a bakery to help them bake better bread. Recently they have had a problem with the yeast they have used. It didn't do its job, and many batches of bread were ruined. The bakery can't afford to make a bad batch of bread, so they want you to develop a quick and easy test to make sure the yeast they use is good before they add it to bread dough. The task is to develop a test the bakers can use to find out how the yeast acts in the laboratory before they add it to dough.

Students learn that baker's yeast is a microbe. Some microbes are bad for us because they cause disease, and some are good. Yeast is a good microbe. It helps us make yogurt, cheese, beer, and bread. Yeast is made of living cells that you can see under a microscope. Yeast cells consume sugar and oxygen to produce carbon dioxide gas and energy. Bread dough is made of flour, sugar, and water. When bakers add yeast to bread dough, the yeast cells eat the sugar in the dough. The carbon dioxide gas they produce makes the dough rise.

Today the students work in groups of four to discuss the task and plan their investigations. The teacher circulates around the room listening to student discussions. They think about how they will determine the effectiveness of the yeast sample. How will they know when it works properly? Will an effective product release a certain amount of carbon dioxide gas? How will they measure the amount of carbon dioxide gas produced?

Students learn about yeast: Life science

These students are experimenting with yeast. They are trying to develop a test to find out how yeast acts in the laboratory before they add it to dough.

Students plan scientific investigations: Science process

As students formulate their plans, they think about how much yeast, how much sugar, and how much water to use in their experiments. They wonder whether they can develop a test using just these three ingredients, leaving out the flour. They discuss their ideas with one another, while the teacher listens and helps them think about their questions.

Another group notices that yeast packages have expiration dates, and they must be certain to test products that expire at about the same time. They discuss other variables they should control, including water temperature and amount of time for the experiment.

The teacher provides many materials for student use, including sugar, water, flour, mixing bowls, measuring spoons, graduated cylinders, thermometers, rulers, empty plastic soda bottles, plastic tubing, modeling clay, balloons, test tubes, test tube racks, a clock, and, of course, packages of yeast. Students can use these materials to conduct their investigations. They examine the materials as they make their plans. The teacher tells his students that once the work is done, each group will summarize its results and write a report to tell about the effectiveness of the yeast sample. The students have an assessment task list, so they know what the teacher expects right from the start (see Table 1.1).

As I observe, I can see that all students are engaged and on task. The teacher continues to circulate around the room, listening to what students are saying,

Table 1.1
Assessment Task List for the Yeast Investigation

Criteria	Comments
Scientific Thought	
Understanding of the topic	
Evidence of research	
Use of science processes	
Presentation	
Clarity and organization	
Impact	
Effectiveness	
Answers the question	
Group Process	
Ability to work together	
All members equally involved	
Members remain on task	
Members document findings	
Members follow classroom safety	
Members help one another	

answering questions as they arise, and posing new ones. He makes notes about what's happening in each group. Things are going well. I'll return to this classroom tomorrow to observe the next phase of the investigation.

Fourth-Grade WebQuest: Native American Three Sisters Gardens

Now I enter the school's computer laboratory, where a group of fourth-graders is engaging in inquiry on the Internet. They are beginning a WebQuest, an inquiry-oriented activity in which much of the information with which they interact comes from Internet resources, sometimes supplemented with videoconferencing. Professor Bernie Dodge of San Diego State University in California originated the idea of the WebQuest. A WebQuest includes the following components:

▶ An *introduction* to provide students with background information about the task

▶ An interesting and do-able *task*

▶ A *set of resources* needed to complete the task

▶ A description of the *process* or steps students should follow to perform the task

▶ *Guidance* on how to organize the information they acquire

▶ A *conclusion* that brings the quest to closure

These fourth graders are solving a WebQuest. They are logged onto the WebQuest Internet site and are investigating the Native American Three Sisters Gardens.

Students use technology in the science classroom

After they log onto the WebQuest home page at http://edweb.sdsu.edu/ webquest/webquest.html, students move through the menu to a collection of WebQuests. Their teacher directs them to the University of New Mexico collection so that they can begin a WebQuest that enables them to learn about science in combination with Native American culture. This particular WebQuest was designed and written by teachers Marykirk Cunningham, David McDavitt, and Beth Romero from Abingdon Elementary School in Arlington, Virginia.

Students learn about Native American gardening: Life science

The fourth-graders begin to investigate Native American Three Sisters Gardens. They learn that the Three Sisters are not people but corn, beans, and squash, which are planted by traditional Native American gardeners throughout North America. These plants help one another to grow. The Three Sisters Garden forms an ecosystem as it creates a community of plants and animals. The Haudenosaunee, or "People of the Long House," were the first to adopt this gardening technique. The students' task is to investigate the folklore, stories, history, and science related to the Three Sisters gardening method.

The WebQuest requires that students work in groups. Ideally, each group has four students, and in each group is a team of experts: a botanist, an anthropologist, a folklorist, and a museum curator. There are 25 students in the class, so that makes 5 groups with 4 students and 1 group with 5 students. The last group has two botanists instead of one.

Students will learn about the science behind the Three Sisters Gardens and their importance in creating a stable food supply. They will also study how the Haudenosaunee's environment inspired this technique and how Three Sisters gardening influenced their culture, and they will learn the stories and traditions surrounding the use of this agricultural technique. They will present their findings by creating a museum display.

The WebQuest pages provide guidance for the young botanists, anthropologists, folklorists, and museum curators, helping them to understand their roles and learn how to research and carry out their tasks. It also provides online resources, as well as general reference books, magazines, and Native American children's literature for them to use. As students complete their tasks, they are instructed to record their findings regularly. The WebQuest comes complete with an assessment system so that the teacher can assess student work. The room is abuzz with excitement as students begin their first WebQuest. I am impressed with the clarity and level of organization with which the teacher and students begin this investigation.

Back in the College Classroom

Teachers reflect on their lessons

Once we are back in the college classroom, we reflect on what went on in the elementary classrooms. There are many questions:

▶ How did the lesson go?

▶ Was the lesson plan appropriate?

▶ Were the objectives of the lesson met?

> Were state and national standards covered?

> Was the lesson timed correctly?

> Were there any classroom management problems?

> Were the directions given well?

> Were the needs of special learners met?

> Did boys and girls receive equal attention, and were they challenged equally?

The answers to these questions help students plan future lessons, try new techniques, and improve their teaching.

Contexts for Teaching and Learning

Good preparation enables new teachers to answer such questions. The preparation of an elementary science teacher requires solid knowledge in three areas: science content, methods of instruction, and student development. As you proceed through this text, you will gain both practical and theoretical knowledge to prepare you for your career in the elementary school classroom. The goal is to help you gain confidence in teaching science. You will focus on learning science content, methods of teaching and assessing regular and special learners, and developmentally appropriate practice.

A Developmental Approach

This book has several themes, which are woven together in the pages that follow. The ultimate goal is to help you become a knowledgeable, confident elementary science teacher who is part of a community of teachers and learners. My first assumption is that learning and development happen over time. As a teacher, you know that your lessons must match the developmental needs of your students. I believe the same is true for novice teachers. You can't learn everything about science and science teaching in one course or in one book. My philosophy is "less is more." Instead of attempting to pack an unrealistic amount of information into this book, I select pedagogy and content that are appropriate for a novice teacher. If you master this material and put it into practice in your classroom, you will start off with a solid base. You'll be able to build on that foundation as you gain experience in the years to come.

Using this carefully constructed developmental approach, my goal is to motivate you, excite you, and lessen your fear of teaching science. A great deal goes on in an elementary science classroom, and even many veteran teachers shy away from the subject because there is so much to manage. Throughout this book, you will find simple, hands-on activities that you can implement with your students. These manageable activities will allow you to maintain control of your classroom while giving your students the opportunity to explore and discover. The teaching methods that accompany the activities are ones that a novice teacher can implement comfortably. By linking instruction and assessment, you will learn how to listen to what your students are saying so that you can assess their understanding of what's going on in your classroom.

My desire is to help you learn basic concepts of science with the expectation that you will go on to learn more on your own. Once you *learn how to teach and learn science*, you will be able to tackle new topics with confidence when you have your own classroom. You won't be reluctant to teach science. I hope that in this course you will develop a desire to take additional science courses and workshops as you continue to grow as a professional.

Content and Pedagogy Interwoven

Science content and pedagogy work together in this book, with science content integrated with methods of science teaching. For example, you'll *learn about* the human heart as you learn to *teach about* the human heart. You'll learn about mealworms as you learn to teach about mealworms. You'll learn about simple machines as you learn to teach about simple machines. This performance-based approach will give you numerous opportunities to learn as you practice teaching elementary science.

Coordination across scientific disciplines clarifies relationships among concepts: Science process

Since science disciplines are commonly integrated in the natural world, in this text you'll often learn about biology and physics, or chemistry, physics, and biology, or physics and astronomy together. Coordination across biology, chemistry, physics, and earth and space science enables you to see interrelationships as well as applications of important concepts.

Learning from experienced teachers is important when you are a novice. Throughout the text you will meet accomplished teachers who share their knowledge and experience with you. You will also meet practicing scientists who tell you about their work and why they find it so fascinating. You'll learn from their experience as well. You'll learn as much about science and scientists as you will about teaching science.

All of these strands are carefully interwoven throughout this book. To clarify the themes as they develop, I have included two types of marginal notes: pedagogical notes and science content notes. These will help you keep track of key content. Several kinds of activities appear throughout the text:

▶ *Hands-on science activities* that you can use in your college classroom or with your own students

▶ *Reflective activities* that help you think about the content that is presented

▶ *Online activities* that give you practice in using the Internet for teaching and learning and expand your knowledge of content and pedagogy

▶ *Teaching activities* that help you develop expertise with particular teaching strategies

Factors That Influence Science Teaching Today

Many factors are influencing science teaching today. In fact, it's not unusual to pick up a newspaper, magazine, or journal, or log onto an education listserv, and read something about school science reform. Our discussion continues with a look at these factors.

A Brief History of the Current Science Education Reform Movement

In the early 1980s, a perceived crisis in American education was set forth in two documents, *A Nation at Risk* and *Educating Americans for the Twenty-First Century*. These documents stated that our schools needed major reform so that our students could keep up with changes taking place in the world.

The mathematics community was the first to take action. In 1986, the National Council of Teachers of Mathematics (NCTM) began drafting standards for what students should learn in mathematics. In 1989, NCTM published *Curriculum and Evaluation Standards for School Mathematics* and the National Research Council published *Everybody Counts: A Report to the Nation on the Future of Mathematics Education*. At the same time, leaders of several other content-area professional organizations were examining their disciplines. Soon the national standards movement was under way in the United States.

In their scrutiny of practice, science educators asked many searching questions:

▶ Are we keeping up with the advancing technological world?

▶ Are we preparing our students for the 21st century? Will our work force consist of people who are adequately educated in science?

▶ Are we producing a scientifically literate public? Will average citizens understand enough science to make informed decisions about issues that affect them, their families, and their communities?

▶ Are our teachers being kept up to date in their knowledge of science content and teaching methods?

▶ Do students have access to sound curricula in science? Are we ensuring access to scientific careers for *all* students, without regard for race, gender, or socioeconomic status?

▶ Do our administrators create an atmosphere that supports and encourages participation in the improvement of science education?

▶ Do parents and community members support improvement in science education?

After answering these questions, it was clear that science education needed much attention if we were to maintain quality programs.

Recommendations to reform, improve, and change science education emerged. In 1990, the American Association for the Advancement of Science published *Science for All Americans*, the product of a three-year collaboration among hundreds of educators, scientists, mathematicians, engineers, physicians, philosophers, and historians who carefully scrutinized the state of science education and developed a set of recommendations on what "understandings and ways of thinking are essential for all citizens in a world shaped by science and technology."

A serious reform effort thus began. Many state and national agencies responded by providing resources for schools and districts. Most states wrote standards for students and teachers to meet. At the national level, the *National Science Education Standards* (1996) and *Benchmarks for Science Literacy: Project 2061* (1993) guided the reform effort in elementary science. The **standards** describe what all students should know and be able to do upon completion of a 13-year education, providing guidelines, or benchmarks, that describe what students should know and understand as they progress. New teachers often wonder what content they should cover in their courses. Standards provide guidelines for what should happen in classrooms.

Why Do We Need Standards?

But what exactly are standards, and why do we need them? Suppose you are a government official who reads the reports of the problems in our educational system and you want to do something that will benefit the population as a whole. Your first action will be to develop policy. Next, you will need a mechanism that will put the policy into action, leading from your position at the top to the rest of the system. Standards are just such a mechanism. They are a way to raise expectations for all parts of the system, for they are an external force that motivates the system to change.

Standards are a banner, a vision, something to strive for. Science standards provide a vision of what it means to be scientifically literate. They tell us what all students must know and do as a result of their cumulative learning experiences. They provide criteria for judgments regarding systems, programs, teaching, and assessment that can lead to opportunities for all students to learn science in ways that meet the standards. Lessons from past reform efforts tell us that changing any one component of an educational system is insufficient to bring about significant reform (Raizen, 1998). When thinking about standards, we should think **systemically**—in other words, think about *all* parts of the educational system that require change: its structure, operating procedures, ways in which people interact, and distribution of power.

When talking about standards, certain words need clarification. The term *all students* appears frequently in most standards documents. This reflects the social commitment that standards apply to all students, regardless of background, gender, ethnicity, economic condition, circumstance, or ambition. *National* is another term that requires clarification. *National* means there is a nationwide agreement, not a federal mandate, on what defines successful science learning and the school practices that support that learning. *National standards* do not define a national curriculum and do not suggest a form of national standardization of the actual curriculum. The *National Science Education Standards* set goals for programs, teaching, professional development, assessment of teaching and learning, students, programs, science content, and the system as a whole.

Inquiry-Based Science

Elementary school science should be **inquiry based**. Why? Children are filled with curiosity. They come to school with a natural love of learning. They ask questions and seek answers to build on their prior knowledge: Why is the sky blue? Why do fish swim in water? What makes rain come down from the sky? How do planes fly? They observe ants and spiders, explore flowers and leaves, make snowballs, launch rockets, feed hamsters, work on the computer, solve puzzles, and play with blocks. Science is what children do everyday. As teachers, we hope their school experiences foster their natural curiosity and help them continue to inquire and learn more.

In some classes this happens, and in others it does not. To make science come alive, teachers must provide meaningful experiences for children. This includes bringing in materials for them to explore, such as rocks and minerals, batteries and bulbs, liquids, solids, and gases, and toys of all sorts, to name just a few examples. Sometimes teachers can move instruction from the classroom to the real world by providing opportunities for field trips and by inviting scientists, engineers, and other community members into the classroom to work with students. Students need opportunities to engage in age-appropriate activities that mirror those that happen in the real world. They need opportunities to perform so that they can show what they know in a variety of ways. This helps to build the foundation of inquiry-based science, allowing students to ask questions, experiment, develop their own theories about how the world works, communicate their ideas to others, debate and discuss them, and then reflect on the experiences.

Standards documents tell us that science should be inquiry based:

STANDARDS

Engaging in inquiry helps students develop understanding: Science process

In the vision presented by the *National Science Education Standards*, inquiry is a step beyond "science as a process," in which students learn skills such as observation, inference, and experimentation. The new vision includes the "processes of science" and requires that students combine processes and scientific knowledge as they use scientific reasoning and critical thinking to develop their understanding of science. Engaging in inquiry helps students develop

▶ An understanding of scientific concepts

▶ An appreciation of "how we know" what we know in science

▶ An understanding of the nature of science

> ▶ Skills necessary to become independent inquirers about the natural world
> ▶ The disposition to use the skills, abilities, and attitudes associated with science

---

The *National Science Education Standards* say more about inquiry-based science, explaining that

STANDARDS

> When engaging in inquiry, students describe objects and events, ask questions, construct explanations, test those explanations against current scientific knowledge, and communicate their ideas to others. They identify their assumptions, use critical and logical thinking, and consider alternative explanations. In this way, students actively develop their understandings of science by combining scientific knowledge with reasoning and thinking skills (p. 2).

This statement is important because it describes science as scientists know it, and it applies to the classroom as well.

This active, thought-provoking approach is new to many elementary science teachers who look at science education as a passive experience. The **traditional science classroom** is one in which direct instruction is the predominant instructional strategy. In such a classroom, the teacher is a strong leader who "directs student activity, approaches the content in a direct and businesslike way, organizes learning around teacher-posed questions, and remains the center of attention" (Rosenshine, 1979, p. 71). With **teacher-centered methods of instruction,** the student has less responsibility for his or her own learning than in the inquiry-based classroom. Teacher-dominated methods include lecture, recitation, teacher-directed small groups, sharing time, and seat work (Weinstein, 1991).

In the past, large numbers of elementary school teachers relied solely on textbooks, and the textbooks of the past included general information about science, focusing on teaching vocabulary and facts rather than on providing opportunities for inquiry. Elementary science teachers often felt pressured to have students engage in drill and practice so that they could perform well on standardized tests. Unfortunately, many students memorized such facts and forgot them after the test was over, becoming bored and disenchanted with science along the way.

Recent research in language learning gives us some insight into why learning science by memorizing vocabulary words isn't the best approach. When language is learned in the context of some meaningful activity, it is quite successful. Through adolescence, children learn about 13 new words per day. Traditional approaches used in school, which include memorization, allow them to learn only 100 to 200 words per year, which is far fewer than the nearly 5,000 words they can learn from meaningful activity (Miller & Gildea, 1987). Vocabulary learned by rote memorization is not integrated into everyday life; rather, it exists as small bits of information that students memorize but do not apply. The vocabulary acquired through active learning helps children express meaning, and therefore is useful—and used.

Learning should be active, not passive

Current conceptions of science learning differ from those of the past. A large body of knowledge tells us that learners are not passive receivers of knowledge but active learners who bring their own views of the world into the classroom (Driver, Guesne, & Tiberghien, 1985; Shymansky, Hedges, & Woodworth, 1990; Tobin, Capie, & Bettencourt, 1988). Classrooms should be places where students think about and solve real-world problems and have opportunities to investigate the natural world. They should see interrelationships across scientific disciplines and integrate mathematics and technology with science. This is a big change from the traditional science classroom.

Although research findings suggest that direct instruction promotes student achievement (Anderson, 1995; Hirsch, 1996), critics argue that it fosters rote learning and lower-level thinking skills, causes learners to be passive receivers of knowledge, and stifles creativity. Of course, there are times when direct instruction is important and appropriate in a science classroom, but today's vision of elementary science tells us that the classroom should be more student centered and less teacher directed than the traditional model of the past.

Inquiry-Based View of Assessment

The classroom that uses an inquiry-based approach differs from the traditional classroom in many ways. In the traditional science classroom, instruction and assessment are two separate things. Students learn science content, which they memorize for a test. The test generally assesses their recall of facts, and may be administered several weeks after the teacher covers the content.

Alternative assessment should augment traditional paper-and-pencil tests

Much has happened to change elementary science teaching and bring students beyond the limits of the traditional classroom. First, the view of assessment has been expanded. National standards documents emphasize the importance of using alternative assessment strategies *in addition* to traditional paper-and-pencil tests. There is a move away from giving tests where students choose one best answer toward having students show what they know in a number of ways.

Both teaching and testing have changed. The *National Science Education Standards* tell us that assessments are the primary feedback mechanism in the science education system, providing students with information on how well they are meeting expectations. Assessments give teachers feedback on how students are learning, tell school districts how effective their teachers and programs are, and let policymakers know about the effectiveness of policy. The feedback is used in a number of ways, which include changing policy, guiding professional development for teachers, and encouraging students to improve their understanding of science (*National Research Council*, 1996, p. 5).

Alternative assessments focus on higher-order skills

Perhaps the most important change in assessments is their current level of sophistication. Instead of simply testing for memorization of facts, they focus on higher-order skills, such as understanding, reasoning, and ability, to apply knowledge gained through inquiry. Instead of using paper-and-pencil tests to assess understanding by identifying one best answer, teachers now use multiple methods. These include performances, portfolios, interviews, investigative reports, and written essays that are developmentally appropriate, framed in settings that are familiar to children, and free from bias. Even more important, teachers share expectations with students before they begin to work and monitor them as they build understanding. By linking assessment and instruction, students are aware of their achievement targets from the outset and thus are in a better position to meet them.

As you can see, the change in assessment methods drives the change in science instruction. You will spend a great deal of time learning about assessment strategies and developing assessments as you proceed through this text. You will also learn to design science lessons that are developmentally appropriate for children.

The Role of Research in Teaching and Learning Science

Over the past several decades, a great deal of high-quality research on teaching and learning emerged, and you will learn to apply this research as you begin to teach elementary science. This knowledge base developed as a synthesis of principles of neurobiology and cognitive science, informed by the philosophical and cultural contexts of students, classrooms, and schools. We learned from the medical literature and combined that with our knowledge of cognitive science, the field devoted to the study of how people think, reason, remember, and solve problems. The teachings of philosophers John Dewey and of cognitive psychologists Jerome Bruner, Jean Piaget, Lev Vygotsky, David Ausubel, Robert Gagne, and others made important contributions to our knowledge base.

Many researchers believe that learning something new requires children to first develop an awareness of what they are examining, exploring, and inquiring. Only then can they use knowledge and skills and apply what they have learned. The work of Swiss psychologist Jean Piaget, a founder of the field of cognitive psychology, provides important insights into child development.

The work of Lev Vygotsky addresses the sociocultural context of learning, looking at the culture that the child brings to the school. His writings focused on the role the social environment plays in the child's cognitive development, explaining that children begin to learn from those around them. In the social world, children gain experience with concepts, ideas, facts, skills, and attitudes, and they experience their own culture. According to Vygotsky's teachings, knowledgeable adults, siblings, and playmates can help children grow cognitively by encouraging them to work cooperatively and collaboratively in a nurturing environment. As you work through this text, you will learn more about Piaget's and Vygotsky's theories.

Classroom Activities Can Exist Along a Continuum

When you teach science, your students construct and reconstruct what they believe to be true. As we saw in the lessons that opened this chapter, they need opportunities to make meaning for themselves and to ask questions such as "If I do this, what will happen to that?" or "What makes sense and what does not?" When they construct and reconstruct meaning, they take responsibility for themselves as learners.

Constructivist theory encourages you to view your students as active learners and to involve them in their own learning. In a constructivist classroom, you give them problems to solve or something to examine, test, experiment with, or think about. You encourage them to see, study, discuss, wonder, challenge their own thinking, and think about a phenomenon in different ways. You will observe that they experience conflict in their minds, make sense of something, and, all along the way, construct knowledge and their own understanding of the phenomenon. Constructivism, then, is a process of continuously refining existing knowledge, building on an established base of prior knowledge, skills, attitudes, and values.

Piaget was a constructivist who viewed acquisition of knowledge as a process rather than a state. He believed that when people learn, they construct their own representations of existing knowledge. As children grow and develop, the mechanisms by which they construct knowledge develop and mature, and their ways of thinking and constructing knowledge become more sophisticated.

Constructivist teaching drives science education

Constructivism is a driving force behind science education today. Constructivist teachers not only provide rich experiences for students but also think about how they can determine what their students are learning from a lesson. They develop excellent questioning strategies so that students are always thinking and are engaged in dialogue about what they are doing. Through these discussions, the teacher listens to what students say and think. This informal assessment allows the teacher to uncover students' misconceptions and to clarify their ideas.

The constructivist teacher makes the classroom student centered. Instead of focusing solely on "right" or "wrong" answers, he or she elicits the students' thoughts in order to understand what students are thinking and what experiences they need in the future. Standards, curriculum, instruction, and assessment are interwoven so that assessment informs instruction. The constructivist classroom is one in which you hear both student talk and teacher talk.

In classrooms today, instruction occurs along a continuum. Sometimes the teacher does the talking and explains things, and students are passive recipients of knowledge. In such cases, the teacher's role is to be directive. If a new subject is being introduced and students know very little, the teacher might provide basic background knowledge using directive techniques. Once a foundation exists, the teacher might go on to build on what learners already know. Then the teacher assumes the role of coach and mediator, helping students to operate within their own personal worlds to actively construct knowledge. Sometimes students are trying to construct knowledge and become confused. Instead of letting students figure out what's happening on their own, the teacher might decide that it's better to develop a lesson to explain things or to guide them in correcting errors of thinking.

In this text, you will learn to implement standards-based best practice in your classroom and create lessons that draw on the strengths of both teacher-directed and constructivist techniques. You will structure learning for your students in many ways, and use demonstrations, hands-on activities, and whole-class and small-group work in an inquiry-based setting. In this way you will foster the intellectual growth and development of all students in a variety of ways.

Table 1.2 compares the traditional and constructivist elementary science classrooms.

Table 1.2

Comparison of a Traditional Elementary Science Classroom with One That Emphasizes Constructivism

	Elementary Science Classroom That Focuses on Traditional Teaching Methods	Elementary Science Classroom That Focuses on Constructivist Teaching Methods
Student's Role	Memorize facts and vocabulary words (Memorization and drill and practice are not necessarily linked to reinforcing understanding.)	Construct knowledge and understanding; de-emphasize but do not eliminate memorization of facts and vocabulary words (Memorization and drill and practice are linked to reinforcing understanding.)
Teacher's Role	Lecture, present information to students	Provide experiences for active learning; interact with students, seek students' points of view; ask thought-provoking questions; examine, discuss, and critique students' constructions in relation to those of experts and peers; examine, discuss, and critique experts' constructions (scientific concepts) in relation to those of students; help students negotiate meaning through discussions; provide structure for students
Thinking Skills	Look for the "right" or "wrong" answer, emphasize recall of facts	Emphasize higher-level thinking, view students as people who are developing theories of how things work
Curriculum	Emphasize basic skills only	Emphasize big concepts
Instructional Strategies	Emphasize lecture and whole-class discussion	Use a variety of instructional strategies, including cooperative learning
Classroom Social Organization	Students work alone or as a whole class	Students work alone, as a whole class, and in small groups
Assessments Used	Paper-and-pencil tests, multiple choice, fill in the blank, true or false, finding the one best answer	Performance-based assessment, portfolios, projects, observing students at work, student exhibitions, plus traditional assessments

Serving the Needs of Diverse Learners in the Elementary Science Classroom

Teachers need a host of strategies to address learning differences

Humans are characterized by **diversity**—in terms of language, background, ability level, gender, learning style, and personality, to name just a few ways. In the elementary science classroom, there should be equity for all students. This means that every student should have an equal opportunity to learn. Since students are unique, teachers need a host of strategies to appropriately address the differences among learners. You will teach students of various backgrounds as well as those who have special needs.

Currently about 36 percent of school-age children are from underrepresented groups. This includes children of African American descent, Native Americans, Hispanics of all races, and Asian Pacific Islanders. By year 2020, students of color will account for nearly half of the school population. By 2010, one-third of our nation's children will reside in four states—New York, Texas, California, and Florida—and more than half of them will be members of underrepresented groups (Hodgkinson, 1992, 1993). **Exceptional learners** add to the diversity in classrooms. These are students who have special needs and have an individualized educational plan (IEP) to meet those needs. Some of these children have learning disabilities; some have speech, language, or visual impairments; and some have mental retardation, multiple disabilities, hearing impairments, or lack of mobility. Some come from families who live below the poverty line. In the United States, nearly one-fourth of all children live in poverty, and these children tend to be concentrated in inner cities and some rural areas. They are at the greatest risk for not succeeding in our schools, regardless of race or ethnicity (Jaeger, 1992). You will also work with students who are gifted or talented (and who also have special needs).

My own college classroom includes a young woman named Meri who is a peer to my students and attends class with them. Meri has cerebral palsy and a number of learning disabilities. Her job is to help my students learn about and become comfortable with individuals who are differently abled. She works with them as they develop their elementary science lessons. Meri enriches our classroom and allows the students to develop confidence in their ability to work with diverse learners in the classroom. As a result of being included in a college classroom, Meri has progressed significantly. As we work together, we learn there are more ways in which we are similar and fewer ways in which we differ. You will read more about Meri in Chapter 9. Throughout the text, you will learn to use many methods for addressing the needs of diverse learners in elementary science. As a teacher, you will learn many ways to include all students in classroom activities and to appreciate the value of teaching in a rich, diverse setting.

Using Technology in Teaching and Learning

Technology is changing our world in many ways, including how students learn. **Educational technology**—the use of computers as an instructional tool—can play a number of roles in your classroom. Think about what's on the market today.

Students describe
science learning using
educational technology:
Science process

There is software of all types; Internet tools; multimedia applications, including CD-ROM and videodisc; hypertext applications; programming; word processors, databases, and spreadsheets; videoconferencing; paint and draw programs; and the list goes on. Just think about software alone. There's instructional software that enables students to take part in simulations, tutorials, drill and practice, and educational games (Grabe & Grabe, 1998). Paint and draw programs are easy and fun to use. Two of my students taught a wonderful unit on butterflies to a class of transitional first-graders (students who had passed kindergarten but were not quite ready for first grade). After completing the unit, the children went to the computer room and, using a paint program called Kid Pix Studio, designed their own butterflies. The children's designs allowed the teacher to assess understanding. The students were very excited about their projects, and so was I.

Some schools are technologically advanced; others are not. As a teacher, your role is to learn as much as possible and to take advantage of what your school has to offer. Throughout this text, you will learn how technology can be used to enhance instruction. Chapter 11 is devoted to this topic.

Technology is the
creation of a human-
made world: Science
process

Besides computer technology, or educational technology, there is technology education. **Technology** is innovation or change in the natural environment to satisfy perceived human needs and wants (International Technology Education Association, in progress). **Technology education** involves solving problems based on satisfying a need in a practical way. To determine just what these needs and wants are, a wide range of factors must be considered simultaneously. Thus, technology brings together, or integrates, many different subject areas.

We use technology as a human endeavor to solve problems and modify our environment rather than as science, which is concerned with discovering new knowledge. Technology is about design, and design is the planned process of change. Designing helps us to plan change so that we achieve desired results (Hutchinson & Karsnitz, 1994; Hutchinson & Sellwood, 1996). Design also enables us to develop solutions to problems in a careful, planned way.

Every day we solve problems. Some are easy to solve: What should I eat for breakfast? What's the weather like? What clothes should I wear? Other problems require more thought: How can we develop an efficient delivery system that brings insulin to people with diabetes? How can we grow better crops to feed the world's hungry people? How can we build homes that withstand strong hurricanes? How can we design electric cars that travel long distances to conserve energy? Technology allows us to search for solutions to such problems.

One goal of science education is to provide students with a set of mental tools they can use throughout their lives. The ability to engage in inquiry is one of these tools. Observing a situation, identifying a problem, and formulating and testing hypotheses helps us generate solutions to problems that we deal with in our lives. Technology education offers another tool, called the *design process*, to make problem solving effective. It is an active process that begins by defining the problem and identifying clearly the need that is to be met. The designer then generates several ideas for a solution, keeping in mind the design criteria. In the classroom, students generally work in groups to carry out this process. They select the best or most promising solution, create a model and test it, then reevaluate the solution. Sometimes the solution doesn't work, and the students go back to the drawing board to consider another idea, working by trial and error until they reach a final, workable solution.

Using the design and problem-solving approach, my students recently worked with paper engineering to create pop-up books. As a culminating activity for a unit, they designed a variety of pop-ups, which employ simple machines. One group created a unit about insects for sixth-graders. As an assessment activity, the students participated in a design challenge: create an insect that has two movable parts. Using what they had learned about paper engineering and simple machines, the students wrote and constructed a children's pop-up book about insects. Students integrated their knowledge of simple machines, insects, paper engineering, and the design process to meet the challenge. You can imagine the high level of thinking and creativity these sixth-graders needed to complete this project!

In this text, you will learn about design and problem solving. Some of my students have given me permission to share their work with you, and you will learn how to create and carry out a design challenge with your students. Chapter 12 is devoted to technology as design and problem solving.

Learning to Teach Science: Anxiety Versus Adventure

Learning to do anything new can be a challenge, and anxiety often accompanies such a challenge. Butterflies in the stomach, sweaty palms, and a general feeling of insecurity commonly plague novice elementary science teachers. There is so much to know—how can you possibly know it all? The answer is simple: you don't have to know everything—that's impossible. You do need knowledge of principles of child development, familiarity with many methods of teaching and assessing elementary science, and the ability to learn new content. If you're going to teach something that is new to you, read the science textbook, go to the library, search the Internet, and learn whatever you can about the topic. Talk with accomplished teachers; they will have lots of practical experience to share. Start out by observing successful classrooms in action, and make note of what the teacher does.

As you read this textbook and work with your instructors in your science methods course, you'll learn about science and science teaching. Think of this as an adventure. Each day you'll learn something new. Experiment with your new knowledge when you teach your students. Try out a particular strategy when you teach a lesson. See how it goes. If your lesson doesn't go as planned, think about how you could improve it. I've been a teacher and professor for more than two-and-a-half decades. Each day I learn something new. I always try new things in my class. Sometimes they work, and sometimes they don't. When they don't work, I often ask a colleague to think through the activity, lesson, or strategy with me. My students often help. Together we look for ways to improve. We do this openly, and with good humor. Then I try the lesson again to see if I've removed the bugs.

I look at my own teaching in terms of my own professional development. The world is changing quickly. There is always something new to learn—another seminar, workshop, or course to take. I bring that knowledge to my students. Instead of being anxious because I don't know everything there is to know, I keep on learning, experimenting, and applying what I've learned, both in the college classroom and in the elementary school classroom. If you're feeling a bit anxious as you start to teach, that's normal. If something goes wrong in a lesson, don't blame yourself; find out what went wrong. Try again. Embark on a journey of adventure that will motivate you and satisfy your curiosity for years to come. If you're like me, you will never become bored with your profession.

Constructing Your Own Knowledge of Science and Science Teaching

In this first chapter, you learned a bit about life in the elementary science classroom and examined some of the driving forces behind science education today. I hope you now have some idea of how exciting and motivating science teaching can be. You will find endless possibilities for creativity as you develop your lessons. You should now have started to construct your own view of what elementary science teaching is all about. As you proceed through this course, you will examine each of the topics touched on here in much greater depth, and you will look at many others. You will develop your own theories of what science education is all about, and those theories will emerge from and guide your practice. In addition, this text will provide a wealth of practical information that will serve as a resource for you throughout your career.

Key Terms

performance task (p. 6)
standards (p. 14)
systemic change (p. 14)
inquiry-based science (p. 15)
traditional science classroom
   (p. 16)

teacher-centered methods of
   instruction (p. 16)
constructivist theory (p. 19)
diversity (p. 21)
exceptional learners (p. 21)

educational technology (p. 21)
technology (p. 22)
technology education (p. 22)

Reviewing Chapter 1: Questions, Extensions, Applications, and Explorations

1. Examine the tables of contents of the *National Science Education Standards* and *Benchmarks for Science Literacy: Project 2061*. Discuss the commonalities and differences between them. (Visit the *National Academy Press* web site at www.nap.edu, where you will find the full text of the *National Science Education Standards*. The *American Association for the Advancement of Science* "Triple 'A' 'S'" web site at www.aaas.org is a resource for *Benchmarks for Science Literacy: Project 2061*.)

2. *Science for All Americans* (1990) tells us that science teachers should de-emphasize the memorization of technical vocabulary, explaining that understanding rather than vocabulary should be the main purpose of science teaching. The authors go on to say that "unambiguous terminology is also important in scientific communication and—ultimately— for understanding. Some technical terms are therefore helpful for everyone, but the number of essential ones is relatively small." Discuss

the importance of having students memorize vocabulary words in science class. Think about your own elementary school science classes. Did you memorize many words and facts? If so, how effective was memorization in building your understanding of concepts?

3. One goal of teaching is to help students "know" and "understand." What does this mean to you? How do you know when you "know" or "understand" something? Give an example.

4. You are a food scientist who has been hired by the owners of a bakery to help them bake better bread. Recently they have had a problem with the yeast they've used. It didn't do its job, and many batches of bread were ruined. The bakery can't afford to make a bad batch of bread, so they want you to develop a quick and easy test to make sure that the yeast they use is good before they add it to bread dough. The task is to develop a test that the bakers can use to enable them to compare how the yeast acts in the laboratory with how it acts in the baker's oven. How would you complete the performance task? What tests would you recommend to the owners of the bakery? Set up your own experiment, and see what happens.

5. If you have access to the Internet, log onto the WebQuest home page at http://edweb.sdsu.edu/webquest/webquest.html, and explore.

6. Look at the list of journals in the Print Resources section that follows. Go to the library and familiarize yourself with at least one of these journals.

7. Visit the library and read researcher Senta Raizen's article "Standards for Science Education" (Raizen, 1998). This excellent article will expand your knowledge of science standards.

Print Resources

Berk, L., & Winsler, A. (1995). *Scaffolding children's learning: Vygotsky and early childhood education.* Washington, DC: National Association for the Education of Young Children.

Cavendish, S., Galton, M., Hargreaves, L., & Harlen, W. (1990). *Assessing science in the primary classroom: Observing activities.* London: Paul Chapman Publishing Limited.

DeVries, R., & Kohlberg, L. (1987). *Constructivist early education: Overview and comparison with other programs.* Washington, DC: National Association for the Education of Young Children.

Dewey, J. (1933). *How we think.* Boston: Houghton Mifflin.

Glynn, S., & Duit, R. (1995). *Learning science in schools.* Hillsdale, NJ: Lawrence Erlbaum.

Glynn, S., Yeany, R., & Britton, B. (1991). *The psychology of learning science.* Hillsdale, NJ: Lawrence Erlbaum.

Grabe, M., & Grabe, C. (1998). Integrating technology for meaningful learning. 2nd ed. Boston: Houghton Mifflin.

Mintzes, J., Wandersee, J., & Novak, J. (1997). *Teaching science for understanding: A human constructivist view.* New York: Academic Press.

Neugebauer, B. (1992). *Alike and different: Exploring our humanity with young children.* Washington, DC: National Association for the Education of Young Children.

Novak, J. (1998). *Learning, creating, and using knowledge.* Hillsdale, NJ: Lawrence Erlbaum.

Pennick, J. (1991). Where's the science? *The Science Teacher, 58*(5), 26–29.

Piburn, M., & Baker, D. (1993). If I were a teacher . . . Qualitative study of attitude toward science. *Science Education, 77*(4), 393–406.

Treagust, D., Duit, R. & Fraser, B. (1996). *Improving teaching and learning in science and mathematics.* New York: Teachers College Press.

Print Resources on Standards

American Association for the Advancement of Science. (1993). *Benchmarks for Science Literacy: Project 2061.* New York: Oxford University Press.

National Research Council. (1996). *National Science Education Standards.* Washington, DC: National Academy Press.

Journals for Science Teachers

Journal of Research in Science Teaching, School of Education, University of Missouri—Saint Louis, 8001 Natural Bridge Road, Saint Louis, MO 63121-4499

School Science and Mathematics, Science and Mathematics Education, Oregon State University, 237 Weniger Hall, Corvalis, OR 97331-6508

Science, American Association for the Advancement of Science, 1200 New York Avenue, NW, Washington, DC 20005

Science and Children, National Science Teachers Association, 1840 Wilson Boulevard, Arlington, VA 22201-3000 Phone: 703-243-7100 Fax: 703-243-7177

Science and Society, Guilford Publications, 72 Spring Street, New York, NY 10012

Science Education, Box 506, Peabody College, Vanderbilt University, Nashville, TN 37201

Science News, Science Service, 1719 N Street, NW, Washington, DC 20036

Science Scope, National Science Teachers Association, 1840 Wilson Boulevard, Arlington, VA 22201-3000 Phone: 703-243-7100 Fax; 703-243-7177 Fax: 703-243-7177

The Science Teacher, National Science Teachers Association, 1840 Wilson Boulevard, Arlington, VA 22201-3000 Phone: 703-243-7100 Fax: 703-243-7177

The Sciences, New York Academy of Sciences, 2 East 63rd Street, New York, NY 10021 Phone: 212-838-0230

TIES Magazine, Technology Education, The College of New Jersey P.O. Box 7718, Ewing, NJ 08628-0718

Electronic Resources

Houghton Mifflin Web site
http://www.hmco.com
This is the Houghton Mifflin web site, which offers a wide variety of resources for teachers.

Stevens Institute
http://k12science.stevens-tech.edu/curriculum/curichome.html
This is the Stevens Institute web site, where you can access science experts, a wide range of curricula, and the best real-time data sources and projects available on the web.

Safety on the Internet—Blocking Software
http://k12science.stevens-tech.edu/safety/safety.html
This site discusses safety on the Internet.

National Science Teachers Association
http://www.nsta.org
This is the National Science Teachers Association web site.

http://www.gsh.org/nsta_SSand C/
This is the NSTA Scope, Sequence, and Coordination Project for secondary science.

Association for the Education of Teachers in Science
http://science.cc.uwf.edu/aets/aets.html
This is the site of the Association for the Education of Teachers in Science.

American Association for the Advancement of Science
http://www.aaas.org/

This is American Association for the Advancement of Science web site and is the home of *Benchmarks for Science Literacy: Project 2061.*

National Science Foundation
http://www.nsf.gov
This is the National Science Foundation web site, where you can find information about programs and grants for elementary science.

CHAPTER 2

Scientists at Work: Inquiry and Discovery

Stand in a beautiful woodland, listen to a bird's song, see the dappled sunlight magnifying the grandeur of the trees. This is more beautiful when one realizes that the bird is communicating with others, looking for a mate, defending its territory, and the reason the trees are so tall is that they are reaching for the sky, competing with each other for the most precious of all resources—sunlight. Many of the wildflowers bloom in the spring because that is when the trees have no leaves; then they can receive the gift of sunlight. In a dense forest with very few flowers and bushes under the tall trees, if one of those trees happens to fall, magically that space will fill with flowers and leaves and brush. This vegetation grows from seeds that may have been transported there by birds or by the wind.

Observe the creatures in the woodland. What are they? How do they find food? How do they find their mates? What do they need to survive? How do they communicate with each other? How do they survive in the winter? How did they evolve to be the way they are?

Look into the sky and see the glory of the countless little diamonds glittering against the black void. Realize that each little diamond is a star like our sun, each with its own size and brightness. The hazy glow of the Milky Way is the huge galaxy of 100 million stars in which we live, seen from our place within it. We see the Milky Way as a band across the sky, because the galaxy is flat and thin. The overwhelming grandeur of the universe makes us want to explore, just in the same way that a child wonders what's in the next room or how a toy works. Just in the same way that a teacher wonders how a child's mind works and develops.

What you just read are the words of Nobel Prize–winning physicist Russell Hulse in response to my question "What motivates you to study science?" Then he added, "Scientists are often motivated by aesthetics."

As you read through this chapter, think about the answers to these questions:

1. **What is science?**
2. **What are the branches of science?**
3. **How do scientists think and work?**
4. **What is the role of creativity in the work of a scientist?**
5. **What makes a person scientifically literate?**

The Nature of Science and Scientists

To teach science, you need to have an understanding of the nature of science and scientists, and you need to construct meaning for the term *science*. This involves looking at how scientists work, the skills they need to do their work, and what motivates them. In this chapter, you will meet several scientists who will tell you why they study science and what it means to them. They will also tell you about their disciplines. As the chapter continues, you will become familiar with multiple views of what makes a scientifically literate person.

Following the theme of this book, in Chapter 3 you will move into science teaching with a series of simple, hands-on activities that you can use in your class-room to help your *students* become familiar with some of the processes scientists use. This is important because it will enable your students to begin to construct an accurate view of the nature of science.

Benchmarks for Science Literacy: Project 2061 (American Association for the Advancement of Science [AAAS], 1993) says:

STANDARDS

Liking science is important

From their very first day in school, students should be actively engaged in learning to view the world scientifically. That means encouraging them to ask questions about nature and to seek answers, collect things, count and measure things, make qualitative observations, organize collections and observations, discuss findings, etc. Getting into the spirit of science and liking science are what count most. Awareness of the scientific world view can come later (p. 6).

What Is Science?

Science is a cultural force

What *is* **science?** For many years intellectuals have debated the answer to this question, and many perspectives have emerged. Here is one viewpoint:

Simply put, science is knowledge of nature and pursuit of that knowledge. Yet this pursuit involves a great deal. It involves, among other things, a history, a method of inquiry, and a community of inquirers. Today, especially, science is a cultural force of overwhelming importance and a source of information indispensable to technology. (Kneller, 1978, p. 1).

Science: Inquiry and Discovery

Science is about inquiry and discovery: Science process

People are curious about the world. They ask questions and seek answers so that they can understand how things work. Science is a way of looking at the world and seeking explanations so that we can understand how the world operates. It is a way of solving problems and using the solutions to those problems to explain why things happen as they do. Solving problems and seeking explanations often lead to unexpected discoveries and more unanswered questions. The process of asking questions, seeking answers, and discovering new things can be quite exciting, making science a field for explorers who chart new territory. In short, science is about inquiry and discovery.

Science is developed through a range of discoveries: Science process

Sometimes great scientific breakthroughs occur, but most of the time progress is made slowly and steadily as a result of the contributions of many people. Dramatic discoveries sometimes change ideas about how the world works in more sudden, fundamental ways. While such discoveries are very important and famous, such as the work of Albert Einstein, most of science progresses through a range of discoveries, from the very small to the very large.

Through the processes of science, the body of knowledge grows; therefore, it is not surprising that the word *science,* derived from the Latin word *scientia,* means *knowledge.* Science is an activity undertaken by people who are involved in the accumulation of knowledge about the universe. More than a collection of facts, scientific knowledge involves understanding, analyzing, and explaining facts, emphasizing physical cause and observed effect.

Benchmarks for Science Literacy: Project 2061 (AAAS, 1993) says:

STANDARDS

Scientific knowledge accumulates gradually: Science process

History provides another avenue to the understanding of how science works. . . . Although [it is important to emphasize] the great advances in science, it is equally important that students should come to realize that much of the growth of science and technology has resulted from the gradual accumulation of knowledge over many centuries (p. 4).

Science: A Way to Discover Something New

The discovery of a cure for cancer, the mapping of the human genome, and the development of new drugs to treat and cure diseases are examples of scientific discoveries. When I started my career in the early seventies, the scientists whom I worked with discovered a new material that could be used to make soft contact lenses. Hard lenses existed at the time, but it was clear that soft contact lenses would have several advantages. Our company collaborated with what is currently one of the country's largest producers of soft contact lenses, which used the new material to make a variety of prescriptions. It was necessary to test the new lenses on people, and eyeglass wearers (I was not one of them) had the opportunity to volunteer to try the first soft contact lenses. I recall hearing stories by people who tested the soft lenses and saw rainbows when looking at light. When looking at "test" traffic lights, they saw beautiful colors, but were not sure whether the light was red, yellow, or green. So research and development continued. The class of chemicals appropriate for this purpose was discovered, an application existed, and research continued. Today high-quality soft contact lenses are widely available, and millions enjoy the benefits of this discovery.

Science: A Systematic Approach to Uncovering Knowledge About the Universe

One purpose of science is to help us guard against the common mistake of fooling ourselves. It protects us against believing something is true when it is not true. As we observe the world, we use our senses to take in and interpret information. Suppose you observe a young child playing ball near the side of a road, and the ball rolls into the road, right in the path of an approaching car. In this situation, you make both an observation and an inference. You observe the situation and infer that danger is near, and you act quickly: you shout at both the child and the driver to stop. You have used the skills of observation and inference to gain knowledge.

In other situations, however, observation and inference do not work quite as well. Here is an example. A group of students is playing in the schoolyard, and a disagreement erupts between two students. The students who observe what happened are asked to describe and interpret what they saw. It is unlikely that they will all describe and interpret the situation in exactly the same way. In fact, it is common for people to bring their own personal thoughts and feelings into such a situation, therefore affecting what they observe.

Science is a way of thinking and inquiring: Science process

Situations like these bring about the need for a *way of thinking* or *method of dealing* with information that is reliable and truthful, where evidence is gathered in a systematic, controlled manner. Science provides such a process, called the **scientific method**. It is a *way of thinking and inquiring* that allows us to investigate and explain natural phenomena. In this view, science helps to protect us against believing something is true when it is not.

Benchmarks for Science Literacy: Project 2061 (AAAS, 1993) says:

STANDARDS

By gaining lots of experience doing science, becoming more sophisticated in conducting investigations, and explaining their findings, students will accumulate a set of concrete experiences on which they can draw to reflect on the process. At the same time, conclusions presented to students (in books and in class) about how scientists explain phenomena should gradually be augmented by information on how the science community arrived at those conclusions. Indeed, as students move through school, they should be encouraged to ask over and over, "How do we know that's true?" (p. 4)

A Word About the Scientific Method

The scientific method is not a series of steps that scientists follow rigidly, although some people have this mistaken impression. Russell Hulse explains,

[The scientific method] is an approach to seeking knowledge in which scientists weave their way back and forth as they inquire. They begin by gathering data and asking questions. Asking questions is an essential part of science. The world is a complicated place, and without prior knowledge, scientists won't know enough to ask the right questions. They must figure out what sorts of knowledge would help in the quest, find out what is already known, and how it is known. They benefit from knowing what others have already discovered and use it as a framework on which to build.

Then scientists form ideas about the answers to the question being investigated. This is when a hypothesis is formulated. Hypothesis formation is the creativity in the process. It comes from a whole life's experience. Once the hypothesis is tested and a conclusion results, the conclusion is studied. If something really new has been discovered, a scientist must be sure to have built a good, solid foundation for adding to or modifying what is known. In essence, this is the scientific method. As you can see, it is a creative, rather than a rigid, process.

Activity 2.1   Online: What Is Science?

Explore the following web sites and answer the question "What is science?"

> http://www.nova.edu/ocean/biol1090/W2SCIENCE.htm
>
> http://www.enews.com/magazines/discover/

At this site you can find *Discover* magazine, a monthly general science journal.

Search the Internet for additional sites that provide answers to this question. Visit the library or use the Internet to familiarize yourself with the journal *Science* or the weekly science magazine *Science News*. ■

Scientists at Work in the Sciences

Earth and space science, life science, and physical science are divisions of science: Earth and space science, life science, physical science

There are three widely accepted divisions of the domain of science: earth and space science, life science, and physical science. Table 2.1 on page 32 contains the *National Science Education Standards* for these three divisions, or branches, of science. The subject matter in each area focuses on its science facts, concepts, principles, theories, and models (National Research Council, 1996, p. 106). Note that many of the divisions of science overlap, and scientists in different fields often look at the same problem from a different view.

In the paragraphs that follow, you'll meet three scientists who will tell you about their work. Martin Becker, a paleontologist and stratigrapher, studies earth science; Marcia O'Connell, an embryologist, studies life science; and Jill Foley, a graduate student in physics, studies physical science.

Table 2.1
***National Science Education Standards* for Earth and Space, Life, and Physical Science**

Earth and Space Science Standards	
Levels K–4	**Levels 5–8**
Properties of earth materials	Structure of the earth system
Objects in the sky	Earth's history
Changes in earth and sky	Earth in the solar system

Life Science Standards	
Levels K–4	**Levels 5–8**
Characteristics of organisms	Structure and function of living systems
Life cycles of organisms	Reproduction and heredity
Organisms and environments	Regulation and behavior
	Populations and ecosystems
	Diversity and adaptations of organisms

Physical Science Standards	
Levels K–4	**Levels 5–8**
Properties of objects and materials	Properties and changes of properties in matter
Position and motion of objects	Motions and forces
Light, heat, electricity, and magnetism	Transfer of energy

Martin Becker Studies Earth Science

Martin Becker explains that earth science is a conglomerate of a number of fields of study (see the box below for some that you should know about). He believes that studying earth science is a good starting point for elementary science students because the field contains elements of most other branches of science. To gain a good understanding of minerals, a student must learn about the chemical elements that comprise them. To understand fossil organisms, a student must turn to biology. To understand earthquakes, a student needs an understanding of the physics of waves. Studying earth science leads a student to the other sciences, shows how the domains of science overlap, and leads to acquisition of knowledge of the field itself. This process should begin in elementary school.

Earth science is a conglomerate of a number of fields: Earth and space science

- ▶ **Geology** is the study of the solid earth, including rocks and minerals.
- ▶ **Meteorology** is the study of weather systems and the air or atmosphere.
- ▶ **Astronomy** is the study of the objects in the sky and their motion.
- ▶ **Historical geology** and **oceanography** are the study of fossils and evolution, change over time, and the oceans and seas.

These Duke University scientists are engaged in cancer research. Measurement is an important tool in their work, and you will teach students how to measure in the science class.

When asked what motivated him to become a scientist, Dr. Becker explained that as a child, he spent summers at the seashore with his parents and older brother. At age 12, his parents urged their sons to find a way to earn some money. He and his brother were avid boaters who loved salt-water fishing and marine environments, so they started a small business: They became clammers.

At the time, the movie *Jaws* was quite popular. Dr. Becker explained that to clam by treading, one must jump overboard. After seeing the movie, he recalled hearing the *Jaws* theme song "playing in his head" each time he jumped into the water. "We were often chased out of the water by small sharks," he said, adding that he had a "deep fear that the 'big one' would be near."

Fascinated by the many varieties of sharks and the species' ability to remain on earth for 400 million years, he began to study sharks and collect sharks' teeth. Today he has a collection of more than 100,000 sharks' teeth. Studying the "ultimate predator" is a major part of his work. As a paleontologist, he studies fossilized sharks' teeth from the Atlantic and eastern Gulf Coast regions of the United States, including New Jersey, Georgia, and Alabama. He studies the Upper Cretaceous time period, when *Tyrannosaurus rex* roamed the interior of what was then the North American continent. At that time, the region from Texas to New Jersey was a shallow ocean where sharks swam. It is this region, now a terrestrial environment, where he finds the teeth that he studies. As a stratigrapher, he studies sedimentary rock deposited in the earth's layers. This allows him to interpret changes that have occurred in the earth over its 4.7 billion years of history.

Activity 2.2   Hands-on Science: Motivating Your Students to Learn About Earth Science

Overview: Here are some things you can do to get your students to think about earth science.

Materials: Piece of sheet rock (ask school custodian if there is some in the school), galvanized nail (check with the custodian), rock salt used as a de-icer (available in supermarket or hardware store in cold-weather areas), piece of aluminum foil, piece of glass

Procedure: Pass these objects around the room. Ask students where they think the items come from. (These are all minerals. They come to us from the earth, volcanoes, evaporative processes, as erosive products in rocks.) Sheet rock is made of the mineral

Table 2.2
***National Science Education Standards* for Science in Personal and Social Perspectives**

Science in Personal and Social Perspectives Standards	
Levels K–4	**Levels 5–8**
Personal health	Personal health
Characteristics and changes in population	Populations, resources, and environments
Types of resources	Natural hazards
Changes in environments	Risks and benefits
Science and technology in local challenges	Science and technology in society

gypsum. A galvanized nail is made of iron coated with zinc. Rock salt is made of the mineral sodium chloride. Aluminum foil is made from the element aluminum (found as aluminum ore, or bauxite). Glass is a solution composed of sand, soda ash, limestone, and borax. Let students think of other rocks and minerals that we routinely use.

Students need a context for understanding that minerals have an economic importance. People import and export minerals; they are made into products, thereby affecting the global economy. This is a good lead into a discussion of science in personal and social perspectives, including what our natural resources are, where they come from, and how important they are to us (National Research Council, 1996). (See Table 2.2.)

Natural resources meet the needs of society: Earth and space science

Assessment: Listen to your students as they take part in the discussion. Have they grasped the idea that resources are things that we get from the living and nonliving environment to meet the needs and wants of a population (National Research Council, 1996, p. 140)?

You might discuss the fact that people have always used rocks and minerals to make tools and weapons. Point to the development of human culture as plotted by the kinds of rocks and minerals used. Point out that the earliest stages of civilization are called the "Stone Age" and the "Bronze Age." Mention that strong rocks make good building materials. Rocks such as granite are carved for a variety of purposes in construction: thin slabs of slate are often used to make a roof, bricks are made of baked clay, and limestone is a key ingredient in cement (Dixon, 1996). ■

Marcia O'Connell Studies Life Science

Marcia O'Connell studies life science, which she describes as the investigation of the biological world—the world of living things. Biology is generally divided into these major areas: the study of plants, the study of animals, and the study of fungi and microorganisms. The following box lists some major areas of life science.

▶ **Genetics** is the study of heredity and gene regulation.
▶ **Cell physiology** is the study of the structure and function of cells.

> ▶ **Biomedical engineering** uses physics and engineering to build devices to help us study biology and medicine.
> ▶ **Molecular biology** is the study of living things at the molecular level.
> ▶ **Microbiology** is the study of microbes such as bacteria and viruses.

Marcia O'Connell is an embryologist. She studies the ways in which organisms develop from fertilization to birth. She works with zebra fish, the kind you can purchase in the pet store for 50 cents each. She looks at the genetic events that lead to the development of the zebra fish embryo. What she enjoys most about her job is the ability to explore and discover new things.

Dr. O'Connell believes that the elementary science classroom should be a place where students can explore and find new answers. It should be a place where discovery happens rather than one where students focus only on what is known. She says that as a child, she was always fascinated by the world: "I wondered why things are the way they are." Explanations fascinated her, and she always looked for new answers.

Although she had an early interest in science, she did not begin her career in embryology until graduate school. There she realized that she could move from "learning what's known to participating in finding new things that are not known." She explains, "I found that the textbooks don't have all of the information. There's more information to be discovered, and with a little confidence, I learned that I too could become a part of making new discoveries." To make *your* classroom a place where discovery happens, she recommends the next activity.

Activity 2.3   Hands-on Science: Motivating Your Students to Learn About Life Science

Overview: Marcia O'Connell says that your students can begin to learn about life science by studying fish. Start with several male and female zebra fish. (Just buy ten from the pet store and you'll have some of each.) Once they mate, your students will be able to watch the embryos develop into baby fish.

Materials: A fish tank, a good aeration system, one male and one female zebra fish, and flake food (from the pet store). At the bottom of the tank, place a container filled with marbles sitting on a sieve. Once mating occurs, the eggs will be deposited on the marbles and fall through the sieve into the container.

Procedure: Prepare the fish tank, and add the fish. (The pet store can give you directions for setting up the tank and equipment that you purchase. If you purchase a tank from a science supply house, it will come with directions.)

If you want to study the fish embryos, place the container with marbles on a sieve and place the whole apparatus into the fish tank in the evening. The following morning the fish will deposit eggs on the marbles. Remove the container and pour the eggs through a second sieve with a finer weave to catch the eggs. Place the eggs in a petri dish, and observe them under the microscope. You will be able to watch each one grow from a single cell to a little fish in two days. If you don't want to remove the eggs and view them under the microscope, simply allow your students to watch the baby fish as they grow in the fish tank.

Assessment: Have students keep a journal charting the development of the offspring. How do students react to the study of life science? What questions do they ask? ■

Jill Foley Studies Physical Science

Jill Foley is a graduate student who studies **physical science,** the study of the composition and properties of matter and energy. There are two main branches of physical science: chemistry and physics. Jill studies **physics,** which she describes as the search for the most fundamental laws of nature, those that explain the behavior of the entire physical world from a few basic ideas. **Chemistry** is the study of matter and its changes. Changes in matter occur everywhere—in our bodies, in the environment, and all over the universe. In the laboratory, chemists take molecules apart and put them together in new ways to form new products. This is one way in which they study chemistry. Like the life sciences, physical science has many interrelated subdivisions. The box gives a couple of examples.

> ▶ **Physical chemistry** applies physical principles to the reactions that chemical compounds undergo. Astronomy and geology are based on principles of physics.
> ▶ **Engineering** uses the principles of physics and chemistry to develop devices for use in society. Even biology is based on physical science principles.

As a child, Foley was interested in understanding the physical world, but she doesn't remember being exposed to it very much in elementary school. She recalls her introduction to the atom as being in an episode of the sitcom "WKRP in Cincinnati." The "planetary" model of the atom, with negatively charged electrons orbiting a positively charged nucleus of protons and neutrons, was being explained to one of the main characters, Venus Flytrap. At age 9 or 10, Foley was fascinated and wanted to learn more, but unfortunately that didn't happen in elementary school. She hopes other children will have more opportunity to study physical science in the early grades, where she feels it can be understandable and fun.

Jill wants you to know that "physics is for everyone—it's the most basic science, underlying all others. You don't need an advanced degree to know about how the world around you works." Currently she is a graduate student in the program in plasma physics at Princeton University. She is learning about fusion power, which she hopes to help develop into an environmentally friendly, abundant power source.

Physics is the study of the natural world at the most fundamental level: Physical science

What motivated Jill to study physics? She explains that physics is the study of the natural world at the most fundamental level. It requires analytical thinking, putting together an experiment, and focusing on what's important. It also requires a great deal of critical thinking: "You have to separate important from unimportant information, and look at a situation and try to make a prediction about what will happen based on past experience. You get a feeling for what's going on." She enjoys thinking in this way.

Like other physical scientists, Jill has the opportunity to answer many questions: Why does an ice cube float on water? What makes a hot-air balloon rise and fall? What causes lightning and thunder? How does a microwave oven, radio, television set, or cellular phone work? How does a computer process information? How does HDTV work, and how will it bring us a clearer television picture?

Jill believes that physical science makes life less of a mystery. It helps us determine cause-and-effect relationships. It tells us what's going to happen and why. She says that thinking about and doing their own experiments can be empowering for elementary school students: "It's the student's own little universe, and he or she can have control over it." She recommends that teachers work with their students as co-investigators. Together they can figure out what's happening in an experiment. To make *your* classroom a place where physical science happens, try the next three activities.

Activity 2.4   Hands-on Science: Motivating Your Students to Learn About Physical Science

Overview: Some of the most important concepts in physical science, such as the structure of the atom, may at first seem inaccessible to elementary science students, because they are abstract and not on the scale of everyday life. While this is a difficulty for teachers who try to help students learn about such concepts, Jill Foley believes that one of the most fascinating aspects about physical science is trying to visualize and comprehend things that we can't see directly. Of course, we do feel the effects of the structure of matter all the time.

Students can't see electric charges, but they can feel their effects: Physical science

After introducing your students to the **protons, electrons, neutrons,** and structure of the atom, try this activity, which will let your students feel and see some of its consequences. In this activity, students learn about **electric charges** and how they interact. Although students can't see the charges, they can feel their effect.

Materials: For each student, you will need an empty soda can and a balloon.

Procedure: Blow up one student's balloon, and tie it. Then rub the balloon against your hair or a student's hair (this works best if the hair is clean and free of spray, gel, or cream). The balloon now has more electrons than protons and picks up a negative charge.

Like charges repel; unlike charges attract: Physical science

Place the soda can on its side on the table. Hold the balloon near the can, and slowly move it toward the can. Some of the electrons in the can are free to move. Charges that are the same (like charges) repel, so the electrons go to the other side of the can, leaving a positive charge on the balloon side. Opposite charges attract (unlike charges), so the can rolls toward the balloon, which picked up a negative charge when you rubbed it on hair.

Have students repeat the procedure with their own balloons and cans. Now show students how you can make your balloon follow you around the room, or let them have a balloon race.

Next, slowly move your balloon toward someone else's balloon. Do they attract or repel? Try this with other students' balloons. Do all balloons behave in the same way? Think about and devise an explanation for what's happening.

Rub the balloon on your hair (or a student's hair) some more. Does the hair stand up? If it does, it's because the hair picks up a charge, and the charges get as far away from each other as possible. Did you ever move around on a rug and zap your friend with your finger? If you did, your finger released excess electrons, which you picked up from the rug. Did your clothes ever stick to each other when you took them out of the dryer? That happened because clothes pick up a charge when they rub against each other as they dry.

Assessment of understanding can begin by writing in a science journal

Assessment: In your journal, draw the balloon and the can. If the balloon has a negative charge, what are the charges on the can? Label your drawing with "plus" and "minus" charges. Why does the can move toward the balloon? (The can moves toward the balloon because the positive charges on the can are closer to the balloon than the negative charges in the can. The strength of the attraction depends on the distance.) ▪

Activity 2.5   *Hands-on Science: Experimenting with Sound and Light*

Overview: In this activity, students learn about how sound and light travel. Although they can't see sound and light waves, they model them.

Materials: A Slinky™.

Light and sound travel in waves: Physical science

Procedure: Choose two students and have each hold one end of the Slinky. The students stretch the Slinky so that it is a little less than two feet long. Then they shake it up and down so that it makes waves. These are the types of waves you find in water. They are called *transverse waves*. Light also travels in transverse waves.

Next, you will demonstrate how sound travels through the air. Have the two students kneel down on the ground, with each student still holding an end of the Slinky and pressing it against the floor. One student compresses the coils, then releases them, causing the spring to pulse back and forth. This creates a *longitudinal wave*, which is like a sound wave. Sound causes air molecules to compress, then expand. The compressed and expanded area in the air is the medium through which energy is transferred. This allows the vibrations that cause sound to move through the air.

Now have another pair of students connect two cups with a string. Have one student talk into a cup while the other one listens. Ask them if the sound travels faster through the air or via the string that connects the two cups. Then ask all the students to place their fingertips on their throats and then talk. They will feel their throats vibrating. The vocal cords in the throat move as they speak, causing the air in the throat and mouth to vibrate. The vibrating air makes the sounds we hear.

Finally, have students create a variety of musical instruments. Ask them what parts all musical instruments have in common. (They all have parts that move, which cause vibrations.)

Students use journals to explain their thinking

Assessment: Have students draw pictures of longitudinal and transverse waves in their journals. They should explain in their own words how they think sound travels through the air. Ask them what else they would like to learn about sound or light. Have them develop investigations for further study. ▪

not be enough information to form a good question. The scientist might say, "This is a very interesting and important area to study. It is worth the effort to compile information as a basis for further study. I'll go and see what I can find out. I'll write it all down and organize it." This process yields data of all sorts. That scientist, or future scientists, will refer to these data to learn more.

Framing Questions

Scientists' questions are sustainable: Science process

When scientists are ready to pose a question for study, they often require a great deal of time and creative thought. Their questions are rich in scientific content, interesting, and important to them. They often address real-world issues that have real-world consequences. The questions scientists pose are sustainable. This means the scientists must engage in research and pursue solutions over a long period of time, because the solutions require much detail.

When you and your students pose questions for study, spend a good deal of time thinking about how and what you will ask. Be sure the question is broad enough to require that students learn a good deal of science content as they seek solutions. Look at the state and national standards documents, and see if the question helps you to meet standards. Think about the **subproblems**—the smaller questions—that will come up as your students attempt to answer the broader question. Be sure that the question leads your students to investigations that they can actually undertake in the classroom or at home. Sometimes students come up with questions that are good but simply can't be answered by an elementary student.

Students' questions should relate to the real world: Science process

Like scientists' questions, questions posed by students should be related to the real world. This provides context so that the student can see the worth and consequence of the question and how it relates to his or her life. Answering good questions leads to interesting investigations that last for a few weeks or even months. To help your students frame such questions, you can introduce them to a topic and direct them in investigation and exploration. Once they are engaged, allow them to brainstorm new questions for study.

Some examples of good questions for study are:

▶ What kinds of pets do the students in my school have?

▶ What's in our water supply?

▶ Is the air the same all over our state?

▶ What kinds of trees do we have in our town?

▶ What's in the foods we eat in the school cafeteria?

▶ How do the children in our school care for their pets?

▶ How do we use electricity in our homes and in our school?

Each of these questions leads to an investigation that children can undertake. They cover content and skills that are outlined in the state and national standards, have real-world applications, and require a good deal of detail to answer thoroughly.

The story of Brynn Olsen illustrates how a kindergartner formulated and answered an important question, which became a science investigation for her.

Brynn Inquires About Skeletons

On Halloween, Brynn Olsen and her kindergarten classmates learned about skeletons. They had a guest speaker who brought a real skeleton to class so they could see and feel the bones. Brynn thought about the skeletal system for a long time. She asked, "Why do people have skeletons?" She had many subquestions: "How many bones are in a skeleton?" "How do our skeletons get bigger as we grow?" "Do boys and girls both have the same skeletons?" "Do the foods we eat make our skeletons stronger?" "Is it hard to make a skeleton?"

One evening, her mother cooked pasta for dinner. Brynn helped. As she held the uncooked pasta in her hands, Brynn thought it felt like a bone: it was smooth and hard. Ever since she saw the skeleton on Halloween, she wanted to make one and learn more about them. This became an important investigation for her.

She thought that beads could make a good skeleton, but they were too small and easy to lose. The uncooked ziti, though, would be perfect. She asked her mother to help her make a ziti skeleton, and Mom agreed. They started out with a long string and threaded the string through the openings in the pasta. That was the spine. They made the skull by turning a shorter chain of pasta into a circle and connecting it to the top of the spine. There were two pasta chains for the arms and two for the legs. Since males and females have similar skeletons, and Brynn wanted people to know that her skeleton was a female, she used red nail polish to paint its fingernails and toenails.

When they were done, Brynn and her mother made a pasta skeleton that looked somewhat like a real skeleton; it was about the size of an average kindergartner. Creating her own skeleton was important to Brynn. She learned that bones have different lengths. She discovered that there are 206 separate bones in a human skeleton. Bones give people support and structure. The skeletal system gives the body shape and protects the organs inside.

Brynn learned that bones work with muscles to help the body move. Joints connect one bone to another bone. Ligaments keep bones together and hold them in place. She also learned that children must eat foods like milk and cheese to keep their bones strong.

Brynn wants to be a veterinarian, and she wants to learn more about bones in the future. She plans to investigate animal skeletons next.

Designing an Approach

A literature review provides information about a topic

After formulating important questions, the scientist next decides how she or he will go about finding the answers by designing an approach. First, the scientist reviews the literature on the topic to find out what is already known about it. Next, the scientist plans the research, estimates how much it will cost, and determines what instruments are needed. Once these considerations are well thought out and the funding is available for the project, the investigation begins.

Designing an Experiment

Hypotheses should have testable consequences: Science process

Sometimes scientists undertake exploratory studies in which they observe and write about what they study. In most cases, they formulate **hypotheses,** statements taken to be true for the purpose of investigation. They formulate hypotheses that have testable consequences. To test their hypotheses, scientists often design experiments, calibrate instruments, carry out trial runs, and then perform experiments. They make **observations** (facts gathered by experiment), then **collect, analyze,** and **interpret** data. They construct **experiments** to test the factors related to the question under investigation. These factors, called **variables,** change, or vary. In an experiment, all variables are kept the same except for the one being tested. This is the process of **controlling variables**. If variables are not controlled, the experiment is not a true assessment of the work. Manipulated variables are **independent variables,** and responding variables are **dependent variables**.

Scientists collect data under reproducible conditions, because scientists routinely test one another's work. The data either *support* or *do not support* the original hypotheses. Scientists generally try to disprove hypotheses, for if a particular hypothesis cannot be disproved after extensive testing, it is likely to be accepted as true.

Analyzing and Sharing Work

Scientists share work and offer criticism

Scientists propose explanations, consider alternative explanations, make conclusions, report findings in journals, and share their results at conferences. When they share their work, other scientists react to it and offer criticism. This allows the scientist to reflect on his or her findings and move on to the next steps. These steps might include repeating the research, this time with a new hypothesis.

Scientific Facts and Natural Laws

Scientific facts are established truths: Science process

What happens when a particular hypothesis is tested over and over again and experimental results confirm the hypothesis? When this happens, we say that scientists establish truth, which we call a **scientific fact;** it can be reproduced at will anywhere in the world. When large numbers of related facts are combined, we develop **natural laws**. You are familiar with many natural laws—gravity,

These children are conducting an investigation about mass. They are gathering data and will explain their findings to the class tomorrow.

conservation of mass, conservation of energy. Natural laws apply in all observable cases; therefore, we conclude that they apply to all possible cases. Here is the story of the development of one natural law.

Law of Conservation of Mass

The **law of conservation of mass** tells us that mass is neither created nor destroyed in an ordinary chemical reaction. This law was tested by extensive experimentation; the work of the French chemist-physicist Antoine Lavoisier provides evidence for this conclusion.

Lavoisier performed many experiments involving matter. In one instance, he heated tin in sealed jars that contained air. He measured the mass of his starting materials (tin and air), and when the reaction concluded, he measured the mass of the products (tin and a powder). In every case, the mass of the oxygen from the air in the jar plus the original metal (tin) equaled the mass of the remaining metal

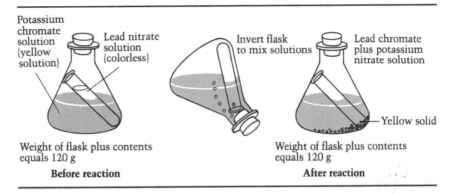

Potassium chromate solution (yellow solution)

Lead nitrate solution (colorless)

Invert flask to mix solutions

Lead chromate plus potassium nitrate solution

Yellow solid

Weight of flask plus contents equals 120 g

Before reaction

Weight of flask plus contents equals 120 g

After reaction

Figure 2.1
Saw of Conservation of Mass   An experiment like Lavoisier's. An experimenter puts a test tube containing a lead nitrate solution into a flask containing a potassium chromate solution. The experimenter weighs the flask and contents, then turns the flask upside down to mix the two solutions. A chemical reaction takes place, producing a yellow solid. The experimenter weighs the flask and contents again and finds no change in mass.

plus the powder. (Stop for a minute and think about what this means.) Lavoisier concluded that when a chemical change occurs, matter is neither created nor destroyed; it just changes from one form to another. This is a statement of the law of conservation of mass (Sherman & Sherman, 1999). Figure 2.1 illustrates another experiment supporting this principle.

Laws of Gravity and Conservation of Energy

Other familiar natural laws include the **law of gravity,** which describes how objects behave when they fall, and the **law of conservation of energy,** which states that in any chemical or physical change, energy is neither created nor destroyed; it is simply converted from one form to another.

The Skills That Guide the Processes of Science

Scientists use process skills: Science process

As an elementary science teacher, you should become comfortable with the ways scientists work when they carry out their investigations so that you can bring this process to your classroom. When at work, scientists use skills called **science process skills,** or simply **process skills.** These skills include observing, estimating, classifying, inferring, measuring, collecting data, making charts and graphs, analyzing data, communicating, predicting, defining operationally, making hypotheses, controlling variables, experimenting, and formulating models (see Table 2.3). These process skills are among the tools of scientists, the tools that help them do their work. In the next chapter, you'll have the opportunity to learn more about these skills and practice them in the classroom.

Table 2.3
The Science Process Skills

Process Skill	Description
Observing	To watch attentively and make a systematic scientific observation
Estimating	To make an educated guess or approximate calculation about a quantity
Predicting	To state, tell about, or make known in advance on the basis of special knowledge
Forming and testing hypotheses	To formulate an explanation that accounts for a set of facts that can be tested by further investigation
Measuring	To make a comparison between an object and a standardized or an unstandardized unit
Choosing and controlling variables	To manipulate one factor while holding the others constant to determine the outcome of an event
Collecting data	To collect information organized for analysis or used as a basis for decision making
Classifying	To arrange or organize data according to category
Making charts and graphs	To display data in a visual format
Analyzing data	To examine data methodically and separate the data into parts or basic principles to determine the nature of the whole
Inferring	To conclude from evidence or derive a conclusion from facts
Communicating	To express oneself in a way that is readily and clearly understood
Defining operationally	To describe the nature of basic qualities of an object or a phenomenon based on information or experience with it
Formulating models	To create a tentative description of a system or theory that accounts for all of its known properties.

Putting This All Together

Now that you know a bit about science, scientists, and how they work, our discussion turns to the idea of scientific literacy. One goal of science teaching is to nurture our students so that they become literate adults who can make sound, well-thought-out decisions. The skills they practice in the science classroom move with them when they enter the real world as adults who can think and reason. We begin our discussion of scientific literacy with a short scenario.

Scientific Literacy: Using Scientific Knowledge to Make Sound Decisions

While shopping in the supermarket, you pick up a can and notice a health claim on the label. The claim is about nutrients. The label says, "Diets low in fat and high in vegetables, especially those containing vitamin A, C, or fiber, may reduce the risk of certain types of cancer." You pick up another can, and the label says, "A diet containing sufficient levels of calcium helps maintain good bone health and may reduce the risk of osteoporosis in later life." How do you know if these claims are true? Will either of these products make you a healthier person? How do you decide which product, if any, to buy?

Being scientifically literate helps. In 1990, the Nutrition Labeling and Education Act (NLEA) empowered the Food and Drug Administration (FDA) to regulate health claims on labels, and initiated "Nutrition Facts" labels. Health claims can appear on labels only if "there is significant scientific agreement to support the claim, the food contains the correct amount of the nutrient that is linked to the disease, the food doesn't contain high levels of damaging nutrients such as fat, saturated fat, cholesterol, or sodium, and it isn't a junk food" (Liebman, 1997). Knowing and understanding this information helps you make good decisions about which foods to eat. It also helps you separate fact from fiction. As a teacher, you will help to develop scientific literacy in your students so that they use scientific knowledge to become good decision makers throughout their lives.

Defining *Scientific Literacy:* Multiple Perspectives

Our nation embraces a number of important goals for science education. One goal is that all students should achieve scientific literacy, enabling them to share in the "richness and excitement of comprehending the natural world" (National Research Council, 1996, p. IX). According to the *National Science Education Standards,*

STANDARDS

Once we meet this goal, students will be able to make personal decisions based on scientific principles and processes, and they will be able to participate in discussions of scientific issues that affect society. They will be able to examine local and national issues and identify underlying scientific issues, expressing positions that are informed by science and technology, and they will be able to use the scientific method to think critically, solve problems creatively, work collaboratively with others, and understand the value of technology (National Research Council, 1996, p. IX).

Scientific literacy means employing scientific thinking in decision making: Science process

People routinely face situations that require decision making. They can best handle such situations if they have knowledge of scientific principles and competence in employing scientific thinking in the decision-making process. Scientific literacy entails the ability to ask questions, observe, talk to people with knowledge in a certain field, read and understand what one is reading, refine original questions, ask new questions, gather and analyze new data, understand the situation, make an informed decision, and act on it. Situations that require scientific literacy are wide ranging:

▶ How much exercise do I need to stay healthy?

▶ If I want to lose or gain weight, what foods should I include in my diet? How often should I eat?

▶ Is it safe to live under high-tension wires?

▶ Should nuclear power be utilized as an energy source?

▶ When faced with illness, what treatment is best? What are the right questions to ask health care providers?

▶ When is a species endangered, and what can we do to save it?

▶ How should we manage our natural resources?

▶ Should school buses have seat belts?

▶ What knowledge do teachers need to purchase the best scientific equipment for an elementary science laboratory?

Characteristics of a Scientifically Literate Person

A scientifically literate person gathers information, asks questions, and makes informed decisions about situations such as those just listed.

 STANDARDS

The *National Science Education Standards* define *scientific literacy* as the "knowledge and understanding of science concepts and processes required for personal decision making, participation in civic and cultural affairs, and economic productivity." This means that a "person can ask, find, or determine answers to questions derived from curiosity about everyday experiences." Such a person has the ability to "describe, explain, and predict natural phenomena" and can "read with understanding articles about science in the popular press and engage in social conversations about the validity of the conclusions" (National Research Council, 1996, p. 22).

When scientific information is presented, the literate person evaluates the source and quality of the information and uses technical terms appropriately, applying basic scientific concepts and processes. As an elementary school teacher, you will help your students begin their development as scientifically literate individuals; the process will continue throughout their lives.

Viewing Science as a Human Activity That Reflects Diversity

To become scientifically literate, students need an accurate vision of science. As a teacher, you will help your students view science as an activity that involves all kinds of people; you will provide an understanding of the types of problems that our society must tackle; and you will help students distinguish between science and science fiction.

Unfortunately, children sometimes think that scientists become involved with outlandish situations that are of no practical value to humanity. I recently watched a rerun of one of my favorite movies, *Back to the Future,* starring Michael J. Fox, who plays Marty McFly, an ordinary person; and Christopher Lloyd, who plays Doc Brown, a stereotypical scientist. Doc is an eccentric, middle-aged white male who is well-meaning and quite intelligent, but lacking in social skills and a bit absent-minded. He builds a time machine that takes the two main characters back into their past and then back to the present (i.e., the future). The movie is very entertaining, but it does not accurately portray the important work of science or scientists.

Scientists represent the diversity of society. They can be women, people of color, and people of all ages.

Table 2.4
***National Science Education Standards* for History and Nature of Science**

History and Nature of Science Standards	
Levels K–4	**Levels 5–8**
Science as a human endeavor	Science as a human endeavor
	Nature of science
	History of science

Another familiar character is Spock, the science officer in *Star Trek*. He is impeccably groomed, logical, all-knowing, authoritative, and devoid of emotion. Spock is a wonderful character, but he does not portray a real scientist. Still another stereotypical scientist is The Professor, whom you can meet if you watch reruns of "Gilligan's Island." No matter what the problem, others call on him to formulate the solution, whether it be to construct a weather station, a Geiger counter, or a radio. He completes each task successfully and systematically, and shows no emotion, even when all attempts to rescue the group from the island fail.

Scientists represent the diversity of society

The work and lives of real scientists are far removed from the images portrayed by movies and television. Women as well as men work in the scientific disciplines. Scientists represent all age, racial, ethnic, economic, social, and political groups. This diversity is the message you should bring to your students (see Table 2.4).

Each child comes to your class with an ethnic identity. As a teacher, it is important for you to recognize the ethnic identities of your students; instead of ignoring differences, you should be conscious of them and include the work of people of all backgrounds in your lessons. You will help your students as they learn to recognize, respect, and appreciate their own ethnic heritages and those of their classmates. You will also assess students' prior knowledge before planning for instruction, and recognizing individual ethnic identities is part of assessing your students' prior knowledge.

Activity 2.9   Online: Scientists Are a Diverse Group

Explore the following Internet sites and become familiar with the diversity of the scientific community.

African Americans in the Sciences

> http://www.lib.lsu.edu/lib/chem/display/faces.html

Archives of Women in Science and Engineering

> http://www.lib.iastate.edu/spcl/wise/wise.html

Girls and Women in Science

> http://www.beloit.edu:80/~gwsci/gws.html

Multicultural Science Resource

> http://205.203.3.9:80/multicultural.html

Students' Understanding of Themselves

Scientific literacy develops through the years

Helping students to develop an understanding and appreciation of their own ethnicity is a first step. As students grow older, they begin to develop a national identity, which includes commitment to the ideals of a democratic society. Students who attain a strong national identity are able to develop a global identity, which occurs when they understand how our nation fits into the global picture. They will then be able to view the actions of each nation and understand how the actions of one nation affect other nations around the world (Banks, 1990). This is a tall order for elementary school students, but as an elementary teacher, you will plant the seeds that will grow as they do. It is also an important factor in the development of scientific literacy. As scientifically literate adults, students will understand how decisions made locally and regionally have both a national and a global impact.

Youngsters who are developing their individual, national, and global identities are well served by a curriculum that focuses on the contributions of scientists of diverse ethnic groups. They need to know that women and men of all ages participate in all areas of science and technology, and have done so for centuries. Throughout the text, we will focus on such accomplishments.

Activity 2.10   *In the Elementary Classroom: Your Students Draw a Scientist*

Overview: In this activity, your students will draw a scientist. The activity works best with students who are in grades 2 and above.

Materials: Paper, crayons, or markers

Procedure: Ask students to draw a scientist. This activity can be done individually, in pairs, or in groups. Once the drawings are finished, have students move from table to table to view one another's work.

Assessment: Ask students to describe one another's drawings. Look for patterns or stereotypes, such as drawings that depict scientists as middle-aged white males with unkempt hair and white lab coats. If students produce many such drawings, talk about stereotyping. Explain that when people rigidly assign stereotypical roles or attributes to a group, they limit the abilities and potential of that group. Stereotyping denies us a knowledge of the diversity, complexity, and variation among humans (Lerner, 1997). Explain that scientists can be women, people of color, and people of all ages. ▪

Constructing Your Knowledge of Science and Science Teaching

As you reflect on this chapter, think about what the term *science* means to you. Did its meaning change as you read the chapter? What are your impressions of scientists? How do they think? What is the role of creativity in the work of a scientist?

Developing scientific literacy in your students is one of your major goals as an elementary science teacher. It is a goal that you won't be able to accomplish in a year, but you will be able to give your students a good beginning or move them along a path that has already been paved. Developing scientific literacy is not simple. It requires presentation of and understanding of scientific concepts in a developmentally appropriate way. It requires careful lesson planning and good utilization of resources.

Also think about what the term *scientific literacy* means to you. Did its meaning change as you read the chapter? What decisions have you made in your own life that required knowledge of science and technology?

Key Terms

science (p. 28)
scientific method (p. 30)
geology (p. 32)
meteorology (p. 32)
astronomy (p. 32)
historical geology and
   oceanography (p. 32)
genetics (p. 34)
cell physiology (p. 34)
biomedical engineering (p. 35)
molecular biology (p. 35)
microbiology (p. 35)
physical science (p. 36)
physics (p. 36)
chemistry (p. 36)

physical chemistry (p. 36)
engineering (p. 36)
protons (p. 37)
electrons (p. 37)
neutrons (p. 37)
electric charges (p. 37)
reactants (p. 39)
products (p. 39)
subproblems (p. 41)
hypotheses (p. 43)
observations (p. 43)
collecting data (p. 43)
analyzing data (p. 43)
interpreting data (p. 43)

experiments (p. 43)
variables (p. 43)
controlling variables (p. 43)
independent variables (p. 43)
dependent variables (p. 43)
scientific fact (p. 43)
natural laws (p. 43)
law of conservation of mass
   (p. 44)
law of gravity (p. 45)
law of conservation of energy
   (p. 45)
science process skills (p. 45)
process skills (p. 45)

Reviewing Chapter 2: Questions, Extensions, Applications, and Explorations

1. Write your own answer to the question: What is science?

2. In the 15th century, the Greeks, Chinese, Koreans, and Europeans observed nature but did not engage in science. In the 16th and 17th centuries, the view of science changed as people began to "do" science. Using the Internet or the library, learn more about this changing nature of science. Check these history of science web sites:

Beginner's Guide to Research in the History of Science
http://www.kaiwan.com/~lucknow/horus/guide/tp1.html

18th Century History of Science Links
http://www.english.upenn.edu/~jlynch/18th/science.html

Autumn Hall
http://users.deltanet.com/~rblough/

3. You wake up in the morning and watch the sun rise. In the evening, you watch the sun set. You wonder why this happens. In your classroom, ask some of your students to answer the question: Why does the sun rise and set? They will make up stories. Record their stories. Some of the stories will be true, and some won't. How will you help them decide whether to accept their stories as true or to seek greater understanding?

4. Think about a decision you made in the past year that required knowledge of science and technology. Were you able to make a sound decision based on your understanding of scientific principles?

5. Over the next week, scan the local newspaper for articles that deal with issues requiring scientific literacy. Find some situations or events that you could discuss with your students.

Print Resources

American Institute of Physics. (1997). *The best of wonder science: Elementary science activities*. New York: Delmar Publishers.

Dixon, D. (1996). *Rocks and minerals*. London: A Quarto Children's Book.

Dorling Kindersley. (1993). *Science Encyclopedia*. London: Dorling Kindersley Ltd.

Hamilton, L. (1996). *Child's play around the world*. New York: Berkley.

Nye, B. (1993). *Bill Nye the Science Guy's big blast of science*. New York: Addison-Wesley.

Ostlund, K. (1992). *Science process skills: Assessing hands-on student performance*. New York: Addison-Wesley.

Science and Technology Department of the Carnegie Library of Pittsburgh. (1994). *The handy science answer book*. Detroit: Visible Ink Press.

VanCleave, J. (1997). *Play and find out about nature: Easy experiments for young children*. New York: John Wiley & Sons.

Willow, D., & Curran, E. (1989). *Science sensations: An activity book from the Children's Museum, Boston*. New York: Addison-Wesley.

Electronic Resources

Expect the Best from a Girl
http://www.academic.org/

Exploring Your Future in Math and Science
http://www.cs.wisc.edu/~karavan/afl/home.html

4,000 Years of Women in Science
http://crux.astr.ua.edu/4000WS/4000WS.html

Campbell-Kibler Associates, Inc.
http://www.tiac.net/users/ckassoc/

Ask Rafael
http://www.chias.org/www/edu/asksraf/askraf/html

Bill Nye, the Science Guy
http://nyelabs.kets.org

Girls and Women in Science
http://www.beloit.edu:80/~gwsci/gws.html

Multicultural Science Resource
http://205.203.3.9:80/multicultural.html

Children's Literature

Dispezio, Michael
Awesome Adventures in Electricity and Magnetism
(Sterling Publications, 1998)
ISBN: 0-8069-9819-9
Preschool–Grade 3

Riley, Peter
Electricity (Franklin Watts, 1998)
ISBN: 0-531-11511-9
Preschool and Grades K–3

Lunis, Natalie
Discovering Electricity: Student Book
(Newbridge Communications, 1997)
ISBN: 1-56784-477-4
Grades 2–6

Richards, Elsie
Turned on by Electricity (Troll Associates, 1997)
ISBN: 0-8167-4254-5
Grades 3–6

Evento, Susan (ed.)
Matter and Energy: Mini Book (Newbridge
Communications, 1997)
ISBN: 1-56784-348-4
Preschool and Grades K–2

Kerrod, Robin
Matter and Materials (Thomson Learning, 1995)
ISBN: 0-7614-0031-1
Grades 5 and up

Patten, John
Solids, Liquids, and Gases (Rourke Books, 1995)
ISBN: 1-55916-126-4
Grades 1–4

Patten, John
Matter Really Matters (Rourke Book Co., 1995)
ISBN: 1-55916-124-8
Grades 1–4

Glover, David
Solids and Liquids (Kingfisher Books, 1993)
ISBN: 1-85697-845-1
Grades 1–4

Time-Life Book Editors
Structure of Matter (Time Life, 1992)
ISBN: 0-80949-662-3
Grades 3 and up

Darling, David
From Glasses to Gases: The Science of Matter
(Dillon Books, 1992)
ISBN: 0-87518-500-2
Grades 5 and up

Lafferty, Peter
Matter & Energy (Ferguson, 1991)
ISBN: 0-02-941141-6
Grades 3–6

CHAPTER 3

Introducing the Processes of Science

Halloween is just around the corner, and Linda Zalewitz's fourth-grade classroom is decorated for the event. Mrs. Zalewitz bought pumpkins from a local merchant, and pumpkins seem to be everywhere. She just completed a lesson on pumpkin geography, in which her students used thin strips of masking tape to mark the equator and the meridians, then carefully measured and taped lines of latitude and longitude to their pumpkins. Next, they drew the continents and the oceans to create little globes. That activity lasted for several days.

As they located the oceans, some of her students began to wonder whether pumpkins float or sink. She realized this was an excellent topic for investigation, so today she will allow her students to begin to answer the question. This student-directed investigation will take a couple of days to complete. They will plan today and experiment tomorrow.

Mrs. Zalewitz's students work in groups of four. Here's what happens in one group. The students begin by stating the question: Do pumpkins sink or float in water? They discuss what they must keep in mind when answering the question. First, each student's pumpkin is different. Some are bigger than others, and their shapes are slightly different. The students wonder what effect the size and shape of the pumpkin will have on whether it sinks or floats.

Next, they make a prediction. Based on the size of the pumpkins, they think that the two smaller pumpkins will float and the two bigger pumpkins will sink. How will they test this? They will need a big bowl of water: perhaps a bathtub, a kiddy swimming pool, the classroom sink, or just a fish tank. They will fill it with water. They will do two trials for each pumpkin. In other words, they will do each test twice. The water will be the same temperature for each pumpkin and each trial. The students

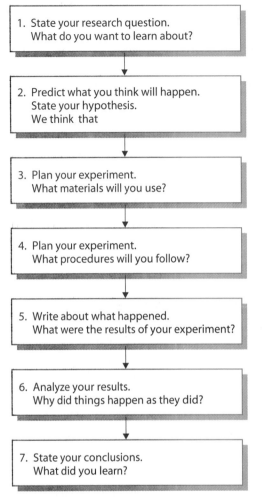

1. State your research question.
   What do you want to learn about?

2. Predict what you think will happen.
   State your hypothesis.
   We think that

3. Plan your experiment.
   What materials will you use?

4. Plan your experiment.
   What procedures will you follow?

5. Write about what happened.
   What were the results of your experiment?

6. Analyze your results.
   Why did things happen as they did?

7. State your conclusions.
   What did you learn?

Figure 3.1
Using Science Process

will place the pumpkin in the water carefully to avoid splashing and losing water. They will record their data on a chart (see Figure 3.1).

Mrs. Zalewitz discusses the plan with the group. She has a big fish tank that they can use. She tells them they are ready to experiment. Tomorrow they will answer the question and expand their understanding of floating and sinking. Mrs. Zalewitz is thrilled that her students are so enthusiastic about the experience. It has clear connections to their lives and is interesting and fun to think about. She believes they are developing the skills necessary to become independent inquirers about the natural world.

When they carry out the experiment the next day, the students are amazed. *All* of the pumpkins float, even the biggest ones! The students wonder why, so they ask more questions: "What's inside a pumpkin?" "Is it solid all the way through, or is there some space inside?" "Is the space filled with air?" "Do big pumpkins have more space inside than small pumpkins?" "Do pumpkin seeds float?"

The students notice that when the pumpkins float, each pumpkin seems to find its own favorite position—usually on one side. Someone wonders whether this has anything to do with the way the pumpkin grew. There are lots of new questions to answer and much to think about. Tomorrow Mrs. Zalewitz will let them dissect their pumpkins and look inside. It will be a bit messy, but they will learn from the experience. She will give them magnifying glasses so they can examine the pumpkins' insides carefully. Mrs. Zalewitz says to herself, "My students are thinking, asking questions, investigating, acting like scientists, and enjoying science class. This experience couldn't be better!"

The example you just read encapsulates much of the information that will be presented in this chapter, which provides practice with the science process skills.

Throughout the chapter, you will find hands-on activities that you can use in your college classroom or with students in your elementary science classrooms.

As you read the chapter, think about the answers to these questions:

1. **How do elementary science teachers help students become familiar with the science process skills?**

2. **What are some ways to practice observation, description, estimation, measurement, and classification skills in the classroom?**

3. **How can I help my students use multiple process skills to answer a question?**

4. **In what ways do students communicate science explanations in the elementary science classroom?**

5. **How do students use the processes of science to construct knowledge?**

Bringing Inquiry and Discovery to Your Classroom

Throughout this chapter, you will learn about scientific inquiry. You'll also find ways to teach several science topics. In addition to learning about how the senses help us to communicate, you will learn ways to teach your students about the senses. Using scientific inquiry, you'll discover ways to classify animals by what they eat. Then you'll engage in a simple experiment. When given three different brands of bubble bath, you will determine which one makes the best bubbles.

Science as Inquiry

Science process skills facilitate investigation: Science process

Using the science process skills will enable your students to engage in scientific inquiry and carry out investigations so that they will have a way to study the natural world on their own.

STANDARDS

The *National Science Education Standards* point out that inquiry "refers to the activities of students in which they develop knowledge and understanding of scientific ideas, as well as an understanding of how scientists study the natural world" (National Research Council, p. 23). *Benchmarks for Science Literacy: Project 2061* tells us that by the end of the second grade, "students should know that when a science investigation is done the way it was done before, we should expect to get a very similar result. Science investigations generally work the same way in different places. By the end of the fifth grade, students should know that results of similar scientific investigations seldom turn out exactly the same. Sometimes this is because of unexpected differences in the things being investigated, sometimes because of unrealized differences in the methods used or in the circumstances in which the investigation is carried out, and sometimes just because of uncertainties of observations" (American Association for the Advancement of Science, 1993, p. 6.)

Inquiry is a technique used in classrooms since ancient times; Socrates, Aristotle, and Plato employed this method of teaching to get students to think and to become involved in learning and creating. John Dewey (1933) described this process as one in which we "bring facts before the mind that enable a person to reach a conclusion on the basis of evidence" (p. 13). Dewey's view of inquiry became popular during a conference of scientists and later inspired the publication of Jerome Bruner's (1960) classic book *The Process of Education.*

Process skills facilitate thinking and problem solving: Science process

All of those who write about inquiry and discovery tell us that certain basic processes are found in every episode that involves inquiry. These are the science process skills (review Table 2.3 on page 46). They help us to think and solve problems. As a teacher, you will help your students learn to think and become actively involved in their own learning so that they can construct knowledge.

To accomplish this, you will structure learning situations so that your students become aware of the processes of science and have opportunities to practice them. They will learn to ask questions, since questioning is closely related to inquiry teaching. Your goal is to have your students learn to think like scientists and to apply the same thinking process to reading, language arts, world languages, visual and performing arts, mathematics, social studies, health and physical education, to the workplace, and to life in general as they become literate adults. Students should learn to observe carefully, interpret what they observe, understand a situation in its context, and feel good about this experience. They should begin to understand the nature of science and to develop an appreciation for "how we know" what we know in science.

Using the Process Skills in Your Classroom

In this section, you will investigate the science process skills in greater depth as we define them and suggest activities that will enable your students to engage in inquiry-based science. Once you have experience with the process skills, you can begin to help students combine process skills and scientific knowledge so that they can think critically and expand their understanding of science.

The activities selected for this section are particularly easy to implement. They require only a limited amount of preparation and provide good practice for novice teachers. In the chapters that follow, the activities become slightly more complex. Since asking questions is related to engaging in inquiry, suggested questions to guide students in constructing knowledge accompany each activity.

Recycle and reuse materials for science investigations

Many of the materials necessary for the activities in this chapter are commonly found in an elementary science classroom; others are generally available around the house or dormitory, or in a local food market or pharmacy. Some of the materials you will use are items you might normally discard as refuse. Recycle

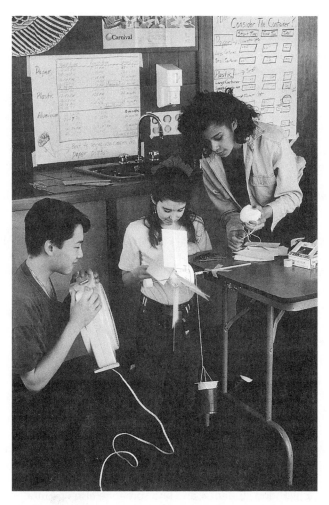

You can implement hands-on science on a low budget if necessary. Be creative. You can examine materials you use in your daily life and reuse them in your lessons.

and reuse such materials so that you get into the habit of looking at everyday items with a careful eye. In this way, you will develop skill in gathering resources for your science classroom and developing creative ways to use them. The cardboard inside of a paper towel roll, an old shoe box or empty tissue box, paper plates, paper cups, and paper clips are all examples of materials that you can use and reuse.

One experienced teacher told me, "I never throw anything away without first examining it and thinking about how I could use it in my classroom." This mindset saves money and allows the teacher to supplement equipment, materials, and supplies provided by the school or district for science instruction. When budgets are lean, teachers can still engage students in hands-on science without spending too much money. As a new teacher, you can bring hands-on science to your students at a very low cost by using this approach. In addition to being friendly to the environment, being creative and resourceful is an important habit for a teacher to develop.

Practicing Observation and Description

Our five senses—sight, touch, taste, smell, and hearing— enable us to observe and to gather information. To be able to practice the skill of observation, students need to engage in simple hands-on activities. We'll begin with an activity that you can use in any of the primary or intermediate grades, called the Peanut Activity, in which students observe peanuts in shells and describe them.

Young children's observations are often descriptive

Young children's observations are generally descriptive or qualitative. In kindergarten, students use pictures or simple words, both spoken and written, to describe peanuts. As students grow older, their observations become more sophisticated and are not only qualitative but quantitative as well. In later grades, they make measurements and create charts and graphs to communicate their observations about peanuts. The Peanut Activity is a good way to start practicing the skills of observation and description.

Activity 3.1 Hands-on Science: How Do You Describe a Peanut?

Overview: Students first work individually, then in groups to observe and describe peanuts in their shells.

Materials: For each student, you will need one peanut (in its shell), one index card, a paper or plastic cup, and a pencil or marker.

Be aware of allergies to peanuts

Procedure: Students work in groups of four or five. (Note: Allergies to peanuts can be quite serious, even if a person just inhales the aroma without eating them, so find out if any of your students have peanut allergies before doing this activity. In this activity, no one eats a peanut, and the peanuts remain in their shells.)

1. Each group of students lists as many uses of a peanut as they can. Encourage students to *brainstorm*—to contribute ideas quickly, even silly ones; suspend judgment; and include everyone's ideas.

2. Each group now gets one cup filled with eight peanuts so that there is one peanut (in its shell) for each student and a few extras, which remain in the cup. Each student chooses a peanut to observe. Students observe their peanuts, describe them, and write descriptors on the index card. (This part takes about 10 to 15 minutes.)

3. Students put the peanuts back in the cup and shake them up. Then each student finds his or her own peanut. (This takes less than five minutes.) Next, students return the peanuts to the cup, exchange index cards (or pictures if they are early childhood students), and find someone else's peanut using the description (or drawing) on the index card. (This takes about five minutes.)

Assessment: Here are questions you can use with students to assess the activity when the observation phase has been completed. Students spend a few minutes answering these questions on their own, share them in their small groups, and then discuss them with the whole class.

Shape, size, texture, and odor identify objects: Science process

1. If you were to describe a peanut to someone who has never seen one before, what characteristics would you use? (Color, shape, size, texture, odor, special identifying marks)

2. Were you successful in finding your own peanut? Were you successful in finding someone else's peanut?

3. As a scientist, what skills have you used to do this? (Observation, communication, collecting data, analyzing data) ∎

Activity 3.2 Hands-on Science: What Does Your Liquid Look Like?

Overview: The teacher pours about a quarter-cup of a different liquid into each of four saucers. Students first observe the liquid in its pure form. Then a drop of food coloring is added to each liquid, and students make a new observation. Students work in pairs in grades K–2, in teams of three to four in grades 3 and 4, and in teams of four to six in grades 5 and 6.

Materials: You will need (per class) two different types of milk (choose from skim, 1 percent, 2 percent, whole, light cream, half-and-half, heavy cream, powdered milk, and canned milk), 1 liter of water, 1 liter of seltzer (or any clear, carbonated beverage), food coloring (one box per class), four shallow saucers (per group; these will be cleaned and reused). (Check with school cafeteria personnel to find out if they can supply the milk. You will need no more than two pints of each type.)

Procedure:

1. Use the placemat (see Figure 3.2) to line up and identify the content of each saucer. Write the names of the liquids that you will observe.

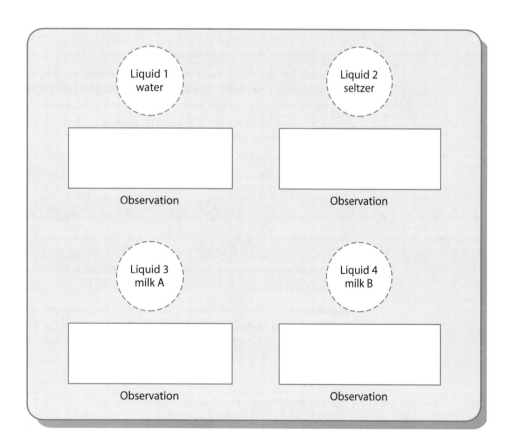

**Figure 3.2
Placemat for the
Observing Liquids
Activity**

Students use a word web to record observations

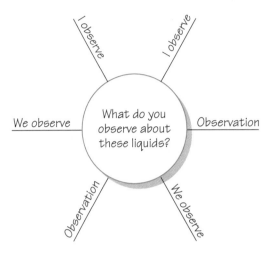

Figure 3.3 Word Web

What do you observe about these liquids?

I observe / I observe / We observe / Observation / Observation / We observe

2. Students need about five to ten minutes to observe the four liquids in their teams. Team members discuss their observations with one another. Then teams share their results in a whole-class discussion (about ten minutes). The teacher uses a word web to record team contributions (see Figure 3.3).

3. Next, one drop of food coloring is added to each liquid. Students observe what happens and record their observations on the placemat. Once again, members of each team share their observations with one another; then teams share their results with the whole class.

Assessment:

1. What were the characteristics of the liquids before the food coloring was added? (Students describe texture, color, odor, shine, fizziness, etc.)

2. What happened to each liquid after the food coloring was added? (The food coloring dispersed in the water; dispersed, but more rapidly, in the seltzer; and remained intact in the milk. Since milk is a mixture of water and varying quantities and types of fat, depending on the type of milk tested, the food coloring is dispersed to a different degree.)

3. What other science process skills besides observation were used in this activity? (Inferring, communicating, collecting data, analyzing data) ▪

Activity 3.3 Hands-on Science: The "Squishy Touch": What Does It Feel Like?

Nerves send stimuli to the brain: Life science

Overview: In this activity, students use the sense of touch to make observations. When the skin is touched, nerves receive stimuli that are sent to the brain and are then translated as messages that the brain understands. This activity is appropriate for students in the primary grades and takes about 45 minutes to complete.

Materials: A variety of household objects: hot (not too hot!) liquids (in sealed jars), cold liquids (in sealed jars), soil (in a small bag), sand (in a small bag), sandpaper, paper towels, tissues, sponges, fabrics, waxed paper, or any items available for students to touch and feel. Be creative!

Procedure:

Integrating science and literature

1. The teacher reads the poem "Squishy Touch" from *A Light in the Attic* by Shel Silverstein, (HarperCollins, 1981).

2. The teacher puts the objects in a large shoe box and passes the box from student to student. Students close their eyes as they put their hands in the box to feel the objects.

Young children must learn to use their senses. This young man is learning to use the sense of touch.

Assessment:

1. In a whole-class discussion, students identify and describe the objects they have touched. The teacher asks, "What kind of object is it? What does it feel like?"

2. As a whole class, students develop a classification scheme for the items. The teacher asks, "How are these objects alike? How are they different?"

3. The teacher leads students in a review of the process skills used in this activity (inferring, communicating, collecting data, classifying, analyzing data). ▪

Activity 3.4 Hands-on Science: What Does It Sound Like?

Integrating science and literature

Overview: In this activity, primary students will learn about hearing. Before class, the teacher prepares a cassette tape with examples of different sounds. As the lesson begins, the teacher reads *The Very Quiet Cricket* by Eric Carle (Philomer Books, 1990). This book is about a cricket that does not talk. The book also focuses on the other four senses. The reading leads into a discussion of sounds that children might hear during a day at school. Some sounds are pleasant, and others are not. Sounds can be loud or soft, or high pitched or low pitched. The class brainstorms examples of each. Then the teacher plays the tape of various sounds. As the children listen, they classify the sounds into different categories. Students then close their eyes as the teacher moves to different parts of the room, plays the tape, and has students identify the direction from which the sound is originating. The next part of the lesson includes a hands-on activity.

Materials: Five shoe boxes, each containing only one of the following suggested objects: (1) marbles, (2) coins, (3) uncooked pasta, (4) pebbles, (5) cotton balls. (Items may be changed, depending on what is available.)

Procedure: Small groups are formed, and students pass the boxes around so that each student has a chance to shake the closed box and make predictions about its contents.

Studying same *and* different

Assessment: In a whole-class discussion, students describe the different sounds they heard when they shook the boxes. The teacher asks, "What sounds did you hear?" Students record the observations, and the class works together to develop a classification scheme for the sounds. The teacher asks, "How are these sounds the same, and how are they different?" Students then brainstorm additional objects they could place in the shoe boxes. ■

Activity 3.5 Hands-on Science: Same and Different

Overview: This activity is about diversity among children. Children learn that not everyone can see in the same way and that blind people "see" with their hands by touching. They will also learn that all people do not hear in the same way and that deaf people have the ability to communicate even though they cannot hear the spoken word.

Materials: Blindfolds (one per child), Braille alphabet cards (Braille is a language that uses raised dots in different patterns instead of letters), books (like Holub, J. [1996]. *My First Book of Sign Language.* NY: Troll Assoc., or Wheeler, C. [1997]. *Simple Signs.* NY: Puffin) or a video such as *Sign Language for Everyone* (1997), starring Cathy Rice.

Procedure: The teacher blindfolds students while they sit at their seats. Students attempt to write and color while wearing the blindfolds. Next, they read (or view a video, if available) about children who must use sign language to communicate.

Assessment: In a whole-class discussion, students discuss how people who are blind and people who are deaf gather information about the world. To begin to move from a teacher-centered to a student-centered lesson, have students create a picture that a blind person could "see" using his or her fingers. This will enable students to apply what they learned in the earlier experience. Conclude by teaching students a few words in sign language. The suggested readings at the end of the chapter provide good reference sources. Have students invent a new way for people to communicate. Students might create a new language that uses more than one sense. ■

Estimation and Measurement

Estimation, measurement, and problem solving are related: Science and mathematics

Three of the tools needed to engage in inquiry—estimation, measurement, and problem solving—are closely related. Asking questions and solving problems leads to collecting data and making measurements. Estimating an answer before coming up with a solution makes problem solving more meaningful.

Estimation

Estimation involves finding an answer that is sufficiently close that decisions can be made. Instead of producing an exact answer, students first determine a ball-park figure. This encourages us to look at the problem and decide what a sensible answer would be. It provides a check on the final answer, which *will be* the exact solution or measurement.

Think of what happens when students omit estimation. The use of a calculator serves as a good example. Suppose a student enters numbers into the calculator with little thought. When an unreasonable answer results, the student is not aware of the error because she or he did not employ estimation as a first step. Estimation allows us to decide when a number is reasonable and expected and when it is not.

Estimation also produces greater appreciation of number size. When teaching your students about estimation, use words such as *about, close to, just about, a little less than, a little more than,* and *between.*

Measurement

Scientific inquiry involves accurate measurement: Science and mathematics

Engaging in scientific inquiry involves observing accurately and measuring carefully. Since the time of the French Revolution, there has been an effort to have all scientists around the world communicate using the same system of measurement. This effort produced the **metric system,** which is quite logical and easy to use; most countries have adopted this system. You can convert units by simply moving a decimal point. Standards of measure are based on natural phenomena; for example, length is determined by a particular wavelength of light, which never changes.

Americans use the English system of measurement: Science and mathematics

In the United States, people use the **English system** of measurement instead of the metric system, although currently there is a move to change to the latter. In the metric system, the foot is the unit of length; it is divided into 12 smaller units called *inches.* We measure longer distances in *yards.* Weight is measured in *pounds,* and pounds are divided into 16 smaller units called *ounces.* Larger weights are measured in *tons.* The unit of volume is the *quart.* To measure smaller quantities, we divide the quart into 32 smaller amounts called *fluid ounces.* Larger units of volume are the *pint* (2 pints = 1 quart) and the *gallon* (4 quarts = 1 gallon). (See Table 3.1.)

Table 3.1
The English System of Measurement

Length	Weight	Volume
12 inches = 1 foot	16 ounces = 1 pound	16 fluid ounces = 1 pint
3 feet = 1 yard	2,000 pounds = 1 ton	2 pints = 1 quart
5,280 feet = 1 mile		4 quarts = 1 gallon

In 1960, the International Bureau of Weights and Standards adopted the International System of Units (SI), setting the standards by which all scientific measurements are made. Based on the metric system, SI consists of a set of standard units of measurement for distance, weight, volume, time, electric current, temperature, light intensity, and amount of substance (see Table 3.2). In addition, there is a set of prefixes that express larger or smaller multiples of these units; the prefixes represent multiples of 10. Other units, called *derived units,* are composed of combinations of these units; for example speed, measured in meters per second, is derived from the unit for distance and the unit for time.

Table 3.2
The Seven Fundamental Metric (SI) Units

Quantity	Unit	Symbol
Length	Meter	m
Mass	Kilogram	kg
Time	Second	s
Electric current	Ampere	A
Temperature	Kelvin	K
Light intensity	Candela	cd
Amount of substance	Mole	mol

Table 3.3 lists the commonly used SI prefixes. To use one of the prefixes, simply add it to the metric unit, indicating that it is a multiple of that unit. For example, the prefix *kilo* has a multiplier of 1,000, so 1 kilometer = 1,000 meters, 1 kilogram = 1,000 grams, and 1 kiloliter = 1,000 liters. The prefix *centi-* has a multiplier of .01. Therefore, 1 centimeter = .01 meters (1/100 of a meter), 1 centigram = .01 grams, and 1 centiliter = .01 liters.

Table 3.3
Table of Metric (SI) Prefixes

Prefix	Symbol	Multiplier
nano	n	0.000000001
micro	Greek *mu*	0.000001
milli	m	0.001
centi	c	0.01
deci	d	0.1
deka	da	10
hecto	h	100
kilo	k	1,000
mega	M	1,000,000

Estimation is an important tool in science teaching: Science process

Estimation is a tool that will help you understand the metric system (SI) and the English system and how they are related. Without using exact numbers, these ballpark estimates will help you make sense of these systems of measurement. For example, a nickel weighs about 5 grams. When dealing with volume, 1/2 cup is about 120 mL, and a cup is about 240 mL. A quart and a liter are very close in volume, so a quart of milk and a 1-liter bottle of soda represent almost the same amount of space. Picture a 2-liter bottle of soda and you will know the volume of space equivalent to 2 liters. A teaspoonful of sugar is equivalent to about 5 mL. Length is easy to estimate: a centimeter is the thickness of a finger, and a millimeter is the thickness of a fingernail.

The following activities will help your students practice the skills of estimation and measurement.

Activity 3.6 Hands-on Science: How Do I Estimate and Measure Length with Handspans?

Integrating science and mathematics

Overview: This activity helps children in grades K–1 learn the skills of estimation and measurement. The teacher asks, "How many handspans wide are your desks?" First, students measure their handspans, and then they estimate how many handspans wide their desks are. Since most students of this age are beginning to conserve length, this activity is developmentally appropriate.

Materials: Paper and pencil to record the data, several pairs of scissors, a chalkboard or sheet of chart paper to record class results

Procedure:

1. Students trace their hands on a sheet of paper and mark off the handspans (see Figure 3.4 on the next page).
2. With scissors, students cut out their handspan templates.
3. Students estimate how many handspans it will take to go from one end of their desks to the other. The estimates are recorded by each student individually and by the teacher on a whole-class chart.
4. Students measure the width of their desks, first using their hands and then using their handspan templates.

Assessment: Students discuss their answers, first with a partner, then in a whole-class discussion. Find out how close predictions were to actual results, and ask students to discuss what strategies they used in making their predictions. Be sure to observe students as they work so that you can assess performance. ■

Activity 3.7 Hands-on Science: How Do I Estimate and Measure Length with the Metric System?

Using math as a tool for science

Overview: This activity is appropriate for students in grades 2 through 4. It teaches them to estimate and provides an introduction to the metric system. The teacher asks, "How many centimeters long is your desk? Estimate first, and then measure."

Materials: Paper, pencil, centimeter rulers, a chalkboard or large sheet of chart paper to record the data

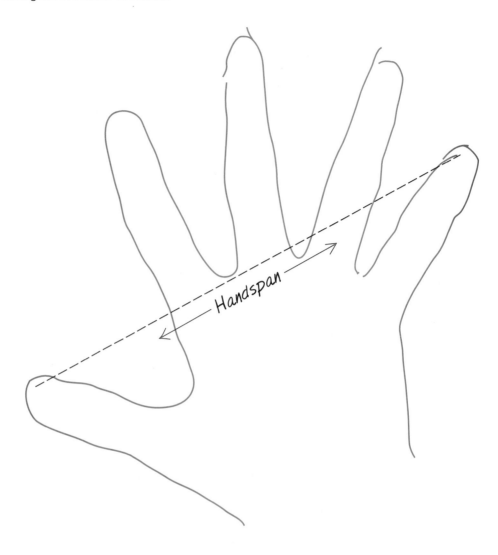

Figure 3.4
The Handspan

Procedure:

1. Each student is given a centimeter ruler.

2. Students estimate how many centimeters (cm) it will take to go from one end of their desks to the other. They record their estimations individually, and the teacher records the data on the chalkboard or a whole-class chart.

3. Students measure the width of their desks first using their hands, then using their centimeter rulers.

Assessment: Ask students what strategies they used to formulate their estimations. Then discuss how close their estimations were to the actual measurements. Choose several additional objects in the room and have them repeat the activity. Did they improve their estimations as they practiced the skill? How accurately did they measure? Be sure to observe each student as he or she carries out the activity so that you can assess performance. Make notes about each child's performance (see Figure 3.5). ■

These youngsters are learning to estimate and measure. They estimated the length of a piece of yarn and now they are measuring it.

Student Name	Your Comments and Observations

Figure 3.5
Teacher Log for Assessing Student Performance.   Use this sheet to record observations of students performing the activities described in this chapter.

Activity 3.8 Hands-on Science: How Does a Single Pan Balance Measure Mass?

Constructing a single pan balance

Overview: Some teachers are lucky enough to have classrooms filled with science equipment, and others are not. Balances are important tools that help students make measurements. If your classroom doesn't have balances, you can easily make them. Students can take their balances home with them and use them to carry out a variety of inquiry-centered activities on their own.

Materials: Each child will need an empty shoe box with a lid, one medium-size rubber band, two paper clips, 50 cm of string (kite string is good), light-colored construction paper, a dark marker, and a paper cup. Visit the school cafeteria and find out if empty process cheese spread boxes are available; these boxes (which are generally discarded) make great balances in the elementary science classroom and can be used instead of shoe boxes.

Procedure: Cover the lid of the shoe box (or empty cheese box) with light-colored paper. Using your centimeter ruler, make a line down the center of the box. About 10 cm from the top of the box, poke a hole through the lid. (If your students can't do this on their own, use a nail with a blunt tip to poke the hole. Keep the nail in your possession throughout the construction phase.) Feed one end of the rubber band through the hole. Inside the lid, attach a paper clip through the loop of the rubber band to keep it in place. Attach the top of a paper clip to the bottom of the rubber band on the outside of the lid. Poke three holes in the top of the cup (they should be equidistant from one another), tie a piece of string through each hole, and tie the strings together at the bottom of the paper clip. Place the lid on the box, and you now have a single pan balance.

To calibrate the balance so that it measures correctly, you need to construct a scale. With the empty cup attached to the rubber band, make a mark on the vertical line that you drew down the center of the box by touching the bottom of the paper clip to the lid. Draw a short horizontal line at this point, and call it "0". If you don't have a mass set available, you can use nickels to calibrate the scale (a nickel has a mass of about 5 grams). Put two nickels in the cup and see how far down the rubber band is stretched. Mark this point "10 grams." Keep adding nickels until you have marked off "20 grams," "30 grams," etc.

Remember that this is not a professionally constructed balance. The measurements are only approximate. As the rubber band ages, the measurements will change, so you will need to replace the rubber band and recalibrate the scale when this happens. Still, considering that balances cost about $30 each, this is a suitable alternative. It takes about 30 minutes to create the balance. Younger students will need help, but those in grades 4 and above can work on their own.

Assessment: Place an object of unknown mass in the cup. Have your students see how far down the rubber band is stretched, and determine that mass of the object. ■

Activity 3.9 Hands-on Science: Creating a Double Pan Balance to Measure Mass

Constructing a double pan balance

Overview: This is a version of the single pan balance that contains two paper cups instead of one.

Materials: Each child will need an empty shoe box (or process cheese spread box) with a lid, three medium-size rubber bands, four paper clips, a plastic straw, light-colored construction paper, a dark marker, and a paper cup.

Procedure: Cover the lid of the box with light-colored construction paper. Using your centimeter ruler, make a line down the center of the box. About 10 cm from the top of the box, poke a hole through the lid. (If your students can't do this on their own, use a nail with a blunt tip to poke the hole. Do this part yourself, and keep the nail in your possession throughout the activity for safety reasons.) Feed one end of the rubber band through the hole. Inside the lid, attach a paper clip through the loop of the rubber band to keep it in place. Attach the top of a paper clip to the bottom of the rubber band. Open the bottom end of the paper clip and use it to poke a hole through the center of the plastic straw. Wrap rubber bands around each end of the straw. Attach each of the two remaining paper clips to the paper cup. Use the two remaining rubber bands to hold the paper clips in place at each end of the straw. Place the lid back on the box, and you now have a double pan balance.

To calibrate the balance, you will place a known mass in one cup and an object with an unknown mass in the other cup. A nickel has a mass of about 5 grams. Use nickels in one cup to counterbalance the mass of the object in the other cup. Count the number of nickels used, and determine the mass of the unknown object. Jelly beans or popcorn kernels can be used to achieve masses of less than 5 grams.

Assessment: To ensure that your students know how to use the balance, place an unknown object, such as a handful of uncooked rice or a handful of raisins, in one cup. Ask students how they will determine the mass of the unknown object. Using nickels (or jelly beans or popcorn kernels) as the known mass, have students determine the mass of the rice or raisins. ■

Activity 3.10 Hands-on Science: Does Popped Popcorn Weigh More or Less Than Unpopped Popcorn?

Estimation and prediction are related: Science and mathematics

Overview: This activity helps students understand the concepts of mass and volume. It is appropriate for grades 3 through 6. Students are given a question and use the materials provided to solve the problem. This activity is done in groups of four students.

Materials: A double pan balance, 2 ounces of unpopped popcorn per group of students, a hot-air popper for the class

Procedure: 1. Pose this question to students: " Does popped popcorn weigh more or less than unpopped popcorn?" (Using the double pan balance, students are likely to place equal masses of unpopped popcorn in each cup. They estimate the mass of the popcorn kernels before and after they have popped. The popcorn weighs less when popped, as the moisture inside of each kernel is released during popping.)

2. Students design their own experiments to answer this question.

Assessment: Visit each group and observe what is happening. Use a chart such as the one in Figure 3.5 to record your observations. ■

Activity 3.11 Hands-on Science: Popped or Unpopped: What's the Difference in Volume?

Volume is the space an object occupies: Science and mathematics

Overview: Volume is the amount of space an object takes up. In this activity, you will begin with one-quarter cup of unpopped popcorn, measure the volume, and estimate the volume of the kernels after they are popped.

Materials: Unpopped popcorn, a hot-air popper, a measuring cup, tools for measuring volume

Procedure: Measure a quarter-cup of unpopped popcorn in a measuring cup. Students estimate how much volume it will take up when popped. Pop the popcorn.

Assessment: Have students compare their estimates with what actually happened. How close were the estimates? ■

Using Observation, Description, and Classification

Now that students have practiced observation and description, and have some background in measurement, they are ready to begin to use multiple process skills to categorize objects. In the following three activities, students will observe, describe, and classify.

Activity 3.12 Hands-on Science: How Do Coins Differ?

Overview: In this activity, students will collect and classify coins.

Materials: A variety of coins

Procedure: Collect a variety of coins (pennies, nickels, dimes, quarters, foreign coins if available). Students observe, describe, and sort them.

Assessment: How did students sort the coins? Did the observations and descriptions of the coins help them in their sorting? Ask students if they could sort the coins in any other ways. ■

Activity 3.13 Hands-on Science: How Can You Classify Potato Chips?

Overview: In this activity, students will classify potato chips.

Materials: Each pair of students needs about 20 potato chips.

Procedure: Students work in pairs to classify their potato chips. Then they share classification schemes with the class.

Assessment: Ask students how they sorted the potato chips. What characteristics did they identify? Can they classify them in any other ways? ■

Activity 3.14 Online: Classifying Animals

Animals can be herbivores, carnivores, or omnivores: Life science

Overview: You can classify animals by the kinds of food they eat. Herbivores eat mainly vegetables and plants, carnivores eat mainly animal flesh, and omnivores eat plants, vegetables, and animal flesh. Students will be given six animals and will search the Internet to find out whether the animals are herbivores, carnivores, or omnivores.

Materials: A computer hooked up to the Internet, paper, and pencil

Procedure: Students visit the library or search the Internet to find out whether the following animals are herbivores, carnivores, or omnivores: alligator, baboon, beaver, coyote, hippopotamus, human.

These students are doing an Internet search to find out whether the animals they are studying can be classified as herbivores, carnivores or omnivores.

Assessment: After classifying the animal, students are to find out what type of teeth it has. Ask them: (1) Is there a relationship between what an animal eats and the type of teeth it has? (2) What is your hypothesis? (3) What is the basis for your hypothesis? (4) What do you have to know to test your hypothesis? ■

Using Multiple Process Skills to Answer a Question

Students are now ready to move to the next step and carry out a simple experiment.

Activity 3.15 Hands-on Science: Which Bubble Bath Produces the Most Bubbles?

Students engage in problem solving

Overview: This activity presents a problem to solve that uses the science process skills. Though simple, it generates a great deal of discussion and debate as students try different ideas.

Materials: Three different kinds of bubble bath, water, cups, items to measure bubbles with (e.g., rulers, thin strips of paper), drinking straws

Procedure: Students work together to determine which bubble bath produces the most bubbles. Instead of directing the activity, the teacher acts as question asker and facilitator. Be sure your students define the term *most bubbles*. They should all agree on what *most* means. It could mean the highest column of bubbles, the widest column of bubbles, the most bubbles that remain after a minute or two, or something else.

Students discuss variables

When you start this activity, have your students talk about variables. This experiment makes students aware that variables exist and must be controlled. It is also easy to repeat several times as they decide on which variables to control. For example, if they decide to add some bubble bath to each cup and blow the bubbles with a straw, they will notice that the amount of bubble bath added to each cup and the amount of time for blowing bubbles should be controlled. If not, they won't be able to tell much about which type of bubble bath produces the most bubbles. The type of bubble bath varies from cup to cup and the amount of bubbles produced depends on the brand used if they control all other relevant variables.

Assessment: Observe your students and listen to them as they plan, think, and carry out the experiment. What process skills do they use? What variables do they identify? Do they control variables? Do they make a prediction? Do they answer their question? Is there discussion and debate about the procedure and the solution? After they do the experiment once, have them discuss what happened. When my students perform this experiment, they repeat it a few times, each time learning something new about performing an experiment.

Using math as a tool for science

Have students graph their results on a bar graph. Graph the independent variable—type of bubble bath—on the x axis and the dependent variable—let's say you decide it's the height of the column of bubbles that determines the "most" bubbles—on the y axis. In this case, the independent variable is a qualitative variable measured on a nominal scale. A **nominal scale** classifies objects into categories based on some defined characteristic, such as type of bubble bath. Then you count or measure the number of objects in each category. In this case, you measure the height of the bubble column to find out which bubble bath produces the "most" bubbles. Elementary students often classify objects, so learning to make a bar graph to represent data is a good first step in using mathematics as a tool for scientific understanding.

Extension: Allow your students to formulate additional questions for study based on this investigation. ▪

Constructing Knowledge and Communicating Scientific Thought

When implementing inquiry-based instruction, it is important that students analyze their results, arrive at generalizations, and communicate their findings to others so that they can construct knowledge. They should use scientific evidence when developing an explanation. Be certain that your students leave the experience with knowledge of the content as well as the process, for coming away with one and not the other is not enough.

Students need feedback from the teacher

Students learn the content by performing activities and using the process skills. As they work, students must have feedback from teachers and peers, *because sometimes students formulate incorrect conclusions or omit something that should be considered;* by having them communicate their ideas, you can help them clarify their thinking. When students present their ideas to teachers and classmates, they are like scientists discussing ideas and presenting papers to their colleagues. This is part of the process of science, which will enable you to know what your students think and know.

Not every student comes to the science class with the same level of cognitive preparedness, so look for variations in how your students think and act. Some students respond better to some teaching strategies than to others. Therefore, learning to examine your own practice is an important skill to develop. This will enable you to match students with particular modes of instruction. In the following chapters, you will learn more about how to select the proper strategies for your students.

Students Communicate Findings

Multiple methods of communication

As part of scientific inquiry, students should think about relationships between evidence and explanations, construct and analyze alternative explanations, and communicate scientific arguments. They can do this in a number of ways.

One teacher told me that her fifth-grade students act like scientists as soon as science period begins. They keep laboratory notebooks, formulate research questions, generate hypotheses, design experiments, record and analyze data, and derive conclusions. They even prepare a budget to "finance" their research. Before going on to the next topic, a science conference is held in which students present papers and critique one another's work.

Some teachers engage students in writing. One teacher I work with has students write reports about their science investigations. She reads the reports and immediately knows what they understand and what they must relearn and review. Another teacher has his students record observations, which the students refer to as "observational notes."

Students can also apply their scientific knowledge to create stories of their own. If they learn about the geology of a region, for example, they can write tales that take place in that region, using the geology they learned to build the story. Applying the knowledge allows the students to "own" that knowledge.

Integrating science, technology, and assessment

Teachers often work together to allow students to make connections from one subject to another. The art teacher can have students make projects that bring science lessons to life. The music teacher can help to integrate science and music. Two of my students integrated science and technology in an interesting way. Their first-graders studied about dinosaurs. After spending a week learning about different dinosaurs, their student teacher brought them to the computer lab and gave each student a card bearing the name of a particular dinosaur. Using a program called Kid Pix 2, the first-graders created the dinosaurs. As I observed the lesson, each first-grader was able to present and discuss his or her dinosaur, providing an impressive level of detail. At every grade level, students can communicate findings and think like scientists. As you proceed through this text, you will learn many ways for students to think about and present their work.

Constructing Your Own Knowledge of Science and Science Teaching

This chapter contains a great deal of information. It is now important for you to reflect on it. Building a science teaching portfolio and keeping your own journal will assist you with this task. *Portfolios* are purposeful collections of selected work and student self-assessments developed over time. They document progress in achieving goals and objectives. *Portfolio assessment* is the process by which we develop, review, and evaluate portfolios. Make notes about the artifacts you would choose in creating your own science teaching portfolio. As you select those artifacts, place them in a special folder or notebook.

What are the science process skills, and how can your students practice them in the classroom? How do you assess your students' use of science process skills? How do students use multiple process skills to construct scientific understanding? What are the elements of a simple science experiment? How can students refine an experiment as they construct and reconstruct their understanding of science as inquiry? As you think about this chapter, these are some of the questions you should ask yourself.

Key Terms

estimation (p. 65)   English system (p. 65)   nominal scale (p. 74)
metric system (p. 65)

Reviewing Chapter 3: Questions, Extensions, Applications, and Explorations

1. You asked your primary students to bring a favorite object to class today. Your goal is to have them observe the object. Make a list of five questions you will ask your students to help guide their observations.

2. You are teaching a lesson to your upper elementary grade students, which you introduce with a motivating demonstration. You open a new 1-liter bottle of seltzer and pour out (or drink) about a half-cup. You place 20 raisins into the remaining seltzer in the bottle and close the cap. The raisins immediately begin to dance up and down in the seltzer. Make a list of five questions you will ask your students to guide them in inquiry.

3. Your students are learning about conserving natural resources. You pose this question: "Do we use less water when taking showers or baths?" Create a lesson to help your students answer this question.

4. You learn of an invention convention being sponsored for elementary school children. You would like your class to enter, since it offers them an opportunity to engage in inquiry.

How will you prepare your students for this experience?

5. Gathering resources is an important first step in teaching elementary science. Containers such as shoe boxes are useful for holding objects. Make a list of other items that can be reused, recycled, or used differently that will function as containers.

6. This chapter provides several activities that will help your students practice the skill of observation. Make a list of ten additional items that your students could bring to school to observe scientifically. Choose one of these items and write a brief activity, including overview, materials list, procedure, and assessment.

7. As you observe your students using process skills, create your own benchmarks to guide you in the assessment process. Use Table 3.4 to record your work (the first row is completed as illustration).

Table 3.4
Assessing the Science Process Skills

Process Skill	Proficient	Apprentice	Novice
Observing: To watch attentively and make a systematic scientific observation	Can differentiate an observation from an interpretation; identifies patterns and regularities; uses instruments to gather data	Differentiates between useful observations and false observations; uses instruments to gather data	Uses the senses to describe; can't differentiate an observation from an interpretation
Estimating: To make an educated guess or approximate calculation about a quantity			
Predicting: To state, tell about, or make known in advance on the basis of special knowledge			
Measuring: To make a comparison between an object and a standardized or unstandardized unit			
Choosing and controlling variables: To manipulate one factor while holding the others constant to determine the outcome of an event			
Collecting data: To collect information organized for analysis or used as a basis for decision making			
Classifying: To arrange or organize data according to category			
Making charts and graphs: To display data in a visual format			
Analyzing data: To examine data methodically and separate the data into parts or basic principles to determine the nature of the whole			

Table 3.4
Assessing the Science Process Skills (continued)

Process Skill	Proficient	Apprentice	Novice
Inferring: To conclude from evidence or derive a conclusion from facts			
Communicating: To express oneself in a way that is readily and clearly understood			

As you observe your students using process skills, create your own benchmarks to guide you in the assessment process. (The first row is completed for you.)

Print Resources

American Institute of Physics. (1997). *The best of wonder science: Elementary science activities.* New York: Delmar Publishers.

Axelson, D., & Nichols, C. (1996). *Managing technology in the classroom.* Huntington Beach, CA: Teacher Created Materials.

Bennett, S., & Bennett, R. (1993). *The official Kid Pix activity book.* New York: Random House.

Hamilton, L. (1996). *Child's play around the world.* New York: Berkley.

Lifter, M., & Adams, M. (1997). *Kid Pix for terrified teachers.* Huntington Beach, CA: Teacher Created Materials.

Lifter, M., & Adams, M. (1997). *Integrating technology into the curriculum.* Huntington Beach, CA: Teacher Created Materials.

Ostlund, K. (1992). *Science process skills: Assessing hands-on student performance.* New York: Addison-Wesley.

VanCleave, J. (1997). *Play and find out about nature: Easy experiments for young children.* New York: John Wiley & Sons.

Willow, D., & Curran, E. (1989). *Science sensations: An activity book from the Children's Museum, Boston.* New York: Addison-Wesley.

Electronic Resources

Just Think: Problem Solving Through Inquiry
New York State Department of Education, Office of Educational Television, Cultural Education Center 10A75, Albany, NY 12230
This video shows how teachers mediate learning in inquiry-centered classrooms.

Elementary Science Lesson Plans
http://tikkun.ed.asu.edu/coe/links/lessons.html
This site links to lesson plans in just about every science discipline.

Nye's Lab Online
http://nyelabs.kcts.org/
This site contains hands-on activities for children and resources for teachers.

Science Power
http://www.luc.edu/schools/education/science.htm
This site is a great science resource for teachers and includes links to lesson plans.

Children's Literature

Fey, James and Anderson, Catherine
Filling and Wrapping: 3-Dimensional Measurement
(Dale Seymour, 1997)
ISBN: 1-57232-39-5
Grades 7 and up

Markle, Sandra
Measuring Up: Experiments, Puzzles and Games Exploring Measurement (Athenium, 1995)
ISBN: 0-689-31904-5
Grades 3–7

Carlson, Donn
Physical Science Measurement Student Activity Book (Education Systems, 1990)
ISBN: 1-878276-12-3
Grades 6 and up

Mandell, Muriel
Simple Experiments in Time with Everyday Materials (Sterling Publications, 1997)
ISBN: 0-8069-3803-x
Grades 4–6

Ash, Russell
Incredible Comparisons (DK Publishing, 1996)
ISBN: 0-7894-1009-5
Grades 4–6

Carrie, Christopher
Measurement (fiction) (Crayola Activity Book, 1987)
ISBN: 0-86696-206-9
Grades 3–6

DiPaola, Tomi
The Popcorn Book (Holiday House)
ISBN: 0-823-40533-8
Preschool and Grades K–3

Aliki
Corn Is Maize (Harper Trophy, 1986)
ISBN: 0-064-45026-0
Preschool and Grades K–3

Thayer, Jane
The Popcorn Dragon (William Morrow and Company, 1989)
ISBN: 0-688-08340-4
Preschool and Grades K–3

CHAPTER 4

Guiding Inquiry

How do you bring inquiry-based instruction to your students? How do you help them design investigations that are meaningful, important, interesting, and easily carried out in the classroom or home? As this chapter begins, you will read stories about students who engaged in inquiry. I asked each of them how they got the idea for their research. Each investigation was sparked by a real-life event: Lea's stuffy nose, Philip's interest in the human body, and Anjali's questions about how fourth-graders get cuts and scrapes. For each of these students, the investigation was meaningful because it answered a question of interest to them.

You will then read about how to bring inquiry-based science to your classroom. You'll learn how to motivate your students, uncover their preconceived notions about how things work, and guide them so that they ask good questions. You'll hear from a scientist who talks about framing good questions. Then you'll explore ways to help your students engage in exploration and develop understanding of a concept. As you read through the chapter, think about the answers to these questions:

1. **How do I bring inquiry-based instruction to my classroom?**
2. **What does teacher-directed inquiry look like?**
3. **How do I move from teacher-directed inquiry to student-directed inquiry?**
4. **What are some ways to motivate students in the science classroom?**
5. **How and why should I uncover students' preconceived notions about science concepts?**
6. **How do I help my students formulate good questions for study?**
7. **What happens when students investigate? How do they make sense of their work? How can I help them figure things out?**
8. **How do children carry out investigations that involve life science?**

Children Engage in Inquiry

An inquiry-based classroom is one that fosters exploration of ideas, experimentation, creativity, and lots of thinking. The *National Science Education Standards* say that inquiry into authentic questions generated from student experiences is the central strategy for teaching science. (National Research Council, 1996, p. 2) Teachers should focus on inquiry as it relates to the real-life experiences of their students and guide them as they create their own investigations (Edwards, 1997). As you read the accounts of student-directed inquiry that follow, reflect on the children's thinking and reasoning. How did they make sense of their data and arrive at their conclusions?

Inquiry should relate to life experience

Lea Asks About Taste and Smell

Lea Steinman is in second grade. In January, she had a cold. Her nose was stuffed up, and she couldn't taste anything. She wondered why she couldn't taste anything, so she went to the library to find some books on the sense of taste. She read the books and kept a science journal in which she wrote about the most important things she learned. She learned that people usually smell and taste food at the same time. When people sniff air that contains odors, the odors are detected by certain cells in the nose. Those cells send messages to a part of the brain that detects the odors and tells the person what she or he smells. Taste works in a similar way, but the tongue, not the nose, is the body part that brings the messages about different foods to the brain. Then the brain interprets the messages and gives the person information about the taste of the food in his or her mouth.

Check with teacher before tasting in science class: Safety

The following week Lea's cold was gone, and she could taste again. She wanted to find out what happens if a person holds his or her nose and tastes something at the same time. Would that person be able to taste? Lea designed an experiment to help answer this question. She knew from science class that she should never taste anything that was part of a science experiment unless the teacher said it was safe. She checked with her teacher before she began, and since the teacher said her materials were safe to taste, she proceeded.

Lea prepared several cups with liquids. The first was water, the second was water and sugar, and the third was water and salt. She added food coloring to each solution so they looked the same. Her mother was having a party, and there were many guests at her house, ranging from 8 to 70 years old. She invited them to participate in her experiment. She also asked several friends to participate.

Lea gave each person a sheet of paper to record his or her age and test results. She had her participants hold their noses and taste the solutions. She found that older people were able to distinguish taste better than younger people. Now she began to wonder what happens to the sense of taste as people get older. She asked this question: Does the sense of taste change with age? She hypothesized that it does change with age, and she designed a new experiment to test her hypothesis: The sense of taste gets better as people get older.

This time Lea wanted to test more than just plain water, sugar water, and salt water. So in addition to these three liquids, she had people taste apple juice, grape juice, almond extract, maple syrup, and banana syrup while holding their noses. She gave them another sheet of paper to record their findings. Again, older people did better than younger people.

First, Lea concluded that the sense of taste improves with age. The older a person grows, the better his or her sense of taste. Then she began to talk to the people in her study. She learned that the younger people were unfamiliar with many of the foods they tasted. They couldn't identify them because they had never tasted them before. Now she hypothesized that familiarity with items has more to do with recognizing taste than the person's age. She learned that even when people hold their noses, they can still taste things. Lea wondered whether having a cold with a stuffy nose and tasting something is the same as holding your nose and tasting something when you don't have a cold. Perhaps the cold affects smell *and* taste.

Lea enjoyed doing this research and plans to do more in the future. She wants to learn more about how taste and smell are related, because she doesn't have all of the answers yet.

Philip Investigates Life Without Thumbs

Test hypotheses by experimentation: Science process

Philip Artis is a third-grader who is very interested in science. He wondered what life would be like if we didn't have our thumbs. Would we be able to do all

The children are investigating what happens when three different liquids are mixed. They used food color to make it easier to see what happens when they mix them.

the things that we do? Would we be able to play baseball, fly an airplane, or create a work of art? Philip hypothesized that without thumbs, it would be more difficult for people to accomplish many tasks. He developed a series of experiments to test his hypothesis.

Philip first asked his subjects to hold out a hand and move the thumb in different directions. They did that with ease. Then he asked them to move their fingers in the same way. He found that fingers don't have the same range of motion that the thumb does. Next, he asked his subjects to button and unbutton a pair of pants, tie shoelaces, write their names, and pick up a flashlight and turn it on and off, all with the full use of their thumbs and fingers. All subjects accomplish these tasks with ease. Then he strapped a piece of Velcro around each subject's hand, eliminating the use of the thumb. Philip was careful not to make the Velcro so tight that it would cut off the person's circulation. He asked his subjects to repeat the preceding tasks, this time without the use of their thumbs.

Philip found that they could not accomplish the tasks easily without the use of their thumbs. Simple tasks became harder to do, took longer, and were not neatly done. His hypothesis was supported. He learned that only primates have hands that can grasp and hold objects, because of the presence of an opposable thumb—one that moves opposite to the other fingers. In humans, the thumb is set at an angle in relation to the other fingers. In apes and humans, the thumb rotates on the carpometacarpal joint. Among primates, humans can move their thumbs farthest across their hands.

Philip knows what it's like to tie shoelaces with the use of the thumb, but he wonders what would happen without the use of the thumb.

Philip enjoyed this research a great deal. He wants to learn more about science and eventually become a doctor.

Anjali Researches Cuts and Scrapes

Anjali Nandakumar is in fourth grade. She wanted to know how fourth-graders get cuts and scrapes. She also wanted to know how long their cuts bleed. She started off by visiting the library and doing an impressive search on the topic of bleeding. She asked her mother to photocopy some articles for her, using sources such as the *New England Journal of Medicine*. Although you might think such a source is way too advanced for a fourth-grader, after spending a half-hour with Anjali, you would realize it is not. Anjali learned about platelets and how they help stop bleeding. She also learned how we get fevers and how white blood cells attack germs.

Math as a tool for scientific inquiry: Science process

Anjali then began her study of cuts and scrapes. She sent a letter announcing her study to fourth-grade teachers and students at her school. She asked them to record when they got their cuts, how they got them, where the cuts were located, whether they bled, and how long they bled. When a student had a cut, Anjali recorded every two days how the cut was healing. She recorded all of these data in her journal. Then she graphed the results and analyzed the data (see Figure 4.1).

Anjali found that school materials such as paper, scissors, and binders were the number one source of cuts among students. Cans, boxes, and furniture were the number one source of cuts among fourth-grade teachers. The hand was the site of most cuts and scrapes among students, followed by the wrist, the leg, and the arm. Most cuts bled for a minute.

Anjali learned a great deal about blood cells. She enjoyed engaging in inquiry and plans to study medicine when she's older. I'm sure she'll be very successful!

Bringing Inquiry-Based Instruction to Your Classroom

How do you, as a novice teacher, bring inquiry-based instruction to your class? Recall that in Chapter 1, you learned that classroom activities fall along a continuum. Sometimes you have to provide direct instruction, and sometimes you let students figure things out for themselves. Sometimes you and your students work together to make sense of something.

Inquiry teaching falls along a continuum

Bringing inquiry-based instruction to your students is similar. Sometimes you direct the investigation, and sometimes your students take charge and investigate on their own. There are three ways to do this, which fall along a continuum: (1) teacher-directed inquiry, (2) teachers and students acting as co-investigators, and (3) student-directed inquiry (see Figure 4.2) on page 86.

Teacher-Directed Inquiry: A Starting Point

Teacher as question answerer

Sometimes you guide students in a **teacher-directed,** step-by-step process in which you structure learning experiences for students. When using this form of inquiry, you provide a set of guided experiences and expect your students to make generalizations about these experiences. Students usually carry out experiments following step-by-step instructions regarding procedure, equipment, and data to collect; then they analyze the data and make generalizations. You explain the concept as it develops and act as a question answerer rather than a question asker.

1/18/99

Dear 4th graders and 4th grade teachers,

As a part of my Science Fair project I would like to survey you about cuts and scrapes you get in the next few weeks. This will involve questions like: When did you get it, how did you get it, where is it, did it bleed, if so, for about how long, etc. I will ask you every 2 days how it is healing.

This survey is optional so it's your choice to participate.

Thank you.
Anjali Nandakumar.

P.S.
Please be careful, try not to get any cuts or scrapes!!

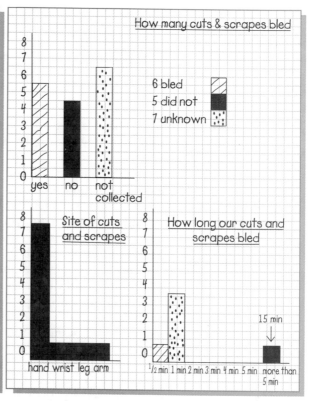

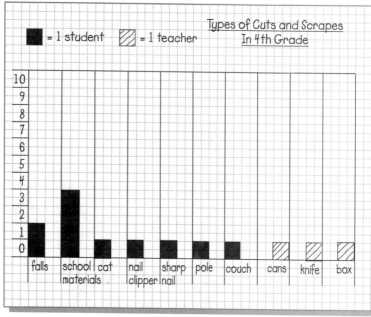

Figure 4.1
Anjali's Investigation

**Figure 4.2
The Continuum
of Classroom
Inquiry**

Teacher-directed
inquiry

Teachers and
students as
co-investigators

Student-directed
inquiry

While this method is commonly used in elementary science classes, as you read on you will learn that you need to move beyond teacher-directed methods. When teachers rely too much on teacher-directed inquiry, they usually fail to build in opportunities to find out what their students really think or how they build meaning. If you don't know how or what they think, it's difficult to help them develop or change their thinking. If your students don't understand what's happening in the classroom, you probably won't have the opportunity to find out or help them if the lesson is teacher centered. Despite these drawbacks, however, teacher-directed methods do have some positive aspects.

The teacher-directed inquiry process is useful when students have little understanding of a topic and need a great deal of guidance and explanation from you. Some students, especially special learners, do best with direction from the teacher. It is also a good way for novice teachers to begin to practice teaching inquiry-based science. You maintain a great deal of classroom control while allowing your students to investigate and discover. You lead them through the development of a concept, guiding them along the way. This often helps you to understand the concept more deeply. My students find that beginning with teacher-directed inquiry is one way to practice teaching science while gaining confidence in their ability to implement hands-on activities. But it is not the only method they use. Once they practice this technique, they quickly move on to other methods that are more like the way in which scientists do science. Such methods give students more responsibility for their own work, allow them to practice the skills necessary to become independent inquirers, and give the teacher an opportunity to find out what students think.

Avoid overemphasis on teacher-directed inquiry

Norine Seiden, an elementary science supervisor, explains that:
[S]ome things are taught more easily by telling. Some concepts are too difficult for students to explore, and not every student can construct meaning from experience. Sometimes teachers feel more comfortable using this approach. When using this strategy, the teacher first defines the concept or principle, then students carry out activities to illustrate the idea. This approach is frequently used in science classes, where a lecture and discussion precede the hands-on activities. Students learn about the concept before they engage in experimentation. Teachers guide students through the process of inquiry, helping them construct meaning along the way. Teachers should be careful

and avoid relying on this technique too much, as learners should also experience student-centered instruction. (Personal communication)

As soon as you gain experience with teacher-directed inquiry, move on to try other methods that enable your students to have more responsibility for their own work and the freedom to ask their own questions, explore, and direct themselves. Such student-centered methods give you more opportunity to observe your students at work and allow you to become aware of their embedded ideas of how the world works.

Activity 4.1 Hands-On Science: How Fast Does Your Heart Beat?

Overview: In this activity, you will practice teacher-directed inquiry. Your students will answer the question: "How fast does your heart beat?"

Materials: Watch with second hand, computer or pencil and paper for recording data

Procedure: Begin the lesson by telling your students about the human circulatory system. Explain that it is a vehicle that relies on blood to transport the oxygen from the air you breathe, food, and important chemicals to all parts of your body. After dropping off these products, your blood picks up waste from cells and removes them.

In the classroom the students are engaged in inquiry that is directed by the teacher.

Plasma, platelets, and red and white blood cells are blood components: Life science

Then discuss the components of blood: plasma, platelets, red cells, and white cells. The red cells give blood its red color and are oxygen carriers. White cells are larger than red cells and help to fight disease. Platelets allow the blood to clot when an injury occurs. The plasma is the clear, yellow-colored substance that contains red cells, white cells, and platelets.

Continue by telling students that the heart pumps the blood around the body. The heart is a strong muscle that contracts and then relaxes. When blood that is low in oxygen flows into one side of the heart, the powerful muscle pumps the blood into the lungs, where they pick up oxygen. Now that the blood is rich in oxygen, it flows back to the other side of the heart, where it is pumped to the rest of the body.

Watch your students as you talk to them. Are they interested? How do you know what they understand? As you continue the lesson, tell them that they are going to do an activity to feel how fast the heart pumps blood. Give specific directions for the activity. Let students work in pairs. Have one person act as recorder and the other as experimenter.

Step 1: **The experimenter presses two fingers on the inside part of the wrist.**

Step 2: **The experimenter counts the number of pulse beats felt in one minute.**

Step 3: **The recorder records the pulse on paper or in the computer.**

Step 4: **Students switch roles.**

Once the activity is over, students return to their seats. Ask them to reflect on what they learned from the activity. Have them answer this question: "What have you learned about your pulse rate?" They probably will be able to tell you how many beats per minute they recorded.

Assessment: Think about this activity. Did it go well for you? Were your students able to carry it out successfully? How did you assess their understanding? How did you feel as you implemented this teacher-directed technique? How did your students respond as learners? ■

The activity probably went very well for you. It was easy to carry out, and classroom control should not have been a big issue. The materials were easy to gather, and the directions were simple. Unfortunately, there wasn't much for students to think about. You told them what to do and provided the questions for them to answer. Is there another, more thought-provoking way to carry out such an activity? Yes, there is—read on.

Students and Teachers Acting as Co-investigators

Students take more responsibility for their work

The next step along the continuum involves **students and teacher as co-investigators.** With this method, you choose the topic and set guidelines for inquiry, and students have a question to answer and materials to use. You provide guidance, but not as much as you give when working in the teacher-directed mode. There are no step-by-step instructions to follow. Students work in a more independent

In this class the students and teacher act as co-investigators.

fashion to answer the question. They first think about how they will answer the question. They engage in discussion and decide how to proceed. Sometimes their ideas are good, and sometimes they need to make modifications. What's important is that your students learn to take responsibility for their own learning. This is an important quality that will lead to your students' development as learners and that will carry through into other classes and aspects of life.

As with teacher-directed inquiry, students explore the topic, formulate hypotheses, analyze data, search for patterns, make generalizations, and formulate conclusions. They discover things on their own as they construct knowledge. They communicate with their peers to benefit from the generalizations arrived at by others. You act as a co-investigator and resource provider instead of one who directs the activity. As students answer their questions and draw conclusions, you and they work together to find out whether their conclusions are valid. This often leads to new investigations and new conclusions. Results of new investigations often lead to revising conclusions reached earlier.

Activity 4.2 Hands-on Science: Are My Classmates' Pulse Rates the Same or Are They Different?

Overview: In this activity, you and your students will act as co-investigators as you answer this question.

Materials: Watch with second hand, computer or pencil and paper for recording data

Procedure: To introduce the lesson, have students sit still for 10 minutes; then take their pulses. Have them do 20 jumping jacks, and record their pulses again. Ask, "Are your pulses the same or different?" Then ask, "What causes a pulse?"

You can explain the basics of the circulatory system as described earlier. Give students time to answer the question "Are your pulses the same or different?" They will tell

Humans require more oxygen when exercising: Life science

you that they are different before and after exercise. Ask them why. Lead them in a discussion as they discover that when they exercise, their bodies require more oxygen. Since the blood carries oxygen to the cells, the heart beats faster to respond to the increased need for oxygen and to remove wastes. Since the heart beats faster, the pulse increases.

Now pose another question: "Are pulse rates of the children in the class the same or are they different?" Allow your students to answer the question on their own. They will need to determine how to answer it, since you won't provide step-by-step directions. You may choose to have them work in pairs. Give them some time to plan. Walk around the room and listen to what they are saying. Do their ideas make sense? Once they are ready, let them carry out their investigations, record the data, and make sense of it. How do they answer their questions? Allow students to present their findings to one another. Encourage discussion and debate.

Assessment: How did this method of introducing the topic work? Were students more interested? Did more thinking go on in the classroom? Were you able to manage the activity? Did you get a better idea of what your students were thinking? Did this method work as well as or better than the teacher-directed method? ■

Student-Directed Inquiry: The Student as Investigator

With **student-directed inquiry,** students decide what to study, ask questions, gather the materials for the investigation, set the research agenda, and freely explore the topic individually or in a small group. This happens best when students have prior experience with inquiry-based instruction and are familiar with working in this way. Once students have questions they wish to answer and hypotheses they wish to test, they design experiments to test their hypotheses. They design proper controls, make careful measurements, and clearly define the independent and dependent variables on their own. They pay attention to data collection and analysis, and they present their results to others. The stories you read about Lea, Philip, and Anjali are examples of student-directed inquiry.

Teacher acts as a mentor and guide

When using this technique, you carefully avoid providing excessive structure. The focus of the activity should be on inquiry and investigation, not transmission of information from teacher to student. You act as a mentor and a guide. As questions arise, the students address them with help from you, if necessary. Students should make decisions and draw their own conclusions. They should also decide how they will communicate their findings to others (Edwards, 1997).

At first, this method can be a bit difficult for the novice teacher to manage, as students need a wide range of resources to carry out their own investigations. They also need to be given the freedom to explore. As a new teacher, it helps to have experience with teacher-directed inquiry before allowing your students to explore on their own.

Student-directed inquiry brings additional considerations for a new teacher. It requires a significant amount of time, and since the choice of research topic is left up to the students, it may not fit exactly into the curriculum. You should definitely practice teaching using this strategy, but it's best to have experience in a more controlled setting first.

> Norine Seiden explains that:
>
> [S]ome teachers begin by posing questions and allowing students to structure their own activities to learn about the concept instead of preparing activities for them. Others allow students to formulate their own questions and structure their own activities as they learn about the concept. A student can often derive the concept on his or her own. When the student needs some guidance and direction, students and teachers often act as co-investigators. (Personal communication)

New Teachers Should Learn Multiple Methods of Inquiry

Teachers need multiple strategies

Since multiple approaches and teaching strategies are needed to help students gain understanding and construct knowledge, exposure to all three forms of inquiry teaching helps students to learn about science, but in different ways. Each method has its place in providing a complete experience for elementary school students.

The Elements of Inquiry-Based Instruction

How do you motivate students? What should you know about your students' thinking before you introduce a new concept or topic? How do you help your students begin an investigation? How do you help them build understanding of the concept or topic they are investigating? This section will answer these questions.

Motivating Students

In order to motivate students, it's important to find out what interests them. You can simply start a class discussion that permits your students to talk about what they like and what they want to learn about. New information becomes more meaningful to students when they can connect it to existing knowledge, so take some time to find out what they already know when you begin (Abdi, 1997).

Questioning motivates students

You can use questioning to help motivate your students. Clifford Edwards (1997) suggests that you provide students with something interesting to observe, such as a very engaging demonstration, and stimulate them to ask questions about what they see. You can have them read interesting articles to stimulate dialog and research on topics of interest. Finally, you can generate a list of possible questions for study, helping them to focus on exactly what they would like to investigate.

Consider Grace Fong, whose bedtime reading inspired an investigation:

Interesting article stimulates inquiry

Grace Fong is in fourth grade. One night before going to sleep, she read an article about smell and odor. The article made her curious. She wanted to know why people sometimes have odors, especially in their feet, armpits, and mouth. She wondered whether washing helps to eliminate odor. She also wondered whether the odors coming from children's bodies are as strong as those coming from adults'. She read that bacteria cause odors, and hypothesized that the greater the number of bacteria, the stronger the odor. Grace talked with her father, a microbiologist, who helped her design an experiment.

They filled plates with agar, a medium in which bacteria can grow. Grace collected bacteria from a child's and an adult's armpits, feet, and mouths and let them grow in the plates. Then each person bathed and used mouthwash, and she resampled. Some plates remained untouched. Her father brought the cultures to his laboratory so that they could grow. When the experiment was over, he properly disposed of the plates.

Grace found that the bacteria from the foot looked similar to the bacteria from the mouth, but they were bigger. Bacteria from armpits grew several big colonies. After people washed, fewer colonies grew. She also learned that children's bodies, which don't produce odors as strong as those coming from adults' bodies, produced fewer bacteria.

Grace enjoyed her research project. It brought up many questions for further study, and she plans to learn more in the future. She especially enjoyed the opportunity to work with her father in his laboratory. She said that she now understands more about his job.

Presenting Students with Discrepant Events

Discrepant events stimulate thought

Another way to motivate students is to present them with discrepant events. A **discrepant event** is something the child observes that puzzles him or her and stimulates thought. For example, take a cardboard tube from an empty roll of paper towels and a ping-pong ball. Put the ping-pong ball in the cardboard tube. Swing the tube quickly across your body in a horizontal plane until the ball flies out of the tube (being careful not to point it at anyone) and curves sharply. This happens because the air pressure is greater on one side of the ball than on the other, causing the curvature in its path. (This a way to demonstrate Bernoulli's principle.) Students don't expect this to happen, and it excites them and makes them think.

Grapes sink in plain water and float in salt water: Physical science

A negative charge on a balloon attracts the positive side of a water molecule: Physical science

Here's another example of a discrepant event. Prepare one glass of plain water and one glass of salt water. Place a grape in each glass. It will sink in plain water and float on salt water. Your students will wonder why, leading to a lesson on density.

As still another example, blow up a balloon and rub it against your hair. You have just put a negative charge on the balloon. Now go to the sink and turn on the water. Move the balloon near the stream of water. A water molecule has a geometry that causes it to have a positive end and a negative end. The water stream curves toward the balloon, because the negative charge on the balloon attracts the positive side of the water molecule. Students wonder why, and then begin to think and ask questions. This leads into a discussion of atoms and molecules.

If you spend some time in the children's science section of a library or bookstore, you will find dozens of books that show you how to demonstrate discrepant events.

You can also find a number of web sites for discrepant events:

http://www.vcu.edu/eduweb/newhomepage/faculty/website/discrep.html

http://scienceinquiry.com/demo-main.htm

http://www.mdsci.org/demos.html

http://www.educ.kent.edu/deafed/law-009.htm

http://www.fi.edu/qanda/amy8-9/amy8-9.html

Look through them and select activities that are appropriate for your classroom. You might even ask your students to find and demonstrate some activities for their classmates.

Identifying Alternative Frameworks and Misconceptions

One of the most important aspects of being a good elementary science teacher is finding out what your students already know and understand when they "do" science. A lesson can go awry if you are unaware of what students think and believe. What should you know about your students' thinking *before* you introduce a concept or topic? To begin, you must uncover their **preconceptions,** or preconceived notions about how things work. These are the private understandings that students develop concerning the meanings and applications of science concepts (Driver, 1990; Driver, Guesne & Tiberghien, 1985). Cognitive scientists report that students often have misconceptions about science (Pressley & McCormick, 1995). What are some of these misconceptions?

▶ When sugar dissolves in water, does it disappear or is it still there? Some students think it is gone forever.

▶ Does Styrofoam have weight? Some students think it doesn't.

▶ Do all living things have blood? Some students think they do.

▶ Do plants have blood? Some students think they do (until they dissect one).

▶ Do plants make their own food? Some students think they don't (but by using the chlorophyll in their leaves—chlorophyll is the green pigment—plants can make their own food).

▶ Where do misconceptions come from? Scientist Russell Hulse says: The world is a complicated place, and while simple generalizations and conclusions are sometimes correct, very often they are wrong. That's why science is so important to human understanding in all areas of human endeavor. It takes you to the next step, which is to verify your hypotheses and build a mental model of the world, understanding the world as it really is.

Often people think this scientific approach makes the world cold and sterile, but just the opposite is true, because it opens your mind to the real depth, richness, and beauty of the world around us. You are as sure as you can be that you have the right answer when right answers really matter. (Personal communication)

As a teacher, you need to know what your students think in order to help them inquire and construct knowledge. If they start out with erroneous ideas, you need to know, because it's hard to build understanding when you start with misunderstanding. Erroneous preconceptions can lead to misconceptions.

Preconceived Notions and Alternate Conceptions

Students sometimes construct misconceptions, which are better thought of as alternate conceptions

Constructivists believe that students actively construct knowledge. The knowledge they already possess affects their ability to learn new knowledge. If what your students are learning conflicts with what they already know, it may be difficult for them to recall or apply this new knowledge in a useful way (von Glasersfeld, 1989, 1992). When their preconceived notions conflict with what they are learning, they commonly construct **misconceptions,** which are better thought of as **alternate conceptions.** It is important for you to probe the knowledge your students already have so you will know whether it conflicts with what they are learning.

What happens if the prior knowledge conflicts with the new knowledge? Your job is to help students to reconstruct knowledge so that things make sense (Mestre, 1994). How do you do this? The first step is to determine students' prior knowledge by asking **open-ended questions,** which make them think and synthesize what they already know (Abdi, 1997). Here are some examples of open-ended questions: How does rain form?; Why do we have day and night?; What makes a plane fly?. More generally, you can ask, "What's going on here? How does this work?"

Activity 4.3 Hands-on Science: Is Soda Good for Your Teeth?

Overview: You are going to introduce a unit on good dental health, and some of your students think that drinking lots of soda poses no problem to their teeth. It tastes good, so they think it is good for them. You want them to know that cutting down on sugary foods is a good way to care for their teeth. You set up an experiment so they can see what happens to a tooth when it sits in soda overnight.

Like teeth, eggshells are made of calcium: Life science

Materials: Two jars, one filled with soda and one filled with water; two baby teeth or two clean eggshells (which contain lots of calcium, like teeth)

Procedure: Place one baby tooth (or eggshell) in the jar filled with soda and the other tooth in the jar filled with water. The next day, remove the teeth. The tooth that sat overnight in the jar of soda is being eaten away. The tooth that sat in plain water looks as it did yesterday.

Assessment: Your students discuss this finding and conclude that drinking lots of soda may not be so good for their teeth, despite its good taste. They certainly wouldn't want to drink a glass of soda and then go to bed without brushing their teeth. This activity provides a great lead into the discussion of good dental health. ◼

Ask open-ended questions

Before you begin teaching a topic, think of several open-ended questions to ask students. You can ask questions to the whole class, and you can break students into small groups. The chapter on cooperative learning, Chapter 10, presents numerous ways to encourage your students to share their thoughts and communicate their ideas.

If you find that students have misconceptions, you should consider explaining concepts first and guiding students through a series of activities to build understanding. This is one situation where teacher-directed instruction is important. If your students have misconceptions, it would be risky to have them try to discover a concept on their own, because they are not starting on a level playing field. You might choose to structure learning experiences for students and guide them in a step-by-step fashion as they investigate. After you develop the concept with them, you ask them to generate their own questions for further study. Then you move on to a more student-centered approach. Once they have an understanding of the concept, they can begin to ask new questions about the topic and to investigate further on their own.

Asking Questions

If you assess students' prior knowledge and they have a solid understanding of a concept, they can formulate questions, design investigations, and generate explanations. Be sure your students formulate questions that they can answer. Sometimes students don't generate testable questions. If this happens, allow them to think about how realistic their questions are. Have them share questions with one another and challenge one another's ideas.

Inquiry-based teaching centers around allowing your students to ask questions. This might be difficult for those students who are unaccustomed to asking questions or for those who are shy or reserved. As a teacher, you should provide many opportunities for *all* students to ask questions as a natural part of your class.

Internet sites stimulate thought

One method of encouraging students to ask questions is to provide magazines and books for them to read. They can check out good Internet sites. You can also show them interesting science demonstrations. Have them discuss what they read or observe. Then they will be able to formulate appropriate questions. Another method of bringing forth questions for study is to suggest several topics for investigation to them (Edwards, 1997).

At one elementary school, students in grades K–2 and 3–4 gather for a hands-on science assembly before they select topics to investigate. There they observe dozens of interesting demonstrations, which are often centered around a particular theme, such as the "human body" or "all creatures big and small." As they participate in the assembly, they begin to formulate questions about phenomena that interest them. Before they leave, each student has at least one idea to develop. Ideas change, and students often investigate something else, but they do leave the assembly with a good start.

Russell Hulse says that asking good questions and coming up with ways to answer them requires creativity:

Pose well-formulated questions: Science process

Some questions are well posed and others are ill posed. Let's say that you want to grow the best fruits and vegetables that you can. You might want to try different fertilizers and different ways of pruning the plants. One way to find out what works best is to run experiments. You ask, "What makes my fruits and vegetables grow the best? This is an example of a poorly posed, ambiguous question. Does *best* mean tallest? Does *best* mean the most leaves? Does it mean the most fruit? Does it mean the biggest fruit? When your students pose questions, be certain that the questions are well formulated. (Personal communication)

Starting an Investigation

How do your students start an investigation? After they formulate their questions, they read about the topic. They can go to the library to get articles from journals and newspapers, search the Internet, read the textbook, or talk with experts such as scientists. The end of this chapter provides a list of Internet sites that put you in touch with experts in various scientific disciplines. In some cases, students will explore the topic, make observations, gather data, and try to classify their data. That's all that is appropriate for some topics. In other cases, once they know something about the topic, they will make a prediction or hypothesis about how they think things work, or they will predict what will happen as a result of an experiment.

Young children engage in exploration

To test the hypothesis, students can design an experiment. The sophistication of the experiment depends on the student's grade level. A kindergartner won't develop an experiment that is as sophisticated as a fourth-grader's. But even in the early grades, students often formulate a question, study about the topic, gather data, and classify those data, engaging in exploration. That's a big accomplishment for five- and six-year-olds! Consider this investigation carried out by kindergartner Jessica Meagher.

Jessica likes to work on the computer. She has two favorite computer games. One, called Dinosaur 3D, is about dinosaurs, and the other, called Skeymour Skinless, is about humans. Jessica began to wonder how dinosaurs and humans are the same and how they are different. She told her parents about her question, and they took her to a museum to see dinosaur skeletons. The skeletons were very big. Her parents bought her a tee shirt with a picture of a dinosaur on the front. They also bought a model of a dinosaur, but the bones weren't connected. Together they and Jessica built a model. Then they bought a model of a human skeleton and built it, too. Jessica also read about dinosaurs in a big book.

After learning about humans and dinosaurs, she began to answer her question on her own. She started by thinking of things that people could do that dinosaurs couldn't do, and classified her thoughts into two categories: (1) People can make their own habitats; dinosaurs couldn't. (2) People can use tools; dinosaurs couldn't.

Jessica found out there were many different kinds of dinosaurs. Some were very, very large and moved slowly. Others were much smaller and very active. Some looked like birds. People are much more alike than dinosaurs were, Jessica thought. Dinosaurs became extinct; people still live on the earth. Then she thought of ways in which people and dinosaurs are similar. Both people and dinosaurs need food and water to survive. Both breathe air. Both need a place to live.

Jessica told me that she likes being a scientist. She plans to learn more science as she grows older. She also plans to continue her study of humans and dinosaurs.

Older students design experiments

Older students can formulate hypotheses and design experiments, if doing so is appropriate for their investigations. Because they often have difficulty identifying and controlling variables, you should expect to assist them as they define the variables in their studies. You may also need to help them build in controls so that they have a basis for comparison and a way to judge change. They make measurements, record their measurements, and analyze the data. Then they can draw conclusions about what happened, find out whether or not their hypotheses were supported, and develop questions for further study. Consider Kunal Ranadive's work.

Kunal, a fourth-grader, is interested in engineering. He wanted to find out how muscles, bones, and joints work together. More specifically, he wanted to know if the human body works like an efficient machine, which expends little energy to do a large amount of work.

Kunal visited the library to do research. He found that engineers who design moving and lifting machines such as cranes and mechanical diggers use the principle of mechanical advantage, in which a small movement is turned into a large one. He decided to study the arm as a mechanical system, looking at the shoulder joint, the elbow joint, and the biceps muscle, a skeletal muscle attached above the shoulder joint and inserted an inch below the elbow joint. He wanted to learn whether the shoulder-biceps-elbow system uses the principle of mechanical advantage. His research question asked: "Is the biceps muscle positioned such that it expends the least amount of energy to do the greatest amount of work?" He hypothesized that the answer is yes.

To test his hypothesis, Kunal had to build a **model**. Using two strips of cardboard, a cutting mat, a craft knife, a ruler, a pencil, a pair of scissors, two strings (one red and one yellow), colored paper, metal wires, nuts and bolts, glue, and clay, he built a replica of a human arm. He studied about levers and learned that a lever is a rigid bar or rod that turns on a certain point, called the *fulcrum*. The lever moves a weight (load), using a *force*, or effort.

To find out whether the human arm operates as a lever that produces the greatest mechanical advantage, Kunal had to create an experiment in which he could test the actual human arm against another design. Each new experiment would be a trial. He repeated each trial twice. In each trial, he would change one part of the experiment and keep everything else the same; in other words, he controlled the variables.

First, he created a cardboard arm with the biceps muscle positioned in a location that is different from the position of the human biceps. He tied one end of a piece of red string to the forearm and the other end to a point on the "misplaced" muscle. Next, he made a replica of an actual human arm. Using yellow string, he tied one end to the forearm and the other end to the actual location of the human biceps. He held the upper arm and pulled each string separately from its "muscle" to raise the forearm by 45 degrees.

Kunal observed that both "muscles" pulled the forearm up, but the yellow string, which was connected to the "real" muscle, traveled a shorter distance than the red string, which was connected to the "misplaced" muscle. He concluded that the real muscle raised the forearm with the lesser amount of contraction; therefore, it had the greater mechanical advantage. The human arm, he concluded, works like an efficient machine, which spends the least amount of effort to do the greatest amount of work.

The human arm works like an efficient machine: Life science, physical science

To extend his research, Kunal said he could position the red string in other locations. In this way, he could find out if there are other places where a muscle could be positioned such that it has mechanical advantage, gathering more data to test his hypothesis.

Kunal sincerely enjoyed his research—I could tell just by speaking with him. He plans to continue learning more about science and engineering as he grows older.

Sharing results with peers is very important. Students can share in small groups, with the whole class, or with the school community. You must listen to them as they share their findings. This is how you will know what they think.

Helping Students Build Understanding of Concepts

Once you assess students' prior knowledge, begin to clear up alternate conceptions, and allow them to investigate, your job is to help them develop understanding of new concepts. You can do this in many ways. You can explain the concept to them, they can explain the concept to you and to one another, and you can ask questions that allow them to apply and analyze their thinking. Such questions are more specific than open-ended questions. Here are some examples.

What do you predict will happen? Why did you make that prediction? What's happening in this experiment? Why is it happening? Challenge their answers.

You can also ask more specific questions as they draw conclusions based on evidence.

How does the color of clothing that a person wears affect the person's comfort level on a warm day? What is the effect of a diet that lacks calcium on the strength of a child's bones? How does the amount of light a plant receives affect its rate of growth? Tell me what you know about the effect of acid rain on marble statues.

Students analyze one another's results

Next, use the information from their answers to assess their understanding. Have them check their results carefully. Be sure that the conclusions they formulate are based on the evidence they collect. Encourage them to speak and write about their findings. Allow them to present their results to the whole class. Let them challenge one another's thinking. Encourage them to analyze one another's results. Have them reflect on their work. Listen carefully to what they say. You use your professional teaching knowledge to judge whether or not they understand.

Activity 4.4 Teaching Skills: Observing an Experienced Teacher

Overview: For this activity, you will need to find an outstanding elementary science teacher who uses inquiry-based instruction. Get permission to observe this teacher's class. Record all of the questions she or he asks while involving students in an investigation.

Assessment: What types of questions does the teacher ask? How does he or she assess prior knowledge? How does the teacher know when students understand a concept? Does she or he challenge students' conclusions? Does the teacher check to see that their conclusions are based on the data they collect? ◼

Activity 4.5 Hands-on Science: Engaging in Your Own Investigation

Overview: John Dewey said, "If you have doubt about how learning happens, engage in sustained inquiry; study, ponder, consider alternative possibilities and arrive at your belief grounded in evidence" (Dewey, 1933). Think of a topic that you would like to investigate. Start with a question. I will suggest some possibilities, but it is preferable that you choose your own questions. Make predictions, hypothesize, design an experiment, make a model, collect and analyze the data, and draw conclusions. Reflect on your findings. Think about this experience.

Questions for study:

1. You are an elementary teacher preparing your students for the end-of-year field day activities. The event will take place outdoors in mid-June, when the temperature is expected to be in the 90s. You don't want your students to become overheated too quickly. Design an investigation that allows you to determine the best color of clothing for them to wear.

2. You will teach a lesson on water conservation. Design an investigation that will help you determine whether taking a shower or a bath uses more water.

Assessment: What question did you ask? How did your investigation go? What did you learn? Did your conclusions follow from your evidence? How will you bring this experience to your students? ■

Your Development as an Elementary Science Teacher

As an elementary science teacher, you will pass through several stages in your own development. You will start out at one level and continue to progress as you move along in your career. You are not expected to know everything at the start. As you gain teaching experience, you will learn more and become better at all aspects of teaching. Your subject matter knowledge will grow as you continue to plan lessons and attend courses, seminars, and workshops. Your ability to teach inquiry-based science will develop as well.

Some elementary science teachers don't start out with a solid background in science. They have a difficult time determining when students have misconceptions because their own science backgrounds are weak. They may even share some of their students' alternate conceptions. Many teachers learned from textbooks, had little experience with hands-on science, and never experienced inquiry-based teaching in any form.

If you lack a solid science background and think of science as a subject taught in lecture fashion from a textbook, you are not alone. Your preconceived notions about how to teach science may conflict with how you should teach science because you are affected by your prior experience. This course and this text probably are quite different from your own school science experience and will help you to teach and learn science in a different way. Once you have an understanding of what teaching science involves, you can build your content knowledge slowly.

Many beginning teachers fear teaching science because they believe they don't know enough and never will. In my work with experienced, outstanding science teachers over the years, I learned that many of them started out with little interest in science, having taken just a few courses. Starting slowly, gaining confidence, trying new experiments, building a collection of materials and supplies, and enjoying the spirit of inquiry and discovery hooked them. They found out how much fun teaching science can be, and they continued to grow as elementary science teachers.

Constructing Your Knowledge of Science and Science Teaching

After completing this chapter, begin to reflect on your new knowledge. You should now have a basic understanding of the essential aspects of inquiry-based teaching. Review them. What are the essential aspects of inquiry-based teaching? What are some of the methods teachers use to bring inquiry into the elementary school classroom? What is the role of the teacher in an inquiry-centered classroom?

How do you help your students begin an investigation? What support do they need? What pitfalls might you anticipate? If they arise, how will you deal with them?

I suggest that you make notes about the artifacts from this chapter that you would choose in creating your science teaching portfolio entry on inquiry-based teaching. As you engage in scientific inquiry, include the results of your experiment in the portfolio.

Key Terms

teacher-directed inquiry (p. 84)
students and teacher as
   co-investigators (p. 88)
student-directed inquiry (p. 90)

discrepant event (p. 92)
preconceptions (p. 93)
misconceptions (p. 94)

alternate conceptions (p. 94)
open-ended questions (p. 94)
model (p. 98)

Reviewing Chapter 4: Questions, Extensions, Applications, and Explorations

1. Pair off with a peer and discuss the elements of inquiry-based science. What must you know about your students before you begin an investigation?

2. Read through the chapter and analyze the student research summaries. What motivated each student to investigate his or her topic? I interviewed these students two and three months after they presented their research to their peers. What can you say about how well they retained what they learned?

3. *Benchmarks for Science Literacy: Project 2061* tells us that scientists differ greatly in how they do their work. There is no fixed set of steps that they follow, but they do collect relevant evidence, employ logical reasoning, and use their imaginations to devise hypotheses and explanations to make sense of their evidence (American Association for the Advancement of Science, 1993, p. 12). Did the student researchers described in the chapter use such scientific thinking?

4. Why is it important to describe things as accurately as possible when "doing" science?

5. Two groups of fourth-graders in your class do the same experiment and collect similar data, but they have different explanations for the findings. How will you handle this situation?

Print Resources

Abdi, S. W. (1997). Motivating students to enjoy questioning. *The Science Teacher, 64*(6), 10.

American Association for the Advancement of Science. (1993). *Benchmarks for Science Literacy: Project 2061.* New York: Oxford University Press.

Bateman, W. (1990). *Open to question: The art of teaching and learning by inquiry.* San Francisco: Jossey-Bass.

Bruner, J. (1961). The act of discovery. *Harvard Educational Review, 31*(1), 21.

Chiapetta, E. (1997). Inquiry-based science. *The Science Teacher, 64*(5), 18–22.

Edwards, C. (1997). Promoting student inquiry. *The Science Teacher, 64*(5), 18–22.

Ginsburg, H. (1997). *Entering the child's mind: The clinical interview in psychological research and practice.* New York: Cambridge University Press.

Ginsburg, H., Jacobs, S., & Lopez, S. L. (1998). *The teacher's guide to flexible interviewing in the classroom.* Boston: Allyn & Bacon.

National Research Council. (1996). *National Science Education Standards.* Washington, DC: National Academy Press.

Welch, W., Klopfer, L., Aikenhead, G., & Robinson, J. (1981). The role of inquiry in science education: Analysis and recommendations. *Science Education, 65*(1), 33–55.

Electronic Resources

A Private Universe Video. Annenberg/CPB Math and Science Collection, Corporation for Public Broadcasting, 901 E Street NW, Washington, D.C., 20004; Phone: 1-800-965-7373.
This video discusses science concepts and alternate conceptions.

Let's Collaborate
http://www.gene.com/ae/TSN
Interact with teachers, scientists, and other classrooms at this site.

MAD Scientist Network
http://medicine.wustl.edu:80/~ysp/MSN/MAD.SCI.html
Scientists from around the world field student and teacher questions and help teachers develop motivating ideas for science classes.

Library in the Sky
http://www.nwrel.org/sky/
This site, sponsored by the Northwest Regional Educational Laboratory, is a wonderful resource for teachers.

Students' Alternate Conceptions
http://ascilite95.unimelb.edu.au.SMTU/ASCILITES95/abstracts/Akerlind.html
This site discusses students' alternate conceptions.

Explore Science
http://www.explorescience.com
This site includes online activities and experiments.

Access Excellence
http://www.gene.com/ae/
This site includes life science resources for teaching and learning.

Children's Literature

Swan, Erin
Primates: From Howler Monkeys to Humans
(Franklin Watts, 1998)
ISBN: 0-531-11487
Grades 4–6

Lewin, Roger
Human Evolution: An Illustrated Introduction
(Bladwell Science, 1999)
ISBN: 0-632-043091-1
Grades 6 and up

Merriman, Nick
Early Humans (Knopf, 1989)
ISBN: 0-394-82257-9
Grades 4–6

Wond, Ovid
Experiment with Animal Behavior
(Children's Press, 1988)
ISBN: 0-516-02214-2
Grades K–4

Cole, Joanna
The Magic School Bus: Inside the Human Body
(Scholastic Trade, 1990)
ISBN: 0-590-41426-7
Preschool and Grades K–3

Hawcock, David
The Amazing Pull-Out Pop-Up Body in a Book
(Dorling Kindersley Publishing, 1997)
ISBN: 0-789-42052-X
Preschool and Grades K–3

Wyse, Liz and Haslam, Andrew
Body: The Hands-On Approach to Science
(World Publications, 1997)
ISBN: 0-716-64711-7
Grades 6 and up

Hewitt, Sally
Growing UP (Children's Press, 1998)
ISBN: 0-0516-21180-3
Preschool and Grades K–3

Greenway, Shirley
How Do I Move? (Ideal Children's Books, 1992)
ISBN: 0-9249-8578-8
Preschool and Grades K–3

Rakow, Donald, & Warner, Philson
Grow with the Flow (Com Coop., 1993)
ISBN: 1-57753-218-x
Grades 5–7

Marzollo, Jean
How Kids Grow (Cartwheel Books, 1998)
ISBN: 0-590-45062-X
Grades 3 and up

CHAPTER 5

Children's Learning

While on a hike, you stop at an outcropping of rocks. You find what looks like an old jaw bone with teeth embedded in the rock. You wonder how it got there. If you are a child, you might offer any of these explanations:

▶ The jaw bone comes from an animal. The animal was killed by another animal. His body was melted into the rock by the sun, and we found its jaw bone.

▶ Some animal was chewing on a rock, but the rock was too big, so the animal choked. After awhile, more rock showed up around the animal, and it got buried. Its skeleton broke apart, and we found its jaw bone and teeth.

▶ There was once a cute, fuzzy little four-legged animal who was nibbling on some grass for dinner, when suddenly a big dinosaur snuck up on the little animal and stomped it into the rock. We found its jaw bone.

How would a scientist answer this question? The scientist would systematically reconstruct the environment in which the organism lived. He or she would begin by determining whether the teeth are those of a herbivore, a carnivore, or an omnivore. Using a field guide to fossils, the scientist would do research to match the fossil with a particular animal. The next step would be to determine the age of the sediment in which the fossil was deposited. This would offer additional information that helps to identify the organism as living during a particular age. The scientist would then reconstruct the environment of deposition. Was it put there by a freshwater process or by a river flowing into a dry basin, or did a completely terrestrial process deposit it? The scientist would also use isotopic dating to determine the numerical age of the fossil.

These students are on a hike. They're studying rocks and collecting samples.

In this chapter, you will read about the theory of Jean Piaget, who emphasizes the child's personal construction of reality and actual developmental level. Then you'll learn about the work of Lev Vygotsky, who extended Piaget's teachings to include the influence of language, interaction with adults, and the social and economic system. As you read through this chapter, think about the answers to these questions:

1. **What is constructivism? How does it relate to science teaching?**
2. **How does Piaget's theory contribute to your understanding of science teaching?**
3. **How does Vygotsky's theory of social constructivism expand Piaget's view?**
4. **How do I put constructivism into practice in my elementary science classroom?**
5. **What does a constructivist classroom look like?**
6. **How can we use constructivist theory to teach about earth science topics?**

Children Construct Knowledge

Children construct their knowledge

Look back at the scenario that opens this chapter. Are the answers the children provided incorrect and the one given by the scientist correct? In fact, the children's answers are just as correct as the scientist's. Children *construct* their knowledge, rather than receive it, fully formed, from the physical world and from their many social encounters, which include interactions with parents, relatives, friends, teachers, classmates, and even media personalities. Constructions are personal, and each child's construction is unique.

Children's constructions are different from those of adults. To understand how a child thinks and constructs meaning, you can't rely on your adult experience, modes of thinking, and values (Ginsburg, 1997). You must discover what is in the child's mind and how that child builds his or her own understanding. Then you can begin to understand the child's response. This is the essence of **constructivism**.

Learning About Constructivist Theory

Constructivism takes many forms and styles, and theorists disagree widely about what these forms and styles are. Nevertheless, according to Herbert Ginsburg (1997),

[D]espite the many forms and styles of constructivism, and the theoretical disagreements, there is widespread consensus among psychologists that the child does not develop concepts and ways of thinking primarily because the world imposes them, parents or teachers inculcate them, culture provides ways of thinking about them, or the mind innately contains them. Instead, the child actively uses information from the world, the lessons provided by parents and schools, the cultural legacy, and the species' biological inheritance as bases for constructing knowledge. (p. 59)

Nature and Nurture Working Together: The Cognitive Growth of the Child

Knowledge of cognitive development is essential in lesson planning

To understand how children learn science, it is important to consider the development of children's cognitive abilities and skills. The process of knowing, called **cognition,** includes perception, memory, and thinking. **Perception** is the process by which we recognize patterns and begin to know objects, events, people, and processes. **Memory** is the process by which we recall, or keep experiences that we have learned in mind. **Thinking** is the process of considering ideas and using such skills as comprehension, analysis, synthesis, and evaluation. As a child grows cognitively, the process of knowing grows as well (Wakefield, 1996). As you plan developmentally appropriate science lessons for your students, you will use your knowledge of cognitive development.

When psychologists describe human development, they often divide the effects of nature into maturational plateaus, or stages. The stages correspond to approximate age ranges. Stage theories of cognitive development help you to understand what you should expect as a child matures, and enables you to plan instruction appropriately. In this chapter, you will learn about two major models of cognitive development: Piaget's theory of cognitive development and Vygotsky's theory of social origins of thought. These theories provide insights into the stages of cognitive development as well as into the social contexts in which children develop. An understanding of developmentally appropriate practice, which is based on our knowledge of cognitive development, will help you to understand how children learn science. Being aware of broad developmental sequences—what nature provides—and using this knowledge as a starting point for improvement will help you move your students along as they develop.

The Role of Theory in Education

Theories examine patterns and relationships: Science process

Before examining each of these theories in depth, let's first consider the role of theory in education. In general, **theories** examine patterns and relationships and provide explanations for phenomena that we observe in nature. Sound theories explain known relationships and are useful in making predictions about the world that will be verified later. Based on application of theory, we know what is likely to happen when we observe a pattern or a relationship. Confidence in a theory grows as new situations arise and the theory is useful in making predictions. Once scientists disprove a theory, it is modified or replaced by a better theory. Scientists value simplicity, and simpler theories are often more acceptable than complicated ones.

As a teacher, it is important to be aware of numerous theories of teaching and learning so that you can make informed, intelligent decisions about providing instruction for students. Just as doctors turn to such fields as chemistry, biology, physics, and psychology to gain knowledge that they can apply to their practice, teachers turn to such fields as biology, psychology, sociology, and anthropology to inform their practice. As a teacher, you will view learners through multiple lenses, looking at what happens as the mind and body develop while being aware of the effects of the social world. Let us now turn to the theory of Jean Piaget to learn more about the cognitive development of children.

Piaget's Theory of Cognitive Development

Jean Piaget was a researcher whose pioneering work was instrumental in the development of cognitive science. Born in 1896 in the small town of Neuchatel, Switzerland, the son of a history professor, he exhibited an early interest in observing animals in their natural habitats. As he grew older, he attended the University of Neuchatel, where he earned both his undergraduate degree and Ph.D. by age 21. He developed an interest in psychology and expanded his knowledge by studying in Zurich. Later he went to Paris to study abnormal psychology. There he began to investigate the development of thinking in children. He later moved to Geneva to direct the Jean-Jacques Rousseau Institute, where he devoted himself to the study of cognitive development. His research continued until he retired in 1975. Piaget died in 1980.

Jean Piaget works with children.

In the early 1960s, Piaget's work became popular in the United States, and his theory of cognitive development dominated the field of cognitive psychology for about 20 years. One of the most important tenets of his theory of intellectual development is *constructivism*, which views the learner as a builder of knowledge. Students are seen as active constructors rather than passive receivers of knowledge. Through constructivism, Piaget helps us to understand how children learn and develop.

Piaget's model is important for teachers. It says that students come to us not with blank minds but with previous learning. They learn a great deal before they come to school, including learning to speak, learning to move about in their own space, and familiarizing themselves with the logic used by their parents and other caregivers. Piagetian theory also reminds us that teaching is not telling. Instead, his constructivist philosophy urges us to view the learning process as one that is active. It asks us to engage students in their own learning and to act as facilitators who enhance the learning process. All students are not the same; each child builds his or her own version of reality. This happens in different ways and at different ages, a fact that led Piaget to develop a *stage theory* of cognitive development.

Activity 5.1 Reflective Activity: Thinking About Your Own Experiences with Constructivism

Overview: Constructivist theory is quite popular in education today, but it is not new to teaching. In this activity, you will consider your own school experience and try to identify teachers who used a constructivist view in their classrooms.

Connecting new learning to previous learning is essential

Procedure: Reflect on your school experience. Think of teachers you have studied with who are student centered and who focus on individual student learning. These teachers' classrooms have a healthy, positive climate in which students solve problems, ask questions, create their own investigations, work cooperatively, discuss and debate ideas, reflect on their work, exercise creativity, and are encouraged to take risks. New learning is built on previous learning, and stories, whole-class discussions, good examples, and anecdotes are used to help students see the relevance of the content. New learning is connected to previous learning as students retrieve previously learned materials from memory and use this knowledge to facilitate current learning. Students have opportunities to practice and solve problems that are similar to those they will eventually have to solve in life. Such teachers use a variety of teaching strategies to help students learn, and they allow students to converse with one another, with the teacher, and with others so that they can construct understanding.

Assessment: Use a journal to record your reflections. Does this type of teacher serve as a role model for you? Is there a particular teacher whom you described? ■

Key Processes in Human Development

Piaget's theory is based on his interests in biology and cognition. He assumed that humans inherit two basic tendencies: the ability to systematize or combine processes into coherent, logically related systems, called **organization,** and the tendency to adjust to the environment, called **adaptation**. As children grow they develop **schemes,** or organized patterns of behavior or thought. A child's schemes are his or her concepts of reality.

As a child progresses through life, he or she encounters new situations. Sometimes these situations fit existing schemes, and sometimes *adaptation* occurs. When this happens, the child creates a match between existing schemes and new experiences. Piaget proposed two subprocesses to achieve adaptation: assimilation and accommodation. When *assimilation* occurs, the child adapts by interpreting an experience so that it fits an existing scheme. When *accommodation* occurs, the child adapts by changing the existing scheme to fit the new experience (Biehler & Snowman, 1997, pp. 49–57).

Consider 9-year old Kelly, whose existing scheme tells her that the sun rises in the morning and explodes into little pieces at night. That's why it becomes dark at night. During the night, the little pieces of the sun gather, and by morning, the sun is put together again. When that happens, the sun rises, and we see its light. Kelly developed this idea a few years ago, and since she hasn't thought about it in awhile, this is her current understanding and is what she tells her teacher when asked to explain why day and night occur.

The sun is a star: Earth and space science

In class today, Kelly learns that the earth is a planet, one of nine planets that orbit, or go around, the sun. The sun and its nine planets make up the solar system. The sun is a star, one of many hundreds of billions of stars that make up the Milky Way galaxy. The teacher shows the class a model of the solar system so they can think about what it means for planets to orbit the sun. She shows her students what it looks like when the earth revolves around the sun. Tomorrow she'll give them more time to work with the model. Today she has another goal: to help her students to understand what causes day and night. So she develops an activity to help students explore this concept. She breaks the class into groups of four. Each group has a flashlight to act as the sun and a small ball that is a replica of the earth. She asks the children to use the flashlight and the ball to make a model that shows how day and night might occur.

In Kelly's group, the children try different things. Some work and some don't. Finally, someone comes up with the idea that if the earth spins, it gets the light from the flashlight when facing it, and when it doesn't face the flashlight, it is in darkness. The students test this idea with the flashlight and the earth ball. It works. They spot the teacher's swivel chair and remember that it too spins around. They decide to take turns sitting in the chair and spinning around. This will give them a better test of the model. One person shines the flashlight at the chair while the other spins around in the chair. Half of the time the person spinning in the chair sees the light, and the other half of the time he doesn't. The students decide that if the chair spins around once a day, this would explain why we have day and night.

Modeling the earth's rotation on its axis: Earth and space science

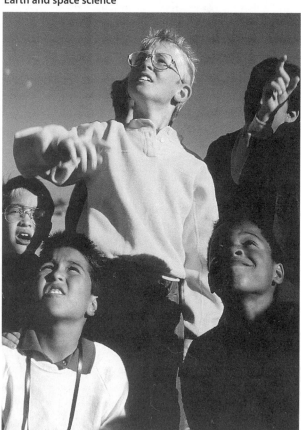

These students are wondering why we have day and night.

Kelly begins to assimilate as she fits a new experience into an existing scheme. Next, she modifies her existing scheme and adjusts her understanding, in light of the new experience, as accommodation takes place. She learns that if the sun shines all the time and the earth spins around, rotating on its axis once a day, we have day and night. The earth doesn't have to stand still while the sun explodes into little pieces for night to occur. The little bits of sun don't have to come together for day to occur. Other things are possible. According to Piaget, adaptation is the process of repeated assimilation and accommodation.

Equilibration, Disequilibrium, and Learning

Piaget explained that there is a mechanism that regulates the development of understanding, or accommodation, called *equilibration*. When a discrepancy occurs between what is understood and what is perceived, a condition called *disequilibrium*, or imbalance, exists. Equilibrium must then be restored by activating the individual's ability to *accommodate*. This continues until a new state of *equilibrium*, or balance, is reached. The concepts of disequilibration and equilibration are important in the learning process.

In thinking about Kelly's experience, you can examine the concepts of equilibration and disequilibration. When her original idea is challenged, she is thrust into a state of disequilibrium. This activates accommodation, which continues until she develops a new understanding and reaches a state of equilibrium once again. She has a new idea of how things work that makes sense to her. Let's now turn to Piaget's theory of cognitive development to understand how to apply these mechanisms.

Piaget's Stages of Cognitive Development

Reviewing Piaget's stages of cognitive development

Piaget's theory identifies four stages of cognitive development. We order the stages such that successive stages incorporate the development of preceding ones; the stages therefore are hierarchical. We associate each stage with a particular age range. Note, however, that the ages represent an average. Not all children reach the stages at the same age, and rates of cognitive development vary from child to child. Thus, a child who develops more slowly than another will not necessarily lag behind in development as an adult.

Piaget's first stage of development is the **sensorimotor period,** which deals with how children adapt to reality by sensing and moving. Children reach this stage between birth and 2 years of age. Next in the hierarchy is the **preoperational period,** which concerns itself with how the child forms concepts before the ability to use logic develops. This generally occurs between ages 2 and 7. From ages 7 to 11, children generally enter the stage of **concrete operations,** in which they use applied reasoning and logical thought structures to solve concrete problems. The last stage, which typically occurs between ages 11 and early adult, is **formal operations**. In this stage, children use systematic reasoning to solve problems. Table 5.1 summarizes the four stages.

Table 5.1
Characteristics of Piaget's Stages of Development

Stage/Age Range	Characteristics
Sensorimotor (Birth to two years)	Uses senses and movement to develop schemes. Object permanence develops.
Preoperational (Two to seven years)	Cannot reverse mental operations. Incapable of operational thought.
Concrete operations (Seven to eleven years)	Capable of operational thought. Uses concrete operations to solve problems. Not capable of abstract thought.
Formal operations Eleven to early adult	Capable of abstract thought. Can think systematically.

Sensorimotor Stage (Birth to 2 Years)

Perceiving by using the senses and moving about are the ways in which children from birth to 2 years collect data about their world. During the first months of life, objects exist for a baby only when they are in sight. Sometime between ages 9 and 18 months, the infant develops *object permanence,* or the knowledge that an object exists even when it is out of sight.

Children at this age exhibit a great deal of curiosity. Even though they lack sophisticated language and have limited ability to think about objects, they are able to gather data about the world. When they play with rattles, they use the sense of hearing. When they manipulate objects and place them in their mouths, they gather data about the way things feel and taste. As they employ their developing motor skills, they find out more and more about their world. Youngsters at this age are *egocentric,* meaning they derive information about the world from their own experiences.

As children near the end of the sensorimotor stage, they develop more elaborate schemes. At the beginning of this stage, means-end, or causal, relationships were not possible—but now they are. Once object permanence exists, they investigate features of objects, and "out of sight" is no longer "out of mind." The ability to crawl or walk about their surroundings enables children to develop spatial schemes. The concept of time develops as they become able to coordinate what happened in the past to what is happening in the present and what will happen in the future. The development of language enables children to name objects, and through play, the use of gestures, and the development of mental images, they can conceptualize objects in a variety of ways.

Preoperational Period (2 to 7 Years)

During the preoperational stage, language develops and intellectual growth centers around mastery of symbols, including words. Piaget believed that mastery of symbols involves mental imitation derived from visual images and bodily sensations, building on what the child experienced in the sensorimotor stage. Early language development involves naming objects, such as "dog," "cat," "milk"; socializing, which includes greeting others by saying "hi" and "'bye"; and making requests, such as "go out," when the child wants to go outside, or putting together words, such as "me milk", to request a drink of milk. By the time children are ready for kindergarten (about age 5), language development advances so that they make requests, give instructions, and formulate explanations.

Adults may perceive a child's thoughts and actions to be illogical

Although preschoolers and children in the primary grades are able to use language well, since they are at the preoperational, or prelogical, stage, adults often perceive their thoughts and actions to be illogical. Three characteristics of this stage—*perceptual centration* (focusing on only one aspect of a problem at a time), *irreversibility* (being unable to move back and forth reversibly when solving a problem), and *egocentrism* (being unable to consider another person's point of view)—are impediments to operational behavior, or actions carried out with the use of logic. These characteristics are easy to observe as children carry out traditional Piagetian tasks, which are simple experiments. These include conservation problems, in which we test children on the ability to recognize that certain properties remain unchanged even when appearance or position changes. You will examine several conservation problems so that you can carry them out with your students and reflect on your own findings.

One of the best-known conservation problems involves conservation of a liquid substance, such as water. To do this task, you will need two short, wide glasses of the same size and one tall, narrow glass that holds the same volume of liquid as the short glasses. You will also need two drops of food coloring in two different colors, a pitcher of water, and a 4- or 5-year-old. To minimize disturbances, carry out the task in a quiet location.

To begin, position the two identical short, wide glasses next to each other; then add exactly the same amount of water to each glass. Color the water in each glass with a different food color. Give the child a few minutes to observe the situation; then ask if both glasses contain the same amount of water. When the child replies, ask, "Why do you think so?" It is likely that the child will tell you that both glasses contain the same amount of water. If he or she doesn't think so, provide a medicine dropper or a teaspoon and let the child add water until she or he believes both glasses contain equal amounts. Then pour the water from one short, wide glass into the tall, narrow glass. Ask if the tall glass and the short glass contain the same amount of water. When the child replies, ask, "Why do you think so?" (See Figure 5.1.)

**Figure 5.1
Assessing
Conservation
of Liquid**
When the water is poured from the short, wide glass to the tall, narrow glass, nonconservers believe there is more water in the tall glass.

A preschooler is likely to tell you that the taller glass holds more water because it is taller. A 6- or 7-year-old, on the other hand, will likely tell you that both glasses hold the same amount of water but it only *looks* like the taller glass holds more. The younger child has difficulty understanding that both glasses hold the same volume of water because of *perceptual centration;* that is, the child's ability to focus on more than one quality or aspect of an object at a time has not yet developed, so he or she focuses on height but not on width or volume.

Irreversibility is another impediment to logical thought. Although the child can *physically* pour from the short, wide glass into the tall, narrow glass and back to the short, wide glass, he or she cannot *mentally* reverse the operation.

Finally, preschoolers are egocentric and self-centered, meaning they can see things only from their own perspective and not from the perspectives of others; it does not mean they are selfish or conceited. When using language, we tend to assume that others listen to and understand what we are saying. In the case of the tall glass and the short glass, a preschooler is likely to insist that the taller glass holds more water, and any attempts to explain another view are futile. The following activities will enable you to work with young children and develop further understanding of how they think.

Activity 5.2 Hands-on Science: Assessing Conservation of Number

Overview: Piaget believed that children do not conserve number before ages 6 or 7. This means that when you arrange a fixed number of objects and then rearrange them to make the arrangement appear longer or shorter, the child who does not conserve number thinks that the number of objects, not the position of the objects, has changed. Picture two rows of coins, each containing the same number of coins lined up one above the other. When you rearrange one row so that there is more space between coins and it appears longer, the child who is a nonconserver cannot understand that the number of coins is the same and that only the position and spacing between the coins has changed.

Materials: 20 pennies

Procedure: Make two rows of pennies, one above the other, as shown in Figure 5.2. Ask the child which row contains more pennies. The answer should be "Both rows contain the same number of pennies." Next, spread out the pennies in one row. Now ask the question again. If the child does not conserve number, he or she will say that there are more pennies in the row in which they are spread out.

Figure 5.2 Assessing Conservation of Number
When the pennies are moved so that there is more space between them, nonconservers believe there are more pennies in the bottom row.

Assessment: Repeat the activity again. If the child answers in the same way, he or she is a nonconserver. If the answers are inconsistent, the child may be in a transitional stage. If the child tells you that the number of pennies did not change, she or he does conserve number. ■

The preoperational child sees things from his or her own perspective

In general, the preoperational child sees things from his or her own perspective and has difficulty seeing things from another viewpoint. When discussing the conservation tasks, the child will often look at you in a puzzled way if you attempt to explain errors of logic. As the child enters the next stage of development, these characteristics change as emphasis on perceptual centration, irreversibility, and egocentrism diminish and logic continues to develop.

Concrete Operations (7 to 11 Years)

As the child grows older, operational thinking develops and is characterized by the ability to master certain conservation tasks. When pouring water from a short glass to a tall glass, the child now knows that the amount of water stays the same. However, other tasks, such as conservation of length, are still in question. Activity 5.3 provides an example of a task that children usually master between ages 7 and 8. As you administer the "conservation of length" task, as well as the activities that follow, use simple words and be sure the child understands what you are asking. Each task requires that equivalence be established first, so don't go on to change or vary anything until the child agrees that both starting materials are exactly the same. If you don't establish this condition, it is pointless to continue the task. Be careful not to pressure or lead the child. Some children are not ready and are unlikely to understand the task, so go no further if you encounter such a situation. As a new teacher, getting feedback concerning your work with children is important. You may want to videotape yourself working with children or have a classmate observe and give you feedback as you administer the tasks.

Activity 5.3 Hands-on Science: Assessing Conservation of Length

Figure 5.3 Assessing Conservation of Length
When the bottom string is moved to the right of the top string, nonconservers believe the bottom string is longer.

Overview: Before age 7 or 8, children generally do not conserve length. If two objects are exactly the same length, the child thinks they differ in length, depending on position. For example, if you place two pieces of string of identical length one above the other, as shown in Figure 5.3, then shift them so that one string moves ahead of the other, the child will believe the string that you moved forward is longer than the other.

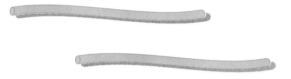

Materials: Two pieces of string of exactly same length

Procedure: Position the string such that one piece is directly above the other. Ask the child to describe the length of each piece. The child should tell you that they are both the same length. Now shift the top string so that it moves to the right. Ask the child about the length of each piece of string. A child who does not conserve length will tell you that the string you shifted to the right is longer than the other string.

Assessment: Repeat the activity, this time swirling one string into a spiral. Ask about the length of each piece of string. Once again, the nonconserver will tell you that the original string is longer than the other. ■

Activity 5.4 Hands-on Science: Assessing Conservation of Amount of a Solid

Figure 5.4 Assessing Conservation of a Solid
When the sphere of play dough is flattened into a pancake, nonconservers believe there is less solid.

Overview: Piaget believed that children under age 7 or 8 generally do not conserve the amount of solid substance. Two objects that contain exactly the same amount of a solid are thought to contain different amounts of the solid depending on the shape of the material.

Materials: Two small cans of play dough or modeling clay. Since play dough is colorful and quite easy to mold, I prefer to use it when administering these tasks; however clay works just as well.

Procedure: Open each can of play dough in front of the child. Ask if both cans contain the same or different amounts of play dough. Ask the child to explain his or her answer.

Remove the play dough from the can and roll the contents of each into a ball. Ask if the balls contain the same or different amounts of play dough; then ask the child to explain his or her answer. Next, roll one lump of play dough into a pancake. Ask if the ball and the pancake contain different amounts of play dough; then ask for an explanation.

Assessment: If the child can conserve the amount of a solid, he or she will tell you that both lumps of play dough are the same and only the shape changes. To be sure the child understands the concept, change the shape of the ball to a "snake," and ask the questions again. You might try dividing the play dough into little pieces and repeating the questions. ▪

Manipulating concrete objects is important

Children at this stage are not yet capable of abstract thought. They solve problems by manipulating concrete objects. For example, when learning mathematics, it is important for children at this stage to work with a variety of manipulatives such as pattern blocks, base ten blocks, tangrams, geoboards, and cubes that link together. The experiences with concrete objects help them to understand mathematical concepts. In the science classroom, working with hands-on materials and engaging in experimentation are very important. When studying about length, mass, volume, and temperature, the child should have experience with measuring real objects. At the beginning of this stage, children's investigations are primitive and unsystematic. They often try to derive relationships from their work, but are generally unable to do so. Transferring information from one situation to another is often difficult. At the latter part of this stage, children develop the ability to organize investigations and define variables, then measure them as they record data, form tables and charts, analyze data, make predictions, and develop generalizations. They begin to be able to think scientifically. Somewhere between ages 9 and 12, children develop the ability to conserve weight, and between 11 and 15 years of age, they often develop the ability to conserve volume. Activity 5.5 guides you through a weight conservation task.

Activity 5.5 Hands-on Science: Assessing Conservation of Weight

Overview: Piaget believed that children generally develop the ability to conserve weight between ages 9 and 12. Before developing this ability, when given two lumps of play dough of the same shape and of equal weight, the child believes that the weight changes if the shape changes.

Materials: You will need two small cans of play dough and a balance. If your school does not have a commercially constructed balance, use the double pan shoe box balance described in Chapter 3.

Procedure: Open each can of play dough in front of the child. Remove the contents of each can, and have the child roll each lump into a ball. Find out if he or she believes that the two balls have the same weight (are equally heavy). Have the child weigh each sphere of play dough, using the balance, to verify his or her answer. Next, ask the child to flatten one sphere into a pancake. Ask whether both lumps of play dough still have the same weight, and be sure to get an explanation. The child may or may not believe that both the sphere and the pancake have the same weight.

Assessment: If the child believes that the weight remains unchanged when the shape changes, you can try another experiment. Break the play dough pancake into several smaller pancakes. Ask if all of the small pancakes weigh the same as the sphere did, and ask for an explanation. Use the balance to help your student find out if a change in weight has occurred. ■

Now that you have experience with administering Piagetian tasks, you should be aware of some criticisms of his work. Some critics believe that the tasks are too complex and do not represent children's real-life experiences; therefore, they are difficult for children to understand and carry out. The tasks also hone in on skills and abilities that children lack rather than on those they have mastered. Such is the case with children at the preoperational level. On the other hand, some researchers believe that Piaget overestimated the capabilities of adolescents, who are expected to exhibit formal thought (Kamii, 1984). While we assume that high school seniors and college freshmen are capable of using higher-level thinking and can deal with abstractions, some studies show that large percentages of students in these age ranges cannot think in this way. A look at the characteristics of the formal operations stage will provide clarification.

Formal Operations (11 Years to Early Adulthood)

Working with hypotheses requires scientific thinking: Science process

As the formal operational stage begins, children pass into adolescence. According to Piaget's theory, they can now engage in formal operations. Instead of solving problems haphazardly using trial and error or by manipulating concrete objects, the formal thinker is capable of dealing with abstractions about concrete objects and events. Piaget stated that during the period of formal operations, thinking changes so that it "no longer bears exclusively on directly perceivable objects and realities, but also on 'hypotheses,' that is to say, on propositions from which it is possible to draw necessary consequences without deciding on their truth or falsity before having examined the result of these implications" (Piaget & Inhelder, 1969, p. 51). Thinking hypothetically, formulating hypotheses, and expressing relationships are characteristic of formal thought. The ability to work with hypotheses requires scientific thinking, not only in science but in other areas as well.

Piaget proposed the idea of the "structured whole," a condition that must be met if an individual is to be considered a formal thinker. Ann Parsons, a translator of Piaget stated, " . . . the structured whole, by virtue of which the subject is able both to combine parts into a whole and to separate them from it, might be impressionistically characterized as a sort of mental scaffolding held up by a number of girders joined together in such a way that an agile subject can always get from any point—vertically or horizontally—to any other without trapping himself in a dead end" (Inhelder & Piaget, 1958, p. xx). The structured whole takes many forms. For example, once adolescents reach the stage of formal operations, they understand that it is important to control variables. They can use proportional reasoning when thinking about physical situations and have a concept of mechanical equilibrium, a notion of probability, and an understanding of correlation.

Piaget and Inhelder developed a number of tasks to assess formal operations. In the chemical task, the student is asked to mix four colorless, odorless chemical solutions—1, 2, 3, and 4—with solution g, which is also colorless and odorless. The object of the task is to produce a colored solution. The color is produced by mixing solutions 1 and 3 with g. Solution 2 has no effect, and solution 4 inhibits the color. As the task begins, the teacher presents the student with two cups, each containing a colorless solution. The first cup contains solution 2, and the second contains solutions 1 and 3. Solution g is then added to each cup as the student observes. When g is added to the first cup, nothing happens. When it is added to the second cup, the solutions turn yellow. The student is then asked to duplicate the yellow color by mixing solutions 1, 2, 3, and 4 with g and to identify the function of each solution.

A student at the concrete level generally attempts to solve this problem using one-to-one correspondence: combining each solution separately with solution g. More advanced concrete thinkers might attempt two-by-two correspondence or three-by-three correspondence, using trial and error. The formal thinker uses a systematic approach to generate all 15 possible combinations and will be able to draw conclusions about the relationships among the solutions.

Although Piaget believed that children can handle problems that require formal operations by age 15, many studies show that this is not the case. At the start of high school, not all students are capable of considering all aspects of a problem and reasoning about possibilities that cannot be perceived in a systematic way. Studies indicate that when asked to solve Piagetian tasks that require formal operations, up to 50 percent of college freshmen function at the concrete level of thought (McKinnon & Renner, 1971; Sherman, 1979). Other studies examining the ability of college students to use formal operations have found that only 20 percent are able to do so (Schwebel, 1972, 1975; Siegler, 1981).

Results such as these have led researchers to seek ways to extend Piaget's theory. For example, psychologists challenge Piaget's belief that instruction by adults with expertise will not significantly alter cognitive development. Recent reviews of the literature (Sigelman & Shaffer, 1991; Sprinthall & Sprinthall, 1994) report that good instruction *can* help children assimilate and accommodate new experiences when they are in the process of developing schemes that will bring them to the next stage of cognitive development. Researchers believe that by providing simple explanations, furnishing concrete objects to manipulate, and providing time for students to work with the objects, teachers can foster cognitive growth in children.

Although educators routinely consider the work of Piaget when examining the development of logical thought in social studies and the sciences, they turn to the work of Byelorussian psychologist Lev Vygotsky to extend Piaget's teachings. Vygotsky examines the relationship between language arts and the development of cognitive thought, with a focus on the effects of social influences. While Piaget speaks of stages of cognitive development, Vygotsky proposes *zones* of development. Our discussion now turns to Vygotsky's work.

Vygotsky's Theory: The Role of Social Interaction in Cognitive Development

Basic concepts of Vygotsky's theory

Educators commonly cite the contributions of **Lev Vygotsky** when studying the theory and practice of constructivist education. Born in 1896, Vygotsky believed learning can be structured so that children are active learners while teachers or other adults use their advanced knowledge to meaningfully guide learning. Four basic concepts are integral to his work: (1) children construct knowledge; (2) learning can lead development and pull children along; (3) development cannot be separated from its social context; and (4) language plays a central role in cognitive development (Vygotsky 1976, 1978, 1987). Vygotsky believed that through social interaction, children gain knowledge from peers, older children, and adults who know more and have more experience than they do. When faced with a concept they don't understand, with instruction they will be given tools to help them understand, and they will learn.

The theories of Lev Vgotsky are often applied in constructivist science classrooms.

The Zone of Proximal Development

Teaching in the ZPD provides a view toward the child's future

Vygotsky believed that when aided, a child can learn more. The difference between what a child can produce *unaided* and what that child can produce *with aid* is called the **zone of proximal development,** or **ZPD**. From the standpoint of cognitive development, Vygotsky believed it is more important to know what a child is capable of with aid than what she or he can already do unaided. This provides the teacher with a view toward the future, focusing on what the child will be able to accomplish with good instruction.

When planning for instruction, the teacher should be aware of the zone of proximal development for the child so that the child's potential can be reached. Suppose you have a student who cannot think through a problem. If you ask the right questions and provide good hints, the child will likely be able to solve the problem. Suppose you are teaching two 10-year-olds about why we have seasons. You ask challenging questions that are meant for older children, which neither student can answer at the start. You ask leading questions and help them to recall prior knowledge. Both students are now able to answer some of the questions. One answers questions intended for a 12-year-old, and the other answers questions intended for a 13-year-old. The zone of proximal development is 2 for the first student and 3 for the second student; the second student therefore has a wider ZPD than the first student. Vygotsky would recommend that when you plan further instruction for these students, you challenge them at a level just above that of a 10-year-old—just beyond the level of their competence.

Instructional strategies that help students move beyond the zone of proximal development include good questioning techniques. In addition, having students work together in a peer tutoring situation, where one student is higher achieving and the other is lower achieving, can help the latter student transcend the zone of proximal development. One new teacher used this technique when a new student entered her class. The newcomer was unfamiliar with certain content, and the teacher decided to have a student who had already mastered that content act as a tutor. The result was that the new student caught up, and the two students established a friendship.

Internalization

Internalized discussion becomes thought

Vygotsky put forth the idea that we convert social discussion into thinking by a process called **internalization**. He proposed that during social discussions with other people, we eventually transform those discussions into useful problem-solving strategies. Thus, through the use of language, higher-level thinking develops. Once we internalize discussion, it becomes thought, and when we externalize thought, it becomes discussion.

In the classroom, teachers should encourage students to express ideas and views without fear. In the early grades, children need structured and unstructured experiences. Having children bring an object from home to class, such as a science show-and-tell item, and asking them to describe the object and explain why they chose it is one way to *structure* communication. A child might bring a favorite shell or rock, or even a pet. Allowing the child to express an idea and give an opinion is a way to promote *unstructured* communication. You might engage your students in a discussion of a science-related event that is occurring and have them express their opinions. After completing a science activity, students in the older grades can discuss results with classmates, then complete their individual laboratory reports. Working with partners and in teams provides additional opportunities for communication of language and thought.

Scaffolding

Teachers support student learning by scaffolding instruction

When workers construct or renovate a building, the structure requires a great deal of support. When teachers support students as students construct knowledge, they **scaffold** instruction. In this process, the student and the teacher work together to set goals for the student. It is important that these goals be student centered and ones that the student desires to achieve. At first, the teacher and the student work together within the student's zone of proximal development. Then the teacher challenges the student just beyond his or her level of competence. If the student needs assistance, the teacher provides whatever is necessary. As the student moves to the next level, the teacher gradually withdraws support. Once the student masters the skill, the teacher no longer needs to provide support.

The earth is a watery planet: Earth and space science

In preparing a lesson that utilizes scaffolded instruction, one of my students searched the Internet and found a lesson idea. She was teaching a unit on the earth and wanted her students to understand that the earth is a watery planet, with oceans covering a very large amount of its surface. While oceans consist of salt water, rivers supply us with fresh water for drinking, washing, and growing crops. The teacher wanted her students to explore fresh water and salt water, and to find out how they differ. She also planned to have her first-grade students learn how scientists work and think, but she wanted to be sure the motivation and interest came from the students and not from her. She showed them pictures of people swimming in a lake. In one picture, the people were floating on top of the water. The students wondered why this happens.

The teacher gathered two clear, 9-ounce plastic cups, a bottle of food coloring, a few teaspoons of table salt, and plain water. She filled two plastic cups halfway with plain water. The other materials were set before the children. The cups of liquid were inviting, and the children were eager to find out what would happen next.

At the start of the lesson, the teacher told the students that they would become scientists. In a whole-class discussion, they talked about how scientists ask questions. Like scientists, the students, too, had a question: why do people sometimes float on water and sometimes don't?

Scientists perform experiments: Science process

The teacher asked them to say more about how scientists work. The students knew that scientists "make experiments." The teacher wanted the children to understand that as part of scientific thinking, scientists make predictions about what is going to happen, then set up experiments to test those predictions. But she found that the children did not possess this knowledge. She decided to work within the zone of proximal development for each child to scaffold instruction.

Using drawings to record data: Science process

She picked up the bottle of food coloring and asked the children what would happen if she placed a drop of food coloring in the first glass, which contained plain water. She explained that this was like the fresh water people find in rivers and lakes. The students discussed the question and predicted that the food coloring would mix with the water. She told them that, acting like scientists, they would watch carefully, write or draw what happens, and discuss their experiments. Her students would record data by drawing pictures. She gave each child a crayon and a sheet of paper and asked that they draw the plain cup of water. Once the food coloring was dropped into the cup, the children drew the results. There were no surprises: the food coloring moved in spirals through the plain water and, within a few minutes, colored the liquid.

After discussing the results, the teacher asked the students to add two teaspoons of table salt to the second cup of water. She said that this is the kind of water people find in oceans and salt-water lakes. They talked a little about who had ever been to an ocean or a lake filled with salt water, such as The Great Salt Lake. Those students who had talked about what ocean water tastes like described the salty taste.

Scientists make predictions: Science process

Now the teacher asked the students what they thought they should do. One child said they should predict what would happen when she added a drop of food coloring to the second cup of water. "Excellent," the teacher replied, for at least one of the students had caught on and understood that a prediction should be made, then the experiment should be carried out. The teacher asked for predictions. Two students predicted that the same thing would happen in the second cup: the food coloring would mix with the water and the water would turn blue, as in the first cup. She picked up the food coloring, dropped it in the water, and—much to their surprise—the food coloring floated on top of the water.

The students were stunned as they picked up their crayons and drew what they saw. She asked them what they thought had happened. They thought for awhile; then one student explained that the salt probably did something to the water. Since the food coloring was sitting on the salt water, the salt must have made the water heavier. (Actually, salt water is denser than plain water, but these students were too young to understand this concept.) The teacher gave the students time to express their ideas about why the food coloring floated on the salt water. She observed and intervened when necessary so that each child had an opportunity to contribute to the discussion. She listened as they refined their thoughts about why the food coloring mixed with plain water and floated on salt water.

Then she asked her students what they wanted to do next. Many of them wanted to do the experiments again to see if they got the same results. Others wanted to mix the salt water and the plain water together in another cup and see what happened when they added the food coloring to the water. Some students wanted to repeat the experiment and use more salt to make the salt water "stronger," then see what would happen to the food coloring when dropped on the salt water. The teacher allowed each group to experiment and try out new ideas. She asked what they must do before they added the food coloring. "Predict," they said.

As the lesson drew to a close, the teacher began to withdraw support. At the beginning she had provided a great deal of guidance, but as the students took over, she removed some of the scaffolding. In the end, the students began to investigate on their own.

Reciprocal Teaching: Helping Students to Read and Comprehend

How does theory become practice? In this section, you will learn about a teaching strategy that puts constructivist theory into practice in the classroom.

Reciprocal teaching is a procedure that uses small groups and teamwork to improve reading comprehension and understanding of content in the reading materials (Meltzer et al., 1996; Palinscar & Brown, 1984). It offers a way for teachers to provide instruction in the zone of proximal development and is a form of scaffolded instruction. It is a good technique to use when you have students of differing abilities in the same class, and is particularly useful in inclusion settings. You might choose to group together students who are having difficulty and teach them this technique. You might also try this method with groups of students at different ability levels.

Basic strategies used in reciprocal teaching

When applying reciprocal teaching, students learn four basic strategies: summarizing, clarifying, question generating, and predicting. Once internalized, this strategy helps students to take charge and monitor their own understanding. Here is a typical dialogue between a teacher and a group of fifth-grade students who are learning to use reciprocal teaching:

Teacher: Today we are going to learn to use reciprocal teaching. This is a way to help you better understand what you read in your science text. It will also help you understand what you read in *Dragonfly,* your science magazine. Understanding written material isn't always easy, so it's important to have strategies or methods to assist with understanding.

When we use reciprocal teaching, you will read the science text on your own, or sometimes we will read aloud as a group. Then we'll talk about what you've read. Sometimes we'll discuss a sentence, or a paragraph, or an entire passage. After discussing the text, we'll be sure that everyone understands, and if even one person doesn't understand, we'll go over the material again. Next, we'll think about what we've read and ask each other questions about the most important points. We'll take turns answering the questions. Finally, we'll try to predict what the author will say next.

Student: How does this work?

Teacher: We'll take turns being the teacher. When we begin, I'll be the teacher; then you'll each have a turn at being the teacher. When you're good at using reciprocal teaching, you won't need me at all.

The group went on to practice the strategy each day for the remainder of the month. First, they read the text aloud as a group. Next, they summarized the material and clarified confusing points. They then generated questions about important points and answered one another's questions. Finally, they predicted what the author would discuss next.

When they started, the teacher was clearly in charge. Each day the students took more responsibility for the work of the group. By the end of the month, the students were clearly in charge.

Activity 5.6 Teaching Skills: Practicing Reciprocal Teaching

Overview: In this activity you will gather a group of four students of similar ability level, preferably those who have difficulty with comprehension, and teach them to use reciprocal teaching.

Materials: A book that is appropriate for the level of your students

Procedure: Have the group read the book aloud. Follow the steps of reciprocal teaching described above. If time permits, continue to use the strategy each day for four weeks.

Using a journal to assess your classroom practice

Assessment: In your journal, write about your experience with reciprocal teaching. Did it help students understand the content? Did it lower the anxiety level of those who could not comprehend what was being read? Were your students able to take responsibility for their own learning? ■

Constructing Your Knowledge of Science and Science Teaching

Now that you have completed this chapter, it is time to reflect on what you have learned. Reflection is important for you as a teacher, because it affects your understanding of the concepts you are studying. Your reflections enable you to shape and restructure your personal teaching knowledge.

Next, reflect on the theories of cognitive growth discussed in this chapter. How do Piaget's stage theory and constructivism in general relate to your vision of science teaching? How do you view Vygotsky's theory of cognitive development? If you have put the idea of scaffolding into practice, do you see this as an essential part of your teaching repertoire? As you reflect on this chapter, use these questions to guide your thoughts. Are there others that you can add to the list?

Make notes about the artifacts described in the chapter that you would choose in creating your own science teaching portfolio. As you select those artifacts, place them in a special folder or notebook.

Key Terms

constructivism (p. 106)
cognition (p. 106)
perception (p. 106)
memory (p. 106)
thinking (p. 106)
theories (p. 107)
Jean Piaget (p. 107)

organization (p. 109)
adaptation (p. 109)
schemes (p. 109)
sensorimotor period (p. 111)
preoperational period (p. 111)
concrete operations (p. 111)
formal operations (p. 111)

Lev Vygotsky (p. 119)
zone of proximal development (ZPD) (p. 120)
internalization (p. 120)
scaffolding (p. 121)
reciprocal teaching (p. 123)

Reviewing Chapter 5: Questions, Extensions, Applications, and Explorations

1. Select two students and plan a lesson centered around each student's zone of proximal development. Select a task and a model that demonstrates ways in which to complete the task. For example, if you want to teach students how to read a thermometer, develop a lesson and model the skill.

2. Plan and teach a science lesson that uses reciprocal teaching. What were the most successful elements of the lesson? What could you have done better? Did you use materials from a science text, a science magazine, or a newspaper?

3. Why is it important for your students to debate concepts, ideas, and theories of how things work?

4. Why should students share information in both oral and written form in the science classroom?

5. Sometimes a teacher acts as a coach to scaffold instruction. If a student is having difficulty, you might make suggestions to help the student move along. Think of an instance where you acted as a coach to a student. What did you say?

6. Sometimes a teacher makes comparisons to scaffold instruction. For example, when explaining how a river comes from a mountain, you might compare the formation of a river from a mountain to rain falling on a big pile of soil, sand, small rocks, pebbles, and mud. When rain falls, the water finds the quickest way to the bottom of the pile (Nye, 1995). You can even demonstrate this effect. Think of an instance where you made a comparison in order to scaffold instruction.

Print Resources

Baeckler, V. (1986). *Storytime science.* Hopewell, NJ: Sources.

Berman, S. (1993). *Catch them thinking in science.* Palatine, IL: IRI/Skylight Publishing.

Biehler, R., & Snowman, J. (2000). *Psychology applied to teaching.* Boston: Houghton Mifflin.

Kendall, J., & Marzano, R. (1996). *Content knowledge: A compendium of standards and benchmarks for education.* Aurora: CO: Mid-continent Regional Educational Laboratory.

Kenda, M., & Williams, P. (1992). *Barron's science wizardry for kids.* New York: Barron's Education Series.

Meltzer, L., Roditi, B., Haynes, D., Biddle, K., Paster, M., & Taber, S. (1996). *Strategies for success: Classroom teaching techniques for students with learning problems.* Austin, TX: Pro-Ed.

Nye, B. (1995). *Bill Nye the Science Guy's consider the following.* New York: Disney Press.

Wakefield, J. (1996). *Educational psychology: Learning to be a problem solver.* Boston: Houghton Mifflin.

Electronic Resources

The Jean Piaget Society
http://www.wimsey.com/~chrisl/JPS/JPS.html
This site contains information about the work of Jean Piaget.

Information on Vygotsky
http://www.glasnet.ru/~vega/vygotsky/index.html
This site is an excellent resource on Vygotsky.

The Electronic Journal of Science Education
http://unr.edu/homepage/jcannon/ejse/ejse.html
For a historical treatment of constructivism, see Volume 2, Number 2.

Classroom Compass
http://www.sedl.org/scimath/compass
See the article on constructivism in Volume 1, Number 3.

The Case for Constructivist Classrooms
http://129.7.160.115/INST5931/constructivist.
Look for a summary of the *The Case for Constructivist Classrooms* by J. Brooks and M. Brooks (Alexandria, VA: Association for Supervision and Curriculum Development, 1993).

Children's Literature

Berger, Melvin and Gilda
Do Stars Have Points? (Scholastic Trade, 1998)
ISBN: 0-590-13080-3
Grades 4–6

Editors of Klutz
Klutz Guide: Backyard Stars (Klutz Press, 1998)
ISBN: 1-57054-172-8
Grades 3 and up

Royston, Angela
Stars and Planets (Heineman Library, 1998)
ISBN: 1-57572-182-1
Grades 4 and up

Petty, Kate
The Sun Is a Star and Other Amazing Facts About Space (Copper Beech Books, 1997)
ISBN: 0-7613-0593-9
Grades 1–3

Stott, Carole
I Wonder Why Stars Twinkle and Other Questions About Space (Kingfisher Books, 1997)
ISBN: 0-7534-5045-3
Grades K–3

Mahy, Margaret
The Greatest Show Off Earth (Puffin, 1996)
ISBN: 0-14-037926-6
Grades 3–7

Cannat, Guillaume
Be Your Own Astronomy Expert (Sterling Publications, 1996)
ISBN: 0-8069-6131-7
Grades 3–7

Camp, Carole
American Astronomers: Searchers and Wonderers (Enslow Publishers, 1996)
ISBN: 0-89490-631-3
Grades 6 and up

Asimov, Isaac
Astronomy in Ancient Time (Gareth Stevens, 1995)
ISBN: 0-8368-1191-7
Grades 3 and up

Cole, Joanna
The Magic School Bus: Hello Out There (fiction and nonfiction) (Scholastic Trade, 1995)
ISBN: 0-590-88129-9
Grades K–3

Levin, Betty
Starshine and Sunglow (fiction) (Greenwillow, 1994)
ISBN: 0-688-12806-8
Grades 4–7

Gibbons, Gail (illustrator)
The Moon Book (Holiday House, 1998)
ISBN: 0-8234-1364-0
Grades K–3

Instruction and Assessment in a Standards-Based Science Classroom

Part Two extends the background knowledge for science teaching that you developed in previous chapters. Next you will learn to write lesson plans, become familiar with assessment techniques, and develop lessons to include special learners and students with diverse learning styles. You will learn many ways to structure cooperative groups, use computers and technology, and problem solve with your students. As in Part One, you will continue to meet novice and veteran teachers who share their ideas and experiences as you learn more about life, physical, and earth and space science.

CHAPTER 6

Planning for Instruction

LaToya Johnson, a student teacher, is designing a chemistry lesson for her fifth-graders. She begins by deciding what science ideas she wants her students to develop and thinks about the process skills they will use to develop the ideas. She wants them to explore change. She wants them to observe, describe, classify, collect information in an organized way, and examine and make sense of the data. She will arrange three learning stations where the children will engage in interesting activities that allow them to explore this science concept.

At the first station, they will find an empty cup, a bottle of seltzer, and a small jar of table salt. They will pour a half-cup of soda into the glass, then add a teaspoonful of salt. Within seconds, bubbles will form in the seltzer; then foam will rise to the surface as the seltzer effervesces. At the next station, students will find their safety goggles, an empty 35mm film canister, a medicine dropper, a cup of water, and a piece of an Alka Seltzer tablet. They will place the Alka Seltzer tablet into the canister, add a dropperful of water, close the canister, point the cap toward the wall, and shake the canister. Within seconds, the cover of the canister will shoot off forcefully as carbon dioxide gas forms. At the third station, students will find a half-cup of milk, a small bottle of vinegar, and a teaspoon. They will add a teaspoonful of vinegar to the milk, and within seconds the milk will turn into a liquid (whey) and a solid (curd) as the vinegar causes particles in the milk to clump together. All of these phenomena are examples of change.

These are the first steps in planning the activity. LaToya knows there is more to a lesson than planning a fun, exciting hands-on activity. The students must make sense of the activity for the experience to become a meaningful lesson. After completing each part, LaToya wants them to think about what happened. Why did the seltzer foam up after salt was added? Why did the lid pop off of the film canister after water was added to the piece of Alka Seltzer tablet? Why did milk separate into curd and whey after vinegar was added? In each case, change obviously occurred—but *why*? LaToya builds in time for reflection as she designs her lesson. She wants students to discuss, question, rethink, reflect, reconsider, and revise their thoughts as they build understanding.

Examples of chemical and physical change: Physical science

 She thinks about how the activity relates to the real world, because she knows students should connect classroom experiences to existing experiences. She could have the students think about familiar examples of change. Have they baked a cake, made chocolate milk, or cooked an egg? How do these familiar examples of change relate to the changes that took place in the classroom activity? LaToya knows that this lesson ties into *Benchmarks for Science Literacy: Project 2061,* which says that by the end of fifth grade, students should know that "When a new material is made by combining two or more materials, it has properties that are different from the original material. For that reason, a lot of different materials can be made from a small number of basic materials" (American Association for the Advancement of Science, 1993, p. 77).

She stops for a minute, closes her eyes, and pictures herself in the classroom. What questions will she ask? How will she stimulate discussion and debate? How will she ensure that the lesson is student centered rather than teacher dominated? Can she act as a facilitator and transfer responsibility for learning to her students? What about assessment? How will she find out what her students think and understand so that she can give feedback to improve learning? She decides that student journals will be a suitable assessment tool. She designs a performance task for

There's more to a lesson than planning a fun and exciting activity. Students must make sense of the activity in order for it to be meaningful.

students to complete after the lesson. The task requires application of knowledge and will help her assess understanding of the concept of change. As LaToya continues to design her lesson, she makes notes about how she will address each of these questions. Then she is ready to bring the lesson to her students. Figure 6.1 presents LaToya's lesson plan.

In this chapter, you will learn what planning for science instruction involves. As you read the chapter, think about the answers to these questions:

1. **How do I plan for science instruction?**
2. **How do I design meaningful science lesson plans?**
3. **What is a science unit?**
4. **What are some types of units?**
5. **What is a science curriculum? How does it guide a teacher's work?**
6. **How do I introduce my students to the study of chemistry?**

What Are the First Steps in Planning for Science Instruction?

As a new teacher, LaToya is learning to plan for science instruction. Throughout your career, you will plan for instruction in science, as well as in every other subject you teach, so that you can provide students with a coherent, well-thought-out program of study.

Diagnosing student needs

Things to consider when planning for instruction:

▶ What do my students already know?
▶ What are they learning now?
▶ What will they learn in the future?

What Does a Good Science Lesson Plan Contain?

Teachers design lessons on a daily basis. During your years in college, it is important to work with a good lesson plan format. This will make you aware of all of the essential parts of a lesson. As you gain experience in designing and planning lessons, the process will become much easier. This section describes the essential elements of a lesson plan, which are summarized in Figure 6.2 on page 132.

Note that there is no set format for a lesson plan. The format presented in this section, however, works well for my students. I have used it for many years, and highly recommend it.

Figure 6.1

Elementary Science Lesson Plan

Concept: Change

Grade: Fifth

Goal of the Lesson:

To explore change

Specifying Achievement Objectives

After participating in this lesson, all students should be able to observe, describe, collect information about the activities, and display the data in an organized way. Students should be able to formulate explanations about what is happening in each case. They should be able to discuss their ideas with others and defend their ideas. They should be able to relate the examples of change that they observe in the classroom with other examples of change that they encounter in their daily lives. They should be able to work successfully with their peers in carrying out the activities.

Science Process Skills

Observe, describe, classify, collect information in an organized way, examine and make sense of the data.

Assessment Plan

As the lesson proceeds, I circulate around the room, observe students, and discuss their work with them. I will make notes about their work in my notebook.

Once the lesson is over, students will participate in this performance task:
Given a raw egg, a jar, and a pint of vinegar, design an experiment that will remove the shell from the egg without breaking it.

These achievement objectives will be assessed:

- What process skills do you use?

- How do you use the process skills?

- How does your performance on this task reflect what you learned about physical and chemical change?

- What changes happened in this experiment?

Teaching Time Needed

One class period is needed to carry out the activity, and another is needed to analyze and discuss what happened. An equal amount of time is needed for assessment.

Materials

An empty cup, a bottle of seltzer, a small jar of table salt, safety goggles, an empty 35mm film canister, a medicine dropper, a cup of water, a piece of an Alka Seltzer tablet, a half-cup of milk, a small bottle of vinegar, a teaspoon

Introduction to the Lesson

Activity stations are set up around the room. Students are instructed to visit the stations and carry out the activities.

Developing the Lesson

In their science journals, students write about what is happening at each station. They observe, describe, collect information about the activities, and display the data in an organized way. Students formulate explanations about what is happening in each case.

Figure 6.1 (*cont.*)

> **Concluding the Lesson**
>
> Students discuss their ideas with others and defend them. They relate the examples of change that they observe in the classroom with other examples of change that they encounter in their daily lives. There is a whole-class discussion to talk about the lesson. The performance task takes place after the lesson is over.
>
> **Resources**
>
> VanCleave, Janice. (1989). *Chemistry for every kid.* New York: John Wiley & Sons.
>
> **Assessing Your Own Performance**
>
> Once the lesson is over, LaToya will reflect on it.

Figure 6.2

>

Guide for Writing a Lesson Plan
>
>
> **Concept:**
>
> **Grade:**
>
> **Goal of the lesson:**
>
> **Specifying achievement objectives:**
>
> **Science process skills:**
>
> **Assessment plan:**
>
> **Teaching time needed:**
>
> **Materials:**
>
> **Introduction to the lesson:**
>
> **Developing the lesson:**
>
> **Concluding the lesson:**
>
> **Resources:**
>
> **Assessing your own performance:**

Goal of the Lesson

Goals identify what you plan to accomplish

The **goal** of the lesson states what you plan to accomplish and what you intend for your students to learn. You identify your goals when you write your lesson plan. Develop and refine them with your students at the start of the lesson. It is very important that they share the goals, because this will help them to understand and become involved in what they are learning in a particular lesson.

Here are some examples of *broad goals:*

▶ To learn about the three states of matter

▶ To learn to use a microscope

> ◗ To learn about dinosaurs
> ◗ To learn about rocks and minerals
> ◗ To learn about physical and chemical change

Achievement objectives identify results you seek for your students

Teachers translate broad goals such as these into *achievement objectives,* which clearly define what constitutes acceptable performance of each goal. The achievement objectives let students know what is expected of them.

Specifying Achievement Objectives

Achievement objectives and instructional objectives are similar

Achievement objectives are specific statements that (1) set carefully thought-out learning outcomes, (2) specify conditions for learning, and (3) set expected standards for student performance. Well-written achievement objectives clearly spell out the results you seek for your students and tell them what successful performance looks like. If your students don't know what evidence of successful performance looks like, they won't know when they have met their achievement objectives. Achievement objectives are action statements that tell what a student should be able to do as a result of instruction.

You can state learning outcomes in words such as the following:

> ◗ The student will show . . .
> ◗ The student will explain . . .
> ◗ The student will demonstrate . . .
> ◗ The student will recall . . .
> ◗ The student will discriminate between . . .

Conditions describe the circumstances under which learning will occur. In the elementary science classroom, students often use equipment; therefore, you can state conditions in words such as these:

> ◗ Using a thermometer, the student will measure the temperature of a liquid as it cools.
> ◗ Using a battery, wire, and bulbs, the student will create a circuit so that the light bulb is illuminated.
> ◗ Using a concept map, the student will show the interrelationships among parts of a transportation system.

Achievement objectives also specify the level of proficiency needed to perform the behavior after completing the lesson, in another instructional setting, or in the real world. They focus on the important understandings, skills, and attitudes students should acquire from the learning experience. Examples of *measurable achievement objectives* are:

> ◗ After completing this lesson, students will be able to measure the temperature of a cup of hot coffee as it cools to room temperature, record the data in a chart, create a graph to display the data, interpret the data, and explain it to the class.

▶ Using a model of the human ear, students will identify the major parts of the ear and explain how the parts work as a system to enable the human ear to hear sound.

To assess the first objective, your students would begin with a cup of hot coffee and record its temperature over time as it cools, record the data in a chart, create a graph from the data, interpret the data, and then lead a class discussion to explain what is happening. To assess the second objective, your students would need a model of the human ear. They would provide a verbal or written explanation, showing or pointing to the parts of the human ear and discussing how the parts work together. Then you would know something about their understanding of how sound is heard.

Types of Achievement Objectives

Teachers need a wide variety of objectives to address a multitude of skills and behaviors. There are many different classification schemes for objectives. You can write objectives to describe *content; science process skills; physical movement; manipulative skills;* and *attitudes, appreciations, values, and beliefs.* One particularly useful classification system divides objectives into three types or domains: cognitive, psychomotor, and affective. The **cognitive domain** includes intellectual abilities and skills. The **psychomotor domain** consists of basic bodily movements and performance, physical skills and abilities, perceptual abilities, and skilled movement. The **affective domain** includes attitudes, beliefs, values, and feelings. All of these objectives translate into behaviors and performance in the classroom.

The Importance of Writing Clear Achievement Objectives: Linking Instruction and Assessment

Achievement objectives link instruction and assessment

Clear achievement objectives provide a link to assessment. As you teach your lessons, you will determine how well your students meet the aims of the lessons. National assessment standards recommend that teachers assess student performance in a number of ways.

STANDARDS

There are multiple ways to assess student performance

The *National Science Education Standards* say, "Classroom assessments can take many forms, including observations of student performance during instructional activities; interviews; formal performance tasks; portfolios; investigative projects; written reports; and multiple choice, short answer, and essay examinations. (National Research Council, 1996, p. 84)

You might choose **traditional paper-and-pencil tests,** which ask students to do such things as fill in the blanks, match items in one column with items in the next column, or choose the correct answers to multiple-choice exercises. You might choose **performance assessment,** in which students engage in performances such as developing demonstrations, creating products, or constructing responses to situations to provide evidence that they have certain knowledge and skills. "Performance or production requires the student to plan and execute a new work from scratch and to use good judgment in choosing apt content and shaping a quality product—a 'synthesis' leading to a 'unique' creation by the student" (Wiggins, 1998).

Besides developing performance tasks to measure performance that occurs in the classroom, you can create tasks that measure skills and behaviors that students need in the real world. This is **authentic performance assessment**. Students can take on the role of scientist, author of a children's science book, science teacher, science writer for a newspaper or magazine, designer of a science-related product, expert witness giving scientific testimony, science reporter for a TV station, conference speaker, or reviewer of a scientific paper.

Authentic assessment provides motivation for learning

Authentic Assessment

By assuming the role of a scientist, students can apply what they learn in your classroom and introduce them to roles and performances that adults and professionals face in the real world. Authentic performance assessment allows your students to understand why they learn what they do in the classroom, and provides motivation and purpose for learning.

Sometimes you will assess student performance *after the lesson is over;* at other times you will *embed* a performance task in the lesson itself. Embedding performance tasks usually requires that students put together all of the behaviors and skills that they learn. Here is an example of an embedded performance task.

After studying about how scientists think, students formulate a research question, design an experiment, and carry it out on their own. This is a challenging, authentic activity and requires that students meet many objectives. In the next two chapters, you will learn much more about ways to assess achievement objectives.

Learning to write achievement objectives takes practice

Learning to write good achievement objectives is important and requires practice. As you begin to write them, reflect on what you write and compare this with what you observe in your classroom. This is the best way to fine-tune your work. Pairing up with a peer is another good way to assess and refine your work. Observe each other's classrooms and critique each other's lessons. Comment about student performance. Such feedback is essential to you as a new teacher and will continue to be useful as you grow as a professional.

Science Process Skills

Recall from our discussion in Chapter 2 that we use science process skills to define concepts; they help us to make meaning for the information gained when we use our senses. By using the process skills, we better understand our world. In the primary grades, children can observe, communicate, estimate, measure, collect data, classify, infer, predict, and formulate simple models. They can also formulate simple hypotheses, make simple graphs, interpret data, and perform simple experiments. As they grow older, they can carry out investigations. Examples of achievement objectives that incorporate process skills include the following:

Students use process skills to carry out science activities: Science process

▶ Students will measure their heights with a tape measure, record the data on a class graph, determine the most common height of students in the class, and explain their results to the class.

▶ Students will test four different brands of bubble bath, measure the height of the bubble column produced by each brand, graph the results, determine which brand of bubble bath produces the highest column of bubbles, and write a report on their findings.

In this section of the lesson plan, *list* the science process skills that your students will practice.

Assessment Plan

Before you plan your lesson, think about what is acceptable evidence of good student performance. What should your students be able to accomplish once the lesson is over? What should they come away with from the lesson? Once the lesson is over, students should know something new, something they didn't know when the lesson started. It is your job to find out what they have learned. You should share your expectations with them at the outset.

> Things to consider when setting expectations for students:
>
> ▶ What understandings should they develop?
> ▶ What new knowledge should they have?
> ▶ What should they now be able to do?
> ▶ What new skills should they master?
> ▶ What new abilities should they develop?
> ▶ What new attitudes and appreciations should they exhibit?

Focus on what students do know, not just on what they don't know

Traditionally, testing has focused on finding out what students *don't* know. Standards documents stress that it is important for teachers to focus on what students *do* know in addition to what they don't know. Traditional assessment occurs at the end of a series of lessons. Standards-based assessment is ongoing.

> **Standards-Based Assessment**
> Standards documents urge teachers to employ ongoing assessment so that student progress is monitored as learning takes place. In this way, corrections can be made along the way, and it's not necessary to wait until the test is graded to find out about student performance.

If you write good achievement objectives, your assessment will enable you to monitor your students' progress as they achieve the goals you set for them. In the next chapter, you will learn much more about assessment techniques for elementary science.

Teaching Time Needed

Flexibility is important in teaching

Estimate the approximate length of time you will need to teach the lesson. If you need two or three days, be sure to note this. Plan for interruptions; numerous interruptions throughout the day are an inevitable part of the teacher's job. Flexibility therefore is a very important aspect of teaching.

Materials

In the materials section of the lesson plan, simply list the materials you need to carry out the lesson. This is an important organizational step and eliminates the possibility that you will begin an activity without the proper materials.

Introduction to the Lesson

Lesson introductions should be motivating

The introduction includes the ways in which you will motivate your students and arouse their interest. Your motivational strategies should be dynamic, stimulating, and based on natural interests. Examples of introductory activities include demonstrations, thought-provoking questions, films, pictures, models, an exciting story, a timely link with a previous lesson, an interesting current event, a library table, or a learning center. Every lesson should begin with an interest-arousing introduction.

Developing the Lesson

Nurture ideas and concept development in the lesson

In this section of the lesson plan, you will describe how the lesson develops. The lesson flows naturally from the introduction, and it too should be thought provoking and motivating. The development of the lesson is the step in which ideas grow and are nurtured. It includes investigations, hands-on activities, discussions, experiments, and question-and-answer sessions. The developmental phase of the lesson should help students to think and construct understanding.

Concluding the Lesson

In this section, you pull everything together. Be sure that your students begin to build understanding. If they have engaged in an activity, make sure they understand what the activity was about. Question them. Have them discuss the activity. Encourage them to draw conclusions.

Resources

In the this section of the lesson plan, make a list of all the resources you will use. Include books for students, books for yourself, and instructional aids such as songs, dances, audio-visual aids, and other teaching materials. Describe all the ways in which technology will be used. This includes computers, VCRs, audio-visual equipment, word processing (including your use of word processing to compose the unit), spreadsheets, databases, presentation software, science equipment, curriculum-based software, and computer-aided instruction.

Assessing Your Own Performance

When the lesson is over, you should reflect on your own performance. How did the lesson go? What went well? What could have gone better? What did you learn about yourself as a teacher? Is there anything you will do differently next time?

Planning a Series of Lessons

Novices often begin with teacher-directed inquiry

Two of my students, Christina Campagna and Amy Davis, created a series of chemistry lessons for their fifth-graders. As new teachers, Amy and Christina carefully reflect on what they teach and how they proceed. These lessons were written early in the semester, when they felt more comfortable introducing each concept using direct instruction and then providing hands-on activities to reinforce the concepts and enable their students to construct meaning. They assess students each day, and they have the students assess themselves as well. They pay careful attention to classroom management and safety, as each hands-on activity is complicated. Students have very clear directions about how to proceed, and there is order in the classroom throughout each activity.

As novices, Christina and Amy begin with teacher-directed inquiry, since this method gives them more control. If students go off track, the teachers use a quiet signal to call the class to order, then continue with the lesson. Once they are confident that their students can work independently and take more responsibility for their own work, Amy and Christina plan lessons that incorporate student-directed inquiry. Examine their lessons carefully. What do you think about them?

Introduction to Chemistry: Lessons for Fifth-Graders (Estimated Time: Two Weeks)

Overview

These lessons aim to provide fifth-grade students with a basic understanding of chemistry. The topics include scientific thinking, states of matter, and physical and chemical change. They focus on everyday applications of chemistry. Using a hands-on approach to illustrate the principles, students are guided through the activities. Students use cooperative learning in their lab groups. It is our goal for students to gain a solid foundation in chemistry that will spark their interest in science for the future.

Background Information/Content Knowledge

Christina and Amy began their preparation by reviewing some basic concepts of chemistry. Following is their review.

Basics of Chemistry

Chemistry is an experimental science that involves the behavior of matter: Physical science

Chemistry is an experimental science that involves the behavior of matter. Much of the body of chemical knowledge consists of abstract concepts and ideas. Without application, these concepts and ideas would have little impact on society. Chemical principles are applied through technology for the benefit of society. Useful products are developed by the union of basic science and applied technology.

Over the past 200 years, science and technology have moved forward at a rapid pace. Ideas and applications of these ideas are developed through carefully planned experimentation, in which researchers use scientific thinking. This allows researchers to approach a problem and try to come up with solutions in the most effective way possible. In the study of chemistry, we examine the knowledge and understanding uncovered by chemists.

Matter and Energy

Matter and energy describe the universe: Physical science

There are two things that describe the entire universe: matter and energy. **Matter** is anything that occupies space and has mass. That includes trees, clothing, water, air, people, minerals, and many other things. Matter shows up in a wide variety of forms.

Energy is the ability to perform work. Like matter, energy exists in a number of forms. Heat is one form of energy, and light is another. There are also chemical, electrical, and mechanical energy. And energy can change from one form to another. In fact, matter can also change form or change into energy, and energy can change into matter, but not easily.

The States of Matter

Matter exists as solids, liquids, gases, and plasma: Physical science

Matter may exist in any of three physical states: solid, liquid, and gas. A **solid** has a definite shape and volume that it tends to maintain under normal conditions. The particles composing a solid stick rigidly to one another. Solids most commonly form in the crystalline form, which means they have a fixed, regularly repeating, symmetrical internal structure. Diamonds, salt, and quartz are examples of crystalline solids. A few solids, such as glass and paraffin, do not have a well-defined crystalline structure, although they do have a definite shape and volume. Such solids are called *amorphous solids,* which means they have no definite internal structure or form.

A **liquid** has a definite volume, but does not have its own shape since it takes the shape of its container. Its particles cohere firmly but not rigidly, so the particles of a liquid have a great deal of mobility while maintaining close contact with one another.

A **gas** has no fixed shape or volume and eventually spreads out to fill its container. As the gas particles move about, they collide with the walls of their container, causing pressure, which is force exerted over an area. Gas particles move independently of one another. Compared with those of a liquid or solid, gas particles are quite far apart. Unlike solids and liquids, which cannot be compressed very much at all, gases can be both compressed and expanded.

Often referred to as the fourth state of matter, **plasma** is a form of matter composed of electrically charged atomic particles. Many objects found in the earth's outer atmosphere, as well as many celestial bodies found in space (such as the sun and the stars), consist of plasma. A plasma can be created by heating a gas to extremely high temperatures or by passing a current through it. A plasma responds to a magnetic field and conducts electricity well.

Physical and Chemical Properties

Matter—whether it is solid, liquid, or gas—possesses two kinds of properties: physical and chemical. These unique properties separate one substance from another and ensure that no two substances are alike in every way. The **physical properties** are those that can be observed or measured without changing the chemical composition of the substance. These properties include state, color, odor, taste, hardness, boiling point, and melting point. A **physical change** is a change that alters at least one of the physical properties of the substance without changing its chemical composition. Some examples of physical change are (1) altering the physical state of matter, such as melting an ice cube; (2) dissolving or mixing substances together, such as what happens when you make coffee or hot cocoa; (3) altering the size or shape of matter, such as what happens when you grind or chop something.

Chemical properties stem from the ability of a substance to react or change to a new substance that has different properties. This often occurs in the presence of another substance. For example, iron reacts with oxygen to produce rust. This is an example of a **chemical change**. The rusting of iron is a chemical property of iron. That's how we get rusty nails. When you pass an electric current through water, it decomposes to form hydrogen gas and oxygen gas. This reaction is an example of a chemical property of water.

Sometimes it is difficult to differentiate a chemical change from a physical change. In fact, physical changes almost always accompany chemical changes. Some of the signs of physical change that signal the occurrence of chemical change are the presence of a large amount of heat or light, the presence of a flame, the formation of gas bubbles, a change in color or odor, or the formation of a solid material that settles out of a solution. (Sherman & Sherman, 1999)

Matter possesses physical and chemical properties: Physical science

Physical change involves altering the physical state of matter: Physical science

Chemical change results in a new substance that has different properties: Physical science

Introductory Activities

Here is how we motivate our students at the start:

Introductory activities motivate students

Doorway decorations: The door to the classroom is decorated and reads, "Welcome to the Chemistry Lab." The entrance is decorated with pictures of items related to chemistry.

Library table: There are various books selected from the school library on display for students to peruse. We place them on tables around the classroom. Topics include: chemistry, matter, chemical and physical change, and experiments for children. We encourage students to read these books in their spare time.

Bulletin boards: The classroom decorations include several bulletin boards. One focuses on "Thinking Like a Scientist," and it reviews scientific thinking. Another is called "Chemical Change," which discusses chemical change and gives examples. A third bulletin board is called "Physical Change," which discusses physical change and gives examples.

Lab coats: On the first day, students create lab coats from white tee shirts. Each day, when beginning the lesson, they put on their lab coats.

Learning centers: Two learning centers are located in the classroom. They are enrichment centers for students. When students finish work early, they spend time in the learning center. It includes questions for thought and hands-on activities.

Lesson Descriptions

You will now read lesson summaries for seven chemistry lessons. After reading each description (written by Amy and Christina), use the lesson plan format and create a formal lesson plan for each one. Don't hesitate to be creative and change the lessons if you'd like. If you can, try them in an elementary school classroom or in your college classroom.

Chemists at Work. In this lesson, students learn about chemistry; discuss the work of scientists, particularly chemists; and have an introduction to scientific thinking. This is done through direct instruction by the teacher, whole-class question-and-answer, followed by discussions in small groups. We select these techniques because this is our first lesson with the class, and we feel more comfortable establishing classroom control. It is predominantly lecture and small-group discussion. We are gaining valuable experience in presenting a teacher-directed lesson and leading a whole-class discussion. The teachers and students read this scenario, then discuss it:

 Volcanoes

*A*round the planet there are approximately 500 volcanoes that have a record of violent behavior. Currently, however, scientists monitor only about 20 of these volcanoes, and only have the resources to occasionally observe 1/3 of them. As a result, often the first warning signs that come from a volcano that has been dormant for hundreds of years is the initial blast and the flow of the magma down its side. By then it may be too late to save the lives of those living near the volcano as the avalanche of hot ash at a temperature of 1,500 degrees Fahrenheit and moving at speeds of up to 500 miles per hour travels down the mountain.

One solution, developed in the early and mid-1900s and still used today, is a satellite-based system that is able to make infrared and radar observations of volcanoes. Such a system monitors changes in a volcano and alerts scientists on earth to a potentially explosive situation. While a great advance in volcano observation, this system does not have the capabilities that other systems may have to warn of impending disaster.

Enter chemistry. Scientists have discovered that before the initial blast, as the gases rise up inside the volcano, sulfur dioxide gas is emitted from the volcano's dome. Scientists theorize that if they are able to measure the amount of sulfur dioxide coming out of a volcano, they will be able to forewarn residents of nearby towns or villages about an impending blast.

To accomplish this on a planetary level, satellite-based observations are being considered. Current satellite systems, such as the one described above, are able to detect chemicals on earth. However, they are not able to detect the small emissions of sulfur dioxide that are released before a volcanic eruption. New instrumentation developed by Alin Krueger, a NASA scientist at the Goddard Space Flight Center in Maryland, would check sulfur dioxide emissions at a volcano every 15 minutes. If successful, such a system could soon sound the alarm before the next volcanic eruption occurs on the earth. (Sherman & Sherman, 1999)

We begin by discussing this scenario. We ask, "Where's the chemistry?" We talk about what chemists do and how they think. After completing this lesson, our students will be able to define the term *chemistry* and explain what chemists do. Our goal for them is to understand how chemists think, give an example of scientific thinking, and explain this to a peer. They will work cooperatively with a peer and show respect for other students while working. They will share materials, participate in a group discussion, and work independently.

Activity 6.1   Designing a Lesson: Chemists at Work

Overview: In this activity, you will design a lesson based on the description you just read.

Materials: You will use the lesson plan format to design the lesson.

Procedure: Complete these sections:

- State the goal(s) of the lesson.
- Specify achievement objectives.
- List science process skills.
- Create an assessment plan.
- Specify teaching time needed.
- List materials.

- Write an introduction to the lesson.
- Write about the lesson development.
- Write a conclusion for the lesson.
- List the resources you need.
- Assess your own performance.

Assessment: How was the experience? What went well? Was there anything that caused difficulty? After you teach your lesson, answer these questions. How did it go? Compare your lesson with those of your peers. Were they similar?   ■

Stress classroom safety before beginning an activity: Safety

Thinking Like a Scientist: What's in a Mystery Box?   In this lesson, students think scientifically and determine what's inside a "mystery box." We place different objects in shoe boxes, then tape them shut. Students use their senses to gather data about the contents of the boxes and predict what's inside. Rules of laboratory safety are stressed before they begin work. Students reflect on their own performance by completing a performance assessment worksheet. After completing this lesson, students will think scientifically by asking a question ("What's inside the box?"), formulating a hypothesis (make a prediction), designing an experiment to test the hypothesis, collecting and analyzing data, and drawing conclusions. They will practice social skills while working in cooperative groups. They will use problem-solving skills and scientific thinking to solve the mystery. They will appreciate the work of scientists in searching for answers to questions.

Activity 6.2   *Designing a Lesson: Thinking Like a Scientist—What's in a Mystery Box?*

Overview: In this activity, you will design a lesson based on the description you just read.

Materials: You will use the lesson plan format to design the lesson.

Procedure: Complete the sections listed in Activity 6.1. If you have a field placement, teach your lesson. If not, present it to your peers.

Assessment: How is this lesson plan different from the one you wrote for Activity 6.1? What teaching strategies did you use? How did you introduce, develop, and conclude the lesson? Is your lesson student centered?   ■

Thinking Like a Scientist: Paper Towel Testing.   In this lesson, students test four different brands of paper towels to find out which one, when wet, holds the most pennies. The teachers prepare stacks of 10 pennies each, which they tape together. Students pour 10 mL of water on each of the four paper towels. They drop stacks of pennies, stack by stack, from the same height onto each paper towel. They predict which wet paper towel will hold the most pennies without tearing, thereby identifying the strongest paper towel.

Students explore effects of variables in an experiment: Science process

They think scientifically, make predictions, carry out the experiments, collect and analyze data, make inferences, and draw conclusions. They use a laboratory

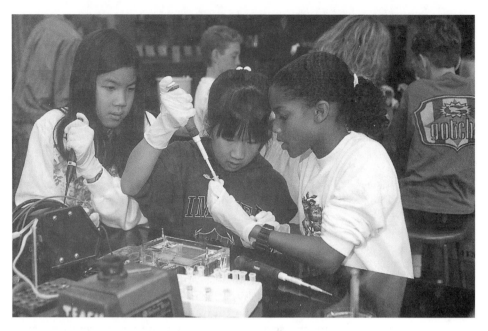

Students use problem-solving skills and scientific inquiry.

notebook as they work. There is focus on managing the classroom during the hands-on activity. After completing this lesson, students will have more practice thinking scientifically. They will explore the effects of variables in an experiment, develop skill in reading a graduated cylinder, and learn the proper use of science equipment to ensure their own safety and the safety of their peers. They will use a journal to write about the experiment and a laboratory notebook to record the data. Once they complete the teacher-directed activity, they test the four brands again, this time designing their own experiments.

Activity 6.3   Designing a Lesson: Thinking Like a Scientist—Paper Towel Testing

Overview: In this activity, you will design a lesson based on the description you just read.

Materials: You will use the lesson plan format to design the lesson.

Procedure: Complete the sections listed in Activity 6.1. If you have a field placement, teach your lesson. Another option is to present the lesson to your college classmates.

Assessment: How is this lesson different from the one you wrote for Activity 6.2? What teaching strategies did you use? How did you introduce, develop, and conclude the lesson? Is your lesson student centered? ■

Ice, Water, and Steam: Three States of Matter. In this lesson, students learn about states of matter. They examine water in three forms: as a solid, a liquid, and a gas. Starting with ice in a plastic bag, they melt the ice, forming water. With help from the teacher, they boil the water to produce steam. They examine the conditions necessary to cause a change in state.

After completing this lesson, students will be able to define the three states of matter and define the properties of solids, liquids, and gases. They will describe how to cause water to change from one state of matter to another. They will practice good safety behavior and proper behavior for a science classroom.

Activity 6.4   Designing a Lesson: Ice, Water, and Steam—Three States of Matter

Overview: In this activity, you will design a lesson based on the description you just read.

Materials: You will use the lesson plan format to design the lesson.

Procedure: Complete the sections listed in Activity 6.1. If you have a field placement, teach your lesson. Another option is to present the lesson to your college classmates.

Assessment: How is this lesson different from the one you wrote for Activity 6.3? What teaching strategies did you use? How did you introduce, develop, and conclude the lesson? Is your lesson student centered?   ■

Using a dramatic chemical reaction to explore chemical change: Physical science

Chemical Change: Blowing Up a Balloon. In this lesson, students learn about chemical change. The lesson begins with direct instruction as the teacher discusses chemical change with the whole class. An experiment showing chemical change follows, and in preparation, the teacher spends a great deal of time discussing safety. Students wear safety goggles. Each pair of students gets a balloon and an empty soda bottle. They pour a quarter-cup of vinegar into the soda bottle and place a teaspoonful of baking soda in the balloon. Students stretch the balloon over the mouth of the soda bottle and let the baking soda make contact with the vinegar. Within seconds, carbon dioxide gas forms and the balloon inflates. Students complete a worksheet to review their work. After completing the lesson, students will discuss the difference between chemical change and physical change. They will perform an experiment and discuss the results. They will practice good safety habits and work cooperatively with a partner to complete the activity. They will appreciate ways in which chemical changes create new substances.

Activity 6.5   Designing a Lesson: Chemical Change—Blowing Up a Balloon

Overview: In this activity, you will design a lesson based on the description you just read.

Materials: You will use the lesson plan format to design the lesson.

Procedure: Complete the sections listed in Activity 6.1. If you have a field placement, teach your lesson. Another option is to present the lesson to your college classmates.

Assessment: How is this lesson different from the one you wrote for Activity 6.4? What teaching strategies did you use? How did you introduce, develop, and conclude the lesson? Is your lesson student centered? ◼

Using growth of crystals to explore physical change: Physical science

Physical Change: Making Rock Candy.   In this lesson, students make rock candy. Since this activity requires close supervision by the teacher, the class works in two groups. While the first half of the class performs the activity, the other half works independently on an assignment. As the lesson begins, the teacher gives explicit directions, stressing proper safety precautions. Students are instructed not to taste any of the materials. They gather the materials needed to begin to grow the rock candy. The teacher prepares a saturated sugar water solution. Students place a string across a pan containing the saturated solution. The students illustrate their work in their notebooks, then complete a worksheet and a reflective performance assessment. Each day for a week, they watch the sugar crystals grow on the string. After completing this lesson, students discuss and give an example of a physical change, review the rules of safety for performing an activity, follow directions, and work cooperatively to complete a task.

Activity 6.6   Designing a Lesson: Physical Change—Making Rock Candy

Overview: In this activity, you will design a lesson based on the description you just read.

Materials: You will use the lesson plan format to design the lesson.

Procedure: Complete the sections listed in Activity 6.1. If you have a field placement, teach your lesson.

Assessment: How is this lesson different from the one you wrote for Activity 6.5? What teaching strategies did you use? How did you introduce, develop, and conclude the lesson? Is your lesson student centered? ◼

Using chocolate to explore change in state: Physical science

Physical Change: Experimenting with Chocolate.   In this lesson, students review physical and chemical change. They practice safety in the laboratory and follow directions. As the lesson begins, the teacher reads "Life Is a Box of Chocolates," a poem by Jill Genio. The teacher explains that the lesson will integrate science and home economics. The students examine the change of state of the chocolate from solid to liquid to solid. They begin by viewing solid pieces of chocolate and identify the state of matter. They then melt the chocolate, pour it into a mold, and let it solidify. They return the mold to the teacher and clean up the work area. They complete a reflective self-assessment and answer questions on teacher-prepared worksheets. After completing this lesson, students discuss and give examples of a physical change, review the rules of safety for performing an activity, follow directions, and work cooperatively to complete a task. They compare the melting and solidifying of chocolate to the melting and freezing of ice.

Students work cooperatively to complete a task.

Activity 6.7   Designing a Lesson: Physical Change—Experimenting with Chocolate

Overview: In this activity, you will design a lesson based on the description you just read.

Materials: You will use the lesson plan format to design the lesson.

Procedure: Complete the sections listed in Activity 6.1. If you have a field placement, teach your lesson. Another option is to present the lesson to your college classmates.

Assessment: How is this lesson different from the one you wrote for Activity 6.6? What teaching strategies did you use? How did you introduce, develop, and conclude the lesson? Is your lesson student centered? ■

In this activity, you will surf the Internet and find lesson plans from a variety of sources. Log onto http://tikkun.ed.asu.edu/coe/links/lessons.html

Here you'll find links to lesson plans from dozens of sources. Select a lesson plan, and analyze it. Does it have sound objectives? Is there an assessment plan? If you can, teach the lesson. How did your lesson go? ■

Science Units

A series of lessons that fit together form a *unit of study*. Students generally complete several different science units each year. Science units should be inquiry based, using a mixture of teacher-directed and student-centered methods. A **unit** is a series of lessons centered on a particular *subject, concept, topic,* or *theme.* For example, a unit can be based on a *theme,* such as transportation. This is a **thematic unit**. Students might view transportation from a systems approach, studying all of the interacting components of the system: trains, planes, cars, trucks, roadways, waterways, airways, traffic management systems, purposes of transportation, and so on. They might engage in mathematics, science, social studies, reading, writing, music, and art—all related to the transportation theme. When teachers design a thematic unit, it usually combines, or *integrates,* several disciplines such as science, mathematics, social studies, music, or art. Such a unit is called an **interdisciplinary thematic unit**.

A unit can be based on a design challenge

Some units focus on having students investigate a topic, ask questions, and solve problems. Others are stand-alones, covering a single subject such as sound, light, electricity and magnetism, biology, chemistry, or physics. You can organize a unit around a **problem** or **design challenge**. A group of third-grade teachers I worked with in a mathematics, science, and technology course recently created a unit on ocean creatures based on *technology design and problem solving*. In this sense, technology is not an instrument, such as a computer, but a field of study that uses design and problem solving to satisfy human needs. The design challenge was to create an ocean creature with one movable part. Besides learning about marine life, their students learned about simple machines as well.

The third-graders solved the problem in a number of creative ways. One group designed a sea creature, while another group used recycled material to design a mechanical robot found in the ocean. The robot's arm moved, and students measured the angles that the arm assumed as it moved. The unit consisted of ten lessons and integrated math, science, and technology. It was quite successful and probably was one of the first times elementary school students asked for more homework; they wanted more time to work on the design challenge.

Some units contain instructions for independent study

Although teachers often encourage students to work in groups, some students prefer to work alone. You can design instructional units for students to work on individually. Such units contain instructions for independent study. Students generally have a problem to solve, and the unit contains materials, a variety of resources, and assessment materials that enable students to work alone on the

This student solved a design challenge.

unit. Having a set of instructional units for individual study is a useful classroom management tool, as some students tend to work more quickly than others and to finish their work early. Those students can begin to work on the individualized instructional units while the rest of the class continues working on the original unit.

When you start teaching, you have few resources in your collection. However, as you continue to teach, your collection grows quickly. When you create something of high quality, save it. You can use it again, revise it, and share it with your colleagues. Others will probably want to share some of their resources with you as well.

A well-written science unit contains several parts and varies in length. A brief unit lasts about two weeks, and a longer unit can last up to a marking period or two. The length of the unit depends on the topic, what appears in the curriculum guide, and the amount and depth of content covered. As a new teacher, creating and teaching a two-week unit is a reasonable starting point. It provides practice in curriculum writing and enables you to understand what planning involves. Principals and accomplished teachers often tell me that students who write curriculum units have a better understanding of the overall planning process. They also know how to connect one topic to another when they plan sequential lessons intended to teach a concept.

As with lessons, there is no set format for a unit plan. Writing a unit of study provides practice in thinking and organizing, and is a good exercise for new teachers. Some teachers never write curriculum at all throughout their careers. In some districts, however, curriculum writing is an ongoing process and a required part of the job. The next time you are in a school, ask one of the teachers if you can see a unit of study. What type of unit is it? What are its parts? How are lessons connected in the unit?

Science Curriculum

A curriculum is a work plan for teachers

Each school or school district should have in place an overall long-range plan for teaching science, which is called a **science curriculum**. A curriculum is a document that serves as a *work plan for teachers*. It describes the content students cover while attending a particular school or school district, and it discusses the methods teachers use to teach and assess the curriculum. In the majority of districts, the curriculum is a document created in the district and written by teachers, administrators, supervisors, and sometimes parents working together.

Examples of high-quality curriculum packages

Today many excellent materials support the elementary science curriculum. In addition to science textbooks developed by publishing companies, the National Science Foundation has funded the development of many science curricula. Many of them are sold as science kits or modules that include materials for hands-on activities. These are sold and marketed by a variety of companies; you can read about them at http://www.col-ed.org/smcnws/msres/cprojects.html. Here are some of these curricula:

- *Great Explorations in Math and Science:* a prekindergarten through grade 10 program developed at the Lawrence Hall of Science at the University of California at Berkeley
- *Science and Technology for Children:* a program for grades 1 through 6 developed by the National Science Resources Center
- *Insights:* a K–6 program developed by the Education Development Center
- *National Geographic Kids Network:* a telecommunications-based student research project for grades 4 through 9 developed by TERC, Inc.
- *Science Curriculum Improvement Study (SCIS-3):* a K–6 program developed by the Lawrence Hall of Science at the University of California at Berkeley
- *Full Option Science System (FOSS):* a K–6 hands-on program developed by the Lawrence Hall of Science at the University of California at Berkeley

In Chapter 14 you will read more about these materials and others.

Some districts create a science curriculum scope and sequence. This is a chart that identifies the grade level at which to introduce a concept or topic and the grade level or levels at which to practice and assess the concept or topic and any related skills. In some locations, the state develops science guidelines, which each school follows; in other locations, local officials establish and mandate local science guidelines. Today many schools and districts adhere to state and national standards. Recall that **national science education standards** provide an overall view of what we should do in the United States to achieve scientific literacy for all citizens. National standards are *not* a national curriculum; rather, they are guidelines to use for curriculum development. For example, the *National Science Education Standards (NSES)* (National Research Council, 1996) contains six chapters that include information about content standards for students, assessment standards for students, science teaching standards, standards for professional development of teachers, standards for programs, and standards for the entire system. The standards serve as a guide for the curriculum development process.

When a district creates a standards-based curriculum, team members first examine all of the state and national science standards and decide how they will meet them. When addressing content standards, they make a decision about which ones to cover and the courses and grade levels in which to teach them. They write the curriculum so that teachers and students cover those content standards in specific courses.

How does a teacher or curriculum writer know when the curriculum covers a content standard completely? This is a difficult question to answer and one that educators grapple with continuously. Fortunately, many excellent elementary science textbooks and National Science Foundation-funded curriculum projects serve as a guide. These materials, developed by teams of scientists, educators, and writers over a long period of time, reflect decades of experience and expertise in a number of disciplines—far greater than the expertise likely to be found in any given school district. Most of these products show how standards-based curricula, instruction, and assessment look. This is why educators routinely select textbooks and curriculum materials to accompany the curriculum. While the curriculum serves as the long-range work plan, the textbook or curriculum materials help put the plan into action and make it a complete instructional package.

Examine your district's science curriculum

As you begin teaching, ask for a copy of your school's science curriculum so that you are aware of your work plan. It is important that you understand what is expected of you and your students. Study the curriculum and ask questions. The best type of curriculum guide is one that is clearly written, hands-on, and easy to follow. Unfortunately, some curriculum guides are vague and impractical. Your thoughtful assessment will enable you to determine the usefulness of your school's guide. If your cooperating teacher or administrator is able to locate the science curriculum guide easily, and if the guide looks like it's been well used, it is probably a useful document. If not, it's probably a seldom used, poorly written, or inadequate product. Since as a teacher you will work with curriculum every day, it is important to understand how teams develop a sound curriculum document and to know what such a document contains.

Constructing Your Knowledge of Science and Science Teaching

Now that you have completed this chapter, it is time to reflect on what you have learned about planning for instruction in elementary science. You will write daily lesson plans that include goals and achievement objectives for all students, as well as objectives to help meet the needs of individual students. As you begin to understand how instruction is planned, consider these elements. Think back on your own schooling. How have your teachers and professors planned for your instruction? Are you aware of the achievement objectives that have been set for you in your teacher education program? If not, find out if there are principles that guide your development as a professional in your college or university.

As you begin to write unit plans and lesson plans, find out if your state has adopted statewide guidelines for elementary science. If so, get a copy of the document. As you write achievement objectives, look at the standards. Do your targets match the standards and proficiencies specified in the document? Finally, familiarize yourself with the curriculum materials on the market today. An excellent resource book is *Resources for Teaching Elementary Science,* created by the National Science Resources Center, which is operated by the National Academy of Sciences and the Smithsonian Institution. This guide is packed with information about high-quality hands-on, inquiry-based curriculum materials and resources for elementary science. Reading this guide will help you understand what is available to you as an elementary science teacher.

Key Terms

goal (p. 132)
achievement objectives (p. 132)
conditions (p. 133)
cognitive domain (p. 134)
psychomotor domain (p. 134)
affective domain (p. 134)
traditional paper-and-pencil tests (p. 134)
performance assessment (p. 134)

authentic performance assessment (p. 134)
matter (p. 139)
energy (p. 139)
solid (p. 139)
liquid (p. 139)
gas (p. 139)
plasma (p. 140)
physical properties (p. 140)
physical change (p. 140)
chemical properties (p. 140)

chemical change (p. 140)
unit (p. 148)
thematic unit (p. 148)
interdisciplinary thematic unit (p. 148)
problem (p. 148)
design challenge (p. 148)
science curriculum (p. 150)
national science education standards (p. 151)

Reviewing Chapter 6:
Questions, Extensions, Applications, and Explorations

1. Send for information about some of the elementary science curriculum projects on the market today. Here are some numbers to call:

   GEMS: 1-510-642-7771

   Science and Technology for Children: 1-800-227-1150

   Insights: 1-800-KH-BOOKS

   SCIS-3 and *FOSS:* 1-800-258-1302

   National Geographic Kids Network: 1-800-342-4460

2. When writing achievement objectives for individual students, what are some things you

should consider? Is it reasonable to expect that your students will meet some objectives for which you did not plan? What happens if your students don't meet the objectives that you set for them?

3. You have spent a great deal of time writing a lesson plan and preparing a science lesson. While you are teaching, your students get into a lively discussion related to the lesson, and you move off track. Should you let this continue, or should you go back to your original lesson plan?

4. How do you know when you have planned enough? How much time should it take to write a lesson plan for a 45-minute lesson?

5. Create a lesson plan for an elementary science lesson using the lesson plan format suggested in this chapter or an alternative format suggested by your instructor.

6. Select a topic for a science unit. Create a concept map to show the relationship among the subtopics that comprise the unit.

Print Resources

Eisenhower National Clearinghouse for Mathematics and Science Education. (1994) *Guidebook to excellence 1994: A directory of federal resources for mathematics and science education improvement.* Columbus, OH: Eisenhower National Clearinghouse.

National Science Resources Center. (1996). *Resources for teaching elementary science.* Washington, DC: National Academy Press.

Science curriculum resource handbook: A practical guide for K–12 science curriculum. (1992). Millwood, NY: Krauss International Publications.

Wiggins, G. (1998). *Educative assessment.* San Francisco: Jossey-Bass.

Wiggins, G., & McTighe, J. (1998). *Understanding by design.* Alexandria, VA: Association for Supervision and Curriculum Development.

Electronic Resources

Rowe, Mary Budd. (1993). Science Helper K–8: Version 3.0 (CD-ROM). Armonk, NY: The Learning Team. This CD contains thousands of hands-on science activities.

Annenberg/CPB Case Studies in Science Education
- Elementary Science Case Studies
- Middle School Case Studies

Annenberg/CPB Minds of Our Own Videos
- Can We Believe Our Eyes?
- Lessons from Thin Air

Annenberg/CPB Science IMAGES Library (Classroom videos)
(1-800-965-7373)
- Darlene Norfleet, 1st grade—Working through a unit on the human body, students compare and contrast features of their own bodies.
- Sister Gertrude Hennessey, 2nd grade—Students develop a theory about force and motion by working with various moving objects.
- Chris Collier, 3rd grade—The class engages in a variety of activities and keeps journals of data and their thoughts while examining the five senses.
- Marc Heuer, 4th grade—Research about water facts and the water cycle.
- Linda Hallenbeck, 5th grade—Population data they collect from gravestones in the local cemetery help students examine the process of scientific inquiry.
- Dorcas Gonzales-Lantz, 6th grade—Students learn about matter and molecules as they investigate the relationships between energy and changes of state by observing water change from ice to steam.
- Kathy Brown, 7th grade—An actual case history from 1904 of a Chicago patient who suffered from fatigue teaches students about the human circulatory system.
- Doug Kirkpatrick, 8th grade—Students use computers to observe, graph, and analyze data, then confirm predictions via email with university scientists during a lesson on "What happens to light as you move away?"

Lesson Plans Page
http://www.lessonplanspage.com/
This site contains hundreds of lesson plans.

Chemistry for Kids
http://www.chem4kids.com/
This excellent site focuses on teaching chemistry to elementary school children.

Children's Literature

Burns, G., & Woodman, N.
Exploring the World of Chemistry
(Franklin Watts, 1995)
ISBN: 0-531-20119-8
Grades 4–6

Kramer, A., & Harvey, P.
How to Make a Chemical Volcano & Other Mysterious Experiments
(Franklin Watts, 1991)
ISBN: 0-531-15610-9
Grades 5–8

Newmark, A.
Eyewitness Science: Chemistry
(Dorling Kindersley, 1993)
ISBN: 1-564-58231-0
Grades 4–6

Vancleave, J.
Janice Vancleave's Molecules
(John Wiley & Sons, 1992)
ISBN: 0-471-55054-X
Grades 4–6

Peters, E.
Alien Chemistry (Troll Associates, 1999)
ISBN: 0-816-75036-X
Grades 4–6

Cole, J.
The Magic School Bus Gets Baked in a Cake: A Book About Kitchen Chemistry (Scholastic Trade, 1995)
ISBN: 0-590-22295-3
Grades 3–4

Arnold, N., & Desaulles, T.
Chemical Chaos (Scholastic Trade, 1998)
ISBN: 0-590-10885-9
Grades 4–6

Shellenberger, S., & Johnson, G.
Lockers, Lunch Lines, Chemistry, and Cliques
(Bethany House, 1995)
ISBN: 1-556-61483-7
Grades 6 and up

CHAPTER 7

Linking Instruction and Assessment

Day 1

It is late fall, and 22 young scientists, including several special learners, are studying classification, which is part of a first-grade unit on plants. The unit is part of the year-long first-grade curriculum that integrates science, math, social studies, reading, writing, music, and art. It also focuses on helping students develop social skills. This particular unit, designed by a team of first-grade teachers, takes four weeks to complete. Central to the design of the unit is the link between instruction and assessment.

When designing the unit, the teachers selected a number of science process skills appropriate for first-graders. Children in the first grade can observe, communicate, estimate, measure, collect data, classify, make simple inferences, predict, and formulate simple models. They can also make simple graphs and data tables, interpret data, and engage in simple experiments. Today's lesson involves developing the ability to make observations, classify, and create simple graphs to display data. To understand the concept of classification, the students first classify buttons by color. Later they will classify beans, then plant them.

The teacher, Ms. Green, introduces the lesson by reading *The Button Box,* a story about a young boy who has an imaginative adventure as he sorts through his grandmother's button collection. After listening to the story and discussing it as a whole class, students work in pairs to sort a pile of buttons. Each pair of students has about 25 buttons. They sort the buttons into groups by color. With help from their teacher, they later create graphs to reflect their findings.

A great deal of planning goes into the unit. Since the class includes students with special needs, Ms. Green and the special education teacher, Dr. Ramirez, work together to modify the lessons in the unit so that they are appropriate for each student. The teachers decide to have the class create a *data chart* to organize the information they present in the story. Data charts are useful for recording information, documenting what students learn, or categorizing information (McKenzie, 1979; Tompkins, 1998). When creating a data chart, students brainstorm the characteristics of the topic, which they write across the top of the chart; then they list examples in the left column. The rest of the chart contains words, pictures, or sentences (see Figure 7.1).

KINDS OF BUTTONS	DESCRIPTION
Buttons with flowers	There are ten of them. They look like Grandma's china dishes.
Sparkly buttons	I pretend they're jewels.
Cloth buttons	They are made of cloth, satin, or corduroy. They remind me of fancy clothes.
Metal buttons	From overalls and jeans
Leather buttons	From cowboy shirts and sweaters
Winter coat buttons	Like the ones on Grandpa's winter coat
Small buttons	From shoes worn long ago
Shiny buttons from uniforms	Mr. President buttons
Pearly ones	I make a rainbow
Buttons with shanks	Buttons for puppets and stuffed animals
Round, flat, thick buttons	Grandma's buttons in the button game
Round, flat, thin buttons	My buttons in the button game
Seashell buttons	Buttons that were seashells
Glass buttons	Buttons that came from sand
Wooden buttons	Buttons from trees
Deer buttons	Buttons from antlers

Figure 7.1
Data Chart to Go with *The Button Box*

The teachers anticipate that students may encounter difficulty creating graphs that reflect how the buttons are sorted by color. To solve this problem, they decide to show the students examples of graphs completed by other students. They also devise another strategy. Moving from concrete to abstract, students take a sheet of grid paper and place all buttons of the same color (or shades of the same color) in the same column (see Figure 7.2). They prepared the grid paper earlier, so it has a title, a space for the student's name and today's date, and a key.

Accommodating students with special needs

Some students have difficulty with fine motor skills, so those students use a computer to create their graphs, with appropriate help from the teachers. Many of the students are quite computer literate and can move along more rapidly than others. The teachers encourage these students to use the computer to create their graphs as well. Students who finish the task earlier than the others move on to activities for further challenge. These activities enable them to move along and think about the work more deeply. These students reclassify the buttons using first two attributes (for example, size and color), then three attributes (size, color, and number of holes).

Day 2

Classifying beans: Process skills

Today's lesson involves bean classification. Ms. Green purchased a package of 16-bean soup mix in the supermarket for 85 cents. The young scientists continue to

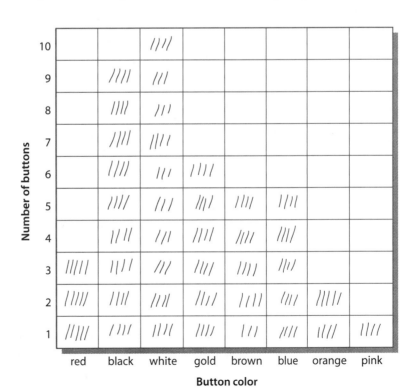

**Figure 7.2
Grid for Button
Classification**

work in pairs. Each pair gets a variety of beans in a small plastic bag. The teacher tells them to classify the beans into groups. Unlike with the button classification, where they formed groups by color, the students now choose their own classification schemes. This is challenging for some students, as the packets contain many different kinds of beans.

Some interesting classification schemes emerge. Many teams group the beans by type—kidney, black turtle, lima, lentil, peas, split pea, yellow pea, to name a few. Others group by bean size, and some sort by color. On a sheet of paper, students trace around the beans in each group and color them. Their next task is to create a graph to reflect their findings. Yesterday they created graphs with assistance. Today they will create them on their own. This, too, is a big step for some students.

Before they work on their graphs, the teachers ask everyone to sit on the carpet in the front of the room. Once students gather, they review expectations as they assess prior knowledge. Since some students have difficulty following directions, it is necessary to explain and model the assigned task. This exercise will benefit all students, however. The teachers know that giving good directions is essential if all students are to understand.

Using wait time

Ms. Green begins by asking students to identify the parts of a graph. Elissa raises her hand first, but she is not called on immediately. The teacher uses wait time so that all students have a chance to think about the answer before raising their hands. *Wait time* refers to the amount of time the teacher gives the students to think before calling on someone to answer a question (Rowe, 1974, 1986). When wait time increases, students have more time to think, and they can give longer, more detailed responses. Students volunteer more responses, and fewer questions are left unanswered. Students also ask more questions. Once a student responds, Ms. Green lets time pass before responding to the student and asking a follow-up question. In this case, Ms. Green waits five seconds after asking the first question. She then calls on Tyree, who tells her that the first item to place on the graph is the student's name and the date. "That's correct," Ms. Green replies, and then waits three seconds before calling on Elissa, who says that every graph needs a title. Within five minutes, the class lists all of the essential items on a graph. They learned yesterday's lesson well. They then discuss each part of the graph, thinking about how an expert first-grader (***), a proficient first-grader (**), and a novice first-grader (*) would perform. When discussing name and date, the class decides on the following criteria:

Name and Date

*** My name and the date are in the proper place on the graph.

** My name and the date are on the graph, but they are in the wrong place.

* I forgot to write my name and the date on the graph.

When discussing the title, here is what they decide:

Title

***   I have a title that describes the graph well.

**   I have a title, but it could describe the graph a little better.

*   I forgot to include a title.

Clarifying expectations
for students

The students and the teachers work together until they have created a complete assessment task list for a graph (see Table 7.1 on page 160). Assessment and instruction are linked. As they go back to their seats to complete the bean classification activity and create their own graphs, the students have a clear idea of their expectations and how their work will be assessed. Along with their teachers, they participated in linking instruction and assessment.

In Chapter 6, you learned about how to write lesson plans. A good lesson includes an assessment plan. In this chapter and the next, you will learn how to create such a plan as you read about linking instruction and assessment. As you read this chapter, think about the answers to these questions:

1. **How can I scaffold instruction by using assessment?**

2. **How do I assess student understanding to uncover misconceptions?**

3. **What methods should I use to assess student progress as I teach?**

4. **How do I evaluate overall student performance?**

5. **How do I use assessment information to provide feedback to students and improve instruction?**

6. **How do I link instruction and assessment while exploring the ideas of floating, sinking, and density with my students?**

Assessing and Evaluating Student Learning

Assessment is a term that describes all of the ways in which educators gather information about student learning. They **evaluate,** or *interpret*, this information, then use it to guide decisions and actions in education (Hibbard, 1996).

Teachers use assessment information to

▸ Decide whether students meet achievement objectives

▸ Form learning groups

▸ Evaluate their own teaching

▸ Determine whether a student needs special testing or additional help

▸ Provide feedback to students on their progress

▸ Formulate report card grades

Table 7.1
Assessment Task List for First-Graders

1. **Name and Date**
   - ***   My name and the date are written in the proper place on the graph.
   - **   My name and the date are written in the wrong place on the graph.
   - *   I forgot to write my name and the date on the graph.

2. **Title**
   - ***   I have included a title that describes the graph well.
   - **   I have included a title, but it could better describe the graph.
   - *   I have forgotten to include a title.

3. **Labels**
   - ***   I have labeled clearly and correctly, including number and type of beans.
   - **   I have labeled only the number.
   - *   I have forgotten to use labels.

4. **Entering the Data**
   - ***   I have accurately entered the data.
   - **   I have entered the data, but I have not done a good job.
   - *   I have forgotten to enter the data.

5. **Key**
   - ***   I have correctly labeled the key.
   - **   I have incorrectly labeled the key.
   - *   I have forgotten to include the key.

When you are aware of the strengths and weaknesses of your students, you can plan instruction accordingly. Sometimes the curriculum needs to be adjusted; information gained from assessment and evaluation enables you to make those adjustments. Sometimes you are moving too quickly or too slowly; assessment and evaluation help you to pace your instruction. Parents and guardians need to know how their children are progressing, and sharing assessment information with them engages them in their child's education. It also enables them to join you in helping the child succeed in school. Most important, children need feedback on their progress, and the assessment process allows you to include them in their own learning; it lets them know how they are progressing.

Assessments can be formal or informal

Assessment is an ongoing process that takes many forms. It can consist of **informal** information that you gain from observation of student characteristics, conversations with students, informal interviews, class discussions, group discussions, and informal question-and-answer sessions, or it can be **formal.** As a teacher, you will rely on both formal and informal assessments. Formal assessments have a special purpose: when designed properly, they provide fair, unbiased information about student behavior and achievement. In an elementary science class, formal assessments include such items as homework, quizzes, systematic observation of students, formal interviews, oral reports, essays, performance appraisals, performance tasks, journals, learning logs, laboratory notebooks, self-assessments, and portfolios of work. You will use the information gained from formal (as well as informal) assessments to make an overall evaluation of student progress when you complete report cards for your students. Other formal evaluation tools include teacher-made tests, local and state assessments, and standardized tests. In this text, you will learn how to use these tools.

Assessment is a major topic in education today and one that teachers deal with on a daily basis. It is estimated that teachers spend 20 to 30 percent of their time in assessment activities (Gage & Berliner, 1998). Research in the area of assessment is plentiful; pick up any educational journal or scan the list of offerings at just about any professional conference for educators, and you will see assessment on the agenda. If you do so, you will find that there is ongoing debate in the field, as some researchers believe traditional paper-and-pencil tests are best, whereas others argue that such tests should be replaced by assessments that are performance based.

Performance Assessment

Using performance assessments to show what you know

Performance assessments require your students to translate their knowledge and skills into action. To demonstrate problem solving or decision making that

Using a journal to record observations during a field trip.

requires application of content, it is often better to engage in a performance. To find out if a student can set up an experiment or use a balance to make a measurement, the student performs the action. There are other reasons for the emergence of performance-based assessments. As constructivist theory gained support, new needs surfaced and additional means of assessing student learning were necessary; traditional means of assessing students were not a good match for the constructivist classroom. While traditional multiple-choice and paper-and-pencil tests effectively assess knowledge of facts and concepts, teachers find that application of content, science process skills, manipulative skills, attitudes, and habits of mind are difficult to measure in these ways. This led to interest in developing a variety of other assessment approaches to expand teachers' ability to plan instruction and make classroom decisions. Recall from Chapter 6 that students engage in performances such as developing demonstrations, creating products, or constructing responses to situations to provide evidence that they have certain knowledge and skills.

Linking Child Development with Instruction and Assessment

In Chapter 4, you learned about inquiry-based approaches to science teaching and the importance of identifying alternative frameworks and misconceptions. In Chapter 5, you acquired knowledge of principles of child development and constructivist theory. Chapter 6 focused on planning for instruction, which included learning how to write lesson plans. You will now read about linking instruction and assessment to improve student performance. You have knowledge in a number of fields. You must put this all together and ask, "How do I apply and use this information to teach elementary science?"

To do this, you will study the concept of density and see how it develops from early childhood, when students first examine floating and sinking, to adolescence, when they begin to understand the concept of buoyancy. You will work through a series of lessons, each linking principles of child development to knowledge of instruction and assessment, and you will learn a variety of methods to assess student understanding. After working through the hands-on activities and learning about many different assessment techniques, you will create your own lessons, complete with an assessment plan that suits the needs of your students.

Constructivist learning theory is the basis of the design of this series of lessons, which focus on student thinking and problem solving. Students take responsibility for their learning and engage in dialogue with their peers and their teachers as they ask questions and seek answers. The assessments are both formal and informal. In some cases, you will ask questions, engage in conversations with students, and assess understanding informally. In other cases, assessment will be formal, including science logs, journals, concept maps, portfolios, and tests of all sorts. As you read through the activities and plan your own lessons, ask yourself these questions:

1. What principles of child development or models of learning must I keep in mind to plan a developmentally appropriate lesson? For example, might a theory of Piaget or Vygotsky be used to design a particular lesson? Does this lesson use a constructivist approach to teaching?

2. What are the appropriate achievement objectives to set for my students? What will I accept as evidence of student understanding?

3. What is the best way to assess whether or not my students meet the achievement objectives I set for them?

4. How do I use feedback from informal and formal assessment to improve instruction?

5. How should my next lesson reflect this information?

You will begin by reading a story about Archimedes, who is famous for his thoughts about floating and sinking. It's a classic story that your students will likely find interesting. After you read the story, you will learn about informal assessment techniques. Following that discussion, you will read about formal assessments, then work through a series of hands-on activities to develop the concept of density. Then you will design your own lessons.

Floating and Sinking: A Story to Illustrate the Concept

Archimedes was one of the first experimental scientists: Physical science

You have probably heard of Archimedes, the Greek mathematician and inventor who lived in the third century B.C. (approximately 287 to 212 B.C.). He is thought to be one of the first experimental scientists because he used scientific thinking and experimentation to solve problems and gain new knowledge. Historians credit him with discovering how levers and pulleys work. This discovery led to the construction of large machines that were based on the use of simple machines. In his time, people knew Archimedes for his work as an adviser to Hiero, the king of Syracuse, Sicily.

You may be familiar with a particular problem that Archimedes solved for the king, who commissioned a goldsmith to make a new gold crown. When he received the crown, the king suspected that it was not pure gold but a mixture of gold and less valuable silver. Archimedes was given the task of finding out whether the crown was made of pure gold. He needed a way to make some measurements. He knew that if he had two pieces of gold that were exactly the same size and weighed each piece, he would find that their masses were the same. If you have two bars of pure gold and they are both the same size, they should have the same weight if both are made of pure gold. The problem was that the crown was irregularly shaped, so it was difficult to calculate its volume.

Being a true scientist, Archimedes was always thinking. One day while taking a bath, he realized that when he got into the tub, some water spilled onto the floor. He knew that this overflow occurred because he took up space in the tub. He reasoned that the same logic could be used to calculate the volume of the crown. He could fill a pan with water to the very top. When he placed the crown in the pan, the water would overflow. He would catch the overflow, which was the same as the volume of the crown. He could weigh the crown and divide that number by its volume, which he would now know. He should get the same number if he weighed a piece of pure gold and divided its mass by its volume. That's how he could determine whether or not the crown was real. Archimedes was so excited by the idea that he jumped out of the bathtub, shouted, "Eureka, I have found it!", and ran through the town with no clothes on (or so the story goes). He tested the new crown and compared its **density** (mass per unit volume) with the density of a piece of pure gold, and found that the crown was indeed a mixture of gold and silver. The king had been cheated by the goldsmith!

The Science Concept Behind the Story

A body placed in a fluid displaces some of the fluid: Physical science

Archimedes continued to work with fluids. He asked why an object seems to get lighter when lowered into a fluid such as water. He discovered Archimedes' principle, which explains why this happens. According to this principle, a body placed in a fluid displaces, or pushes away, some of the fluid. That's what happened when he stepped into the bathtub and sat down. The weight of the displaced fluid is equal to the weight that the object seems to lose when placed in the fluid. The object seems to lose weight because the fluid is pushing up on it, supporting some of its weight.

Consider this example. A hard-boiled egg floats on water. The floating egg displaces a small amount of water. If you weigh the displaced water, you will find out how much less the egg seems to weigh. The water pushes up on the egg and supports some of its weight. This force is called *upthrust*. The force pushing up on the egg is equal to the weight of the water pushed away, or displaced by, the egg. This is an example of Archimedes' principle. An object floats if the force of the water pushing up on it is equal to or greater than the weight of the object. If an object weighs more than the force pushing up on it, the object sinks.

The concept of density explains what's happening. If the mass per unit volume, or density, of an object is less than that of the fluid in which it is placed, it will float. If the density of an object is greater than that of the fluid, it will sink.

In the sections that follow, you will learn about informal and formal assessment techniques. You will learn how to use these techniques as you develop lessons for your students to help them understand the concept of density.

Informal Assessment

Asking questions and conversing with students is informal assessment

As a natural part of your classroom work, you observe your students, converse with them, listen to them interact with their peers, and informally assess their prior knowledge and their progress. It is important to ask questions and listen to what they say. Encourage them to ask one another questions as well. When you place your students in groups, they have many opportunities for discussion and interaction. Listen carefully to group discussions. Circulate around the room and ask about their observations. Scaffold their understanding with questions that lead them to the proper conclusions. (Which developmental psychologist taught this to us?) Help them move forward as they gain understanding. Ask questions such as "What do you observe?" "Why do you think this is happening?" "Can you explain what's happening?" Listen to their answers, and think about what they say. Ask yourself, "What does this student's answer mean?" When your students ask you a question, ask yourself, "What does this question tell me about this student's understanding?" You will learn a great deal about their thinking in this way.

Ask yourself if you believe your students understand the concepts. Do they seem confused? If so, ask more questions to find out what they think and why they might be confused. Ask yourself, "What else might I do to help this student grasp this concept?" Sometimes a student is not ready to understand a particular concept; the concept may be too advanced for the child. In some cases, the student does not have the background or experience with which to connect the new knowledge. What will you do in this case? Will you provide the student with more concrete experience? Will you think of other ways to help that child learn? Will you reintroduce the same concept a few days later and see if any growth occurs? All of these approaches are viable solutions.

This teacher is using informal assessment to find out what his students think.

When your students are investigating floating and sinking, you may find that some have lots of experience and are ready to think about what makes an object float or sink. Young children often experiment with floating and sinking while playing with toys in the bathtub. But some students may not have experimented with floating or sinking before. Some may have misconceptions and need some time to experiment and think. For these students, investigating objects that float and others that sink is an appropriate first experience.

Approaches to Equity and Diversity

Set appropriate objectives for students with special needs

Students with special needs may have difficulty understanding the concepts and carrying out the activities. Be patient. If you set appropriate objectives for children with special needs, you will help them to progress at their own rate. Speaking slowly and using repetition and appropriate vocabulary are important when working with students with learning disabilities. Processing information often takes longer for special learners, and if you provide a safe, secure environment in which they are not afraid to try something again or ask the same question more than once, you will often find that they will begin to understand. Being part of a small, well-run, cooperative group will encourage students to ask more questions if they don't understand. Give the students confidence, be supportive, pace instruction effectively, and above all be patient. This is also an important strategy to use when teaching students for whom English is a second language. You will learn more about working with students with special needs in Chapter 9, and you will read about cooperative learning in Chapter 10.

Questioning as Informal Assessment

As you work through the activities involving floating and sinking, pay particular attention to the ways you can use information gained from informal student assessment to assess prior knowledge, identify misconceptions and scaffold instruction. When helping your students work through an activity and build understanding, your questions are a vital part of bringing them from confusion or misconception to understanding. By asking the right questions, you can determine what your students understand.

Questioning students helps to clarify understanding

Here are some questions that you might ask students as they think and experiment.

A classifying question

- How are these alike?
- How are these different?

A conjecturing question

- What if . . . ?
- What might be true?

A generalizing question

- What patterns do you see?

A specializing question

- Can you give a special example of this?

A convincing question

- How do you know this is true?
- Why did this happen?

An analyzing question

- What is this all about?
- What is the cause for this?

Practice your questioning skills with a peer before working with your students. Think about the questions you will ask. State them clearly. Ask for one response at a time. Many new teachers like to compose a set of questions and place them in the lesson plan.

Formal Assessment

Learning logs and journals help students reflect on their work

Using formal assessment tools such as learning logs, journals, observation checklists, and portfolios provides concrete data to supplement what you learn from the informal assessment. You will now read about these tools.

Learning Logs and Journals

Using learning logs and journals is an excellent way to learn about what your students think. Learning logs give students an opportunity to record key ideas during a discussion. You can have them connect new ideas with prior knowledge by writing in their logs. You can also have students record the questions that remain after the lesson (see Figure 7.3 on page 168).

Journals help students to reflect on what they learn (see Figure 7.4 on page 169). They provide an opportunity to express opinions, react to findings, and explain observations. A child's journal can be a resource that provides information about how that child's thinking, skills, and attitudes change over time (Hein & Price, 1994, p. 104). Whereas learning logs are more structured, journals invite students to express themselves in greater depth.

Students can share learning logs and journals with their classmates. When they discuss their ideas with one another, they may clarify their thinking or uncover concepts that they don't understand.

If you have students with special needs, you should definitely consider using science journals. Special learners often require extra time for processing, and with a journal a student can have as much time as needed to complete an entry, perhaps starting it in school and finishing at home. Besides expressing scientific thought, writing skills will improve with practice, and a journal fosters writing. Using a journal to process what happened in a lesson allows you to see if your students came away with key ideas. When involved in experimentation, students can write about their predictions in a journal. If they have questions, they can record them. You might pose questions during the lesson and ask students to respond to them in their journals. If students solve difficult problems, they can write about their solutions.

Name: Lauren

Concept: Acids

1. Outline the key ideas from this lesson.

Acids are very common in our world. Acids taste sour. Some places that we find acids are in ants, fruits, soda, car batteries, and stomachs. Some acids are strong and some acids are weak. Strong acids can burn through things. They are dangerous. Weak acids are safe. We can even eat them, like in fruits. Scientists use the pH scale to find out how strong or how weak an acid is. The pH scale goes from 1 to 14.

2. Can you connect this with something that you already know?
   If you can, write about it.

We have acids in our stomachs. Even though they are strong acids, they don't burn through our stomachs. This is because there is a lining in our stomachs that protects us from the strong acids.

Sometimes people get upset stomachs. Too much stomach acid can cause an upset stomach. When people get upset stomachs because of too much acid, they take medicine to counteract or neutralize the acid.

Acids can be mixed with water. This makes them weaker or more dilute. The orange juice container says it is from concentrate. This means that strong orange juice was mixed with water to dilute it.

3. If you have any additional questions, write about them.

Strong acids can be made weaker by adding them to water. If you add enough water to a strong acid, can it become as weak as a weak acid?

(Lauren: A very dilute solution of a strong acid and a very concentrated solution of a weak acid can have the same pH. — Mrs. S.)

Figure 7.3
Science Learning Log

Monday: Today we started to learn about acids. It was kind of fun. The teacher had lemons for us to taste. She also had oranges and grapefruits for us to taste. They were sour. We learned that acids taste sour.

Tuesday: Today we learned that there are different kinds of acids. I was interested to learn that ants make an acid called formic acid. A very long time ago, when people wanted to make formic acid, they boiled ants. People use this acid to make paper. I wonder what happens when a stinging ant bites a person.

Wednesday: Acids can also be in rain. This is acid rain. It comes from gases made by pollution. The gases mix with the water in clouds. When it rains, acids come down from the sky. Acid rain can ruin buildings and statues. This is very interesting.

Thursday: Today we had some fun. We learned how cakes rise. Cakes are made with baking powder. When baking powder mixes with water, a gas called carbon dioxide forms. This gas makes the cake rise. We made a cake in class to see how this works. We put the cake in the oven in the teacher's room, since we don't have an oven in our classroom.

Friday: Today we used pH paper to test acids to see how strong they are. We tested lemon juice, orange juice, milk, seltzer water, and rainwater. We recorded the pH of each acid. They were all different. Then we had an unknown liquid. We had to test its pH and predict what we thought it was. I predicted lemon juice, and I was right.

Figure 7.4
Science Journal

Sharing a learning log or journal with a classmate is a way for students to interact socially. Working in small groups, students can brainstorm new ideas and record them in writing. Journals and learning logs can serve as study aids when preparing for more comprehensive assessments. Most important, when you read students' journals or learning logs, you will quickly know whether or not students are on track or if they are confused.

When your students record their thoughts in a journal, you must first provide a journal *prompt*. This is a statement or a question that focuses their writing. Here are some examples of journal prompts:

▶ Review our last lesson. Do you have any unanswered questions?

▶ What are the main points of today's lesson?

▶ Now that you are familiar with this topic, is there anything else that you would like to learn?

▶ Write about how easy or difficult this lesson was for you.

▶ Think of ways in which you will use what you learned today in another way.

▶ What did you like about this lesson? Was there anything you disliked?

Observation Checklists

Observation checklists formalize your observations

You can monitor your students' progress on an ongoing basis by observing them at work. You can also have your students monitor their own performance or the performance of their peers. Table 7.2 provides an observation checklist for the elementary science class. In this instance, students are assessed on comprehension, listening to a speaker, and appreciating science work. Table 7.3 provides another format for an observation checklist. This format allows you to comment on all of the students in the class. This observation checklist is useful for monitoring progress in the development of science process skills.

Concept Maps

Concept maps add a visual dimension to written text

Concept maps are knowledge representation tools that your students can use as they construct knowledge and understanding. When listening to a lecture, working on a science project, engaging in an investigation, or planning an experiment, your students can create concept maps. These tools add a visual dimension to written text and provide a way for students to organize their thoughts. Teachers often use concept maps to organize the topics they will teach in a unit. Curriculum developers map out the curriculum with a concept map.

You should read a concept map from the top to the bottom. Concepts move from more general topics, which are placed at the top of the map, to more specific topics, which are placed below the general topics. Crosslinks are lines that connect concepts, showing how ideas in different parts of the map relate. Short phrases such as *is based on, stresses that, relates to, discusses, made of, when, in, into,* and *by* explain how ideas are connected (Novak, 1998).

As an elementary science teacher, you can use concept maps in at least two ways. First, you can use them as a developmental tool to see what your students think and how they relate one concept to another. Once the maps are finished, students can present them to you as an end product. Figure 7.5 (see page 173) shows an example of a concept map. Think about some other ways in which you can use concept maps.

Portfolios

Portfolios are purposeful collections of student work

Portfolios are purposeful collections of work gathered in a systematic way. They are assessment tools that allow students to reflect on their work. Since portfolios are produced over a long period of time, students can chart their development as their portfolios progress. A portfolio shows a student's "habitual and historical pattern of competence" (Kline, 1998a, p. 2). You should work with your students to help them decide which samples of work to include in their portfolios.

Table 7.2
Performance Task Assessment List for Comprehension, Listening, and Appreciating Science

Element	Possible Points	Self-Assessment	Teacher Assessment
Comprehension			
Can explain the main idea			
Supports the main idea with details			
Can answer questions about the topic			
Can explain science terms			
Uses diagrams to clarify explanations			
Can communicate ideas verbally			
Listening in the Science Class			
Can tell you what the speaker said			
Expresses the speaker's feelings about an issue			
Knows what is a fact and what is an opinion			
Puts ideas into categories			
Considers cause and effect			
Makes generalizations about the content of the presentation			
Applies information to other experiences			
Appreciating Science			
Shows enjoyment while participating in experiments			
Shows enjoyment when thinking scientifically			
Enjoys working with others in the science classroom			

Table 7.3
Observation Checklist for a Science Activity

Ratings:

✔+ means very frequently   **A** = States the problem

✔ means frequently   **B** = Makes a prediction

✔− means often   **C** = Formulates an experiment

no means not evident   **D** = Carries out experiment

     E = Collects data

Name of Student	A	B	C	D	E	Comments
1						
2						
3						
4						
5						
6						
7						
8						
9						
10						
11						
12						
13						
14						
15						

What are some samples of work that students can collect? To begin, the portfolio is a place to display and think about the products of performance assessments. These include journal entries, learning logs, laboratory worksheets, photos of experiments, concept maps, descriptions of key ideas, reports, drawings, poems, songs, and other samples of student work.

A portfolio is a forum for thinking and writing about one's work. When my students create their own science teaching portfolios, they write a brief reflective piece to help them think about each piece of work they include. They explain why each artifact is a part of the portfolio. The portfolio becomes a source of conversation, just as an elementary science student's portfolio is a source of conversation between student and teacher. Together you and your student discuss the student's work. The student critiques his or her own work and makes plans for improvement. The student can share the portfolio with his or her parents, and you can use it as a source of discussion during a parent-teacher conference. If you are keeping a portfolio in this course, how have you made your selections? Have you reflected on your progress to date?

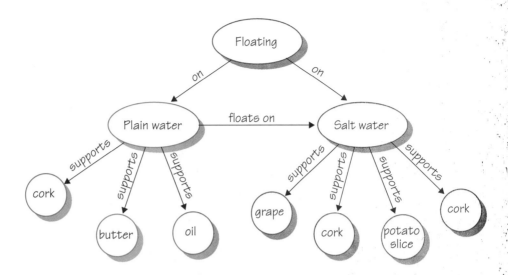

**Figure 7.5
A Concept Map**

Exploring Floating and Sinking

Your students are now ready to engage in activities and explore this science idea. We begin with activities for students in the early grades. First, they will investigate several items to determine whether the objects float or sink. Here is how you might set this up in your classroom.

When they enter the room, students find a variety of materials on their desks, including a pan of water, a grape, and a slice of potato. You give them some time to examine the objects and then begin a class discussion.

Grape and potato slice sink in plain water: Physical science

Your questions are important. At the start, you might ask, "Do you think that the potato slice will float in water?" Once you have a response, ask, "Why do you think a potato slice floats in water?" or "Why do you think a potato slice sinks in water?" Wait for an answer. Let your students perform the experiment. The potato slice sinks in plain water. Ask why it sinks. Youngsters are likely to think of variables such as the object's size, shape, or texture. Then ask, "Do you think that the grape will float? Why or why not?" Have students try the experiment. They will see that the grape also sinks in plain water. Ask, "Are a potato and a grape alike in any way?" Then ask, "If they are, in what way are they alike? Why do they both sink in plain water?"

Your students might focus on what comprises a potato and a grape. They might think about the objects' high-water content or about their size, shape, or texture. They might also tell you that the water in the container has something to do with whether something floats or sinks. Encourage them to develop ways to test their hypotheses. Give them time to think and investigate. There are other objects on their desks that they can explore.

Grape and potato slice float in salt water: Physical science

You might ask if they think there would be a change if you placed the objects in something other than water. Ask what they think would happen if you placed the grape and the potato slice in water, then added salt to the water. Let them

This youngster is studying floating and sinking.

predict what would happen, then try the experiment. They can add salt to the water a teaspoonful at a time and then stir. Both the potato slice and the grape will float in salt water. Encourage your students to think about why the potato slice and the grape float in salt water and sink in plain water. They will have many different explanations. Some may think the salt made the water heavier or thicker; therefore, the grape and the potato slice float on the thicker liquid. (This happens because sodium chloride, or table salt, dissociates, or separates, into charged particles called *ions* when placed in water. There are now more particles in the same volume of water, increasing the mass of the water. Salt water has a greater density than plain water, and it exerts more upthrust than plain water does. That makes the grape and the potato slice float on salt water.)

The following activities offer a number of ways to help your students think about density. Try them on your own; then select a few and try them with your students. Observe the children at work and see where their natural curiosity leads them. These activities may bring to mind how a person floats more easily in an ocean than in a lake. Students might think of a bottle of salad dressing made of oil and vinegar, or of bobbing for apples in a pan of water at Halloween. They might make connections between other familiar experiences and their classroom activities. As you work through these activities, you will probably come up with some of your own ideas to explore.

Activity 7.1 Hands-on Science: Floating and Sinking in Plain Water

Overview: In this activity, students in the early grades examine a variety of objects to see which ones float and which ones sink. They gain experience with floating and sinking.

Table 7.4
Will It Float or Sink in Plain Water?

Object	Prediction	Actual Result
Peanut		
Cork		
Uncooked egg		
Hard-cooked egg		
Stick of butter		
Raisins		
Peach		
Other items		

What happened? Why? Were your predictions correct? Why or why not?
What do you think happened?

Materials: A pan of water, an uncooked egg, a hard-cooked egg, a slice of butter, raisins, a cork, a slice of peach, a plastic cube, a small stone, other objects of your own choosing

Procedure: Ask students to predict and then find out which objects sink and which ones float. They then record their predictions and the actual results in a data chart.

Assessment: Students complete Table 7.4. You assess the results and gain information about what the students know. Questions are likely to arise as you assess your students' understandings of floating and sinking. Have them record their thoughts in a journal. They may not be sure of what properties make an object float. Some may think the size of the object makes it float or sink. Following this logic, they may reason that if a large piece of potato sinks, a smaller piece of potato floats. Let them test this idea. They may think that the texture of the object causes it to sink or float. Can they think of a way to test this? A child may reason that a sugar cube will not float because it soaks up water when it gets wet. Others may think that the shape of the object determines whether it sinks or floats. For example, a piece of aluminum foil shaped into a ball sinks, whereas an aluminum foil boat floats. Finally, some may think that the composition of the liquid in which they place it determines whether something sinks or floats. For example, the grape sinks when placed in plain water but floats in salt water. Your students will think about many possibilities, and it's your job to help them understand each one. To help your students construct their knowledge of floating or sinking, encourage them to test each variable, one by one. ■

Activity 7.2 Hands-on Science: Floating and Sinking in Salt Water

Overview: Students in grades 2, 3, or higher can learn more about floating and sinking by changing the liquid in which the objects are placed. It enables them to test the hypothesis that "The liquid in which we place an object determines whether or not the object floats or sinks."

Table 7.5

Will It Float or Sink in Salt Water?

Object	Prediction	Actual Result
Peanut		
Cork		
Uncooked egg		
Stick of butter		
Hard-cooked egg		
Raisins		
Peach		
Other items		

Were your predictions correct? Why or why not? What do you think happened?

Materials: A pan of salt water, grapes, raisins, a cork, an uncooked egg, a hard-cooked egg, a stick of butter, a plastic block, pieces of different kinds of wood. (Note: You can have students add salt to water on their own, or you can make a large quantity and have it ready for them. To make the salt water, heat plain water in a saucepan. As it cools, add table salt and stir. Stop when salt starts to accumulate on the bottom of the pan. Cool the water to room temperature before using it. You will need to add about two pounds of salt to a gallon of hot water to make a saturated salt water solution.)

Procedure: Ask students to predict and then find out which objects sink and which float. They then record their predictions and the actual results in a data chart. Talk about what is happening. What do students say? What do they think?

Assessment: Students complete Table 7.5 or create graphs on their own. They write about what is happening in the next journal entry. You assess the results and gain information about what your students know. A discussion takes place in which comparisons are made about objects that did not float in plain water but did float in salt water. Some students may wonder whether plain water floats on salt water. This leads to the next activity, in which they combine plain water and salt water. Combining plain water and salt water is tricky, so read the directions carefully. Your students should be able to do this on their own if they are in the upper elementary or middle school. ■

Activity 7.3 Hands-on Science: Does Plain Water Float on Salt Water?

Overview: In this activity, students in grades 2 through 6 find out if plain water floats on salt water.

Materials: A small, clear plastic or glass jar, food coloring, a cup of plain water, a cup of saturated salt water, a spoon or stirring rod

Procedure: Place a few drops of red food coloring in the plain water and a few drops of blue food coloring in the salt water. Pour the salt water into the clear jar. Slowly pour the plain water down the side of the stirring rod or the back of the spoon into the jar. If your students do this carefully, there will be two fluid layers.

Plain water floats on salt water: Physical science

Assessment: Your students will observe that the plain water floats on top of the salt water. Ask them why they think this happens, and have them write about it in their journals. Ask them if they ever thought that two liquids could separate in this way. Talk about helium balloons. Why do helium balloons float in air? (Helium gas is less dense than air, which is a mixture of different gases.) You can begin to introduce the idea of density. At the early grades, it is easier for your students to think about helium being lighter than air. It is actually less dense than air, but students in the primary and early intermediate grades have a difficult time understanding the concept of density. You can begin to build the idea by using the words *lighter than* and *heavier than*.

You can also discuss mixing oil and water to make salad dressing. Oil is less dense than water and floats on top of water. Ice is less dense than water; therefore, when a lake freezes, the layer of ice floats on top of the water. This allows us to be able to ice skate in the winter. Imagine what would happen if ice were denser than water! A lake might never thaw—think about what would happen to marine life! Once this variable is thoroughly discussed, you can have your students think about the effect of size of an object. In the next activity, students discover whether size makes an object float. ∎

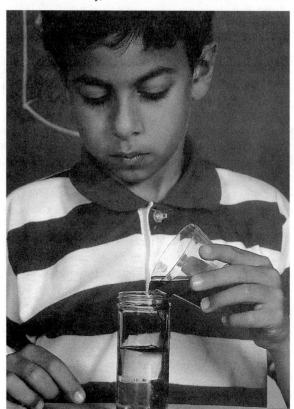

Cooking oil floats on water.

Activity 7.4 Hands-on Science: Does Size Make an Object Float?

Size is not what determines whether an object floats or sinks: Physical science

Overview: In this activity, students in grades 2 through 6 are given equal-size pieces of different solids. Some objects float and some sink, showing that the size of the object is not what determines whether it sinks or floats.

Materials: A bouillon cube, a butter cube, a grape, a glass of plain water

Procedure: Cut the butter and the grape to the size of the bouillon cube. Place each one in the plain water. The bouillon cube and the grape will sink, and the butter cube will float.

Assessment: Question your students to find out if they understand that objects of the same size may or may not float on water. (It is not the size of the object but what it's made of that makes it sink or float.) The journal and learning log are appropriate formats for expressing students' thoughts. ■

Activity 7.5 Hands-on Science: Making a Clay Boat

Overview: In this activity, students in the primary or intermediate grades are given a lump of clay. When rolled into a ball, it sinks. When shaped like a boat, it floats. (You can reshape the clay boat two or three times, but after awhile it loses its elasticity and doesn't mold well. Then you will need new clay.)

Materials: A small lump of modeling clay, a pan of water

Clay ball sinks, while clay boat floats: Physical science

Procedure: Students roll the clay into a ball, place it in the water, and watch it sink. Remove the clay from the pan of water and shape it into a boat. The boat is placed in the water, and it should float. If it doesn't float on the first try, have students reshape the boat until it floats.

Assessment: Ask students why boats float. (They float because of their unique shape. A lump of clay rolled into a ball has a high density, and the force of the water pushing up on it is not strong enough to support the clay and allow it to float. When the clay is shaped into a boat, its surface area is greater, so it displaces more water. Therefore the force of the water pushing up on it [upthrust] is greater than the force pushing down, and the boat floats.) Ask students why a submarine can both float and sink. The discussion might lead them to explore the possibility that submarines have tanks that can be filled with air or with water. When the water is pumped out of the tanks and air is allowed to enter, the submarine floats. When water is allowed to replace the air, the submarine becomes denser and sinks. Have students summarize the experience in their learning logs. ■

Activity 7.6 Hands-on Science: Stacking Liquids

Overview: In this activity, students in the intermediate grades mix three different liquids. The liquids form layers and separate, even when mixed.

Materials: A clear plastic jar with a lid, a half-cup water, a half-cup oil, a half-cup corn syrup, food coloring, three cups, a coffee stirrer or popsicle stick

Procedure: Set out three clear plastic cups. Add one-half cup of oil to the first, one-half cup of water to the second, and one-half cup of light corn syrup to the third. Add a few drops of red food coloring to the water and a few drops of blue food coloring to the corn syrup. Have students predict what will happen when the liquids are combined in the clear plastic jar. (The corn syrup will be on the bottom, the water will be in the middle, and the oil will float at the top.) Combine the liquids one by one, pouring each one carefully into the others by letting it slide down the side of the coffee stirrer or popsicle stick.

Assessment: Using an informal conversation, have students explain what happened. Why did the liquids fail to mix? Have students close the lid tightly and shake the contents. Did the liquids separate again? Why or why not? (They should explain that the objects have different densities.) ■

Activity 7.7 Hands-on Science: Making an Aluminum Foil Boat

Aluminum foil boat can hold pennies and float: Physical science

Overview: This group activity, appropriate for grades 4 through 6, is a design challenge. (You read about design challenges in Chapters 1 and 6 and will learn more in Chapter 12.) It brings together the concepts learned in the earlier activities. Students are given a 15 cm by 15 cm sheet of aluminum foil, 75 pennies, and a pan filled with water. Ask students to design a boat made of the sheet of aluminum foil that will hold as many pennies as possible without sinking. In an earlier activity, they learned that when they rolled a lump of clay into a ball, it sank to the bottom of the pan of water. When they shaped it into a boat with a wide bottom, it floated. Applying this knowledge, they will build an aluminum foil boat that holds pennies and floats. As you observe them in the design stage, ask yourself if you think they are applying what they learned in the earlier activity.

Materials: A pan filled with water, 75 pennies, 15 cm by 15 cm sheet of aluminum foil, 5 index cards per student

Procedure:

1. Form groups of four to six students. One student is chosen to be the group leader. The leader reviews the task with the group and briefly describes how the group will function. Its goal is to allow all group participants equal input. The task is to construct a boat with a 15 cm by 15 cm square of aluminum foil to hold a maximum number of pennies without sinking.

2. The leader gives each group member two index cards.

3. Each group member writes a single idea for building the boat on each index card, expressing the idea in no more than 10 words. Students write a separate idea on each card. Encourage simple pictures that accompany the descriptions. Students are not to write their names on the cards.

4. The leader collects the completed index cards, then hands each participant a new blank index card.

5. The leader shuffles the first set of cards and stacks them. Before reading the cards, the leader tells participants that they will choose two favorite ideas from the

whole stack. The leader reads the cards aloud and numbers them. He or she reads the top card and places it on the table, then reads the rest of the cards one by one and places them on the table. The leader clarifies the basic idea written on the card if necessary, but doesn't change it.

6. On the blank index card, each student records the number of the card (read by the leader) describing his or her favorite idea. If a new favorite idea comes up, participants may change their minds.

7. The leader collects the second set of index cards, then tallies the votes and determines which idea has received the most votes.

8. The group tries the winning idea, building it following the design. If the creation sinks, the boat is redesigned. If it still doesn't float, members look at the other ideas generated. Students work together to try those ideas.

9. Each group assigns a spokesperson to tell the whole class about the design and report how many pennies the boat held before sinking.

Assessment: Students explain why the aluminum foil boat floated and then sank. How an object behaves when placed in water depends both on the object's weight and on the amount of space it takes up. An object that takes up a space greater than the space occupied by an equal weight of water floats on water. The tendency of such an object to float on water is known as **buoyancy.** If the space occupied by the object is less than the space occupied by an equal weight of water, the object will sink. Students should develop an understanding that the weight of a boat and the type of material that composes the boat are important in determining its buoyancy and capacity. Not all students will be developmentally ready to understand this concept. You can have these students think about what they observed, but be patient if they don't understand the concept entirely. Sometimes a student needs to grow intellectually before she or he understands this concept fully, which usually happens at the end of middle school. You can use the observation checklist to assess students during this activity. ■

Activity 7.8 Teaching Strategy: Designing an Assessment Plan

Overview: In this activity, you will select at least one assessment tool (formal, informal, or both) and create your own lesson plan based on your exploration of floating and sinking. You can base your lesson on one of the activities you have just completed, or you can base it on one of your own experiments.

Materials: Paper and pencil, materials needed for your lesson

Procedure: Using the lesson plan format introduced in Chapter 6, create a lesson plan. Focus on the assessment part of the lesson. Use informal as well as formal assessment.

Assessment: Teach the lesson to your students. Is it a teacher-directed lesson? Is it a student-centered exploration? How do you assess student learning? If you were to try the lesson again, would you do something differently? ■

Evaluating Student Learning

Evaluation reports overall progress

In addition to using ongoing formal and informal assessments, you will evaluate overall student progress. Your students will take standardized tests, you will create your own paper-and-pencil tests for them, and you will give report card grades. This section provides information about evaluating student learning with these tools.

Norm-Referenced and Criterion-Referenced Tests

In most schools, students take a variety of tests and quizzes during the year. **Standardized tests** are administered, scored, and interpreted under test-taking conditions that are exactly the same for all students. The Metropolitan Achievement Test and the Iowa Test are examples of standardized tests. Some standardized tests are **norm-referenced,** meaning student performance is reported by comparing one student's performance to those of other students who have taken the same test and constitute a comparison or norm group. **Norms** are records of the performances by groups that have previously taken the test; test-makers use the norms to determine how the score of any individual test taker compares with the scores of other test takers.

Criterion-referenced tests measure a student's ability with respect to some content-based standard or objective (Gage & Berliner, 1998). Instead of providing information about how a student performs in relation to other students, criterion-referenced tests measure the knowledge and skills that a student has acquired. They show how well students are meeting the objectives set for them. When you write the achievement objectives in your lesson plans, you set criteria for student performance. Let's say you teach a unit on dinosaurs to your fifth-graders. You give a test at the end of the unit. You might say that in order to master the subject matter, a student must answer 85 percent of the questions correctly. Criterion-referenced evaluations enable you to determine whether your students have gained the knowledge and skills covered in your lessons, but they don't say anything about how students have performed in relation to their peers. In the past, such tests tended to encourage asking questions with right or wrong answers while discouraging open-ended questions, problems, or tasks that require some type of performance. Newer criterion-referenced tests measure performance as well, and are gaining popularity.

What Makes a Test Meaningful?

Meaningful tests are valid and reliable

Meaningful tests have *validity* and *reliability*. **Validity** is the extent to which a test measures what it's supposed to measure. Testmakers must first define *what* they will measure, then *how* to go about making the measurement. When evaluating a test, the most important criterion is validity (Committee to Develop Standards for Educational and Psychological Testing, 1985; Gage & Berliner, 1998). A test that is valid measures the knowledge and skills that it is supposed to measure. If you teach a unit on plants, a test about animals would not be a valid measure of your students' performance.

When testmakers create norm-referenced and criterion-referenced standardized tests for elementary science, validity is an important issue. Experts in the field examine the test to be certain that it measures the common curriculum in elementary science. This is not an easy task, but it helps to ensure *content validity*. There are other ways to assess validity, which we will not discuss in this text. An educational psychology or assessment text will provide that information for you.

Reliability is the degree to which the results of a test are consistent, stable, predictable, and dependable. Tests should accurately measure a student's performance. When a test is reliable, the student's score reflects his or her knowledge of the subject. If the teacher gives the test again, the student should get the same score or a very similar score. Good tests measure what they are supposed to measure and produce reliable, consistent results. To make your own tests reliable, be sure to give students several opportunities to show what they know. Ask many questions to inquire about the knowledge and skills you teach. If a test is too short and a student makes a careless error or forgets one or two things, he or she will not get a good grade. You won't know whether the student has failed to learn the material or simply made a couple of careless errors. But if you ask many questions on a topic and a student makes an error or two but answers most of the items correctly, you will have a reliable picture of that student's ability. If you don't like the idea of giving long tests, consider giving several short tests on the topic. This will allow you to increase your sampling of items and will be less tedious for you and your students.

Teacher-Made Paper-and-Pencil Tests

Teachers routinely create assessments that are valid and reliable, although they may not realize they are doing so. Here is how this is done. Each time you give an assessment, you look at the scores that students receive, and analyze them. If many high achievers do poorly or many low achievers do very well on a particular test, you investigate to find out why. Were there items that everyone answered incorrectly? Were there items that most students answered correctly? Was something wrong with a particular question or several questions on the test? If so, you do not count these items in the test score. You rewrite them and retest students.

If a test is a good indicator of student performance, it should closely match what you observe to be the general performance in the class. Students who usually perform well should perform well on the test; students who perform less well should perform in a similar manner. If a student's class performance improves, his or her test performance should improve as well. Therefore, you examine the rank ordering of student performance on a test and note unexpected results. You compare this with what you generally know about the students in the class. This is a measure of validity.

In creating a test or an assessment instrument, you usually ask students several questions on a particular topic to be confident that they understand and have mastered the concept. The greater the number of sound questions asked about a particular topic, the greater the reliability and consistency in determining whether the concept has been learned well. Longer tests with more items provide greater reliability than shorter tests. If a test is short and a student gets one or two items wrong, the grade will be quite low. If a test is longer and provides more good questions to answer, its reliability increases.

Report Card Grades

In calculating report card grades, teachers do not evaluate students based on a single test or sample of performance. Combining several trustworthy scores from several different tests will increase the reliability substantially. Teachers base grades on points accumulated from a variety of sources. Therefore, the final grade is likely to be reliable even though a single test may not be.

Report card grades include information from many samples of work

When creating a report card grade, decide what important pieces of work you will count in the grade. Then decide how much weight each element is worth. Tests, quizzes, performance tasks, journal entries, portfolios, and data from informal assessments can all be a part of the grade.

When Assessing Science, Hands-on and Minds-on Go Together

How do you know when your students understand a science concept you are teaching? How do you know when your students can thoughtfully connect prior scientific knowledge with new knowledge? For example, in the activity in which a potato slice and a grape sank in plain water, then floated in salt water, how do you know whether your students understand why this happens? Do they simply memorize what you tell them, or do they grasp the concept first and then commit the knowledge to memory? How do you know when your students understand something completely and can use the knowledge? These are key questions in teaching and learning elementary science and are the challenge of assessment.

When you design instruction and assessment for your students, you must ask this: When I teach a science concept to my students, what do I want them to learn and understand? You start off by writing goals and achievement objectives for your students to meet and you decide what you will accept as evidence of student understanding. Then you design a lesson that allows them to meet these goals and objectives. As you teach, you assess their understanding.

Assessing Misunderstanding

While it's important to assess understanding, it's just as important to assess *misunderstanding*. As you design your lessons, think about what might lead to confusion and misunderstanding. Help your students to uncover misconceptions so they will understand, not misunderstand. You should design your assessment to make your instruction more effective. It must help you judge how well your students understand what they are learning. Your assessment should address these questions:

▶ If a student is just beginning to understand a concept, what will that student say? What words will he or she use to explain the concept?

▶ If a student has an average understanding of a concept, what will that sound like? What will an average learner say and do? How will that average learner act?

▶ If a student has an advanced understanding of a concept, what will that student's explanations and actions be like?

Instead of asking for correct answers only, you must search for understanding as well as lack of understanding. You must differentiate recall of information from true understanding. This helps you find out whether your students seem to understand or truly do understand.

Seeming to understand and truly understanding are different

Seeming to understand, demonstrated by recall, and *truly understanding*, demonstrated by being able to explain, defend an idea, and use the knowledge, represent two different levels of understanding.

When a student answers a question, ask yourself what the answer means. Is the student repeating facts that were memorized? If you challenge the answer, can the student defend his or her reasoning? If you ask the student to use the knowledge in another situation, can she or he do it? Can the student explain his or her thinking?

You can also learn quite a bit from listening to the questions your students ask. All of this information enables you to find out how well you are reaching your students. It tells you if your teaching is going well or if you must try something different to get through to your students.

Writing good objectives is the start of the lesson planning process. Deciding what will serve as evidence of understanding comes next. Teaching the lesson follows. Finding out how your teaching affects your students is the next step. Some students will meet the objectives completely, and you will be 100 percent successful with them; some will meet the objectives only partially; and some won't meet them at all. Your assessment should help you determine the different levels of performance your students achieve.

Constructing Your Knowledge of Science and Science Teaching

After completing this chapter, begin to reflect on your new knowledge. You have an understanding of some of the basic concepts of instruction and assessment, which are linked to your knowledge of models of learning and principles of child development. Think about how instruction and assessment fit together. How will you use the information gained from assessments to guide your students as they grow?

When you introduce a topic, you must assess prior knowledge and uncover misconceptions. What assessment techniques will you use to accomplish this goal? As students inquire and begin to build meaning, you must continue to assess understanding. How will you do this? How will you use information gained from formal and informal assessments to provide feedback to your students? In what other ways will you use assessment information?

Key Terms

assessment (p. 159)
evaluate (p. 159)
informal assessment (p. 160)
formal assessment (p. 160)
density (p. 164)

buoyancy (p. 180)
standardized tests (p. 181)
norm-referenced tests (p. 181)
norms (p. 181)

criterion-referenced tests
 (p. 181)
validity (p. 181)
reliability (p. 182)

Reviewing Chapter 7: Questions, Extensions, Applications, and Explorations

1. What is the purpose of assessment and evaluation? What would your teaching be like if there were no assessment system in place?

2. You would like to see if your students have mastered the concept of density, so you design the following performance assessment. You give them a large, clear plastic cup; three small cups, each filled with a different liquid; a piece of a candle; a small cork; and a penny. The liquids are light corn syrup that has been colored green, milk, and red lamp oil. Have students predict what will happen when they combine all three liquids in the large cup. Then ask them to find a way to determine the densities of the candle, cork, and penny.

3. You are going to teach a lesson about light to third-graders. What informal assessments will you use to diagnose prior knowledge?

4. Your kindergartners would like to learn about the human skeletal system. In order to teach them, you must first assess their prior knowledge. How will you accomplish this?

5. What are some ways to find out if your students understand a concept?

6. You schedule a conference with the parents of your students to talk about their children's progress in elementary science. What information will you share with them?

Print Resources

Burke, K. (1993). *How to assess thoughtful outcomes.* IRI- Skylight. Palatine, Illinois.

Driver, R., Guesne, E., & Tiberghien, A. (1985). *Children's ideas in science.* Philadelphia: Open University Press.

Gage, N. L., & Berliner, D. (1998). *Educational psychology*. 6th ed. Boston: Houghton Mifflin.

Ginsburg, H. (1997). *Entering the child's mind*. Cambridge, UK: Cambridge University Press.

Ginsburg, H., Jacobs, S., & Lopez, L. (1998). *The teacher's guide to flexible interviewing in the classroom*. Boston: Allyn and Bacon.

Hibbard, K. M. (1996). *Performance-based assessment and learning*. Alexandria, VA: Association for Supervision and Curriculum Development.

Meisels, S., Jablon, D., Marsden, M., Dichtelmiller, M., & Dorfman, A. (1994). *The work sampling system*. Ann Arbor, MI: Rebus Planning Associates, Inc.

Rogovin, P. (1998). *Classroom interviews*. Portsmouth, NH: Heinemann.

Rowe, M. B. (1986). Wait time: Slowing down may be a way of speeding up. *Journal of Teacher Education, 23*, 43–49.

Shepardson, D., & Britsch, S. (1997). Children's science journals: Tools for teaching, learning, and assessing. *Science and Children, 5*(34), 13–17, 46–47.

Shymansky, J., Hedges, L., & Woodworth, G. (1990). A reassessment of the effects of inquiry-based science curricula of the 60s on student performance. *Journal of Research in Science Teaching, 27*(2), 127–144.

Tobin, K., Capie, W., & Bettencourt, A. (1988). Active teaching for higher cognitive learning in science. *International Journal of Science Education, 10*(1), 17–27.

Wiggins, G. (1992). Creating tests worth taking. *Educational Leadership, 49*(9), 26–33.

Electronic Resources

The Case for Constructivist Classrooms
http://129.7.160.115/INST5931/constructivist
Look for a summary of the *The Case for Constructivist Classrooms* by J. Brooks and M. Brooks (Alexandria, VA: Association for Supervision and Curriculum Development, 1993) at this site.

ERIC Clearinghouse on Assessment and Evaluation
http://erica.net
Look for information on several assessment topics at this site.

Student Self-assessment
http://www.potsdam.edu:80/educ/glc/eisenhower/seeds/assessments.html.
This site contains worksheets that are self-assessment tools for students.

Martha Borrowman's Alternative Assessment in Science
http://www.cs.rice.edu:80/~mborrow/Lessons/assessls.html
Look for a list of many alternative assessment sites for science education at this outstanding site.

Annenberg/Corporation for Public Broadcast Math and Science Videotape Collection (1-800-965-7373)
- The Science of Teaching Science
- Assessment in Math and Science: What's the Point?
- Will This Be on the Test? Knowing vs. Understanding
- What'd I Get? Scoring Tools
- Is This Going to Count? Embedded Assessment
- That Would Never Work Here! Seeing Assessment Reform in Action (I and II)
- When I Was in School . . . Implementing Assessment Reform

Children's Literature

Bosak, S., Bosak, D., and Puppa, B.
Science is . . .
(Firefly Books, 1992)
ISBN: 0-590-74070-9
Grades 4–6

Daniels, K.
Junior Science Experiments on File
(Facts on File, 1994)
ISBN: 0-816029-210
Grades 6 and up

Fiarotta, Noel, and Fiarotta, Phyliss
Great Experiments with H_2O
(Sterling Publishing Company, 1997)
ISBN: 0-806942-49-5
Grades 4–8

Gardner, Martin
Entertaining Science Experiments with Everyday Objects
(Dover Publications, 1981)
ISBN: 0-486242-01-3
All ages

Liem, T.
Invitations to Science Inquiry
(Science Inquiry Enterprises, 1990)
ISBN: 1-878-10621-X
All ages

Mullin, V.
Chemistry Experiments for Children
(Dover Publications, 1968)
ISBN: 0-486-22031-1
Grades 3–6

Potter, Jean
Science in Seconds with Toys: Over 100 Experiments You Can Do in Ten Minutes or Less
(John Wiley and Sons, 1998)
ISBN: 0-471179-00-0
All ages

VanCleave, Janice Pratt
Chemistry for Every Kid: 101 Easy Experiments That Really Work
(John Wiley and Sons, 1989)
ISBN: 0-471509-74-4
Grades 3–6

CHAPTER 8

Designing Performance Assessments for Inquiry-Based Science

I grew up in a large city, where my grandparents owned a bakery. I spent much of my childhood in the store, playing there in my early years and working there after school and on weekends when I grew older. I also baked cakes, and my grandfather, an expert baker, often judged my creations. He commented on each cake's appearance, taste, and texture. These were his criteria for assessing my work.

To improve the appearance of each cake, I practiced making flowers for decoration; sometimes they looked professional, but much of the time they didn't. I experimented with the ingredients to improve the taste and texture. I changed the consistency of the icing to make the cakes look better, and I used food coloring to improve the appearance of the flowers. My grandfather set standards for expected levels of performance, with criteria and indicators to guide me. In essence he designed a **rubric,** a set of guidelines that helps to evaluate a performance. The criteria told me what I had to do to create a good product. The **indicators** provided concrete examples so I knew when I had met the criteria. Rubrics explain the criteria by which work should be judged, describe the range in quality of performance, and distinguish levels of quality. My grandfather used the rubric to judge my cakes, communicating verbally rather than in writing (see Table 8.1).

Table 8.1
Rubric for Cake Baking

Level of Performance	Criteria and Indicators
3 Expert	The cake is decorated in an expert fashion. The flowers are well formed and are of at least two different colors. The frosting is applied smoothly and evenly. There are no bare spots. The layers of the cake are at least 3" high, and there are three layers. There is frosting between the layers. The layers have risen evenly. The texture is smooth and fluffy. Provides sound evidence of the use of scientific thinking to solve a problem. Interprets and explains information generated by a scientific investigation.
2 Proficient	The cake is well decorated. The flowers are well formed. The frosting is applied smoothly and evenly. There are no bare spots. The layers of the cake are at least 2" high, and there are at least two layers. There is frosting between the layers. The layers have risen evenly. The texture is smooth and fluffy. Provides some evidence of the use of scientific thinking to solve a problem. Interprets and explains information generated by a scientific investigation.
1 Apprentice	The cake is decorated. The frosting is applied smoothly and evenly. There are few bare spots. The layers of the cake are at least 2" high. There is frosting between the layers. The layers have risen evenly. The texture is thick and puddinglike. Shows some evidence of scientific thinking and problem solving.
0 Novice	The cake is decorated. The frosting is applied unevenly. There are many bare spots. The layers of the cake are at least 2" high. There is frosting between the layers, but it is not applied evenly. The texture is thick and puddinglike. Shows little evidence of scientific thinking and problem solving.

As I grew older, my grandfather revised the rubric and raised his expectations; I knew my level of performance would have to rise to meet the new standards. He wrote developmental standards for me as I grew; the criteria for assessment stayed the same, but the expectations and the standards were progressively higher. From the time I started baking, I progressed from novice, to apprentice, to proficient, and finally to expert. I raised my level of performance, and my score on the rubric increased. I once produced a cake judged as a model of excellence—an *exemplar*, or best performance. That is when I earned the "expert" rating (expert for a sixth-grader, that is).

My uncle was a professional cake baker, recognized as one of the best in the city at the time, and the standards he had to meet were much higher than those set for me. The criteria—appearance, taste, and texture—were the same, but the work he produced was truly exemplary. In essence, at the time he set the standard for the

Exemplars are models of excellence

industry. The cakes he produced were exemplars, or models of excellence, based on the industry standard. On the rubric that describes the absolute standard for cake baking, my uncle's work would receive the highest score possible. It would serve as a sample of work that met the highest standard.

Absolute standards provide models of excellence. They are exemplars that show what excellent work and best performance look like. They anchor the rubric to the highest standard. Developmental standards, which are the kind you will set for your students, deal with developmental realities. As a child, I could not produce a cake that was of the quality of my uncle's cakes. While the criteria were the same for both of us (appearance, taste, and texture), the standards set for my cakes varied with my age.

Chapter 1 introduced you to the idea of assessment. In Chapter 6 you learned to write lesson plans with clear achievement objectives, and in Chapter 7 you learned formal and informal means of assessing student work. This chapter extends what you learned in Chapters 1, 6 and 7. You will read more about performance assessment, and you will use scoring rubrics to help you assess student performance. As you read this chapter, think about the answers to these questions:

1. **What is performance assessment?**
2. **How do rubrics help teachers assess and improve student performance?**
3. **How do rubrics help students meet standards?**
4. **What is an authentic performance task? What are the parts of a performance task?**
5. **How do I create rubrics for my students?**
6. **How do I introduce basic concepts of earth and space science?**

The Basics of Performance Assessment

Performance assessments require multiple sources of information

Performance assessments are meant to assess what students know and can do over time. Since this is a continuous process, you can monitor a student's progress over many years instead of just a few times a year, as on a traditional report card. Performance assessments require multiple sources of information and many observations of a particular behavior before you can draw a conclusion about what a child can do. By tapping into this rich source of information about a child's performance, you can document how that child changes over time.

The information gleaned from the child's performance in the school setting provides feedback, which is used to enhance the child's achievement. When engaging in performance assessments, students take what they learn and use that knowledge to solve problems. This is called using *generative knowledge*. In the generative model of learning, learners generate meaning for themselves (Mayer & Wittrock, 1996; Wittrock, 1989, 1991). Instead of viewing learning as a passive process, they view learning as an active process. With this model, you help your students generate relationships between what they are currently learning and their existing knowledge and experience. It is important for learners to do the work on their own; you cannot transmit this knowledge to them or build relationships for them, but you can provide scaffolding (Gage & Berliner, 1998; Wittrock, 1978).

Performance assessments are process oriented

Performance assessments are process oriented, meaning they require students to create a product or engage in a performance. Students are involved in the assessment process: in performing tasks, sometimes developing assessments with you, and often in assessing their own work. Some performance assessments are *authentic assessments,* meaning students solve problems and produce products that involve real-life situations. They solve developmentally appropriate problems using scientific thinking, the same type of thinking scientists use. Their products may include keeping laboratory notebooks and creating web pages, newsletters, newscasts, scientific articles, projects, and portfolios (Gooding, 1994).

Not all performance assessments are authentic assessments

Not all performance assessments are authentic assessments; that is, not all involve real-life situations. Teachers use the term *alternative assessment* to encompass both performance assessment and authentic performance assessment.

Performance assessments can help students develop

1. Understandings—sophisticated and deep understandings of key ideas and theories

2. Technical competence—knowledge of the skills and facts connected to the subject matter

3. Performance skills—mastery of performance skills, which include planning, researching, collaborating with others, and making a presentation

4. Sound habits of mind—perseverance, openness to new ideas, good judgment, and attention to detail (Kline, 1998b; Wiggins, 1998).

When you design performance assessments, you begin with certain goals in mind. Engaging in performance assessments helps students to achieve those goals.

A Performance Assessment Model for Elementary and Middle School Science

A performance assessment consists of a performance task, a response format, and a scoring system.

Performance assessments consist of three parts: the performance task, the response format, and the scoring system (Shavelson and Brown, 1996). The performance task often invites students to solve a realistic science-related problem or conduct a science investigation when given a set of materials. It might ask them to debug a science experiment that hasn't gone well. While investigating and solving the problem, students can learn a great deal. They often find more than one way to solve the problem as they engage in scientific inquiry, using the methods and procedures that scientists use. Authentic performance tasks involve students in challenges that are as similar as possible to those that professionals and other adults encounter in science. Since assessment is built into the activity, students get feedback about their work. That feedback helps them learn more. It also gives you information about how your students learn. This knowledge helps you improve instruction.

An Authentic Performance Task

This section includes a performance task that was developed for sixth-graders. Sixth-grade students often spend a part of the year studying objects in the sky. The *National Science Education Standards* say that students should learn about

▶ Systems, order, and organization

▶ Evidence, models, and explanation

▶ Change, constancy, and measurement

(National Research Council, 1996, p. 105)

Objects have observable properties of size that can be measured: Earth and space science

When students study the sun and the planets, they gain experience with these science ideas. They learn about properties of objects and materials, specifically that "objects have observable properties of size, which can be measured." They study the positions and motions of objects, focusing on the "position of planets and the sun in the real and model solar system." Recall that students should develop the "abilities necessary to do scientific inquiry" and "develop understanding about scientific inquiry." Learning about the objects in the sky helps them to meet these standards as well (National Research Council, 1996, p. 106).

The performance task that follows gives students experience with the sun and the earth. When designing a performance task, you must always decide on the criteria you want your students to meet. The **criteria** match the objectives in your

Learning about the sun and the earth.

lesson plan, which are likely to reflect state and national standards. In this case, students engage in problem solving. They receive feedback about the methods they use to solve the problem, the quality of their work, and the overall impact of their work. Here is the task:

Setting criteria for performance

Earth has four seasons: winter, summer, spring, and fall. The seasons happen because the earth gets varying amounts of sunlight as it orbits the sun. Create a presentation to explain to your classmates why we have seasons. Your presentation should be informative, persuasive, well organized, and thorough.

Students work in groups of four to solve the problem as they complete the task. They know that to be successful, the performance must be informative, persuasive, well organized, and thorough. These are the criteria by which the work will be judged.

Here is how one group carries out the task:

The Earth-Sun System

The earth tilts on its axis at 23.5 degrees: Earth and space science

The students discuss the problem and decide to make a **model** of the earth-sun system. Using a globe (the earth) and a flashlight (the sun), the students make a model of the earth as it orbits the sun. They know that the earth tilts on its axis at 23.5 degrees. If you hold your hand out in front of you and spread your fingers apart as far as they will go, the angle between the third and fourth fingers (counting the thumb as number one) is approximately 23.5 degrees. Placing the sun in the center with the earth orbiting it, they see that the sunlight (from the flashlight) is unevenly distributed, because the earth tilts on its axis. One hemisphere receives more concentrated sunlight than the other. This could account for summer and winter. Now students experiment with the model and test it.

Testing a scientific model to see if it explains why we have winter and summer: Science process

From prior experience, they know that when it's winter in the Northern Hemisphere, it's summer in the Southern Hemisphere. With their model, as the earth orbits the sun, the same portion of the earth always receives a greater amount of concentrated sunlight. This doesn't account for the seasons, however. Their model represents a situation in which it is always summer in the Northern Hemisphere. Their model doesn't work. They analyze the model and find that they have misrepresented the earth's axis; they didn't keep it at 23.5 degrees all the time.

Day and night are of equal length when there is an equinox: Earth and space science

They try another model. This time the earth remains tilted at the correct angle as it orbits the sun. They experiment with the model. Does it explain that during summer, the Northern Hemisphere receives the most concentrated sunshine and the sun is high in the sky? Yes, it does. They test the model again. When it's winter in the Southern Hemisphere, is it summer in the Northern Hemisphere? Yes. Three months later, it's fall in the Northern Hemisphere and spring in the Southern Hemisphere. On September 23, day and night are equal everywhere in the world, and there is an equinox. Three months later, it's winter in the Northern Hemisphere. The sun hits the Northern Hemisphere at more of an angle, and the sunshine is less concentrated. When it's winter in the Northern Hemisphere, it's summer in the Southern Hemisphere. Three months later, it's spring in the Northern Hemisphere and fall in the Southern Hemisphere. On March 21, day and night are equal everywhere in the world, and there is another equinox.

This model works well. The students can't find any cases in which it doesn't explain the seasons.

Now their job is to make a presentation to explain the model to their classmates. As they plan the presentation, they decide to explain how they arrived at this model. They will show the model they tried first, and explain why it didn't work. Then they will demonstrate the model that does work. They decide that their classmates will better understand the model if they have experience with it themselves. As part of their presentation, the students will ask people to come up to the front of the room and try their model. Then they draw a poster to show the position of the earth and the sun during the four seasons, which will be a part of the presentation (see Figure 8.1). Knowing that the presentation must be informative, persuasive, well organized, and thorough guides them in their task. They believe they are prepared for the presentation. What do you think?

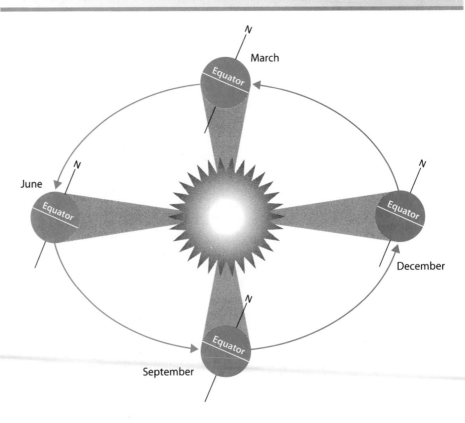

Figure 8.1
Why We Have Seasons

The Response Format and the Scoring System

A response format is a communication tool

To give students a way to communicate their findings, explain their thinking, or justify their results, each performance task is accompanied by a response format. Tables, charts, graphs, laboratory notebooks, journals, and written and oral reports are common response formats. In the example you just read, the presentation is the response format.

A scoring system provides consistency in assessing student work

The scoring system is essential to performance assessment; if well constructed, it provides a meaningful and consistent way to assess student work. A scoring system provides the feedback that serves as a guide to help students improve. When designing a scoring system, teachers must think carefully about the performance so that they communicate to students the purpose of the performance. The criteria in the scoring system should be genuine criteria and central features that describe the goals and objectives of the performance, not necessarily the behaviors that teachers easily observe. The scoring system should describe what matters in the performance. When selecting criteria for assessment, teachers should ask these five questions (Kline, 1998b; Wiggins, 1998):

STANDARDS

What is the intended *impact* of this performance on the audience? Should the successful performance be effective, novel, persuasive, informative, or engaging? Should it solve a problem? Should it create knowledge? (impact)

What is the *quality of work* produced by this student? Is it organized, well crafted, and sound? Is it clear, concise, and polished? (work quality)

What is the *quality of the methods* used to create this performance? Was the student efficient, thoughtful, and thorough? Were students collaborative and cooperative? Is the performance well researched and well reasoned? (methods)

Is the *content correct?* Is it accurate and focused? (valid content)

What is the *level of knowledge* of this student? Does it show sophistication and expertise? (knowledge)

Share performance criteria with students before they begin to work

Not every performance must meet each and every one of these criteria. However, teachers should select two, three, or even four relevant criteria on which to judge the performance. Students can decide on the criteria with their teachers. Unless students know the criteria for performance before they begin, they will not be able to perform as expected. In the performance task explaining the seasons, the presentation was expected to be informative (impact), persuasive (impact), well organized (work quality), thorough (method), and correct (valid content). The criteria on which the work would be judged were clearly communicated at the outset.

Once students perform a task, you need a way to differentiate one student's performance from another. You can describe levels of performance using a rubric.

Designing Scoring Rubrics

Rubrics qualitatively differentiate levels of performance

Rubrics provide a scoring system that is particularly useful during assessment. They give teachers a way to classify students' work into achievement levels, or levels of performance. Instead of using words such as *outstanding, excellent, fair, average, poor, better than* or *worse than*, descriptors of performance explain qualitatively how one level of performance differs from another. Accompanying the qualitative description is a scale, which assigns the points a student will gain for his or her performance. Scales vary along a continuum of quality, with numbers ranging from 0 and 1 at the low end, to 2, 3, and 4 at the mid range, and 5 or 6 at the high end. The higher the score, the better the performance. Rubrics allow teachers to describe concretely what students are capable of doing at each level (see Table 8.2). If work is very well done, the rubric describes in detail just what this means. The criteria stay the same at each level, but the descriptors change.

Table 8.2
Describing Levels of Performance

Level of Performance	Work Quality (Is the presentation organized, well designed and sound?)	Method (Does the work show that the student is thoughtful and thorough?)	Valid Content (Is the work correct and focused?)
Expert	The presentation is clear and concise. The content is effectively communicated to others, and they are engaged.	The investigation is well carried out and well researched. There is evidence of a great deal of thought on the part of the student	The student shows excellent evidence that the work is completely correct and very well focused.
Proficient	The presentation is well organized and interesting. The content is communicated to others.	The student does a good job of carrying out and conducting the investigation. There is evidence of a good deal of thought on the part of the student	The student shows good evidence that the work is correct and well focused.
Apprentice	The presentation is acceptable. The student communicates the content to others with moderate success.	The student carries out the investigation in an acceptable manner. There is some evidence of thought on the part of the student	Most of the work is correct and focused most of the time.
Novice	The presentation is minimally acceptable. The content is not well communicated.	The student carries out the investigation in a minimally acceptable manner. There is little evidence of thought on the part of the student.	Some of the work is correct, and some is not. It is not well focused.

When you rate the student presentation in the "four seasons" performance task, look at the experiments students performed to make decisions about what causes the seasons. This is part of the assessment. Judge their ability to analyze and collect data. A student who scores at the expert level on ability to collect and analyze data doesn't collect more data than a student with a lower score; rather, that student is able to collect and record the data in a way that properly reflects the outcome. A student with a lower rating may not collect or record the data properly, may be unable to do so without assistance from the teacher, or may collect the data but record it in a haphazard fashion. The levels of performance in the rubric reflect quality of performance, not quantity. They permit you to decide on specific criteria for classifying the quality of student work. They also allow you to weigh each criterion in relation to others. If a particular criterion (for example, being persuasive, or thorough, or thoughtful, or accurate) is more important to the overall performance than another, you can reflect that fact in the rubric by weighting it more heavily (Wiggins, 1998).

Activity 8.1 Onlne: Ask Dr. Rubric

Overview: In this activity, you will visit a web site that focuses on alternative assessment techniques.

Procedure: Log onto http://www.classnj.com. Explore the site. If you have questions about rubrics, you can "Ask Dr. Rubric." You will also find many excellent articles on alternative assessment at this site.

Assessment: What did you find most useful about the site?   ▪

Using Rubrics to Help Students Meet Standards

Rubrics allow you to help students meet standards and curriculum aims and goals. You can look at the science standards, decide on a particular standard to address, and develop an instructional activity or performance task that helps the student meet the standard or standards (see Figure 8.2 on page 198). Rubrics give you a way to connect aims, goals, and objectives in the curriculum to specific instructional activities and performance tasks. When you share rubrics with students—or, better yet, develop them together—students know just what is expected of them and understand what the activity is all about.

Tools for Developing a Rubric

You need at least one of the following to construct a rubric: a standards document, a school or district curriculum, or a specific lesson plan. You select the criteria for assessment (impact, work quality, method, content validity, or knowledge). Suppose that students are performing an investigation and presenting their results to their peers in an oral presentation. Three relevant criteria for judging how a student performs are work quality (Is the performance organized, well designed, and sound?), method (Does the work show that the student is thoughtful and thorough?), and content validity (Is the work correct and focused?

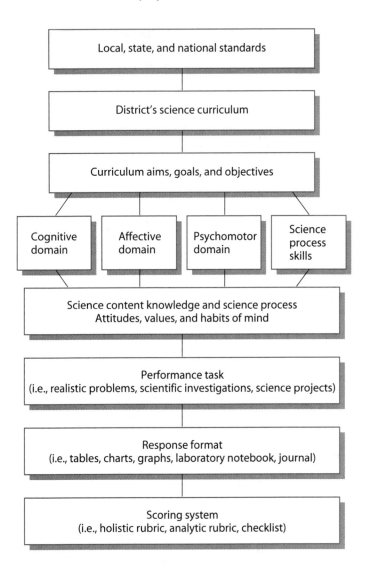

**Figure 8.2
Standards,
Curriculum,
Instruction, and
Performance-Based
Assessment**

*Rubrics connect
student performance
to standards*

Were the experiments well designed and correctly done?). You define what performance looks like at four levels: novice, apprentice, proficient, and expert.

Using a rubric gives you a way to answer the question "What do I know about how this student performs in relation to the standards?" It allows you to look at the curriculum document and ask, "Which aims, goals, and objectives specified in the curriculum are covered in this lesson or activity?" Rubrics also inform you about what students know and understand and about how they think.

Creating a Rubric

As you have seen, creating a rubric means selecting criteria for assessment, then creating a performance task and a response format. Here are a teacher's objectives for a fifth-grade performance task that assesses the chemistry activities presented in Chapter 6:

▶ Students will complete the task by formulating a solution to the problem.

▶ Students will use tools to gather scientific data.

▶ After completing this task, students will learn about different physical properties of the substances.

▶ After completing this task, students will show evidence of using scientific thinking to solve a problem.

▶ Students will use a journal to record responses.

These are the criteria for assessment:

▶ Ability to complete the task (method, work quality)

▶ Provide evidence that shows there is understanding of some of the physical properties of the substances (knowledge)

▶ Use tools to gather scientific data (method)

▶ Provide evidence of the use of scientific thinking to solve a problem (method, work quality)

▶ Interpret and explain information generated by a scientific investigation (work quality, valid content, knowledge)

▶ Write a clear, informative journal entry (impact, work quality)

Here is the task:

On the table before you is a cup containing salt, sand, and iron filings. Your task is to separate the three substances so that each is in its own cup. In your science journal, write about how you solve this problem. Your entry should be clear, thoughtful, and reflect the accuracy of your work.

Holistic rubrics evaluate performance as a whole

You could write two different types of rubrics for this task. One looks at the performance as a whole. This is called a **holistic rubric** (see Table 8.3). If you want to provide a student with an overall picture of his or her performance, you would use a holistic rubric. The second examines the component parts of the performance. This is called an **analytic rubric** (see Table 8.4). If you want to identify a particular aspect (or aspects) of performance and provide feedback on just that aspect, you would use an analytic rubric.

Analytic rubrics identify a particular aspect of behavior

Here is how one student performed the task:

observed the three substances in the cup. I know that iron filings will be attracted to a magnet. Grains of sand are small enough to be filtered by a strainer, a piece of filter paper, or even a paper towel. Salt dissolves in water. When the water evaporates, the salt will be left behind.

Being mindful of safety: Safety

I began by putting on my safety goggles. I tipped the cup on its side, not so much as to have the substances pour out, but just enough to spread them out. Using a magnet, I separated the iron filings from the salt and sand. I had

Using scientific thinking to perform a task: Science process

another cup handy and I guided the iron filings into that cup. The salt and sand remained in the original cup. I added water. The salt disappeared. It dissolved in the water. I took a piece of paper towel and stretched the paper towel over the top of a glass with a wide rim. I held it in place with a rubber band. Then I poured the salt water and sand over the paper towel. The sand stayed on top of the paper towel. The salt water dripped into the glass. I let the paper towel dry overnight and removed the sand. When the water evaporated, the salt was left behind.

Activity 8.2 Teaching Strategy: Using Rubrics to Score Student Work

Overview: In this activity, you will practice scoring student work with the help of an analytic rubric and a holistic rubric.

Materials: Scoring rubrics (Tables 8.3 and 8.4)

Procedure: Decide on a score for the response that you read on pages 199–200. If you can, have your students perform the task. Score their work and refine the rubric.

Assessment: Compare your results with those of your classmates. If you did not have a rubric to help you judge the work, how might you assess the student's response? If two teachers judged the same student work without using a rubric, how might their assessments differ? What are some benefits of using a rubric to judge student work? When would you use the analytic rubric? When would you use the holistic rubric? ■

Table 8.3
Holistic Rubric for the Separating-Solids Performance Task

Expert: Score = 4

The student performs the task in an exemplary manner; provides evidence that there is solid understanding of the different physical properties of solids and liquids; provides concrete evidence of the use of scientific thinking to solve a problem; uses tools appropriately to gather scientific data; communicates very clearly.

Proficient: Score = 3

The student performs the task; provides some evidence that there is understanding of the different physical properties of solids and liquids; provides some evidence of the use of scientific thinking to solve a problem; uses tools appropriately to gather scientific data; communicates clearly.

Competent: Score = 2

The student performs the task; provides some evidence that there is understanding of the different physical properties of solids and liquids; may provide some evidence of the use of scientific thinking to solve a problem; uses tools to gather scientific data; communicates well.

Novice: Score = 1

The student performs the task; provides little evidence that there is understanding of the different physical properties of solids and liquids; provides little evidence of the use of scientific thinking to solve a problem; may use tools to gather scientific data; does not communicate well.

Table 8.4
Analytic Rubric for the Separating-Solids Performance Task

Criteria (Component parts of performance)	Your Rating and Comments
Explains how to perform the task	
Provides evidence that there is solid understanding of the different physical properties of solids and liquids	
Provides concrete evidence of the use of scientific thinking to solve a problem	
Uses tools to gather scientific data	
Communicates clearly	

✔+   means expert-level performance
✔   means proficient-level performance
✔–   means novice-level performance
no   means performance of the task not evident

More Formats for Assessing Student Performance

In this section, you will use a learning log, use a journal, observe a group discussion, and use technology to create a project as you teach about earth and space science. In each activity, you will assess student performance in a different way.

Assessing a Student's Moon Journal

The *National Science Education Standards* tell us that students should know that the "sun, moon, stars, clouds, birds, and airplanes all have properties, locations, and movements that can be observed and described" (National Research Council, 1996, p. 134). "Objects in the sky have patterns of movement. . . . The observable shape of the moon changes from day to day in a cycle that lasts about a month" (p. 134).

Assume your curriculum requires you to cover this standard with your fourth-graders. As you write your lesson plans, you think about which assessment tool would be the best to select. You think about having your students keep moon journals. Elementary school students can use journals to thoughtfully express their ideas. When you read their journals and respond to them, you begin an important conversation with your students. You develop the following performance task as the basis for your lesson:

This young girl is studying the moon through a telescope.

The moon is earth's natural satellite: Earth and space science

Our moon is earth's natural satellite. Each month it goes around the earth once. If you've ever watched the moon, you've probably noticed that each day a different part of the moon is lit. It changes its appearance regularly.

For the next month, I would like you to keep a moon journal. Here are some things to think about: At what time of day does the moon rise? Does it rise at the same time each day? Where in the sky does it rise? Does it rise in the same place or in a different place? What does it look like each day? Does the moon always show its same face to the earth? What happens when it's cloudy or rainy? Can you still see the moon?

Since your class has several academically gifted students, you create this additional task for them:

Creating a task for students who are academically gifted

Work with your partner to make a model of the moon going around the earth. You can use a flashlight as the sun. I will give you a big ball that looks like the earth and a smaller ball that looks like the moon. How will you know that your model is correct? Once you are satisfied that you have a model that works, you can present it to the class.

As you learned in Chapter 7, if you use journals to assess student performance, performance criteria and indicators are essential. They can include quality of descriptive words, number of entries, length of response, clear use of concrete images, quality of dialogue, quality of connections to other subjects, thoughtfulness, originality, and creativity (Burke, 1993, p. 89).

Activity 8.3 Teaching Strategy: Creating a Rubric for Scoring the Moon Journal

Overview: In this activity, you will create a rubric to score the page from the moon journal shown in Fig. 8.3.

Materials: Samples of student work

Procedure: Write the objectives for your lesson. Then decide on the criteria (impact, work quality, methods, valid content, or knowledge) and indicators for performance (listed above, or you can add your own). Establish levels of performance by examining all of the student work samples. Create an analytic rubric and/or a holistic rubric.

Assessment: Use your rubrics to rate the journal responses. Are you satisfied with the result? ■

Figure 8.3
A Page from a Moon Journal

Assessing a Learning Log: Following the Sun

Making a simple sundial: Earth and space science

The next performance task also helps your students meet the standard on earth and space science. They learn more about the sun by studying shadows. They will make a simple sundial and record what happens to a shadow as they trace its path throughout the school day. In preparation for the activity, have your students cut a circle (the base of the sundial) out of a piece of light-colored construction paper (see Figure 8.4). Label the directions: north, south, east, and west. They will also need a lump of clay and a drinking straw. The lump of clay acts as a weight and helps the circle stay on the ground. It also holds the straw in place.

Using a compass to find north, south, east, and west: Earth and space science

Start the activity on a sunny day. Remind your students never to look directly at the sun. At 9:00 A.M., have them go outside. You will need a compass to help them place the circle on the ground so that the directions line up properly. Once the directions are set, place the lump of clay in the center of the circle, then place the drinking straw into the clay so that it stands vertically. Students will need a marker and a ruler to draw the straw's shadow on the circle. Leave the circle on the ground throughout the school day. Unless it's a windy day, the lump of clay will keep the circles from moving. Every hour, go outside and mark the position of the shadow. Although you might think this is too much movement in and out of the classroom for one day, you will be surprised at how excited your students will be about seeing the shadow change. Here are the questions for the learning log:

Before beginning this activity, answer these questions in your science learning log:

Shadows change throughout the day: Earth and space science

What do you know about shadows? What causes a shadow? Do shadows change from morning to night? If you think they change, how do they change?

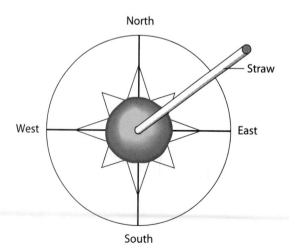

Figure 8.4
Tracing the Path of the Sun

After completing the activity, answer these questions in your learning log:

What do you know about shadows? What causes a shadow? Where is the straw's shadow in the morning? Where is it at noon? Where is it at 3:00 P.M.? How do shadows change from morning to night? Why do they change? Can you think of a practical way to use shadows?

Activity 8.4 Teaching Strategy: Students Assess Their Learning Logs

Overview: In this activity, you will create a student self-assessment for a science learning log.

Procedure: With your students, brainstorm questions to help them assess their own learning logs. They should think about how they answered the questions you posed before doing the activity and after completing and analyzing it. Have them analyze their own thinking. What did they learn about shadows? Does writing in a learning log make them feel more confident in their ability to express this science idea? Does having the learning log available help them to study and review the material? Does it help them to monitor their own progress in science? These are all possible items for the assessment instrument.

Assessment: What is the advantage of having your students assess their own work? ■

Activity 8.5 Online: The Noonday Shadow Project

Eratosthenes measured earth's north-south circumference by measuring shadows at different places on earth: Earth and space science

Overview: Over 2,000 years ago, Eratosthenes accurately measured the earth's north-south circumference by measuring shadows at different locations on the earth. The web site you will visit invites you to join other schools around the world in recreating his experiment. At about the same time of day, you will measure the length of a shadow cast by a meter stick, share this data electronically, and use scale drawings and a spreadsheet to analyze the data. This is a wonderful opportunity to see how mathematics and science work together to explain natural phenomena.

Procedure: Log onto http://k12science.stevens-tech.edu/noonday/noon.html. Explore the site and learn about the project. The explanation and directions are excellent.

Assessment: Did your visit to the site expand your understanding of how mathematics and science work together? ■

Activity 8.6 Online: Viewing Sundial Images

Telling time with a sundial: Earth and space science

Overview: In this activity, you will visit a web site at the University of Wisconsin at River Falls, where you will see a unique sundial.

Procedure: Log onto http://bugs-bunny.anetsrvcs.uwrf.edu/sundial/images.html. Read the instructions, and tell time with this unique sundial.

Assessment: If you have access to the Internet in your elementary school, have your students view the sundial images and the unique shadows. Have them compare the two sets of shadows (the ones they recorded in their activity and the ones from the web site). How are they the same? How do they differ? ■

Assessing a Group Discussion: Making a Solar System Model

Analyzing data and planning an activity in a group discussion

Stimulating discussions happen often in classrooms. From time to time, you may want to assess group discussions. In this section, your students will engage in a discussion in which they analyze data and plan an activity. Then they will create their own self-assessment instrument. Here is the task that stimulates the discussion.

The distances between planets in the solar system are so great that they are almost unimaginable to most of us. The following activity can help your students gain some idea of how far apart the planets are. You present them with a scaled-down version of the distances between the sun and each planet in our solar system. As a group, students plan a tour of the planets. It's their job to determine what form the tour will take.

A data table that contains scaled-down distances between planets: Earth and space science

Break your students into groups of four, and present them with the data set shown in Table 8.5. Have them decide how they will carry out the tour of the solar system. They will need a large space, so the activity may have to take place outside or in the gym. When I presented this data table to my students, one group planned a walking tour of the planets. They put markers on the ground each time they reached a planet. One unit equaled one step. Another group used a roll of toilet tissue, with each sheet being equal to 15 million miles. They marked the planets as they unrolled the paper. For less than a dollar, they had a wonderful model of the distance between planets.

Listen to your students as they discuss the data table and make plans for the activity. Then have them create their own way to assess the quality of the group discussion.

These students are marking out distances between planets to create a scale model of the solar system.

Activity 8.7 Teaching Strategy: Assessing a Group Discussion

Creating a checklist to assess a group discussion

Overview: You will have your students take part in a group discussion, then create an instrument to assess one another's contributions.

Materials: Paper and pencil or computer and word processing program

Procedure: Have students decide what criteria they will use to make their assessment instrument. A checklist is an easy instrument to develop. They might decide to rate each person's contributions to the discussion, show of respect for others, and willingness to share ideas and to modify a point of view when presented with new ideas. They might also assess how well group members got along, how interested and enthusiastic they were, and their willingness to question and challenge the ideas of other group members.

Assessment: What criteria did your students select for their instrument? What is the value of having students create an assessment instrument as opposed to you creating it for them? ■

Using Technology as Authentic Assessment

A data table that contains scaled-down diameters of planets: Earth and space science

The next task requires that your students create a product. They can use technology to present their work. They are limited only by what's available to them.

Not only are the distances between planets hard to imagine, but the sizes of the planets are equally difficult to comprehend. You can help your students

Table 8.5
Distance Between the Sun and the Planets in Our Solar System

Planet	How far is it from the sun? (This is the real measurement in miles)	Scale down the distance from the sun. (Divide by 15 million miles; round to nearest million miles)	How many units from the sun is the planet? (One unit is 1 million miles)
The sun (a star)	0	——	None. You're at the sun
Mercury	36 million	15 million	2
Venus	67 million	15 million	4
Earth	93 million	15 million	6
Mars	142 million	15 million	8
Jupiter	483 million	15 million	26
Saturn	885 million	15 million	50
Uranus	1.8 billion	15 million	100
Neptune	2.8 billion	15 million	156
Pluto	3.7 billion	15 million	206

Using technology as a form of assessment.

Using technology to assess understanding of science concepts

conceptualize the scale of the planets by presenting them with the data shown in Table 8.6 (see page 209). This data table provides the actual diameters of the sun and planets, plus a calculation for a scaled-down version. Now your students can create another model of the solar system, this time with the planets in the correct proportions with respect to one another.

Students can also use technology to create products that allow you to assess their understanding of the concept. Using a program such as KidPix, they can draw the planets. You will be able to look at the drawings and see if the proportions are right. Students can create a solar system model out of clay or different-size balls, take a photo of it, and then scan the photo into a presentation software package such as PowerPoint. My students carried out this activity by blowing up balloons of different colors, each one representing a planet of the proper diameter. They photographed each balloon and created a PowerPoint slide for each planet. When they put all of the balloons together to make the model of the whole solar system, they photographed it and scanned the photo into PowerPoint.

In addition to presentation software, your students can use hypermedia authoring tools such as HyperStudio and HyperCard. These programs allow them to combine words, pictures, sound, and videos. You will learn more about such products in Chapter 11.

You should now have a good idea of the many assessment techniques that are available to you and how to use them. As you continue to plan lessons, you will use these techniques so that you become comfortable with them.

Table 8.6
Diameters of the Sun and the Planets in Our Solar System

Planet	Actual Diameter (in kilometers, not miles)	Size in Relation to Earth's Diameter
Sun	1,392,000	109
Mercury	4,878	0.4
Venus	12,104	0.95
Earth	12,756	1
Mars	6,794	0.5
Jupiter	142,796	11
Saturn	120,000	9
Uranus	50,800	4
Neptune	50,450	4
Pluto	3,400	0.27

Questions to Ask When Creating an Assessment

When creating an assessment, there are some things you should consider because you can make the experience more beneficial to your students. Here is a list of questions for you to think about (adapted from Akers, 1984, and Raizen et al., 1989):

1. Does the problem require students to think? Is there a situation to analyze? Is the problem adequately challenging?

2. Is the problem simple to answer, or does it require more than one step? If it requires only one step, can I think of a way to add another step? Think of the button classification example that opened Chapter 7. Students first classified buttons by one attribute. The teachers then asked them to classify the buttons by more than one attribute, thus adding a step. That extra step made students think more deeply.

3. Do all of the questions have just one correct answer, or do some questions have more than one? It's a good idea to expose your students to questions that have more than one correct answer. Many real-life problems can be solved in more than one way.

4. Have I included problems in which students can use the data they collect? Do students have an opportunity to create their own problems? Recall the pumpkin activity that opened Chapter 3. Students were engaged in inquiry and developed their own problems to solve. They collected new data, analyzed it, and created new problems. That experience was very meaningful to them.

5. Have I encouraged students to use more than one approach to solve a problem? Think back on Lea Steinman's research on taste, which was described in Chapter 4. When faced with a problem, she used more than one approach to reach a solution.

6. Have I given students an opportunity to estimate answers and check results? Recall the measurement activities in Chapter 3. Each one required students to first estimate, then check results. That chapter provides an activity using popcorn that requires an estimation and a check of results.

7. Is the science content in the problem correct? Is the science content in the student's answer correct? Accuracy is important.

8. Have I assessed science content and science process? Do I assess students during hands-on activities, or are all of my assessments done with paper and pencil? It's important to do both.

9. Do I give students opportunities to engage in activities that can be assessed over a long period of time, or do I assess only short-term work? It's a good idea to do both.

10. Do I give problems that purposely contain errors and ask students to find the errors? Do I sometimes ask students to debug an experiment or a problem? These are interesting activities for children.

11. Do I give students opportunities to create their own problems or designs? If I'm teaching about animal adaptations, for example, I teach my students how animals adapt to the environment. Would I then describe a unique habitat and have students design an imaginary animal that could live there so that they apply what they know about animal adaptations?

These are some things to consider when creating your own assessments. Keep them in mind as you visit classrooms and observe assessments given by experienced teachers. Assessments can be a valuable tool for teaching and learning when designed properly. They can also be an enjoyable and meaningful experience for students.

Diagnostic, Formative, and Summative Assessment

Reviewing diagnostic, formative, and summative assessment

We will now review some of the essential elements of assessment so that you have a frame of reference for your knowledge about assessment. Elementary science teachers employ *diagnostic*, *formative*, and *summative* assessments to help them teach.

You use **diagnostic assessment** at the start of a unit or lesson to inform decisions about instruction. This includes making decisions about pacing of lessons, selection of teaching strategies, and focus of instruction. As students engage in the lessons, you continue to use diagnostic assessment to help make decisions about instruction. Talking with students informally, listening to the questions they ask and the answers they give, finding out what they already know, and using performance assessment information are commonly used techniques to diagnose instructional needs.

Performance assessments are **formative assessments** that enable teachers to think about their assessment goals by answering questions such as the following:

▶ Which science standard(s) does this activity help students to meet?

▶ Which curriculum aims, goals, and objectives were met with this activity?

▶ What has this activity helped me learn about students' knowledge and understanding of science concepts?

▶ What has this activity helped me learn about students' understanding of and ability to use science process skills?

▶ How effective was the task or activity?

▶ Was the task or activity clear enough?

▶ How effective was my instructional design?

▶ What adjustments do I need to make in my teaching to help my students meet the instructional goals set for them?

You also learn about student performance as you ask the following:

▶ Are students able to perform this activity? Is the activity functional?

▶ How well did students do on the activity?

▶ Were their answers correct?

▶ What am I learning about this particular student?

▶ What is this student's level of understanding of science concepts and processes?

▶ What did the activity tell me about the level of understanding of this student?

▶ What did the activity tell me about this student's understanding of science process skills?

▶ Did the student meet the aims, goals, and objectives of this activity? How well? Did the activity provide this information?

All of these questions are answered in the formative assessment phase. Formative assessment focuses on meeting specific objectives as each task or activity is completed and on providing ongoing feedback about performance.

Whereas formative assessment is ongoing, **summative assessment** provides a final evaluation. While formative assessment looks at the development of students' understanding at specific stages, summative assessment is an overall evaluation of progress. Recall from Chapter 7 that a summative assessment typically results in a final grade or report card grade. It is a judgment that a teacher makes about a student's overall achievement. The data that result from individual performances, which are a part of the formative assessment, become a part of the summative assessment—the final grade for the marking period. Since formative assessments allow you to assess your own teaching, leading to adjustments in instructional design along the way, should all scores from performance tasks be counted equally in the final grade? Since all performance assessments may not be of equal quality, some may be weighted more heavily than others in the final grade, depending on what you think is fair. If a lesson was not taught particularly well and you think student performance was inferior because the instructional design needed fine-tuning, you would not count that particular performance task as heavily as others in the final grade—or perhaps you shouldn't count it at all.

Summative assessments are usually more comprehensive and complex than formative assessments. They include written examinations, reports, portfolios, or productions that require incorporation of many concepts into a final product.

Constructing Your Knowledge of Science and Science Teaching

After completing this chapter, begin to reflect on your new knowledge. You have an understanding of the essential aspects of performance-based assessment. Review them. Figure 8.2 on page 198 provides another look at the process. At this point in the semester, you can create performance tasks, response sheets, and a scoring system, and you know that this requires a great deal of practice. As you teach, create performance tasks for your students that assess not only their work but also *your* work. You will become more proficient at creating performance tasks as you practice. Using a rubric, you can score samples of student work. Again, this is not an easy task, and it requires much practice.

Instruction and assessment are closely linked. Think about the ways in which they naturally come together. It should be clear that you must assess student thinking on an ongoing basis. What are some ways to find out about your students' thinking? What are some ways to assess their performance? These are some items for reflection.

Key Terms

rubric (p. 188)
indicators (p. 188)
criteria (p. 192)
model (p. 193)

holistic rubric (p. 199)
analytic rubric (p. 199)
diagnostic assessment
  (p. 210)

formative assessment (p. 211)
summative assessment
  (p. 211)

Reviewing Chapter 8: Questions, Extensions, Applications, and Explorations

1. You are teaching a unit on animals that live in very cold places. Name some of these animals. How do they stay warm? Design a performance task that would allow your second- or third-graders to show that they understand how animals that live in cold places stay warm.

2. Have your students design an experiment to determine whether a handful of popped popcorn or a handful of unpopped popcorn weighs more. What criteria will you use to assess their work?

3. How are diagnostic, formative, and summative assessments related?

4. You create and teach a lesson plan. When you assess your students, you learn that your lesson wasn't very good. Your point didn't come across at all. What will you do next?

5. Think about traditional assessment and performance assessment. How does your knowledge of performance assessment affect the way you think about traditional assessment?

Print Resources

Airasian, P., & Gullickson, A. (1997). *Teacher self-evaluation tool kit*. Thousand Oaks, CA: Corwin Press.

Barnes, L., & Barnes, M. (1991). Assessment, practically speaking. How can we measure hands-on science skills? *Science and Children, 28* (6), 14–15.

Burke, K. (1993). *How to assess thoughtful outcomes*. Palatine, IL: IRI Skylight Publishers.

Burs, H., & Marshall, K. (1997). *Performance-based curriculum for science: From knowing to showing*. Thousand Oaks, CA: Corwin Press.

Champagne, A. B., Lovitts, B. E., & Clinger, B. J. (1990). *Assessment in the service of science*. Washington, DC: American Association for the Advancement of Science.

Chittenden, E. (1991). Authentic assessment, evaluation, and documentation of student performance. In V. Perrone (Ed.), *Expanding student assessment* (pp. 22–31). Alexandria, VA: Association for Supervision and Curriculum Development.

Glatthorn, A. (1998). *Performance assessment and standards-based curricula*. Larchmont, NY: Eye on Education.

Ham, M., & Adams, D. (1991). Portfolio assessment: It's not just for artists any more. *The Science Teacher, 58*, 1–18.

Harrington, H., Meisels, S., McMahon, P., Dichtelmiller, M., & Jablon, J. (1997). *Observing, documenting, and assessing learning: The work sampling system handbook for teacher educators*. Ann Arbor, MI: Rebus. Inc.

Hein, G., & Price, S. (1994). *Active assessment for active science: A guide for elementary school teachers*. Portsmouth, NH: Heinemann.

Hogan, K. (1994). *Eco-inquiry*. Dubuque, IA: Kendall Hunt Publishing Company.

Johnson, B. (1996). *The performance assessment handbook: Portfolios and Socratic seminars* (Vol. 1). Larchmont, NY: Eye on Education.

Johnson, B. (1996). *The performance assessment handbook: Performances and exhibitions* (Vol. 2). Larchmont, NY: Eye on Education.

Novak, J., & Wandersee, J. (1990). Special issue on concept mapping. *Journal of Research in Science Teaching, 28* (1).

Ostlund, K. (1992). *Science process skills: Assessing hands-on student performance*. Boston: Addison-Wesley.

Raizen, S., Baron, J., Champagne, A., Haertel, E., Mullis, I., & Oakes, J. (1989). *Assessment in elementary school science education*. Colorado Springs, CO: National Center for Improving Science Education.

Shavelson, R., & Brown, J. (1996) *Assessing hands-on science: A teacher's guide to performance assessment*. Thousand Oaks, CA: Corwin Press.

Wiggins, G. (1998). *Educative assessment*. San Francisco: Jossey-Bass.

Electronic Resources

The Solar System
http://www.hawastsoc.org/solar
This site contains views of the solar system.

The Nine Planets
http://seds.lpl.arizona.edu/nineplanets/nineplanets/nineplanets.html
This site contains information about the planets and moons of the solar system.

Spacelink
http://spacelink.msfc.nasa.gov/Instructional.Materials/.index.html
This NASA site contains all kinds of resources, including lessons you can download.

Lesson Plans for Earth and Space Science
http://www.cea.berkeley.edu/Education/lessons/lessons_teacherdeveloped.html
This site contains numerous lessons on earth and space science, including excellent lesson plans.

Children's Literature

Berger, Melvin & Gilda
Do Stars Have Points? (Scholastic Trade, 1999)
ISBN: 0-590-13080-3
Grades 4–6

Kosek, Jane
What's Inside the Sun?
(Rosen Publishing Group, 1997)
ISBN: 0-8239-5279-7
Grades 4–6

Garder, Robert
Science Project Ideas About the Sun
(Enslow Publishers, 1997)
ISBN: 0-84940-845-6
Grades 4–9

Gibbons, Gail
The Moon Book (Holiday House, 1998)
ISBN: 0-8234-1364-0
Grades K–3

Petty, Kate
*You Can Jump Higher on the Moon and Other
    Amazing Facts About Space Exploration*
(Cooper Beech Books, 1997)
ISBN: 0-7613-0564-5
Grades 1–3

Moroney, Lynn
*Moontellers: Myths of the Moon from
    Around the World*
(Rising Moon, 1995)
ISBN: 0-87358-601-8
Preschool and Grades K–3

Marson, Ron
The Earth, Moon, and Sun
(Tops Learning Systems, 1993)
ISBN: 0-941008-40-1
Grades 5–10

Strategies for Including Students with Learning Differences in the Science Classroom

 Jamie King, a first-year teacher, is preparing a unit on living things for her fifth-graders. She will address the *National Science Education (Life Science) Standard* (National Research Council, 1996), which says:

▶ Living systems at all levels of organization demonstrate the complementary nature of structure and function. (p. 156)

▶ All living things are composed of cells—the fundamental unit of life. Most organisms are single cells; other organisms, including humans, are multi-cellular. (p. 156)

She also wants to address the idea that:

▶ Children learn science over time. (p. 123)

Her lessons will allow students to explore the nature of living things. In this unit, she will revisit and extend the science ideas her students learned in earlier grades. Last year their investigation of the nature of living things led to the study of plants. They learned about seeds, observed a variety of seeds from fruits, dissected them,

Studying about plants:
Life science

identified the parts and functions of each, and studied how the seeds were trans-ported from one place to another. They planted seeds in soil and in water, learned about germination, cared for the plants, and asked questions about plant nutrition and conditions for sustaining life and growth. They observed roots, leaves, and flowers and investigated them. Their exploration of living things did not unfold over a short period of time. It was **sustained inquiry,** which occurs when students carry out an investigation for weeks, months, or even the whole school year. Recall what you have already learned about the nature of scientific investigation in Chapter 2.

Engaging in sustained
inquiry: Science process

Professional scientists routinely carry out their investigations for long periods of time.

This year the students will study pond life. They will visit a nearby pond and observe **macroscopic** organisms that make their homes in the pond, such as frogs, mosquitoes, water plants, and birds that stop by for awhile. Then they will use magnifiers and microscopes to examine samples of pond water and look for **microscopic** organisms living in the pond.

Before they begin this investigation, they must gain experience with a number of important ideas. Ms. King wants them to experiment with the concept of scale, observing things as they appear to grow bigger and smaller. She also wants them to work with lenses, tools that make things appear to grow, shrink, and look different.

Ms. King introduces the first lesson with technology. She has a computer in the classroom and hooks it up to an overhead projection system. Now all of her students can see the computer screen magnified many times from their seats. Whatever is on the 15-inch monitor is projected onto the large, white screen attached to the chalkboard. Students have a brief discussion about the novelty of projecting an image on a small screen onto a larger screen, where it is magnified. She opens the word processing program and makes a large X in the center of the page. It projects onto the wall screen. She asks her students what the letter X can stand for. They reply:

"X-ray."

"eXtra."

"The times sign."

"A railroad crossing."

Ms. King explains, "These are all good answers, but one fits our need best. It's the X in the times sign. $\times$ indicates scale—making an object appear to be bigger or smaller by a certain amount. If I write $10\times$, it means 10 times larger. If I write $1/10\times$, it means ten times smaller."

Her students are interested in this, so they talk about $2\times$, $1/2\times$, $100\times$, and $1/100\times$ and what they mean.

Experimenting with scale:
Science and mathematics

Ms. King asks if they would like to experiment with making things bigger and smaller by a certain amount. They do. She hands each student a piece of centimeter graph paper and a tape measure with centimeter markings. She tells her students they will become the "incredible shrinking fifth-graders." "How?" they ask. "You'll soon see," she says.

Ms. King tells her students they will use the centimeter tape to measure one another. "Let's say you want to draw a life-size picture of yourself. How would you do this?"

They think for awhile and come up with some answers:

"You'd need to measure the length of your head."

"And the width of your head."

"Go on," she says.

"The length of your body from your feet to your head."

"The length of your legs."

"The length of your arms."

"The width of your waist."

"The length of your hands and fingers."

"Yes," she says. "You are all correct."

Collecting data: Science process

Ms. King instructs her students to measure one another as accurately as possible. "Record the measurements on a data chart. Each group is responsible for its own data chart and measurements," she says.

She gives them 20 minutes to take the measurements and complete their data charts. There is much discussion in the classroom. Each student is different and has his or her own set of "life-size" measurements.

When they are done, Ms. King tells them it's time to shrink.

"Shrink?" they ask. "How are we going to do that?"

There is silence; then someone recalls the $\times$ sign. "We can divide our measurements and make them smaller by a certain amount," one student offers.

"How?" asks Ms. King.

After three or four more minutes of question-and-answer, they decide to divide the numbers in the data chart by 2 and find out if they can fit their "scaled-down" measurements on the sheet of centimeter graph paper Ms. King provided. They try this, but it won't work. The scale is still too large. After more discussion, the class decides to take height from head to toe, divide by 10, and see if they can fit a scaled-down version of a fifth-grader on the sheet of centimeter graph paper. This time the scale is correct.

The students work eagerly as they locate each measurement in the data table and divide it by 10. Now they have a new set of measurements. The next step is to make a mark on the graph paper for each measurement. They connect the marks and draw themselves on the centimeter paper (see Figure 9.1). With their colored markers, they draw the clothes they are wearing. There are lots of smiles, giggles, and much excitement in the room. The drawings are terrific; the students can't believe how much like themselves their drawings look. Ms. King gives them some

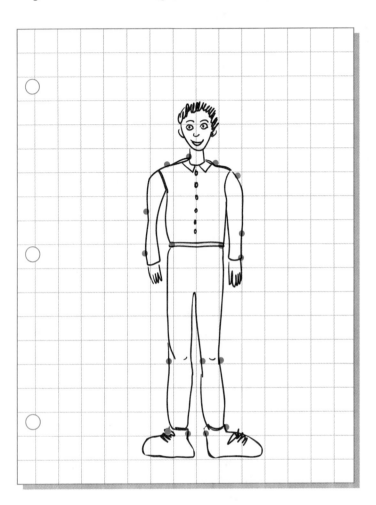

Figure 9.1
Fifth-Graders Shrink

time to personalize the drawings. Then they paste them on sheets of construction paper and decorate the classroom with their artistic creations.

Twenty-six different people are in Ms. King's class. Each student presents his or her drawing to the class. John begins by showing everyone his picture and telling about himself. Ms. King's students celebrate their diversity as they share their drawings with one another. They also have a good understanding of the idea of scale.

You will return to Ms. King's classroom later in this chapter and follow her as she works with her students. Her classroom is very diverse, and she will share her thoughts and lessons with you as she accommodates the needs of individual learners.

This chapter extends much of what you learned in previous chapters and introduces many new ideas. In Chapter 1, you learned that classrooms represent the diversity of society and that your classroom will have many different types of learners. In Chapter 6, you learned about formulating objectives and planning lessons. You know that it's necessary to write objectives to meet the needs of the individual learners in your classroom. This chapter brings you a great deal of information about planning lessons to include (1) students with different learning styles, (2) students with special needs, and (3) students who are gifted. As you read this chapter, think about the answers to these questions:

1. **What different learning styles can I expect to find in my classroom? How do I plan lessons to address the needs of students with these learning styles?**

2. **What is the theory of multiple intelligences, and how do I apply the theory in lesson planning?**

3. **How do I modify science instruction to include students with learning disabilities?**

4. **How do I address the needs of gifted students in my classroom?**

5. **How do I engage students in sustained inquiry as they study living things?**

Diversity in Classrooms

Classrooms are places where diversity flourishes

Schools are places where diversity flourishes. There are students of all ages, of both sexes, from different cultures, racial, and ethnic groups, and of different physical, cognitive, and social ability levels. Your students share both similarities and differences. They may speak different languages, eat different foods, celebrate different holidays, learn different histories, and come from families of different socioeconomic levels. Some prefer hands-on activities, whereas others prefer to listen to a lecture. Some are gifted or talented and can move along quickly, whereas others have special needs and require extra time to process information. Some understand a lesson quickly; others need to hear the lesson explained in more than one way. Some get their work done on time with no trouble, whereas others have difficulty staying focused, staying on task, and completing their work. Some sit calmly, whereas others are hyperactive. Some listen quietly, whereas others call out, demanding special attention. Some communicate easily; others do not. Some have well-developed social skills, whereas others have difficulty interacting with peers. Some are outgoing and friendly, whereas others are shy and reserved. Some like to work in a relatively unstructured environment; others need a great deal of structure. Some like music, some like art, some like math or science, some like reading or writing, and some like a combination of all of these. As a teacher, you will have all types of students in your class, and you need strategies for addressing the needs of *all* learners.

In the past two chapters, you learned about instruction and assessment. Diagnostic, formative, and summative assessments provide a way to gain information about your students, to determine their needs and make decisions about how to teach them. In this chapter, you will learn ways to address the needs of individual learners in your science class. This will help you scaffold instruction as your students construct their own knowledge of science.

Diversity of Learners

Good teachers see things

As a teacher, you are like a scientist: you are a problem solver. You diagnose your students' needs, then choose particular teaching strategies to help learners build understanding. *Good teachers see things.* They are aware of what is going on in their classrooms. They gather data about how their students respond to the learning environment. They analyze the data, make inferences, and draw conclusions about how to teach their students.

Good teachers need a range of teaching strategies so they can adapt instruction to individual needs. Sometimes a strategy works well, but sometimes you have to try something different. Becoming familiar with a range of strategies is what this and the following chapters are about. Starting with a discussion of learning styles, you will learn about student diversity and ways to address differences in the science classroom.

Learning Styles

Traits tell how students prefer to learn

Learning styles refer to the traits that learners exhibit in the classroom. Researchers look at learners' cognitive, affective, and psychological characteristics, and categorize them. These traits tell teachers something about how students prefer to learn. Teachers and researchers then develop teaching strategies that match the preferred way in which a student learns new content and skills. A number of researchers have demonstrated that matching students' learning styles with appropriate instructional strategies improves their ability to learn (Carbo, Dunn, & Dunn, 1986; Dunn, 1996). Instead of focusing on students' weaknesses, teachers work with their strengths and preferences. Several learning styles models exist that suggest teaching strategies to match students' learning styles.

Dunn and Dunn's Approach

Dunn and Dunn's approach to learning styles

Rita and Kenneth Dunn developed a widely used learning styles approach (Dunn & Dunn, 1978). They identify four important variables pertaining to students' cognitive, affective, and psychological characteristics: (1) the learning environment, (2) emotional support, (3) preferred amount of peer interaction, and (4) personal and physical traits and preferences.

▶ Think about the *learning environment* that you prefer. What is it like? Is it a quiet room or one with some noise? Is it a well-lit or a dimly lit room? Do you prefer to sit in a certain place in the classroom?

▶ How much *emotional support* do you require, and what type? Do you need help getting motivated? Are you persistent? Do you take on responsibility or prefer to have others take the lead?

▶ What about *peer interaction*? Do you like to work individually, with a team-mate, or in a group? When you were younger, did you prefer to learn from an adult? Do you prefer to work alone at times and with others at other times?

▶ What are your *personal/physical* traits and your basic *learning modalities*? Are you an auditory learner who likes to hear things, a tactile learner who prefers touch, a visual learner who likes to see things, or do you prefer movement? Are you achievement motivated or perhaps socially motivated? Is there a particular time of day during which you learn best?

These are the variables Dunn and Dunn identified in their research. Keep them in mind as you get to know your students and observe them at work.

Variables Influencing Learning Style

Learning environment:
▶ Quiet/noisy
▶ Brightly lit/dimly lit
▶ A particular location

Emotional support:
▶ Self-motivating/needs motivation
▶ Takes the lead/follows others

Preferred amount of peer interaction:
▶ Works alone/likes a learning partner
▶ Likes group learning

Personal and physical traits and preferences:
▶ Auditory learner
▶ Tactile learner
▶ Kinesthetic learner
▶ Visual learner
▶ Achievement motivated
▶ Socially motivated

A teacher who studies Dunn and Dunn's learning styles approach thinks about his or her students as individuals and gathers information about each one's preferred learning modality, personal and physical traits, preferred learning environment, need for emotional support, and mode of peer interaction. That teacher sets up the classroom and plans instruction with this data in mind. For example, you might organize the science classroom with an area for whole-class work as well as seating areas for small-group problem solving and individual work. Students sometimes work together as a whole class, in small cooperative groups, in pairs, and individually. Sometimes they sit quietly, and sometimes they move around. If a particular student needs to move around more than others, you can take this into account when planning instruction and structuring the day.

Gregorc's Approach

Gregorc's approach focuses on perceptual preferences and ordering abilities

Another approach to learning styles is Anthony Gregorc's style delineator (Gregorc, 1985). His system focuses on perceptual preferences and ordering abilities. **Perceptual preferences** refer to ways in which students prefer to gain information. **Ordering abilities** are the ways in which students order new information (Orlich, Harder, Callahan, & Gibson, 1998). Gregorc identifies two perceptual preferences that students exhibit. *Concrete-oriented* students gain input through the senses; *abstract-oriented* students use logic to gain information. He also identifies two ordering abilities. *Sequential learners* prefer to learn in a step-by-step fashion *Random learners* prefer unorganized information; they will order it and make sense of it on their own. Gregorc developed a typology of learning styles that clusters students by their preferred orientation for processing information (see Table 9.1).

Activity 9.1 Hands-on Science: Using Gregorc's Learning Styles to Teach About the Sense of Smell

Addressing the standard on the senses: Life science

Overview: The second-grade curriculum in Jamie King's school includes a unit on living things. As part of this unit, Dan, a second-grade teacher, is leading his class in the study of characteristics of humans. The *National Science Education (Life Science) Standards* say, "Humans and other organisms have senses that help them detect internal and external cues" (National Research Council, 1996, p. 129). In this activity, Dan uses Gregorc's typology of learning styles to introduce the sense of smell to second-graders.

Table 9.1
Gregorc's Learning Styles

Cluster	Thinking Pattern	Preferred Learning Environment
Concrete sequential	Linear, sequential processing of concrete world	Ordered, linear, and stable
Abstract sequential	Abstract, analytical thinking	Mentally stimulating, but ordered
Abstract random	Emotional, imaginative	Active, colorful, and free
Concrete random	Concrete, world of activity, nonlinear and intuitive	Stimulus-rich, with emphasis on problem solving

Orlich, Donald C., Robert J. Harder, Richard C. Callahan, Harry W. Gibson, *Learning Strategies: A Guide to Better Instruction*, Fifth Edition. Copyright © 1998 by Houghton Mifflin Company. Reprinted with permission.

Materials: Five empty film containers with lids, cotton balls, vanilla extract, lemon juice, cologne, vinegar, bits of chocolate

Procedure: Introduce the sense of smell to his students in four different ways, each one taking advantage of Gregorc's research on learning styles. When you are in the field, you can try this lesson with your class (or you can try it in your college classroom). Observe your students at work. What do you learn from their behavior?

When smelling something, waft the odor toward the nose: Safety

1. Each of four film containers holds a cotton ball soaked with a different scent. The first is soaked with vanilla extract, the second with lemon juice, the third with cologne, and the fourth with vinegar. The fifth container holds small bits of chocolate. Students smell the contents of each container. Remember this safety consideration: when smelling something, students should hold the substance an

Using learning styles research to teach about liquids. This student is gathering information using his preferred modality.

arm's length away and wave their hands past the opening in the container, bringing the odor toward the nose. This is called *wafting*. Never put the substance directly beneath the nose and breathe in, for if the substance is harmful, an injury will result. Find out if your students are allergic to any of these substances before including them in the activity. Send a note home to parents to find out about allergies.

2. Set up four stations and present the lesson in four different ways. Describe the stations to your students and let them choose the one they like best, or let all students rotate through the four stations. Observe the way they respond to each station. Remember that this is a learning experience for you as well as your students.

For concrete-sequential learners who like many concrete examples presented in an organized fashion, provide the prepared film canisters for them to smell. Give them a chart to fill out so they can describe the odors on a response sheet in an organized fashion.

For concrete-random learners, present the prepared film canisters. Tell them they will experiment with the canisters and investigate which odors they like best and which they like least.

For abstract-random learners, set up a cooperative problem-solving session. Ask them to design an experiment to help second-graders learn about the sense of smell.

For abstract-sequential learners, form a discussion group. Have students come up with a series of rules to follow when smelling an unknown substance in a film canister. Then have them create a response sheet to describe and categorize the odors.

Creating an observation checklist for a science activity

Assessment: Create an observation checklist for this activity. What criteria will you observe? How do your students respond? Which station(s) do they prefer? Do you see a relationship between preferred learning style and activity station? ∎

Activity 9.2 Hands-on Science: Creating Your Own Science Activity to Accompany Gregorc's Style Delineator

Overview: In this activity, you will choose the science topic. Create four different ways to design the lesson, one for each of Gregorc's styles.

Procedure: The choice is yours.

Assessment: Examine your lesson. How does it suit the needs of (1) concrete-sequential, (2) random-sequential, (3) concrete-abstract, and (4) random-abstract learners? Is there a particular style that is better suited to your own learning style? ∎

McCarthy's Teaching Model

McCarthy's model integrates learning styles research into an instructional strategy

Bernice McCarthy developed a system that integrates learning styles research into an instructional strategy. Her method is based on the work of Kolb (1983) and Jung (1976), who studied how learners *perceive* and *process* information.

McCarthy synthesized the work of these researchers and others and defined four types of learners based on how they perceive and process information:

Imaginative learners, who perceive information concretely and process it reflectively

Analytic learners, who perceive information abstractly and process it reflectively

Common-sense learners, who perceive information abstractly and process it actively

Dynamic learners, who perceive information concretely and process it actively (McCarthy, 1987)

McCarthy's instructional strategy, called the 4MAT model, incorporates *many* different learning styles into a lesson rather than just a single learning style per lesson (McCarthy & Keene, 1996). It is similar to Gregorc's method in that it focuses on perception (thinking versus feeling) and information processing (hands-on/active versus listening/watching). She believes that a teacher should design every lesson to accommodate the four learning styles. Teachers should keep in mind that imaginative learners prefer sensing, feeling, and watching; analytic learners prefer thinking and watching; common-sense learners prefer thinking and doing; and dynamic learners prefer sensing, feeling, and doing. She also takes into account research on the right and left hemispheres, the two halves of the brain, which process information in different ways (McCarthy, 1987). McCarthy argues that the majority of children who succeed in school are analytic learners who prefer to think and watch, because traditional schools and lessons delivered in lecture style are geared toward these learners.

The four learning styles are incorporated into McCarthy's model of teaching, which follows. As the lesson begins, the teacher organizes a situation that makes students think and reflect. The teacher motivates students and thus creates a reason for learning about a concept or topic. In effect, motivation answers the question "Why should I learn this?" For example, for a lesson about the human skeletal system, students might be asked to select a bone or set of bones and describe their function(s).

As the lesson continues to its second phase, the teacher develops the concept with students. This could be in a lecture format, using direct instruction, or in small study groups. This phase focuses on teaching content and answers the question "What do I have to learn?"

The third phase involves application of the concept. Students might engage in drill and practice of concepts developed in the second phase. In the science classroom, they might engage in inquiry, setting up an experiment to learn more about the topic. This phase focuses on answering the question "How does this work?"

In the fourth phase, students evaluate and refine their ideas. They might make real-world connections, answering the question "How can I apply this information?" Using the principles learned, they might study the bones and muscles in the hand and think about how they work together to enable us to hold things and write. In what other ways can you apply principles of anatomy and physiology with your elementary and early childhood students?

> **McCarthy's Model of Teaching**
> Phase 1:   Why should I learn this?
> Phase 2:   What will I learn?
> Phase 3:   How does this work?
> Phase 4:   How can I apply this information?

Activity 9.3 Lesson Design: Applying Bernice McCarthy's 4MAT Model in the Science Classroom

Overview: In this lesson, students in the primary grades study living things and learn about elephants. Each phase of the lesson suits students with a particular learning style. As a whole, the lesson addresses all four learning styles.

Materials: Music with elephant sounds, videos of elephants, paper and markers for drawing, worksheets on elephants for drill and practice, maps of where elephants live

Procedure: *Imaginative learners:* Begin the lesson by motivating imaginative learners. Students listen to tapes of elephant sounds and move around the room, pretending they are elephants. They use very large construction paper to make a life-size picture of an elephant. They compare their own sizes with that of an elephant. They create stories about elephants and read books about them.

Analytic learners: The lesson continues as students watch content-rich videos about elephants. You might teach about elephants to the whole class. This phase of the lesson develops the content.

Common-sense learners: Students begin to apply what they learn. They locate areas of the world where elephants live and make maps of those areas. They may complete worksheets to practice and review the lesson.

Dynamic learners: These learners like action. As instruction continues, students can select work on elephants for their portfolios, create a gallery of elephant art in the hallway, write stories about elephants, or read stories to parents.

Assessment: How would you assess each part of this lesson? Choose one part of the lesson and create a way to assess it.   ■

The Theory of Multiple Intelligences

Complementing the work on learning styles that we have just reviewed is the theory of multiple intelligences. In the mid-1970s, Harvard University researcher Howard Gardner began thinking about what makes up intelligence. In doing so, he challenged the existing notion that there is a single quality called "intelligence" that can be measured by a single test. The practice of testing for intelligence started just after 1900 when French psychologist Alfred Binet developed the first intelligence test. It was routinely used in elementary schools to identify at-risk students in need of remediation. Gardner questioned the notion of measuring intelligence by asking a person to carry out a series of tasks. He argued that

Imaginative learners have their own learning style.

Gardner proposed seven intelligences

intelligence is related to a person's capacity for solving problems and creating products in particular settings rather than to performing abstract tasks that the person has not encountered before.

In his book *Frames of Mind*, Gardner proposed at least seven basic intelligences instead of one. Gardner mapped the broad range of abilities that fall into the seven categories he calls "intelligences." Table 9.2 (see page 229) summarizes the seven intelligences and their core components. As you design your lessons, remember that your students possess these intelligences, alone and in combinations. Thinking about the seven intelligences as you design your lessons is likely to make them more interesting and engaging. In doing so, you will address the wide range of learning modalities and learning preferences among your students.

When you create your lessons, think about including musical or environmental sounds (musical intelligence); hands-on activities or opportunities for students to move around (bodily-kinesthetic intelligence); visual aids, color, art, sculpture (spatial intelligence); opportunities to use the spoken word in discussions, storytelling, brainstorming, or journal writing (linguistic intelligence); large-group and small-group interactions (interpersonal intelligence); opportunities for individual work (intrapersonal intelligence); and, of course, problem solving, inquiry, and ways to apply the science process skills (logical-mathematical intelligence).

Classroom instructional variables are important factors leading to student success (Wang, Haertel, & Walberg, 1994). Teachers should know many different ways to design lessons. Multiple intelligences and learning styles are two elements that help to inform your instructional decision making. You must now learn how to apply this information in your teaching so that you can become a reflective practitioner. How do you do this? The next section provides a number of science lessons that describe the teaching and learning process and focus on how you can make instructional decisions in light of educational research.

Planning Inquiry-Based Lessons for the Diverse Science Classroom

Teachers make instructional decisions

As an elementary science teacher, you make instructional decisions each time you teach. You consider many variables. Here are some of the questions you ask:

▶ What part of the curriculum am I covering?

▶ What standards am I covering?

▶ What unit am I addressing?

▶ What lessons fit into this unit?

▶ What form of diagnostic assessment will I use?

▶ How should I design this lesson?

▶ Am I considering my students' diverse learning styles when I design this lesson?

In designing an inquiry-based lesson, you ask many additional questions:

▶ What are we investigating in this lesson? Can students state the problem?

▶ Is this problem one that students are interested in solving?

▶ What are reasonable aims, goals, and objectives for this lesson?

▶ Are there objectives for individual students?

▶ How much time will be allowed for this lesson?

▶ What materials and resources are available?

Table 9.2
Summary of Gardner's Multiple Intelligences

Intelligence	Components
Logical-mathematical	Capacity to identify patterns and relationships; ability to reason
Linguistic	Sensitive to sounds, structure, meanings, and functions of words and language
Spatial	Ability to perceive the spatial-visual world accurately
Musical	Ability to produce and appreciate rhythm, pitch, and timbre; appreciation of the forms of musical expressiveness
Bodily-kinesthetic	Ability to control one's bodily movements and to handle objects skillfully
Interpersonal	Ability to identify and respond to the moods, temperaments, motivations, and desires of others
Intrapersonal	Ability to identify and relate to one's own feelings and emotions; knowing one's own strengths and weaknesses

From *Multiple Intelligences in the Classroom* by Thomas Armstrong. Alexandria, VA: Association for Supervision and Curriculum Development. Copyright © 1994 ASCD. Reprinted by permission. All rights reserved.

▶ How will the lesson begin?

▶ How will the lesson develop?

▶ What assessments will I use?

▶ If students have difficulty constructing knowledge, how will I scaffold instruction?

▶ How will the lesson conclude?

▶ What information gained from this lesson will I use to plan the next lesson in the sequence?

These are many of the basic issues teachers consider when planning a lesson or series of lessons. You will now revisit Jamie King's classroom and learn how she makes instructional decisions with these considerations in mind.

Teaching Diverse Learners About Microscopes

Ms. King's lesson on scale was a huge success. Her students learned about making things bigger and smaller by a certain amount and had hands-on, minds-on experience with the concept. They also used math as a tool for science, collected their own data, made their own data charts, and used the data to solve a problem. Today Ms. King is ready to begin a sustained investigation with her students. It will take most of the marking period to complete. As you read the sections that follow, she shares her thoughts with you. You will learn how she plans lessons to accommodate the different learning styles she finds in her classroom.

Introductory Phase of the Lesson

Introducing a science lesson with poetry

In the lessons that follow, students learn to use the microscope. Ms. King recalls what she knows about motivating students who have diverse learning styles. Many of her fifth-graders love poetry, so she starts off the lesson on the microscope with this poem:

I hope you know I'm really small,
But sometimes I look big and tall.
My body's wide from side to side
When I'm swimming on the microscope slide
Want to know why I'm long and wide?
It's because I'm magnified!

A clear soda bottle filled with water acts as a magnifier: Physical science

She knows that many of her students learn best by discussing, so she begins the lesson with this question: "How can you look at something very, very small?" The students tell her that she can use a magnifying glass or a microscope. They begin a discussion on magnifiers. Enid tells the class that she made a magnifier from an empty, clear 1-liter soda bottle. Once the soda was gone, she filled the bottle with water, right to the top, and capped it. She viewed objects through the bottle, and they grew in size. Eduardo adds that he took a piece of cardboard and punched a hole in the center. He put a piece of transparent tape over the hole, then placed a few drops of water on the side of the tape that was not sticky. The water drops acted as a magnifier.

A few drops of water on a piece of transparent tape act as a magnifier: Physical science

Ms. King scans the classroom during the discussion, observing her students to be sure everyone is paying attention—and they are. Not everyone learns best in a large-group discussion, so she wants to be sure that everyone is on task. Then she continues the lesson.

She hands out magnifying lenses, then allows her students to explore objects around the room and discuss their findings with one another. They conclude that they can see small things with their magnifying glasses, but not very, very small things. Sometimes things are in focus, and sometimes they're not.

Ms. King asks, "How can you tell how much bigger a magnifier makes an object?" This is a tough question and causes the students to think. They discuss the question as a whole group. Ann says that you have to look at the same object with your eye, first without a magnifying glass, then with a magnifying glass. You have to compare how much of the object you see without the magnifier with what you see with the magnifier. Ms. King sees this as an excellent opportunity for inquiry and discovery, so she asks her students to develop a way to find out how much bigger their magnifying glasses make an object. (Some students enjoy problem solving, and this is an excellent opportunity for them.)

Using a science log as an organizational tool

There are 26 students in her class, Ms. King forms four groups of 4 students and two groups of 5 students. (She knows that some students prefer to work in

Magnifiers make objects grow in size.

groups.) In each group is a mix of high, average, and low achievers, and equal numbers of boys and girls, with a few exceptions. Since just about every group has students with special needs, Ms. King tells group members to first discuss the problem together and write about it in their science logs. (She knows this organizational tool is important, especially for students who need help with focusing.) Each member should be able to explain the problem to the group. (She wants each group member to be responsible for the work.) This step takes 10 to 15 minutes and is very important in helping students comprehend.

Next, group members brainstorm. Ms. King explains that everyone should have a chance to suggest a solution to the problem. Team members can write suggestions on index cards. The group can discuss the suggestions and try one or more of them together. There is more than one solution to this problem. Her students are eager to get to work.

Day 1: Ms. King Makes Informal Observations

In Chapter 7, you learned about the purposes of informal assessment. Here is how Ms. King uses this technique to gain the information she needs to make instructional decisions. In this case, she gains information about how her students solve problems.

Ann, Brian, Amy, and Sadya are in the same group. After stating the problem and recording it, they decide to experiment. Each has a magnifier. Together they decide to use aluminum foil to create another magnifier, this one having no lens. They do this because Amy reminds them that they will have to make a comparison between the size of an object as seen through the magnifier and with the unaided eye. To allow them to compare correctly, the opening in the "aluminum foil" magnifier should be the same size as the lens in the real magnifier. They decide to roll the foil into a thin strip. Sadya fits the strip around the perimeter of the real magnifier, twisting it at the handle. He makes several twists to produce a handle they can grasp. Now they have a real magnifier with a lens and a replica the same size without the lens. They look at a page of printed text through the lens of the real magnifier, then with the aluminum foil replica.

Calculating magnification: Science and mathematics

Amy tries the experiment first, holding both instruments an equal distance from the page. Sadya doesn't understand why she does this, and Amy explains that to make a true comparison, both instruments must face the same object from the same distance. Sadya thinks he understands and rephrases her explanation in his own words. His teammates tell him that his answer makes sense. Brian says that the print on the page is okay to observe, but an object that could be more easily measured would be better for comparison. Group members discuss this and agree. Brian uses a dark marker to draw a ladder across the page. Its rungs are equidistant from one another. Each team member takes a turn viewing the ladder with the real magnifier and the aluminum foil replica. They find they can see 12 sections of the ladder unaided and 3 sections aided. The magnifier makes the ladder four times bigger, so that's the **magnification.** They write about their discovery in their science logs, then wait until Ms. King brings the class together so each group can share its results.

Practicing informal observation of group work

While her students worked in small groups, Ms. King circulated around the room and listened. She was aware of what was going on in each group. She knew who was talking and who was listening. She watched the groups as they searched for solutions. Most groups solved the problem, each in a different way. Most decided to view an object with the magnifier and with the unaided eye. One group didn't realize that the object should be viewed both times from the same distance. Distance from the object was a variable they had to control. If they didn't, they could not make a fair comparison. Ms. King observed those students at work as they went off on the wrong track. She could have jumped in and explained the flaw in their logic, but she didn't. She decided to let them make the mistake so they could learn from it. Later on they did. In fact, they were very interested to hear what other groups did so they could self-correct this mistake. Ms. King took a risk when she didn't correct them on the spot; however, she reasoned that it was a risk worth taking. In the event they didn't understand that they had made an error, she would work with them later.

Another group did not view an object that was easy to measure, such as a ladder with rungs placed the same distance apart, so its measurements weren't satisfactory. They figured this out on their own as the whole class shared results. After listening to the whole-class discussion, Ms. King gave her students 15 more minutes in which to try something again or begin to record results from their experiments in a data chart. As an extension of the activity, they could use their mathematical knowledge to develop a way to calculate the magnification power of the lens. Those who didn't record their results in class would finish this for homework.

Later on, Ms. King reflected on the lesson The groups were generally good, but things might have been better if she had reconfigured two groups, as two very talkative students were in the same group and two very quiet students were in another. The talkative students were disruptive, and Ms. King had to sit in on the group as members worked in order to get them on task. She was concerned because they weren't engaged in the activity. She should have assigned roles to all group members. Having a responsibility to accomplish something in the group would have changed the group dynamic. Next time she will do this. (You will learn much more about groups and group work in Chapter 10.) The quiet students didn't contribute much to the group, and she decided they might be more apt to contribute in the presence of different students. Again, assigning group roles would have helped.

In general, though, Ms. King is very satisfied with the way her students approached the problem, and she is impressed with their use of scientific thinking and their ability to arrive at the results. This was an excellent activity. She decides to create an assessment task list for the activity. The performance task becomes a performance assessment when she adds the scoring rubric (see Table 9.3 on page 234). She knows that her students should learn more about lenses, which she will cover in her next lesson.

Day 2: Students Learn History and Parts of the Microscope

Today Ms. King moves to a discussion of the microscope. She uses storytelling to talk about its inventor, Anton van Leeuwenhoek. (She knows that some of her students love to hear stories.) Van Leeuwenhoek was born in Delft in the Netherlands in 1632. She points to the map of the world, then asks someone to locate the Netherlands. Sheku locates the country immediately. Ms. King continues by explaining that van Leeuwenhoek was an amateur scientist who prepared hundreds of lenses, grinding them by hand. He started with a glass bead mounted on a metal plate, which served as a magnifier. Why did he use a glass bead or a lens? When light passes from air to glass, it bends. Ms. King knows that her students have some experience with lenses, but now she tells them more. **Lenses** **are pieces of glass or transparent plastic with special shapes.** Lenses can focus light, create images such as the ones students see through their magnifying glasses, and make images larger or smaller. A lens can be thicker or thinner in the center. If it is thicker in the center than at the edges, it's called a *convex lens;* if it's thinner in the center than at the edges, it's called a *concave lens* (see Figure 9.2 on page 235). Once light rays pass through a convex lens, the lens brings the light rays together so that they come into focus. The place where they join is the *focal point*. Ms. King draws this on the board (see Figure 9.3). Her students talk about looking through their magnifying lenses and seeing things in focus and out of focus. A thicker convex lens has a shorter focal length and is more powerful than a thinner convex lens.

As van Leeuwenhoek worked with lenses, he needed an object with standard length to observe. He found that lice have a pretty constant size, so he used the louse as the standard measure with which to compare all other things that he measured, just as one of Ms. King's groups drew a ladder with equidistant rungs

Lenses are pieces of glass or transparent plastic with special shapes: Physical science

Light rays join at the focal point: Physical science

Van Leeuwenhoek used the louse as the standard measure: Science and mathematics

Table 9.3
Checklist for the Magnification Experiment

Element	Possible Points	Self-Assessment	Teacher Assessment
Problem-Solving Ability			
Can state the problem in writing			
Can explain the problem in words			
Can answer questions about the problem			
Can explain science terms related to magnifiers			
Uses diagrams to clarify explanations			
Can communicate ideas verbally			
Formulates reasonable solutions to the problem			
Discusses other people's solutions			
Understands the solution			
Can explain the solution to others			
Appreciating Science			
Shows enjoyment while participating in experiments			
Shows enjoyment when thinking scientifically			
Enjoys working with others in the science classroom			

for measurement purposes. With his lenses, he looked at things such as stagnant water, scrapings from his teeth, and blood cells. He used observation to collect data; he also drew what he saw, and wrote about it as well. (Ms. King thinks to herself that she knows something about van Leeuwenhoek's modes of communication.) In other words, like the students in Ms. King's class, Anton van Leeuwenhoek used science process skills in his work. The class talks a bit about this.

The children become interested in learning about the microscope, and that's exactly what Ms. King wants. They decide that for homework, they will learn

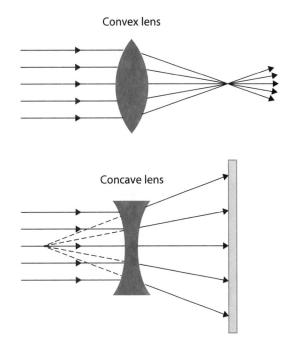

**Figure 9.2
Convex and Concave
Lenses**

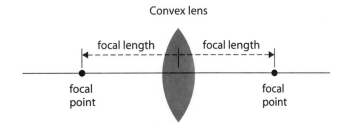

**Figure 9.3
Light Rays Meet at
the Focal Point**

more about the history of the microscope. Some will go to the library, some have resource books at home, and others will search the Internet for information. They will look at how the microscope has helped scientists make progress and learn about the people involved in its development. They will engage in inquiry to learn more.

Ms. King is very happy, as these are the objectives she wrote for the lesson:

▶ After completing the lesson, students will be able to describe the stages in the development of the microscope and learn about the people involved in its development.

▶ After completing the lesson, students will be able to identify and label the parts of the compound microscope.

▶ After completing the lesson, students will be able to explain the purpose of the microscope.

By tomorrow, she will know whether her students meet the first objective. Now she moves on to the others. She wants students to develop the ability to demonstrate proper use of a compound microscope, including handling and focusing. She also wants them to appreciate the advances that the microscope has made for science. It's not long before Juan asks if there are microscopes available for the students to use. There are, and Ms. King is ready to begin the next part of the lesson.

Activity 9.4 Lesson Design: Analyzing the Introductory Phase of the Lesson

Overview: In this activity, you will analyze a part of Ms. King's lesson.

Procedure: Reflect on these questions: What do you think of Ms. King's introduction? Is it engaging? Do the students learn? What do they learn? What learning styles does she address in her introduction?

Assessment: How would you suggest that Ms. King assess student understanding? ■

Developmental Phase of the Lesson

Teaching about the microscope

Ms. King is now ready to begin the developmental phase of the lesson. She points to the question on the board: "How can you look at something very, very small?" The students need direct instruction before they begin. She distributes a diagram of the compound microscope and reviews its parts with them (see Figure 9.4).

Students use microscopes as part of a unit on life science.

The microscopes used in most elementary schools have three main parts: the foot, the tube, and the body. The *foot* is the base of the microscope on which it stands, the *body* is the portion that holds the tube, and the *tube* holds the lenses. At the lower end of the body is a *mirror,* which can be tilted to adjust the light. Above the mirror is a *platform* or *stage* on which to place the *specimen* under investigation. On the stage are *clips* to hold the slide in place. There is an opening in the stage to let the light shine on the specimen. The upper part of the body consists of a *slide* that holds the *tube.* The *tube* holds the lenses, and the *body* holds the tube. A *coarse adjustment knob* allows the user to move the tube up and down, which focuses the microscope. A *fine adjustment knob* moves the tube up and down slightly so that the user can focus completely when using a high-powered lens. The user looks into the *eyepiece.* Just below the eyepiece is the *eyepiece lens.* Microscopes generally have more than one lens, so the *objective lenses* are connected to a revolving *nosepiece* found on the lower part of the tube. The lenses have different *power,* or degree of magnification.

The compound microscope does its work in two stages. First, light shines onto the mirror and is reflected from the area beneath the stage, through the specimen being viewed, into the objective lens, where it is magnified for the first time. The image then moves up the tube through the eyepiece lens, called the *ocular lens,* where it is once again magnified. The image then reaches the user's eye. Most standard microscopes have three objective lenses that magnify objects 4 times, 10 times, and 40 times. Compound microscopes have the additional ocular lens, which magnifies things even more, to magnifications of 40, 100, or 400 times.

The parts of the microscope: Physical science

The compound microscope has greater magnification than the standard classroom microscope: Physical science

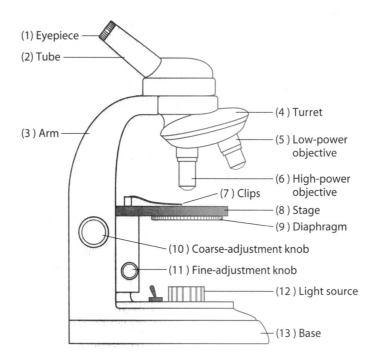

**Figure 9.4
The Compound
Microscope**

(1) Eyepiece
(2) Tube
(3) Arm
(4) Turret
(5) Low-power objective
(6) High-power objective
(7) Clips
(8) Stage
(9) Diaphragm
(10) Coarse-adjustment knob
(11) Fine-adjustment knob
(12) Light source
(13) Base

Practicing safety when using microscopes:
Safety

The students study the microscope's parts and move to the perimeter of the room, where the microscopes are arranged. Ms. King thinks to herself that the hands-on learners will undoubtedly benefit. She also remembers that safety is a major concern in a science classroom. Therefore, students don't all get up at once; they wait for directions, then go. There is a great deal of expensive equipment in the room, and Ms. King wants to be sure that no harm comes to the students or the equipment as a result of having them move through the room in a disorderly fashion. She assigns each student a microscope and a microscope number for which he or she will be responsible throughout the unit. Only a short time remains today, so she must begin to conclude. The discussion took a little longer than expected, so she will have to continue tomorrow.

Students examine the microscopes casually, then return to their seats. They take out their science journals. Tonight's prompt is: Why do you think that people need microscopes? Now it's time for lunch.

Activity 9.5 Lesson Design: Analyzing the Developmental Phase of the Lesson

Overview: In this activity, you will analyze another part of Ms. King's lesson.

Procedure: Answer these questions: What do you think of Ms. King's lesson development? Does it follow logically and naturally from the introduction? Does it make students think? Is it engaging? Do the students learn? What do they learn? What learning styles does she address in the first part of the lesson development?

Assessment: How would you assess this lesson?

Day 3: The Students Investigate

Observing and drawing butterfly wings:
Life science

The students come to class ready to investigate. Ms. King built a good foundation yesterday with the direct teaching part of the lesson, and today students are eager to move ahead. They move efficiently to their microscopes. She asks students to draw a picture of a butterfly wing from memory. Students make drawings, share diagrams, and discuss details. She tells them they will investigate prepared slides of butterfly wings under the microscope and draw new diagrams. They will compare both drawings. Then she demonstrates the proper use of the microscope. Students learn to focus and experiment with different powers. She distributes prepared slides of butterfly wings. They place the slide in the clips on the stage of the microscope. Starting with the lowest power, they focus on the object. Then they focus on medium power, observe, and finally flip to high power. They make drawings and compare what they saw with the naked eye with what they saw

Demonstrating proper use of the microscope:
Safety

with the aid of the microscope. The differences are startling. The views are different, and there is much more detail in the drawings of the magnified butterfly wings. The drawings done with the naked eye clearly depict butterfly wings. The ones done with the aid of the microscope are detailed, but it's not clear that these are butterfly wings.

Todd follows directions and uses the coarse adjustment knob and the low-power objective first. Next, he moves into medium, then high power. Even though

Working with a student who has difficulty following directions

Ms. King tells the class not to touch the coarse adjustment knob when in high power, Todd does so and cracks the slide. She calmly removes the slide, wraps it in paper, and discards it with the refuse. She asks Todd what he would do differently next time. He needs some time to think about this and learn from his mistake. Ms. King does not wish to embarrass him, so she does not reprimand him. Actually, there is no reason to reprimand him. Todd has trouble following directions, and this event is not unusual for him. Instead of making this a negative mark on his performance, she views it as an opportunity for learning. His drawings are good, and she points this out. Ms. King decides that next time students work with slides, she will supervise Todd more closely. Perhaps he needs more help.

Cleaning up after a lesson on the microscope

It's time to clean up. The students put the slides back in the box and return the microscopes to their original condition. They return to their seats and discuss their findings. The microscopes helped them to see detail, but they lost perspective. Focusing was not too difficult. If they focused on low power first, with the shortest objective, then flipped into medium, and then high power without touching the coarse adjustment knob, they would not crack the prepared slide.

Class is almost over, and Ms. King gives this journal prompt: How were the explorations and findings of Anton van Leeuwenhoek and Christopher Columbus similar? She hopes students will say that both were involved in inquiry and discovery. Both opened new doors for others and charted new territories for humanity.

Day 4: The Students Demonstrate Their Knowledge

Ms. King sets new objectives for today's lesson. She wants students to demonstrate their knowledge of the parts of the microscope through hands-on experience. She also wants them to demonstrate that they can handle the microscope properly, view an object, and bring it into focus. Then they will prepare a wet mount. Although some specimens are easily observed without water, many samples look better when water supports the sample and fills the space between the cover slip and the slide.

Preparing a wet mount: Life science

At their desks, Ms. King has the students draw the letter e on a small piece of waxed paper. To make a wet mount, they use an eyedropper to place a drop of water on the letter, then slowly place a cover slip over the letter, using a toothpick to minimize the occurrence of air bubbles. Mary's slide has too much water, and she places a paper towel at the edge of the cover slip to soak up the water. Avinash doesn't have enough water on his slide, so he places a drop of water next to the cover slip. Ms. King circulates around the room as her students work, observing them in action, taking mental notes about who's doing what and how well.

Now the students move to the microscopes, place their slides under the clips on the stage, and view the letter *e*. They draw what they see under the microscope and what they see with the naked eye. The microscope turns the letter *e* upside down. Tyler asks why this happens. He is a student who is academically gifted, and Ms. King decides that this is a good question for Tyler to explore on his own. She will consult some of her resource books this afternoon to decide how she will guide him. She will also phone her friend Barbara, a high school physics teacher, who can help.

Integrating science and language arts

Ms. King concludes the lesson by having her students create an acrostic for the word *microscope* (see Figure 9.5). They review new concepts in small groups and as a whole class. There is a great deal of student talk. In the lessons to come, they will explore what they find in pond water.

Use the letters in the word microscope to describe things associated with the microscope.

Microscopic

Interesting

Compound

Reflected light

Ocular lens

Sense of sight

Cells

Onion skin

Paramecium

Excellent experience

Figure 9.5 Students Create an Acrostic to Describe What They Know About the Microscope

Activity 9.6 Lesson Design: Critiquing the Lesson About the Microscope

Overview: In this activity, you will critique another lesson.

Procedure: Answer these questions: What do you think of Ms. King's lessons about the microscope so far? Has she caused her students to think? Has she attended to students with different learning styles? Do you think her students use the microscope properly? Do they need more practice?

Assessment: Design an assessment for Ms. King's lesson. ■

Teaching Students with Learning Disabilities

As this chapter continues, you will learn more about including all students in the science classroom. Our discussion now moves from addressing students with diverse learning styles to addressing the needs of special learners in the science classroom. Here are the characteristics of some of the special learners in Ms. King's class:

▶ Todd has a learning style that is *impulsive*. He rarely thinks things through; he speaks out quickly, races to get his work done, rarely checks his work, and is always rushing. He doesn't seem to have strategies for organizing his work or his life in general.

▶ Anya is quite passive. She lacks interest in science work, becomes easily frustrated, and is dependent on others to do the work for her.

▶ Josh is quite irritable. He has a quick temper and angers easily. Everything seems to bother him. Ms. King worries when he works on science lessons, because she's afraid he may become angry and cause trouble.

Theories That Guide the Work of Learning Disabilities Professionals

The theories that guide the work of learning disabilities professionals fall into three categories: (1) developmental psychology and maturational theories of learning disabilities, (2) behavioral psychology, and (3) cognitive psychology.

Developmental Psychology

One of the key tenets of developmental psychology is that maturation of thinking ability follows a sequence. The ability to learn depends on the individual's stage of development. This isn't something that can be moved forward; it happens when the individual is developmentally ready for it to happen. Jean Piaget is the developmental psychologist best known for his stages of development. He believed that children move through developmental stages at certain ages. You can turn to Chapter 5 for a review of Piaget's stages of development.

Developmental theory has implications for children with learning disabilities. One assumption is that immaturity is one cause for lack of ability. If a student can't understand or learn a particular concept, it may be that the student simply isn't mature enough to understand. Therefore, teachers must design developmentally appropriate lessons. However, children develop at different rates. Suppose a particular lesson is right for fifth-graders, but some students in the class are not developmentally ready. They may not be able to learn the material. The teacher must keep this in mind when preparing lessons and giving assignments for all students.

Behavioral Psychology

B. F. Skinner is known as the founder of behavioral psychology. The *behavioral unit* is at the core of this theory. The behavioral unit has three parts: (1) the stimulus, which might be a condition set by the teacher; (2) the child's response or target behavior; and (3) the reinforcement, or consequent event, that follows the child's response. According to this theory, a child's behavior is changed by working with these three components. Teachers who use behavioral theory in the classroom use such techniques as direct instruction, mastery learning, or explicit teaching. You identify the academic skills that the student needs to learn and structure the classroom environment such that the student achieves success. The classroom is teacher directed, not student directed. There is focus on learning basic skills. You share goals and objectives with students. Each lesson is timed, you teach the lesson to the students, assess them, provide immediate feedback, and teach the skill until mastery occurs (Rosenshine, 1986; Rosenshine & Stevens, 1986).

Behavior analysis is often used with students with special needs

Behavior analysis is a technique that involves analyzing academic tasks and breaking them into steps. Robert Gagne (1984) advocated this strategy, which divides a complex task into its component parts or subskills. Students learn the subskills in sequential order, practice them, master them, and learn to perform the task. You teach the skills using direct instruction. If the student can perform the task, you did a good job of teaching. Your role is to begin by setting clear goals and objectives for students, breaking larger goals into simpler ones. You sequence lessons so that you can teach the skills. You do most of the talking and most of the work in the classroom. Students listen passively as you explain the work. There are lots of opportunities for drill and practice, and students often complete worksheets to practice the skills. If students make mistakes, you correct them, using assessment to determine whether the students are learning the skills.

Behavioral psychology and direct instruction are often successful with students with learning disabilities. Once you know what skills the student lacks, this method provides a way for you to help the student gain the skills. Ms. King could use direct instruction with Todd, who has difficulty following directions. If she plans his instruction such that she helps him to organize his thinking, things might be easier for him. Even though she believes in student-centered teaching and learning, there is a place for direct teaching methods in her teaching repertoire, especially with certain students. Once she helps Todd to organize and follow directions, he too can explore and investigate.

Cognitive Psychology

Disorders of psychological processing

Cognitive psychology deals with processes by which people learn, think, know, and understand. In the field of learning disabilities, three models from cognitive psychology are especially important: (1) disorders of psychological processing, (2) the information-processing model, and (3) cognitive learning theories. The idea of psychological processing disorders brings forth the view that students are differently abled with regard to processing and using information. This affects their learning. Some students have auditory processing problems, meaning they have difficulty taking in information that they hear. Students with visual processing problems have difficulty with information taken in visually. As a teacher, you will develop lessons for specific students by building processes that are weak and taking advantage of preferred learning styles and areas of strength. In essence, you will strengthen the weakness while focusing on the strength (Lerner, 1997).

Information processing traces the flow of information from point of input to output

The **information-processing model** traces the flow of information from the point of input, through the processing function, to the output. Examples of inputs are a visual, auditory, or tactile stimulus, or something that a student hears or reads, smells, or tastes. Cognitive processes include such behaviors as thinking, memory, and decision making. Examples of outputs are actions and behaviors such as talking, writing, and learning. The human brain takes in information, stores it in the memory, organizes and processes information, and responds to the information (Lerner, 1997). The memory system is important to you as a teacher.

According to the information-processing model, information flows through three systems: (1) the sensory register, (2) the short-term memory (or working memory), and (3) the long-term memory (Atkinson & Shiffrin, 1968).When information comes in through the senses, it is stored briefly in the *sensory register*. Unless the student acts on it, the information is likely to be lost. This is significant for you, because lessons should be engaging enough to cause students to pay attention to what's happening in the classroom—to the information coming in through the sensory register. If a lesson isn't stimulating enough for students, they are likely to tune out.

After passing through the sensory register, information passes to the *short-term* or *working memory*. Once again, students must act on the information or it too will be lost. Organizing and classifying information, rehearsing or repeating it, using drill and practice, or linking the information with prior knowledge are ways in which you can help students retain information that enters the short-term memory.

The *long-term memory* is the permanent storage space for information. To use long-term memory, students must retrieve it and bring it into working memory.

Tapping prior knowledge, using graphic organizers such as concept maps and word webs, and remembering key words helps students to retrieve long-term memory and use it in the learning process (Lerner, 1997).

Modifying Science Instruction to Include Students with Learning Disabilities

The learning strategies approach offers students with learning disabilities a repertoire of strategies that focus on *how* they learn rather than on *what* they learn. Table 9.4 (see page 244) contains strategies for helping students with learning disabilities in the science classroom.

I would now like to share a personal experience with you. Over the past several years, I have included a very special person in my elementary science methods course. You will find that Meredith Saltiel has a great deal to teach elementary science teachers.

When Meredith was finishing high school, she visited me with her job coach to find out if there was a way she could work at our college. She would be 22 years old in August and was eager to begin her life in the real world. I was immediately impressed by Meri's enthusiasm. Her blue eyes sparkled as she told me how she loved to work with children. She explained that her mother teaches the primary grades and her twin sister, Shanna, just graduated from college and was about to enter a graduate program in teaching. Meri shared their love for children and would be happy to work with the students in our teacher education department in any way she could. I told her I'd let her know if something came up.

During the summer that followed, as I wrote my syllabus for the fall semester, I focused on ways to bring issues of multiculturalism, diversity, and inclusion into the science methods course. We generally discussed these topics, studied the research, and developed methods for addressing *all* students in the elementary science class. My students used these strategies as they created lesson plans, then experimented with them in the practicum part of the course. At that point, an interesting thought came to mind. Our college classroom is a pretty homogeneous setting. While we do have some cultural diversity, there are no special learners. What if we were to include a student with a disability in our class for the whole semester? My students would have a unique opportunity to learn. I thought about Meri, because she is a special learner. During her infancy, she developed cerebral palsy and learning disabilities. Meri has a great deal of experience with special education classes, as she spent many years in special education before being included in regular classes in high school. She possesses a wealth of knowledge, and I asked her if she would be willing to share it with my students.

I called Meri in late August and asked if she would like to attend all sessions of my science methods course for the fall semester. She would be a resource specialist in special education, a peer to my students, helping them learn about students with learning differences. Meri would share her expertise with the class as they learned about science and science teaching. She would participate in the hands-on activities, working with my students to give them her view of the activity.

Table 9.4
Learning Strategies for Special Learners in the Elementary Science Class

Self-questioning

Encourage students to ask themselves questions about the material. Here are some organizing questions:

1. What is the lesson about?
2. What problem are we solving?
3. What are the goals of the lesson?
4. How can I solve this problem?
5. Do I have a plan?
6. What is my plan?
7. Am I following my plan?
8. How did I do?

Review Aloud and in Your Head

Listen to what the teacher says and repeat his or her words in your head.

Review what you're learning by saying the words aloud.

Review what you're learning by saying the words in your head.

Determine the Main Ideas

Pay attention to the lesson and pick out the main ideas.

After you have the main ideas, pick out the supporting details.

Try to relate the new information to something you already know.

Memory Tricks

If you have to memorize information, use memory tricks to make things easier.

Modeling

The teacher presents a problem and shows what the student should do to solve the problem. The student knows how to go about solving a problem and solves the next problem using this model.

Checking for Mistakes

Students become accustomed to looking for mistakes on their own before handing in work. This helps deal with students who are impulsive.

Lerner, Janet W., *Learning Disabilities: Theories, Diagnosis, and Teaching Strategies,* Seventh Edition. Copyright © 1997 by Houghton Mifflin Company. Reprinted with permission.

We invited Theresa, my graduate research assistant, to join our team. Her background as a special education teacher, coupled with her undergraduate degree in elementary science, strengthened our collaboration. We formulated a number of research questions to guide our work. We asked, "How can preservice teacher education programs better prepare regular elementary education majors to meet the challenges associated with inclusion of special-needs students in science education?" and "In what ways can teachers modify curriculum and instruction to meet the needs of special learners in the elementary science class?" We also studied ways to address behavioral and instructional challenges associated with inclusive education in elementary science and studied teacher attitudes toward inclusion. Two of my colleagues in regular education offered their classes as a control, since they were not involved in our intervention.

Throughout the semester, we developed and tested strategies for teachers of students with learning disabilities who were included in the science class. We repeated the study in the two subsequent semesters. We collected a range of qualitative and quantitative data. Some data analysis is complete, and some continues.

We found that the students exposed to our intervention had better attitudes toward inclusion than those in the regular program. The study highlighted the importance of thoughtful inclusion for student teachers, which included discussions of unacceptable behaviors and instructional supports intended to counter them. The effect of the intervention on our group was not simple acceptance of individuals with disabilities. Rather, it was acceptance of individuals with disabilities in the elementary science classroom when it is done thoughtfully and with the supports that are likely to make it successful.

Including Special Learners

Over the past 30 years, regular and special education have come together in many ways. While special education students were once isolated from students in regular education, educators and policymakers began to realize that all people live together in society. The idea of placing special education students in the least restrictive environment gained popularity and led to more integration of students and programs.

Models of including students with special needs

The three predominant models of including students with special needs in regular education are (1) mainstreaming (2) the regular education initiative, and (3) inclusion. With *mainstreaming*, a student with learning disabilities is carefully placed in the regular education class for a part of the day. The student might spend most of the day in special education classes and study science with regular education peers. Both the special education and regular education teachers monitor the student. The *regular education initiative* comes from the U.S. Department of Education Office of Special Education and Rehabilitative Services. This initiative suggests that students with learning disabilities spend most of their time in the regular education classroom (Reynolds, Wang, & Walberg, 1987; Wang, Reynolds, & Walberg, 1986). Such a system eliminates the stigma attached to special education classification and makes appropriate instruction available for students with learning problems who are not eligible for special education programs. The **inclusion model** aims to place and teach all students in the regular education class. This would eventually lead to the elimination of special education classes and the elimination of labels for students with disabilities (The Association for Students with Severe Handicaps [TASH], 1993).

The idea of full inclusion for all students in the regular education class meets with some opposition, as many students with disabilities need services that are not easy to provide in regular education settings. Our intervention aims to help the elementary science teacher provide appropriate instruction for the student with learning disabilities in the regular elementary science classroom.

Practical suggestions for working with students with special needs in the regular classroom

In order to understand the frustration, anxiety, and tension often felt by students with learning disabilities, we viewed an outstanding Public Broadcasting System video called *F.A.T. City—How Difficult Can This Be?* In the video, Richard Lavoie, a learning disabilities professional, presents a number of simulations designed to emulate the experiences of children with a range of learning disabilities. The viewer understands how a student with a specific learning disability perceives a particular situation. I highly recommend this video, as I believe it will help you to better understand students with special needs. Here are some practical suggestions that we have found useful in working with students with learning disabilities in the science class:

Access to Content. When a special education student enters the science classroom, you must first determine how that child best accesses the content. Can he listen and comprehend? Can he read and comprehend? Is it best to tape record directions and explanations? Would the child benefit from a side-by-side reading situation in which he works with a peer? Is assistance from the resource or inclusion teacher recommended? Next, you determine the amount of content the student can handle. After conferring with the special education teacher and observing the student, determine how much work the child can complete without frustration.

Support. The student with special needs often requires support. Assess the student, confer with her, and decide whether she will work alone, side by side with a partner, or in a group. This configuration may change from time to time depending on the activity. As the year progresses, the special-needs student may require less support. You may also find that she fits into the regular education class more easily.

Set Evaluation Expectations. Just as you do with students in the regular classroom, confer with the student with special needs and set evaluation expectations. If you use performance assessment, explain the performance task-response sheet-scoring system to the student. Let the student know how you will assess him.

Differentiated Learning. With learners of different abilities, you will need to adapt lessons in various ways. First, determine how much repetition your special-needs students require to learn the material. Find out how much work they can handle, how much time they need to complete an assignment, and how they access the content. It is likely that you will need more than one set of lesson plans. One set is for the regular class and the other set adapts your lessons for special learners.

When a Student Is Stuck. Sometimes special-needs students are stuck. They don't understand, and they don't have strategies that will help. You can set up learning centers around the room to help them access the content. Chapters on tape, reading assignments, and computers with proper software or access to the Internet help to move them forward. Being aware of their learning strategies also helps.

If Students Begin to Get Out of Control. Special-needs students sometimes exhibit aggressive behavior and are difficult to control. Perhaps the most important result of our research is that attitudes toward including special-needs students in the regular education classroom improved following our intervention. We developed ways to help new teachers maintain control of the classroom in difficult situations. Here is one technique that works.

Every teacher needs a *stop* signal. You can hold up your hand or simply tell students to stop in a firm voice. You can ask them to close their eyes. Ask everyone to remain silent for a few seconds. Tell them what you want them to do, then go on. If a particular student causes problems, schedule a one-minute conference. Write unsolicited letters of reference for students who are doing a good job to reinforce good behavior. For some students, behavior is a definite problem. If you establish the rules at the start and adhere to them consistently, you can expect to have fewer problems.

Working with a Short Attention Span. If a student has a short attention span, shorten the task that you assign. Give less homework. You will find that engaging science lessons that encourage thinking and group work often solve the problem of the short attention span.

Handling Distractions. Some students are easily distracted. This can be dangerous when engaging in science activities. Seat such students near you and surround them with quiet students. Scan the room for distracters, and keep them as far away from the students as possible. Give simple directions. We found that some easily distractible students were easier to handle when kept busy. It often helps to cover their desks with a large sheet of paper and allow them to doodle as they listen and work.

Ending the Science Activity. Students with learning disabilities often enjoy hands-on science. They may have difficulty transitioning from the science activity to another activity. Let them know that the science activity will end and another activity will begin. Provide time for transition. Allow them to unwind before moving on.

When a Student Refuses to Work in a Group. Some students with learning disabilities may refuse to work in a group because of unsuccessful prior experiences. Find one other student who can work with the child. Allow the pair to explore together. Then add another student to the group. Gradually build the student's confidence and social skills.

I May Be Paying Attention Even If I Look Like I'm Not. Many students with learning disabilities need extra time to process. They often look like they are bored, not paying attention, or "spacing out." This is especially true in inquiry-based science lessons, which require lots of thought. Meri shared a story of a teacher who constantly reprimanded her and called her lazy because she had a blank stare on her face. We learned by working with Meri that the look was one of deep thought, not boredom or lack of attention. With extra wait time, an excellent answer resulted. It just took a little longer than we thought it would. Be patient and don't be judgmental.

Listening Skills. Be sure the child comprehends what she is hearing. Have the child repeat what she hears. She may hear but not understand. This is something you should assess regularly.

Organizing Work. Organizing work is the number one priority for many science teachers. Students are often unprepared, lose important papers, forget their books, and don't follow directions. Several years ago, I conducted research on how elementary science students follow directions. I observed 84 lessons in one year and found that when the teacher began to give directions, about 50 percent of the students stopped listening. They generally began to search through papers in their desks. It was not a surprise to learn that they could not follow the directions, because they didn't hear them. When you give directions, be sure everyone listens. Don't allow students to do anything but listen to you. Have students repeat the directions; otherwise they are not likely to know what to do. You may choose to tape record your directions so that special learners (and others) can hear them again.

Working with Science Equipment. Working with science equipment can bring challenges you never considered. When working with Meri, we learned that many of the activities we thought were appropriate for all students were difficult for a student with an orthopedic handicap. Assess your activities for developmental appropriateness as well as psychomotor readiness. Some students may have an immature grasp or an inability to manipulate equipment. You may not be able to predict all difficulties, but you will detect them as the lesson proceeds. Make substitutions the next time around.

Classroom Rules, Especially for Safety. As with all of your students, be sure your special-needs students follow all safety rules. At the start of the year, develop a list of safety rules together. Post them in the room. Before each activity, make it a point to talk about safety. Have your special-needs students repeat the rules aloud. If an activity is likely to pose some danger if not carried out properly, and if you believe directions won't be followed, think of ways to substitute another activity.

Timing Activities. We learned from our work that special-needs students require varying amounts of time to complete their work. It often takes them much longer to get organized and get started. If possible, assign a teammate or buddy to help with organization. Provide extra time for completing an assignment, or assign less work to the special-needs student.

Homework.   Completing homework can be a problem for special-needs students. The frustration of organizing, thinking, and completing an assignment can grow when the student is at home and you're not there to help. Be sure the assigment is appropriate. Students who are particularly disorganized often forget their books. Having one set of books at home and another at school is helpful. Conferencing with parents or guardians about homework is essential.

Organizational Calendar.   To help organize your students, post an organizational calendar in the class. Let students record special events and assignment due dates.

A message from a woman with a learning disability

    I would like to conclude this section with a message that Meri wrote for you. It will help you gain insight into the life of a student with special needs.

When I was younger I had a teacher who thought of my learning disability as a behavior problem. It was really hard for me because I was always punished for daydreaming and didn't always understand why.

    I always thought I was a bad kid. I was put on a behavior modification chart for daydreaming. That chart was sent home for my parents to see every day. The teacher always wrote comments on the chart. These comments were about my day. Sometimes they were good and sometimes they were bad. It was almost like blaming me for having a disability.

    My whole school experience was all right. I had some good teachers and some not so good teachers. My teachers always got upset by my slowness. It always became a problem. It was always very hard for me, because I wanted to go faster and wanted to please my teachers. I was always pulled out for therapy and had to miss classes.

    When I was older I went to vocational school for three years. It was OK, but the teachers always told me to go more quickly. They also told me that I wasn't doing things right. However, I do feel that I learned a lot from vocational school.

    I finished my last two years at regular high school. The first year was the best year of my life. I had a great teacher who encouraged me and changed my thoughts about school. The next year I was a postgraduate student. Again I had a teacher who didn't care about disabled students. She always made me feel bad, whether it was not doing a job correctly, being too slow, or not speaking loudly enough.

    My recommendation is for all teachers to understand learning disabilities. You should become aware of the disabilities your students have and work with them to prepare them for life after school.

Activity 9.7 Lesson Design: Adapting a Lesson on the Microscope

Special-needs students use the microscope: Life science

Overview: You have presented a lesson on the use of the microscope and found that three or four students just don't understand. They can't use the microscope properly. You realize that since these are special-needs students, you must reteach the lesson and adapt it for them. You decide to give them step-by-step directions and go very slowly.

Procedure: Plan a lesson on the use of the microscope for your special-needs students. Write step-by-step directions for them. What other adaptations might you include in the lesson? Will you have them explain the directions to you before they work with the microscopes? Will you have them work with a partner who can help?

Assessment: Even though you guide students slowly using step-by-step procedures, you still want them to have an opportunity to use the microscopes to explore. Select something for your students to observe with their microscopes. Have them draw and describe what they see. Let them write about the experience in their science journals. Discuss the experience with them. Plan an appropriate homework assignment for them. ■

Activity 9.8 Lesson Design: Planning a Field Trip to the Pond

Planning a field trip

Overview: In this activity, you will plan a field trip to the pond. You will decide who should accompany you to ensure the safety of your students. You will write a letter to parents letting them know that there will be a science field trip to the pond.

Procedure: Plan the field trip to the pond. Who will chaperone the trip? Write a letter to parents, and include a permission slip for them to sign and return to you.

Assessment: Read the letters written by your classmates. How do they compare? ■

Teaching Gifted Students

In this section, you will learn about addressing the needs of gifted students in the elementary science classroom. Our science theme will continue as you learn about pond life.

What Is Giftedness?

Definitions of giftedness

Intellectual giftedness is related to the concept of **intelligence,** which is the capacity to acquire, process, and use information (Hunt & Marshall, 1999). Early definitions of giftedness required that a student score above 140 on an IQ test. Current definitions are much broader. Paul Witty (1940) suggests that anyone who exhibits consistently remarkable performance in an important area should be considered gifted. An exceptional teacher, a talented basketball player, or an outstanding designer would all be considered gifted.

Joseph Renzulli (1978) argues that creativity and task commitment, as well as a high level of intelligence, are important aspects of giftedness. **Creativity** is the ability to generate unique, imaginative, creative, original ideas. **Task commitment** is the ability to stay focused and stay with a project until its completion. A gifted person must be able to create a product or performance that shows evidence of the giftednes.

Robert Sternberg (1991, 1997) developed a triarchic theory, which states that there are three types of intellectual giftedness: analytic giftedness, creative giftedness, and practical giftedness. An analytically gifted person can effectively analyze, evaluate, and critique a situation. A person with creative giftedness can discover, create, and invent. A person with practical giftedness can implement, utilize, and apply (Hunt & Marshall, 1999).

As you read earlier in this chapter, Howard Gardner (1983) believes there are seven intelligences. According to Gardner, if a person exhibits abundant talent in any of these areas, he or she is considered gifted in that area. Gardner believes that a person can be gifted in more than one area.

Activity 9.9 Online: Internet Resources for Gifted Education

Overview: In this activity, you will explore a web site that has links to information on gifted education.

Procedure: Log onto http://www.cec.sped.org/faq/gt-urls.htm

Assessment: What interesting links did you find? ▪

Addressing the Needs of Gifted Students in the Science Classroom

Addressing the needs of gifted students in the science classroom

Just as you will modify curriculum and instruction for students with special needs, you will modify the curriculum for gifted students. Techniques such as independent study, content acceleration, enrichment, cluster grouping, cooperative learning, and fostering higher-level thinking work well with gifted students.

Independent Study. In Chapter 6, you learned about writing science units. Some units are appropriate for independent study. When you write a unit of study, you begin with a concept map. The concept map outlines all of the subtopics that fit into the unit. If a gifted student is going to work independently on a unit, you might begin by having the student examine the concept map and select the subtopics that are of interest to him or her. You work with the student to decide how the topics will be further explored.

Gifted students need guidance just as any other student does. Sometimes teachers assume that because a student is gifted, no further guidance is needed. If a student is going to work independently, she or he must work with you to develop a work plan. If library research is involved, determine what is required. Be sure to monitor the library research so that you know if the student is on the right track. If the student will do an Internet search, look at the results of the search. Monitor the student's search strategies. If an experiment is to be set up, be sure it is done properly and with respect for safety. A well-monitored independent study project will be much more successful than one performed without enough guidance.

Enriching the Content. Sometimes the regular science curriculum is inappropriate for a gifted student because he or she has already mastered the content or skills you are teaching. The danger of not enriching the content for such a student is that boredom, frustration, or a negative attitude toward the subject may result. If you have a student who already knows what you are teaching, you should allow him or her to explore the subject in greater depth.

When my students teach a science topic, I link them with science experts. If a teacher is teaching about meteorology, I find a meteorologist the teacher can consult. If astronomy is the subject, we locate an astronomer who is willing to help. When a teacher has a gifted student in the class, the professional scientist is always able to provide an extension or exploration to challenge that student. The student can then extend his or her knowledge of the subject. With the Internet so readily available, experts in science can be contacted easily no matter where your school is located. The "Ask an Expert" web sites (see Activity 9.10) are excellent places to find scientists who can help you enrich or accelerate your curriculum for gifted students.

Activity 9.10 Online: Ask an Expert

Overview: In this activity, you will contact experts in various disciplines to find out how to accelerate or enrich content for a gifted student.

Procedure: Develop a question to ask and log onto these web sites to meet experts who can assist you:

http://k12science.stevens-tech.edu/curriculum/aska/science.html

http://www.sciam.com/askexpert/

Assessment: How helpful were the suggestions from the experts? ▪

Accelerating the Student. Instead of enriching the content, you might decide to accelerate the student. This means the student moves ahead to the content that will be covered in a subsequent grade. This is beneficial because the student covers the content more quickly, and the content is likely to be more appropriate. The drawback is that when the student gets to the grade in which that content will be covered, he or she has already covered the material. This may pose a problem for that teacher. If you are going to accelerate a student, be sure that negative effects won't result in the future.

Clustering Gifted Students. You might decide to group gifted students so they can work together. Just as students with special needs often have a resource teacher to guide them, your school may provide a resource teacher to work with a group of gifted students. They remain in cluster groups for part of the time and work in the regular classroom as well.

Cooperative Learning. Gifted students often benefit from working cooperatively in heterogeneous groups. When students work as a team, they have the benefit of sharing ideas with others. They also practice their social skills. If a task is well designed, each member of the team will participate equally and have something to offer others. Chapter 10 focuses on using cooperative learning in elementary science, and you will learn more about managing cooperative groups in that chapter.

Fostering Higher-Level Thinking. One of the best ways to challenge gifted students is to present them with ways to employ higher-level thinking. Elementary science presents unique opportunities for such activities. When students explore, observe, test hypotheses, experiment, analyze data, and draw conclusions, they employ higher-level thinking. How is this done? Let's now return to Ms. King's class to see how she adapts instruction for gifted students.

Studying Pond Life: Lessons for Gifted Students

You will now apply what you learned about teaching gifted students as you join Ms. King and her class on a field trip to the pond. She will share her thoughts as she makes instructional decisions to address the needs of gifted students.

Studying Macroorganisms in a Pond

Gifted students study macroorganisms in a pond: Life science

Ms. King's students are gathered around the local pond. They are working in groups. There are two gifted students, Sarah and José. Ms. King has them work as a pair. They cover the same content the other students do, but she knows they can move along very quickly. She has prepared a list of questions for the whole class and has a separate list for them. Ms. King expects them to finish first, and she wants them to learn more.

Ms. King asks everyone to identify the organisms they see with their eyes. These are macroscopic organisms, which are big enough to see with the unaided eye. She instructs them to create a data chart to organize their observations. They will list what they see, which includes frogs, mosquitoes, tadpoles, plants living both in and around the pond, birds, and dragonflies. She asks them to describe what they see. In a previous lesson she taught about what it means to observe and describe carefully, so most students know what to do.

While the class makes observations, Ms. King speaks with Sarah and José. She wants them to focus on the plant life in the pond. She asks them to think of ways in which the plants are adapted to water. What parts of the plants allow them to live in water? How are those plants different from those that live in soil? How are all plants similar? How are they different (Delta Science Module, 1989)?

Ms. King moves from group to group, monitoring students at work. Sarah and José work well together, and they are enjoying this investigation. When they are finished, she speaks with them briefly to be sure they are on track. She asks them to think about the organisms they see at the pond. How are they the same? How are they different? How do they move around? Do organisms that live in water move differently than those that live on land?

When they get back to class, Ms. King has Sarah and José use the computer to search for sites related to their pond study. They formulate questions for further study. They not only completed the regular assignment; they went beyond and learned more.

Studying Microorganisms

Gifted students study microorganisms in a pond: Life science

As Ms. King left the pond, she took a sample of water in a jar. She wants her students to use their microscopes to observe the single-celled organisms, or *protozoa*, found in the pond.

The next day, students take out their microscopes. Each student gets a depression slide, a medicine dropper, and a cover slip. The depression slide has a small well to hold the sample.

Ms. King instructs the students to observe and draw the microorganisms they see on the slide. Sarah and José have an additional assignment: they study the body structures of the organisms, focusing on how they propel themselves through the water. They also try to determine what the organisms eat and how they are adapted to life in water.

Preparing a hay infusion: Life science

Ms. King knows she can provide students with another way to study these single-celled organisms. She will have Sarah and José prepare a **hay infusion.** They take a few spears of dried timothy grass (a wheatlike grass that is like hay), add a few dried leaves, a quarter-jar of pond water (especially the scum from the pond's surface), and some mudlike soil from the pond. They pour all the ingredients into a jar, cover it lightly with cheese cloth, and let it sit undisturbed in the classroom. Three days later, they add a half-dozen grains of uncooked rice.

Soon the dried grass and leaves begin to decay. The water becomes a little cloudy, and the mixture develops an unpleasant odor as the decay progresses. The one-celled microorganisms from the pond feed off the decayed plant matter and multiply. As long as there is decayed matter to eat in the jar, they live and multiply. When there is no more left to eat, they die.

Sarah and José tend to the hay infusion each day. When it's ready, they use their medicine droppers to get a sample from the bottom of the jar, being careful not to stir up the mixture. They place the sample on the slide. There are many microorganisms darting back and forth. Sarah and José take a few strands of cotton from a cotton ball and place them on the slide. This slows down the organisms that race around too quickly to be observed.

Drawing microorganisms: Life science

Sarah and José wonder whether the microorganisms will be different if they sample the water at the top of the jar. They take a new slide and another sample. Then they compare what they found in the pond water sample with what they found in the hay infusion. The microorganisms look different. The two students wonder whether they will find different microorganisms if they use something other than timothy grass to make the hay infusion. Ms. King is willing to let them prepare another culture. She asks them to draw and identify the microorganisms they have found so far (see Figure 9.6).

Ms. King wants the other students in the class to observe what's in the different cultures. The other students don't move along as quickly as Sarah and José, so she is more patient with them. Sarah and José are moving ahead at their own pace, posing and answering their own questions. She encourages them to

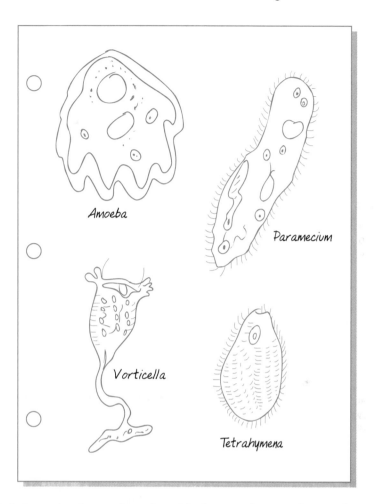

**Figure 9.6
Sarah and José
Observe and Draw
Microorganisms**

pursue their investigation and works with them as they continue to learn more. Armed with this background knowledge, the whole class is ready to begin an in-depth study of cells.

Constructing Your Knowledge of Science and Science Teaching

After completing this chapter, begin to reflect on your new knowledge about teaching all learners in the science classroom. Begin by thinking of the diversity that exists in your own classroom. How is diversity reflected in your work? What do you now know about learning styles? How will you use this knowledge in your teaching?

In this chapter, you read about addressing the needs of special learners in the science classroom. Think about the different theories applied to teaching special learners. How do they differ from methods of teaching students in the regular classroom? Can you use some of these methods to teach students without special needs? You also learned about addressing gifted learners. What strategies will you use to teach gifted students?

Key Terms

sustained inquiry (p. 216)
macroscopic (p. 216)
microscopic (p. 216)
learning styles (p. 220)
perceptual preferences
 (p. 222)

ordering abilities (p. 222)
magnification (p. 232)
lens (p. 233)
behavior analysis (p. 241)
information-processing model
 (p. 242)

inclusion model (p. 245)
intelligence (p. 250)
creativity (p. 250)
task commitment (p. 251)
hay infusion (p. 254)

Reviewing Chapter 9: Questions, Extensions, Applications, and Explorations

1. Now that you have read about learning styles, how would you describe your own learning style?

2. Design a science lesson that uses Bernice McCarthy's learning styles approach.

3. What experience do you have with teaching students with special needs in the science classroom? Describe an experience from your own education or one you have encountered as a teacher. What experience have you had with teaching gifted students?

4. Select an elementary science lesson and adapt it for a student with a special need. Then adapt it for a student who is academically gifted.

5. Describe a specific way in which constructivist teaching and direct instruction come together to address the needs of special learners.

Print Resources

Eisner, E. (1979). *The educational imagination.* New York: Macmillan.

Gardner, H. (1983). *Frames of mind.* New York: Basic Books.

Gardner, H. (1993). *Multiple intelligences.* New York: Basic Books.

Hunt, N., & Marshall, K. (1999). *Exceptional children and youth.* Boston: Houghton Mifflin.

Lerner, J. (1997). *Learning disabilities: Theories, diagnosis, and teaching strategies.* Boston: Houghton Mifflin.

McCarthy, B. (1987). *The 4MAT system.* Barrington, IL: EXCEL, Inc.

Morris, S., & McCarthy, B. (1990). *4MAT in action.* Barrington, IL: EXCEL, Inc.

VanTassel-Baska, J. (1992). *Planning effective curriculum for gifted learners.* Reston, VA: Council for Exceptional Children.

Electronic Resources

F.A.T. (Frustration, Anxiety, and Tension) City: How Difficult Can This Be?
http://www.addwarehouse.com/
This outstanding 70-minute video for teachers, parents, and counselors is designed to emulate the daily experiences of children with a variety of learning disabilities.

Parenting for High Potential
http://www.nagc.org
This web site offers resources for parents who want to help develop the potential of their gifted children.

Biology Lessons
http://www.biologylessons.sdsu.edu/index.html
This site contains lesson plans in a wide range of life science topics.

The Wildlife Discovery Project
http://www.rice.edu/armadillo/Schools/Hisdzoo
This site, created by the Houston Independent School District and the Houston Zoo, contains lesson plans about endangered animals.

Let's Collaborate
http://www.gene.com/ae/TSN/
This site links life science teachers with scientists. You can get involved in online projects, seminars, and discussion groups.

SAMI—Lesson Plans, Projects, and Classroom Ideas
http://www.learner.org/content/k12/sami/lessons.html
This site contains links to lesson plans, online projects, and classroom ideas in life science as well as other areas.

Using Microscopes
http://ofcn.rog/cyber.serv/academy/ace/sci/ceccsci006.html
This site helps you learn to use a microscope.

Staining Cells
http://www.mos.org/sln/sem/staining.html
If you want to learn how to stain a cell, log onto this site.

Making Wet Mounts
http://www.mos.org/sln/sem/wetmount.html
To learn to make a wet mount, check this site.

Children's Literature

Adkins, Jan
Wonder of Light: Big Book
(nonfiction and fiction)
(Newbridge, 1997)
ISBN: 1-56784-450-2
Grades 2–5

Bender, Lionel
Through the Microscope: Atoms and Cells (Franklin Watts, 1990)
ISBN: 0-53117-219-8
Grades 3–7

Horton, Casey
Under the Microscope: Animals
(Gareth Stevens, 1997)
ISBN: 0-83681-605-6
Grades 4–7

Jennings, Terry
Light (nonfiction and fiction)
(Raintree/Steck Vaughn, 1998)
ISBN: 0-81724253-8
Grades 3–7

London, Jonathan
Fireflies, Fireflies, Light My Way (fiction)
(Viking Children's Books, 1996)
ISBN: 0-670-85442-5
Preschool and Grades K–3

Millson, Frank
Light & Color
(Troll Associates, 1996)
ISBN: 0-8167-4048-8
Grades 3–7

Gibson, Gary
Light & Color with Easy-to-Make Scientific Projects
(Copper Beech Books, 1995)
ISBN: 1-56294-634-4
Grades K–4

Gordon, Maria
Fun with Light
(Thomson Learning, 1995)
ISBN: 1-56847-284-6
Preschool and Grades K–4

Challoner, Jack
Light and Dark
(Raintree/Steck Vaughn, 1996)
ISBN: 0-8172-4321-6
Grades 1–4

Tomecek, Steve
Bouncing and Bending Light
(Grosset & Dunlap, 1995)
ISBN: 0-7167-6541-1
Grades 3–7

Murata, Michinori
Water and Light: Looking Through Lenses
(Lerner Publications Co., 1992)
ISBN: 0-8225-2904-1
Grades 1–3

Edom, H.
Science with Light and Mirrors
(ECD Publications, 1992)
ISBN: 0-88110-547-7
Grades 1–4

Berger, Melvin
Light (Scholastic Trade, 1995)
ISBN: 1-56784-105-8
Preschool and Grades K–2

CHAPTER 10

Using Cooperative Learning with Science Instruction

This chapter begins with a lesson presented by Lynette Catalano, one of my student teachers. Lynn is quite proficient at integrating cooperative learning and science, and she has agreed to share her plan for this lesson with you.

Lynn's Plan for a Cooperative Learning Experience

After much thought, I came up with an idea for a culminating project for my second-grade dinosaur unit. We are going on an actual excavation—a dinosaur dig. The objectives of the lesson are:

▶ The students will be able to identify the experts involved in excavating fossils such as dinosaur bones while learning about their jobs.
▶ They will follow the steps involved in a dig by participating in one.
▶ They will collect fossils and classify them.
▶ They will work cooperatively with others throughout the lesson.

I formed the teams six weeks ago, when the unit began. There are one high achiever, two average achievers, and one low achiever on each team, and there are equal numbers of boys and girls. This is a diverse class, and the teams are mixed racially and ethnically.

For the introduction to the lesson, on the day before the dig, I plan to read *Digging up Dinosaurs* by Aliki to my students. I will review the members of a team of experts needed for a dig for dinosaur bones and describe their specific jobs. I will make hats for each team member: the paleontologist, the geologist, the draftsperson, and the worker. If there are five students in a group, I'll add a photographer.

In their cooperative groups, each student will assume the role of one of the team members. I plan to rotate the hats, giving each student an opportunity to experience each job on the dig. Students must work as a team, with each member doing his or her specific task. The groups will work independently at their own pace. I plan to be the timekeeper so that everyone has an equal amount of time on a given task.

Preparing for a science activity

I'll need about 45 minutes to set up the activity and prepare the site before the dig begins. I bought wooden dinosaur skeletons at a local dollar store. All of the bones come separately in the package, and there's a template to follow to construct the dinosaur. The bones will all be buried at the "dig" site. I removed the meat from drumsticks, ham, and beef bones and boiled them in water with one tablespoon of bleach for an hour. Then I baked the clean bones in an oven at 300 degrees

Ensuring that materials are safe: Safety

Fahrenheit for another hour to dry them. I'll use large potatoes to simulate dinosaur eggs. These will also be buried in the dig site. I plan to use five plastic containers, one for each cooperative group. Each container will have cast imprints of footprints and plants (these are intended to be fossils), plastic teeth, boiled bones, dinosaur eggs, and a complete wooden dinosaur broken into skeletal parts scattered through the layers.

The layers consist of a bottom layer of sand, which students won't remove. The next layer up is dry mulch or sawdust. The top layer is crunched-up newspaper representing rock and topsoil. As the dig begins, each group will receive supplies that include a hand rake, shovel, spoons, plastic meat trays, bowls, paintbrushes of various sizes, and plastic bags. As some students find objects in the layers, others will clean, draw, label, and record findings, then graph their results.

Designing a lesson for diverse learners

This project uses many teaching techniques, including cooperative learning, tactile learning (students dig and remove objects), auditory teaching, learning through group interaction, and visual learning. It provides learning opportunities for students with a variety of learning styles and provides experiences for multiple intelligences.

Putting the Idea into Practice

Explaining group roles

After planning the lesson carefully, Lynn presents it to her students. She begins by displaying the different layers of the earth. Each group gets a plastic bag in which to place the layers from the dig. Students take on the role of paleontologist, draftsperson, geologist, and worker. Two groups have a photographer. The geologist shows teammates maps of the region and explains why this is a good place to dig for fossils. The paleontologist studies the prehistoric specimens they find; the draftsperson labels, measures, and draws the fossils; and the worker

A paleontologist studies prehistoric specimens; a geologist analyzes maps of the region: Earth science

does the digging. The photographer snaps photos and keeps a visual record of their work.

Clarifying group roles

Lynn reviews the roles with the children and poses questions and problems that they might anticipate on the dig. In their groups, they discuss the problems that might arise. What if they don't find anything? What if they find something they can't identify? How will they get to the site? They answer these questions together. Once the students have clarified their roles and responsibilities, Lynn distributes the plastic bags, plastic trays, color-coded hats labeled with roles, and plastic dishes.

Establishing classroom rules (safety)

Next, she sets the rules for behavior on the dig. Students can confer, but they must use their six-inch voices, meaning they must speak softly. She reminds them that she will use "clap once" to get their attention. If they hear her clap, they must stop what they are doing immediately. If things get too loud, she can bring them to order in an instant.

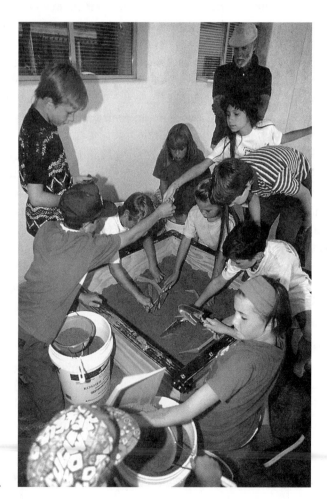

Digging for dinosaur bones in the classroom.

Lynn reviews what will happen on the dig by referring to *Digging up Dinosaurs.* Once again, she reviews each role. She reviews the rules for a successful dig, which she posts in front of the room. Together she and her students review the tools they have. Now she gives workers a shovel, a rake, and a spoon.

Lynn excels in managing the classroom, especially during cooperative learning activities. She gives directions carefully and clearly. She is sure that all students are aware of expectations. Many teachers prefer not to use cooperative learning because they fear they will lose control of the class. Because Lynn has had a great deal of practice, she knows that if she sets and reviews rules with her students and monitors their performance, she will be successful. Once the activity begins, she will circulate among the groups, question students, and scaffold their learning. She can do this only when she is satisfied that there is order in the classroom and everyone is on task.

She tells her students it's time to begin the dig. Excitement fills the classroom. Groups come up to the containers that she set up for the dig. Each group waits its turn to come to the dig site. While the groups wait, they review the classroom rules and the group roles. Lynn circulates around the room and tells students to stop digging after they explore the first layer. Draftspersons return to their seats to label, measure, and draw their findings. Then Lynn tells students they can remove the next layer. She reminds them that they are now in the sawdust layer, and those who are allergic to sawdust should refrain from touching it.

Rotating roles (equity)

Now students change roles. The paleontologist becomes the worker, and the draftsperson becomes the geologist. Lynn reminds students that they should know the responsibilities of their new positions. They can read the rules for the dig or consult with their teammates.

Carrying out an informal assessment and scaffolding learning

Again Lynn circulates among the groups, carrying out an informal formative assessment, asking questions, and scaffolding instruction. She stops at each group and confers with students to find out what they are learning and hear about their specimens. Once again, students change roles and complete the dig.

Observing, classifying, and analyzing results: Science process

Team members now return to their groups to classify and organize. They change roles one more time. Now all students have had a chance to assume each role. The students begin to sort through their findings. Once again Lynn circulates from group to group, asking questions. The children examine their objects and classify them. Each team has a different classification scheme. Some classify by type of object, others classify by size of object. They remove their hats and work together in their "laboratories" to analyze their results. Students confer with one another throughout this process. They then separate the wooden bones. Lynn hands out the template, and they construct a miniature dinosaur.

This hands-on activity is a success. The communication among students is a key factor. Students share ideas as they dig for fossils and dinosaur bones. Classroom management is excellent, and no problems whatsoever arise. Assigning roles to students and having them assume each one is important to the success of the lesson.

Cooperative learning is an instructional strategy that works well with elementary science. It is a way to organize the classroom so that your students work together in teams to accomplish a task. They depend on one another in a positive way, participate equally in the work, and at the same time are accountable for their own work. Instead of standing in front of the classroom and talking a great deal, you turn the classroom over to your students in a highly structured way. Students know what they are supposed to accomplish; as they work, you monitor them, circulating from group to group, listening to students' talk, asking questions, and scaffolding instruction. The groups are student directed rather than teacher directed. You are in control of the classroom every step of the way, but your students have the freedom to inquire and discover as they work.

Lynn's classroom activity encapsulates much of what you will learn in this chapter. As you read on, you will learn more about cooperative learning from a research-based perspective. Then you will learn how you can implement cooperative learning in your science classroom. As you read this chapter, think about the answers to these questions:

1. **What is cooperative learning?**

2. **What cooperative learning strategies are used in elementary science?**

3. **How can I implement them in my classroom?**

4. **How do I use cooperative learning techniques to help my students learn about rocks and minerals?**

About Cooperative Learning

As a new teacher, you know that classroom performance is a prime consideration when providing education for students. One of the toughest decisions administrators and teachers face is how to structure schools to provide the best instruction possible. Should classes be grouped for instruction? Should they be arranged heterogeneously? Should students be grouped according to ability? Should there be grouping within classes? Should classes be self-contained or departmentalized? Should students be separated into different tracks in which they are exposed to different curriculum patterns that vary widely in expectations? Should a mixture of organizational strategies be employed?

Methods other than tracking can provide greater educational benefits for students

Historically, differently abled students were grouped and tracked by ability levels to serve their individual needs and variations. However, research indicates that methods other than tracking can provide greater educational opportunity for students. The use of cooperative learning techniques offers one way to address student diversity in heterogeneous classrooms.

What Is Cooperative Learning?

Cooperative learning uses small groups and teamwork to achieve academic and social gains

Cooperative learning refers to the use of small groups and teamwork to achieve a variety of academic and social gains in the classroom setting. Improved social relations in the classroom, accompanied by improved academic achievement, promote students' self-esteem in the cooperative classroom (Slavin, 1980). Students who participate in successful cooperative learning groups typically experience a strengthened social orientation, characterized by the development of an "attitude of concern for others, a commitment to the values of fairness and social responsibility, and the ability and inclination to act on these values in everyday life" (Solomon, Watson, Schaps, Battistich, & Solomon, 1990, p. 231).

Cooperative learning is beneficial for students whose cultures foster social or group learning

These gains occur irrespective of ethnic background, academic ability level, social class, or gender (Slavin, 1991). In addition, research shows that students who are physically or academically challenged do well in cooperative learning groups (Johnson, Johnson, Tiffany, & Zaidman, 1984; Madden & Slavin, 1983; Slavin, 1991; Stevens & Slavin, 1995). Extensive experimental research documents the positive social effects of cooperative learning on students in hundreds of classrooms at all levels of schooling (Hertz-Lazarowitz & Sharan, 1984). Cooperative learning is also beneficial for students whose cultures foster social or group learning. Many students of color come from cultures where learning occurs in social contexts, and such students benefit from participation in cooperative groups.

Cooperative Learning and Academic Achievement

Cooperative learning techniques in the classroom also promote academic achievement. Most studies show that students of high, average, and low ability gain equally from the cooperative experience (Johnson, Johnson, Tiffany, & Zaidman, 1984; Madden & Slavin, 1983; Slavin, 1991). Research shows that among the most successful approaches to improving students' achievement are cooperative learning methods in which group rewards are based on each group member's individual learning. The best learning effort of every member of the group is necessary for the group to succeed, and the performance of each group member must be clearly visible and quantifiable to the other group members (Slavin, 1983). Each student in the cooperative group is individually accountable for his or her own learning, as well as for the learning of other group members. Each member must contribute equally to the work of the group. In addition, cooperative learning provides a setting for face-to-face interaction among pupils who spend time working and studying together.

These conditions are quite different from those that prevail under teacher-dominated direct instruction. Recall from Chapter 1 that teacher-dominated methods include recitation, teacher-directed small groups, sharing time, and seat work (Weinstein, 1991). Barak Rosenshine (1979) characterizes direct instruction as a method in which "the teacher controls the instructional goals, chooses

With cooperative learning, students take responsibility for their work

materials appropriate for the student's ability, and paces the instructional episode" (p. 38). The teacher is a strong leader who "directs student activity, approaches the content in a direct and businesslike way, organizes learning around teacher-posed questions, and remains the center of attention" (p. 71). With teacher-centered methods of instruction, students have less responsibility for their own learning than in the cooperative group, in which students take a great deal of responsibility for their work.

Ability Grouping

In addition to teacher-centered direct instruction, ability grouping is prevalent in many schools. "Ability grouping exists to deal with one central fact of mass education: students differ in knowledge, skills, developmental stage, and learning rate" (Slavin, 1988). If a teacher prepares a lesson for a class, that lesson ideally should be at the appropriate level for all students. When lessons become too difficult for some students and too simple for others, instructional efficiency is being compromised. Ability grouping limits the apparent range of achievement and levels of performance among students.

Ability grouping has certain drawbacks

Although ability grouping may improve instructional efficiency, it is not without drawbacks that seriously offset its advantages. These drawbacks include misconceptions about learning, misconceptions about individual differences, and errors in judgment that underestimate what children can do. These factors often cause teachers to label students as underachievers and to place them in low-ability groups or slower tracks. Such grouping can stigmatize children and deprive them of future educational opportunities. Misconceptions about individual differences often lead to negative comparisons. While we recognize our cultural and individual differences, we often accompany this awareness with value judgments centering around such things as language, color, and dress. Many of these drawbacks can be avoided by implementing cooperative learning in your classroom.

Girls in the Science Classroom

"In my science class the teacher never calls on me, and I feel like I don't exist. The other night I had a dream that I vanished" (Sadker & Sadker, 1994, p. 14). Statements like these teach us that although Title IX prohibits gender discrimination, many females and members of underrepresented groups report the "disappearing syndrome" when in science class. Although most female and male students sit beside each other in classrooms and study with the same teachers, inequities still exist (Baker, 1987; Becker, 1981; Jones & Wheatley, 1990; Powell, 1994). Sadker, Sadker, Fox, and Salata (1994) report that from elementary school to graduate school, females receive less teacher attention and less useful teacher feedback from teachers, and they talk significantly less in class than boys do, being eight times less likely to call out comments. When they do call out comments, they are often reminded to raise their hands, whereas teachers accept such behavior by boys.

Cooperative learning helps girls foster friendships while working on science activities

Participating in cooperative groups can help to equalize participation in class. It can also help girls to foster friendships while working on science activities with other students who make them feel accepted and comfortable. Girls who are reluctant to report results from science activities to the whole class often find it easier to speak in a small group. Sharing work in groups also improves attitudes about reporting in general (Pickford, 1992).

Cooperative Learning and Racial and Ethnic Relations

Cooperative learning fosters cross-racial and cross-ethnic friendships

Through interaction and communication within small groups cooperating on academic tasks, cooperative learning methods strive to influence students' cognitive learning, along with their attitudes toward learning and thoughts about school. Another goal is to improve relations with members of other groups in racially and ethnically diverse classrooms. In a review of the literature, Robert Slavin examined 14 studies involving students in grades 3 through 12 who were engaged in cooperative learning. He reported that cross-ethnic friendships improved in the cooperative classrooms when compared with the control groups (Slavin, 1983b). You can bring these benefits to your classroom if you implement cooperative learning properly.

You will now read about the elements of cooperative learning in greater depth and apply them to teaching science.

Characteristics of Cooperative Learning Activities

Group goals are common to most cooperative learning methods

Cooperative learning methods share six principal characteristics (Slavin, 1989): (1) group goals, (2) individual accountability, (3) equal opportunity for success, (4) team competition, (5) task specialization, and (6) adaptation to individual needs. *Group goals* are common to most cooperative learning methods. This means the teacher and the students set goals for performance. Group members work together to help one another learn so that the group can achieve its goal. The group often receives an award in the form of a certificate of achievement for doing good work and reaching the group goal. Group members also feel satisfaction from achieving the goal.

Individual accountability is achieved by giving each student a task or responsibility

Individual accountability is achieved by giving each student a unique task and a special responsibility to carry out during group work. You can also structure individual accountability by making each group member individually responsible for his or her own performance on quizzes. You will read more about individual accountability in a few minutes.

Equal opportunity for success is structured by giving each student a role and a responsibility

Equal opportunity for success is structured by giving each student an equal chance to contribute to the success of the team. *Team competition* occurs when teams compete to achieve the best results. *Task specialization* is accomplished by assigning each team member a unique subtask. In Lynn's dinosaur dig, each student had a specific role and a task that accompanied it. Finally, *adaptation to individual needs* is accomplished by adapting instruction to individual students' needs so that each student's needs are met (Slavin, 1989, p. 135).

Once you introduce cooperative learning methods, a change occurs in the classroom organization. You modify the standard technique of teacher presentation and pupil recitation to accommodate for exchange among peers. Whole-group instruction is replaced by interaction among several groups, which is typical of a social system. You relinquish the role of dispenser of knowledge and control as students experience decentralized authority with a focus on promoting direct contact and exchange among students (Sharan, 1990).

Some teachers think that once cooperative learning is implemented in a classroom, no other teaching methods can be used. This is not true. You can use cooperative learning some of the time and still have whole-class discussions and use direct instruction when you think you should. In fact, many of the cooperative learning methods include a mixture of group work and direct instruction. As the teacher, you choose the instructional strategies that fit best with your students and your lessons.

Positive interdependence, individual accountability, equal participation, and simultaneous interaction define cooperative learning

Spencer Kagan (1994) explains that four basic principles define cooperative learning: positive interdependence, individual accountability, simultaneous interaction, and equal participation. For instructional purposes, you will work with Kagan's four principles, engaging in activities to practice each one, then putting all four together, as Kagan says that good cooperative learning activities include all four principles.

Positive Interdependence

Positive interdependence means that for a team to be successful, all members must contribute. Students help one another with learning tasks and interact face to face. If even one team member doesn't participate, the team cannot be successful. How is this arranged in the science classroom? There are several ways.

> **Structuring Positive Interdependence**
> ▶ Limit resources
> ▶ Ensure division of labor
> ▶ Assign responsibility
> ▶ Assign group roles

One way to structure positive interdependence is to *limit resources*. Put each student in charge of one of the materials needed to complete the task: Sara has the paper, Sam has the scissors, and Suhas has the graph paper. Each person is in charge of one of the resources. Here's another way. When your students engage in an activity or a project, each team member has a role; in other words, there is *division of labor*. Students can't finish the activity or project unless they work together to complete each task.

If your students are engaging in inquiry and they need to accomplish certain organizational tasks to do the investigation, put each student in charge of one task. Jhane can be in charge of gathering the science materials, Jon can be in charge

Table 10.1
Team Roles in the Cooperative Group

Role	Description
Materials manager	Manages the materials used during the investigation
Principal investigator	Takes charge of the investigation, asks questions, and keeps the group together
Taskmaster	Keeps everyone engaged and working on the task at hand
Checker	Checks to ensure that each team member can do the work for which he or she is responsible
Encourager	Encourages everyone in the group to work and steps in if group members can't get started or if someone is reluctant to participate
Gatekeeper	Ensures that all members participate in the activity
Praiser	Praises teammates for doing good work
Recorder	Records the work of the group and acts as a secretary

of getting the graph paper and markers, and June can be in charge of setting up the materials. When the investigation begins, there will be other tasks to complete. The group can't move forward unless everyone works together. Like Lynn, you can *assign group roles* so that you divide the task. Common roles in a science class are materials manager, principal investigator, taskmaster, recorder, checker, encourager, gatekeeper, and praiser. The investigation can't be completed unless students do each job. Table 10.1 lists and defines these roles.

Positive interdependence is very different from negative interdependence. In a class where negative interdependence prevails, the teacher makes a point of showing everyone whose work is best, calls on the same student even if others have their hands raised, and rewards some students while failing to recognize others.

Activity 10.1 Lesson Design: Structuring Positive Interdependence While Classifying Mineral Specimens by Hardness

A mineral is a natural solid object with a definite chemical makeup and structure: Earth science

Overview: This activity has two purposes: (1) to implement cooperative learning and (2) to learn a new science idea. In this activity, you will structure positive interdependence while your students study mineral specimens. A **mineral** is a natural solid object with a definite chemical makeup and structure (Christian & Felix, 1998). A **rock** is a mass of one or more mineral substances found in the earth. The minerals in rocks are not always present in the same amount.

Quartz, feldspar, talc, mica, calcite, and pyrite are minerals: Earth science

Materials: A bag of mineral specimens (e.g., quartz, feldspar, talc, mica, calcite, pyrite), a copper penny, a glass plate, newspapers to cover desks

Learning about rocks and minerals.

The Mohs scale classifies minerals by hardness: Earth science

Procedure: Divide your students into teams. Have each team cover its desk with newspaper. Each group needs a bag filled with mineral specimens. (You can get them from a science supply house or have your students bring in any mineral specimens they have collected. Most elementary schools have mineral specimens available. If yours doesn't, check with the local middle school or high school science teachers and see if you can borrow their specimens for a few days.) Have your students classify their minerals by hardness. They can use the Mohs scale to classify them (Table 10.2). The **Mohs scale,** named after geologist Frederich Mohs, is based on the hardness of ten different minerals. Using Table 10.2 as a guide, students can perform a test on each mineral specimen you provide and determine its hardness.

Your task is to structure positive interdependence into the activity. Select one or more techniques (listed in the section you just read) to accomplish this goal. To monitor the implementation of this technique, observe your students as they work.

Assessment: How did the lesson go? What evidence do you have that your students interacted positively with one another? After you are satisfied that you accomplished

Table 10.2
The Mohs Scale

Hardness Rating	Mineral	Test
1	Talc	Can be scratched by a fingernail
2	Gypsum	
3	Calcite	Can be scratched by a penny; cannot be scratched by a fingernail
4	Fluorite	Can be scratched by glass
5	Apatite	
6	Feldspar	Can scratch a glass marble
7	Quartz	
8	Topaz	
9	Corundum	
10	Diamond	Scratches all common materials

Properties of minerals include color, luster, hardness, crystal shape, transparency, and how they split: Earth science

the task of structuring positive interdependence into the activity (the cooperative learning part of the activity), you should extend the science exploration. Have students determine what additional properties of minerals they can observe. (They will need magnifiers. Other properties of minerals include color, luster, hardness, crystal shape, transparency, manner in which the mineral splits.) Now that your students are familiar with the Mohs scale, can they organize their minerals from softest to hardest by scratching one mineral with another? ▪

Individual Accountability

Unless each member of a group is **accountable** for completing his or her own work and for contributing to the work of the group, there won't be a gain in academic achievement (Slavin, 1983a). There are many ways to ensure that your students do their work and contribute to the group, but you must first ask what type of contribution you will expect each student to make.

> **Structuring Individual Accountability**
> ▶ Provide color-coded talking chips.
> ▶ Write summaries of group contributions.
> ▶ Go around the group and share what you heard someone else say.
> ▶ Each student writes with a different-color marker.
> ▶ Each student writes about how well the role was performed.

Color-coded talking chips determine who is talking and how much

To ensure that each student does a fair share of talking, you might give each group member several colored chips, called *talking chips:* Ann gets blue, Anya gets green, Alex gets red, and Angelo gets yellow. Each time a student participates, he or she puts a chip in the center of the table. If there are no yellow chips, Angelo did not talk much; if there are too many blue chips, Ann talked too much. You can also have students write summaries of their contributions to the group and reflect on those contributions.

You might set listening as a goal. Have students go around the group and share what they heard someone else say. This makes students listen, synthesize, and present findings. If students are working together on a project, give each one a different-color marker so you can see what each student contributes. If you have divided the task and assigned group roles, let students write about how well they performed their individual roles.

The following activity will give you practice in structuring individual accountability in your science class.

Activity 10.2 Lesson Design: Structuring Individual Accountability While Describing the Luster of Minerals

Overview: In this lesson, you will structure individual accountability as your students describe the luster of minerals.

Materials: A bag of mineral specimens (quartz, feldspar, talc, mica, calcite, pyrite), magnifiers, newspaper to cover desks

Luster is the way the surface of a mineral reflects light: Earth science

Nonmetallic minerals are dull, glassy, oily, pearly, or silky: Earth science

Procedure: Your students will classify minerals by **luster** (shine). You determine luster by the way in which the surface of the mineral reflects light. Minerals with metallic luster have the shine of metals. Nonmetallic minerals are either dull, glassy, oily, pearly, or silky. Have students think of everyday objects that have different types of luster (pearls, a glass, silk fabric). Then have them classify the minerals by type of luster. Your task is to structure individual accountability into the activity.

Assessment: How did the lesson go? What evidence do you have that you successfully structured individual accountability into the lesson? (Did students make oral presentations to present their results?) What common objects did students identify when they thought about luster? ▪

Simultaneous Interaction

Cooperative learning decreases teacher talk and increases student talk

In traditional classrooms, students often sit silently for most of the day. In 1984, John Goodlad reported that in a traditional classroom, teachers do 80 percent of the talking, with only 20 percent of the time left for students to talk (Goodlad, 1984). Think about what this means. If a lesson lasts for an hour and the teacher talks for 50 of the 60 minutes, that leaves 10 minutes for students to talk. If there are 25 or 30 students in the class, each one has less than half a minute to talk and ask or answer a question. That's not much time! Think about what happens when students work in cooperative groups. If there are four students in a group and the group has even 40 out of the 60 minutes to work, each student can talk for up to 10 minutes. If there are two students in the group, the amount of student talk doubles.

Simultaneous interaction means that instead of one person talking or asking a question at a time, many students can have turns at the same time. Simultaneous interaction goes beyond talking.

Structuring Simultaneous Interaction

▶ Assign a materials manager to each group.

▶ Consult teammates for help.

▶ Have small-group discussions.

If students are going to participate in an activity and the teacher distributes the materials, only one person acts. If students work in groups and there is a materials manager in each group, all groups get materials at the same time. That's more efficient. If there is a whole-class discussion and someone has a question, there is only one question and one answer. If students work in teams and have questions, they can consult their teammates and many students can receive help at the same time (Kagan, 1994). Part of constructing science knowledge is talking about what you think and clarifying your ideas. Cooperative learning enables this to happen in the science classroom.

Activity 10.3 Lesson Design: Structuring Simultaneous Interaction While Observing Streaks of Mineral Specimens

Overview: In this activity, you will structure simultaneous interaction while students observe streaks of mineral specimens.

Materials: Mineral specimens, streak plates, newspapers to cover desks. A piece of unglazed porcelain makes a good streak plate.

Minerals change color because of weathering: Earth science

Procedure: Not every sample of the same mineral looks the same on the outside. Sometimes minerals change color because of weathering or impurities that form in the sample. Even if a mineral has changed color on the outside, when you rub it on a streak

Table 10.3
Streak Tests for Minerals

Color of Streak Powder	Mineral
Colorless	Mica, quartz
Greenish-black	Chalcopyrite, pyrite
White	Feldspar, calcite, halite, sulfur, talc
Gray	Galena

A streak is a colored powder that a mineral leaves when rubbed on a streak plate: Earth science

plate, the color of the streak is the same. A *streak* is a colored powder that a mineral leaves when rubbed on a streak plate. In this activity, your students will perform a **streak test** on their mineral specimens by rubbing them on a streak plate and identifying them by the color of streak powder formed. Table 10.3 lists the streak colors of some common minerals.

Assessment: How did you organize the lesson to be certain that there was simultaneous interaction and that the greatest percentage of class members participated actively at any given time? ■

Equal Participation

Equal participation means students participate equally in their groups

Equal participation differs from simultaneous interaction. When structuring simultaneous interaction, you want to be certain that as many students participate at the same time as possible. When structuring **equal participation,** you want to ensure that students participate equally in their groups. Some students talk more than others. Some students are very quiet or shy. Low achievers may choose not to participate. Some students don't feel good about themselves and fade into the background. There are many ways for inequality to surface, so you have to be aware of them and use strategies to bring equality to the group. You might be thinking that you already know of several ways to structure equality.

> **Structuring Equal Participation**
> ▶ Divide the tasks.
> ▶ Use color-coded talking chips.
> ▶ Use a round-robin strategy.
> ▶ Use a roundtable strategy.
> ▶ Have students pair off for discussions; set the talking time.
> ▶ Rotate roles, and make sure each student has an equally challenging role.

You can encourage division of labor within a group. You can use color-coded talking chips. When you pose a question or when group members have a discussion, you can establish a rule stating that all members must take turns participating. You can use a *round-robin strategy* in which students go around the group from one member to another and everyone takes a turn speaking. Or you can use a *roundtable strategy* in which students go around the group from one member to the next and each student writes a response on the same sheet of paper. If students work in pairs, there can be a **timed pair discussion** in which each student talks for a specified, but equal amount of time.

If you assign roles when dividing the labor, be sure group members rotate roles so that each student has an equally challenging role. Some group roles *attend to the task* at hand, and others *maintain the group process*. Principal investigator, checker, and researcher attend to the task at hand. These students get the work done. Materials manager, encourager, and praiser help to maintain the group

This student is making a careful observation of a rock.

process and are less intellectually demanding roles. Be sure that all students have a chance to experience each role. This is important to keep in mind when equalizing group participation.

Activity 10.4 Structuring Equal Participation While Performing the Acid Test on Mineral Specimens

Overview: In this activity, you will structure equal participation while your students perform the acid test on their mineral specimens.

Materials: Mineral specimens, an empty foam egg container, safety goggles, vinegar, baking soda, medicine dropper

Wear safety goggles when performing the acid test: Safety

Procedure: Another way to gain information about minerals is to use the **acid test.** Vinegar is made of a weak acid called *acetic acid*. When vinegar reacts with certain substances, carbon dioxide gas is released. Your students should start by putting on their clean, sterilized safety goggles. Have them place a different mineral specimen in each well of the empty foam egg container. Then place a quarter-teaspoonful of baking soda in an empty well. Add a few drops of vinegar to the baking soda, and watch it fizz. That's the gas forming. Now that students know what to look for, they can test their minerals. With the dropper, bathe each mineral sample with vinegar. Does any mineral specimen produce carbon dioxide gas? (The mineral calcite will give off bubbles like this when bathed in vinegar.) As you plan for this lesson, think about how you will structure equal participation.

Calcite gives off bubbles when bathed in vinegar: Earth science, physical science

Assessment: Did students participate equally in this activity? How do you know? ■

Activity 10.5 Lesson Design: Using Multiple Cooperative Learning Strategies While Classifying Rocks

Overview: In this activity, you will have your students repeat the tests they just performed (hardness, luster, streak, acid) on a group of unknown rocks and classify them. At the same time, you will design individual accountability, equal participation, simultaneous interaction, and positive interdependence into the activity.

Aquarium rocks, pebbles, rock salt, marble chips, and small stones are good rock samples for students to bring to school: Earth science

Materials: An empty foam egg carton, safety goggles, a streak plate, vinegar, a magnifying glass, small rock samples (aquarium rocks, pebbles, rock salt, marble chips, small stones)

Wear safety goggles when classifying rocks: Safety

Procedure: Have your students bring in their own rock samples. Remember that rocks are made of minerals, but not always in the same amount. Using the tests they performed on the minerals, students classify the rocks. Be certain that they wear their safety goggles. Structure individual accountability, equal participation, simultaneous interaction, and positive interdependence into the lesson.

Assessment: If you can, teach the lesson to your students or your college classmates. How did it go? Compare your lessons with those of your peers. You will see that there are many different ways to structure cooperative learning into a lesson. ■

Characteristics of an Equitable Classroom

Students are likely to feel accepted in a well-managed classroom

A well-managed classroom is one in which students are more likely to feel accepted. In such a classroom, students are more likely to speak out, share opinions, and take risks. This is important because girls are often socialized by parents and teachers to be more passive than boys. If a boy has an opinion and states it freely, his behavior is culturally accepted. If a girl engages in the same behavior, she is often labeled as obnoxious, pushy, or unfeminine. In order to learn, students must ask questions and often challenge things they hear in class. As a teacher, it is important to support and encourage students who feel it is inappropriate to share an idea or express an opinion. Learning and practicing social skills helps all students participate more equally in the science classroom. You will read more about this topic after you complete the next activity.

Activity 10.6 Reflection: Monitoring Yourself to Ensure Equity in Your Classroom

Overview: In this activity, you will check to ensure there is equity in your classroom.

Check to ensure that there is equity in your classroom; continue to monitor yourself in this area

Procedure: Once you implement cooperative learning in your classroom, there are some questions you can ask to ensure that your classroom is an equitable one. Do boys and girls receive the same amount of attention from you in class? Do members of underrepresented groups receive the same amount of attention as those who are of majority groups? Think about comfort in the classroom. Do girls and students of underrepresented groups feel comfortable raising their hands and asking questions? Is a student ever made to feel uncomfortable if she or he gives an incorrect answer? Do students ever tease or ridicule one another in your class?

Assessment: If your classroom is not an equitable one, what can you do to improve it? ■

Practicing Social Skills

I hope that by now you are excited about having your students engage in inquiry and discovery in cooperative groups. If you are like many new teachers—and even some experienced ones—you may be a bit apprehensive about your ability to maintain control of the classroom during group work. Several years ago, I was involved in a two-year study of implementation of cooperative learning in 32 elementary science classes. We gathered all sorts of data and found that one of the major concerns of teachers was their students' social skills. The social skills of so many students were below par that teachers were reluctant to try cooperative learning. Their concerns ran the gamut from students who were too loud, bossy, argumentative, unkind to others, or disrespectful, to those who were unwilling to work with others or unwilling to listen. While some teachers believed their students would acquire social skills as they worked in groups, others preferred to teach the social skills along with the science activities.

You can teach social skills with your science lessons

Our solution to this problem was to have teachers identify the social skills they wanted students to learn and teach one skill each week. They took time to introduce the skill to students, discuss the behavior associated with the skill, and have students practice the skill for a whole week. Teachers developed team roles to match the skills they taught. These are called *group maintenance roles,* as they help students to maintain a well-run group. You already learned about the *encourager,* the *praiser,* and the *gatekeeper.*

The encourager motivates the whole team or individual team members when things are not moving well and says things such as "Barbara has an idea. Perhaps she can help us solve this problem." The praiser shows appreciation for the work of the group and says things such as "Good job!" "Great idea!" The gatekeeper works to bring equal participation to the group. If Sally is the gatekeeper and she observes that Sue is saying very little, she might say, "Sue, what do you think about this?" If Sara is talking too much and Sam is too silent, Sally might say, "Sara, you have some good ideas. Sam, what do you think?"

Another role is that of the *question chief.* One of the main premises of cooperative learning is that students with questions can ask one another for help. What happens if students ask one another for help and they are not sure if their answer is correct or don't know the answer at all? That's where the question chief comes in. One rule concerning questioning is "Ask three before me." This means that in a group of four members, students have to ask the question to three other members before asking the teacher. If group members can't come up with an answer, or if students are uncertain of the answer, the question chief brings the teacher to the group for a consultation.

A very important role is that of the *quiet captain* (Kagan, 1994). When students get too noisy, the quiet captain reminds them to use their soft 6-inch voices, not their loud 12-inch voices.

Finally, there are the *taskmaster* and the *recorder.* The taskmaster keeps the group on task, reminding members how much work they must do in the allotted time period. The recorder acts as secretary for the group.

Once in awhile, a student refuses to work in the group or disrupts the group. Our teachers developed the role of *observer* for such a student. The student works alongside the group, completing all tasks alone, observing the group at work. In some cases, a student leaves a group for two weeks. In just about every case, students decide that it is better to be a part of the group than to complete all of the work alone. Students re-enter the group with a much more positive attitude. Sometimes students need to observe other students at work in a group to see what group work is all about. This helps them to improve relationships with others.

When Do Team Roles Work Best?

Some instances where using team roles is especially helpful are listed in the accompanying box. Can you think of other situations where team roles would be beneficial? How would they be particularly beneficial to quiet students, female students, and members of underrepresented groups?

Team Roles Are Particularly Important When:

▶ One or two students will take over and run the group
▶ Students discuss a topic and you think that some will sit back and listen while others will say too much
▶ You have a team question-and-answer session and you believe there will not be equal participation

Forming Teams

There are several ways to form teams for cooperative learning. These include (1) heterogeneous arrangements, (2) grouping by interest, (3) random groups, and (4) homogeneous arrangements. The most widely used grouping strategy is the heterogeneous team. Such a team allows for a wide range of abilities so that students can help one another learn. It also fosters the development of cross-racial and cross-ethnic friendships. When you construct the team instead of allowing students to self-select, you eliminate the likelihood that students who are unpopular or in a low-status position in the classroom will be left out.

Forming a Heterogeneous Team

Heterogeneous teams are diverse

To form a heterogeneous team, make a list of all students in the class, rank ordering them from the highest achieving to the lowest achieving. The list doesn't have to be perfect, but it should be as accurate as possible. Select a high-achieving student, two mid-achievers, and a low-achieving student. Be sure the group includes boys and girls, as well as students from different ethnic and racial groups. If you know that some students don't get along well, don't place them in the same group; doing so will lead to problems. As the year progresses and your students learn new social skills and practice working cooperatively, you are likely to find that even those that didn't get along well at the start now do. If you keep the team together for four to six weeks, you give students a chance to develop relationships. While they often start out feeling uncomfortable, they grow to know one another over time, developing new friendships and bonding as a group.

Forming Teams by Interest: The Group Investigation Method of Cooperative Learning

Group investigation is a cooperative learning technique in which students group themselves by interest. It focuses on inquiry, data gathering by students, interpretation of information through group discussion, and synthesis of individual contributions into a group product (Sharan & Sharan, 1992). It is an excellent technique for the elementary science class, as it blends inquiry and group work. It consists of six stages, which appear in Table 10.4.

Forming teams by interest level using group investigation

Stage I is an exploratory stage consisting of these four steps:

1. The teacher presents a general problem to the class.
2. The class engages in cooperative planning, thinking of strategies for exploring the problem.
3. Students come up with questions based on the overall problem and sort questions into subtopics.
4. Students form interest groups based on the subtopics.

At this point, students can express their individual interests and talk with classmates about their ideas. The teacher is both leader and facilitator during stage I.

During stage II, students engage in cooperative planning. They decide on their specific research topic, specify roles for each student, decide what they want to find out, and determine their resource needs. The teacher offers help to those who need it and continues to monitor the groups.

During stage III, groups carry out their investigations. This includes locating information, organizing and interpreting this information, and interpreting their findings. The teacher continues to support the groups, providing help when needed and intervening when problems arise.

Table 10.4
The Six Stages of Group Investigation

Stage	Description
I	Class chooses subtopics and forms research groups
II	Groups plan the investigation
III	Groups carry out the investigation
IV	Groups plan presentations
V	Groups make presentations
VI	Teachers and students evaluate projects

In stage IV, groups plan their presentations, identifying the main ideas of their findings and deciding how they will present those ideas. The teacher organizes and coordinates the groups' plans for their presentations and continues to monitor the groups. During this stage the students assume the role of teacher, planning how to teach their classmates what they have learned.

During stage V, students make their presentations. Groups observe one another's presentations, and students have a chance to comment on what their classmates have presented. The teacher serves as coordinator of the groups' presentations, but also functions as a member of the audience.

Finally, during stage VI, teacher and students evaluate the projects, collaborating to evaluate outcomes. They can even work together to construct a test or quiz based on the main ideas of the findings. The teacher then evaluates the learning of new information, higher-level thinking, and cooperative behavior.

Forming Teams Randomly

Random grouping offers variety

Sometimes you may choose to group students randomly rather than heterogeneously. While it is easy to form teams in this way, drawbacks include the chance that teams consisting of many high achievers or many low achievers will result. Students may not benefit from teams that are mixed by gender and ethnicity, and there are limited opportunities for bonding. Nevertheless, you may sometimes decide that a random group would be beneficial for your students, as it offers variety.

Homogeneous Teams

Homogeneous teams are an option

Sometimes you may decide that a particular activity would work better if students of the same ability level worked together. While your students won't have all of the benefits of working in a heterogeneous team, you may be better able to address their needs if the team is homogeneous by ability level. You can still mix students by gender and ethnicity while keeping the ability level the same. There are also some cases where it is beneficial to have friends work together in friendship groups. Again, your students lose the benefits of working in heterogeneous teams, but friendship groups are good to use when your students tell you they are unhappy about working with students they don't know and are more relaxed when working with a friend.

How Many Students in a Team?

The appropriate number of students in a team depends on the ages of your students, the type of activity, and your goals. Generally speaking, in grades K–2 pairs work best. It's often difficult for more than two students to work together in the early grades, although I have observed some teachers do it with success. By the end of second grade, if your students are mature, you can have them work in teams of four. I prefer teams of four to teams of three, because students can pair up and have twice as many opportunities for conversation. In grades six and up, students can work in groups of four to six, although larger groups sometimes become difficult to manage.

> **Recommended Group Size**
> ▶ Grades K–2: two students
> ▶ Grades 3–5: four students
> ▶ Grades 6 and up: four to six students

You should also think about the activity. What is the best group size for the activity? This is something you should decide on by yourself. What happens if you don't have an even number of students in the class? You can form teams of three or five. A team of three allows three different ways for students to form pairs, and a team of four allows six different ways for them to pair up, so either arrangement is beneficial.

Classroom Management for Cooperative Learning

When cooperative learning researcher Shlomo Sharan speaks with teachers, he often asks them, "What are the two things your students like to do most?" They answer, "Talk and move around." Then he asks, "What are the two things they can't do in a traditional classroom?" They answer, "Talk and move around!" Teachers usually laugh as they think about the organization of a traditional classroom. A cooperative classroom is different. There is a great deal of opportunity for conversation and movement. Many classroom management problems disappear as students work in a more relaxed fashion. Here are some strategies that will help make the cooperative classroom run more smoothly.

Quiet Signal

A quiet signal helps to maintain order

You and your students need a quiet signal. This is crucial. When students get too noisy, or if you want to address the whole class, a quiet signal works. Put your hand up in the air, and have your students do the same. Tell them that when they see this signal, they must quiet down. You will find that everyone comes to attention within seconds. When engaging in cooperative learning research, I observed hundreds of classrooms over several years. I carried out an informal survey of how long it took for classes to come to attention when using the quiet signal. The best time was three seconds in a small middle school classroom. At the start, it took up to 20 seconds for students to stop what they were doing. As they practiced, they quieted down more quickly. Quieting down quickly became an unspoken goal among students. The quiet signal works very well. Try it and practice!

Class Rules

Class rules establish acceptable behavior

You and your students must establish class rules. Do this together. Decide such things as student responsibilities, team responsibilities, and acceptable behaviors. I find that five or six rules are enough for a class. Post the rules in the classroom. Discuss them and remind students about them when necessary. (See Figure 10.1.)

Cooperative Strategies

Spencer Kagan and his team have developed dozens of excellent strategies for the cooperative classroom. These strategies can be built into your lesson plans. When to use them depends on your specific objectives. If you are trying to motivate students to work together or to encourage all students to speak, you might use round-robin, roundtable, three-step interview, roam the room, or blackboard share. If your students are reviewing information or studying together, you might use numbered heads together, pairs check, inside-outside circle, or send-a-

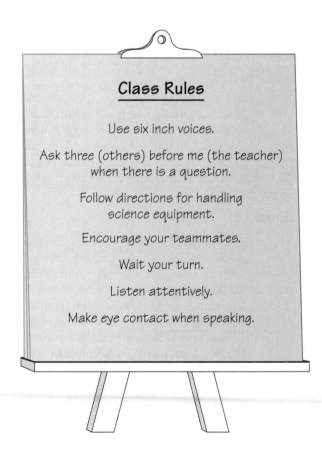

**Figure 10.1
Class Rules for
Cooperative Learning**

problem. Think-pair-share and brainstorming are useful when the goal is thinking. Following are some science activities that show how you can use these strategies.

Strategies for Mastery Learning

Numbered Heads Together

Numbered heads require all students to be prepared

You are teaching a lesson about the different types of rocks, and you want to motivate students while finding out what they understand. You could simply ask questions in a whole-class question-and-answer session, but that would mean only one student would speak at a time. You decide instead to use *numbered heads together*. Your students usually work in teams of four and sit together. You instruct them to number off. In each team, students call off, "One-two-three-four." You ask a question and give students three minutes to discuss it in their teams. Depending on the question, you adjust the time. They discuss the question. Then you call out a number randomly (either one, two, three, or four). Let's say you call out number one. All number ones should be prepared to answer the question. By using this strategy, you structure a situation that requires all students to think about the question and be prepared to answer it, because no one knows which number you will call (Kagan, 1994).

Pairs Check

Pairs check is another excellent strategy that helps students review and study. Have students in each team form pairs. You present a problem. The first partner solves the problem, and the other is the coach. When the student solves the problem, the coach checks the answer. If there is disagreement, they ask you for help. If they both agree on the answer, the coach praises the partner. Partners change roles, you present another problem, and they follow the same steps (Kagan, 1994).

Inside-Outside Circle

Inside-outside circle is a good review technique

Inside-outside circle is another review strategy. Divide the class in half. The first half sits in a circle, forming the inner circle. The other half forms a circle around them; this is the outside circle. Students facing each other form pairs. You pose a problem or a question for review. Students work together to arrive at a solution. You can walk around and monitor the pairs or lead a whole-class discussion to discuss solutions. For the next problem, you can have students rotate so they work with a different student (Kagan, 1994).

Send-a-Problem

Send-a-problem is an excellent strategy for review. Students work in teams to review the lesson or unit. Working together, they create problems or questions for their classmates to answer. Once they write several problems, they "send" them to the next team. Team members solve one another's problems and answer the questions (Kagan, 1994).

Strategies for Developing Thinking Skills

Practicing thinking skills enables your students to create new ideas, apply what they learn, and build understanding of concepts. Unlike mastery structures, which help students review what they learn, thinking skill strategies enable them to think and reflect.

Think-Pair-Share

Think-pair-share is a strategy developed by Professor Frank Lyman. Students are in their teams. You pose a problem that requires thought. Students have some time (you specify the amount) to think on their own. Then they pair off with a partner and discuss their ideas. Finally, students share their thoughts with the whole class.

Brainstorming

Brainstorming fosters creativity

Brainstorming is a strategy that fosters creativity and the development of new ideas. You pose a problem or ask a question. Students work together in their teams. They think quickly and share ideas with others. Silly ideas are included. There is synergy in the group as one student's ideas build on another's. The recorder writes what students say. In the end, students work together to formulate a solution to the problem or an answer to the question (Kagan, 1994).

Strategies for Sharing Information

As students work on science activities, you need ways to foster communication among them. The following strategies work well.

These students are working cooperatively to review for an exam.

Round Robin

When there is something to discuss, students form a *round robin*, taking turns answering and contributing. Everyone gets a turn as you go around the room. It's not necessary to have a recorder, as this is an oral strategy. This is an excellent strategy for kindergartners and first-graders, since writing isn't required (Kagan, 1994).

Roundtable

Roundtable and round robin include everyone in the lesson

Roundtable is just like round robin, except that students write their ideas on paper, and the paper is passed around. There can also be a recorder who writes the contributions (Kagan, 1994).

Three-Step Interview

Three-step interview is one of my favorite strategies. Students pair off; one student is A, and the other is B. You ask a question, have students hypothesize about an activity, or present a problem. A interviews B, finding out what he thinks. Then B interviews A, finding out what she thinks. A shares B's thoughts with the class; then B shares A's thoughts with the class. Think about what happens with this strategy. Student A could report about his own views, but since there is an interview, students practice listening skills, then synthesize what they hear and report to the class. The extra step makes them listen, think, and synthesize information (Kagan, 1994).

Activity 10.7 Lesson Design: Using Cooperative Learning Strategies

Your fourth-graders are identifying rocks. An argument breaks out because Briana wants to use one method of identification, while Bob wants to use another. How will you help your students solve this dilemma? Plan a lesson in which the task is to have your students design a way to identify rocks. Use at least three cooperative strategies (select one or more that you just read about) in the lesson so that you are sure there is simultaneous interaction, positive interdependence, individual accountability, equal participation, and face-to-face interaction. ◼

Activity 10.8 Online: Earth Science Activities

Overview: In this activity, you will adapt two excellent online lesson plans by adding cooperative learning strategies.

Wear safety goggles when making metamorphic rock pancakes: Safety, earth science

Procedure: Log onto these sites and view two excellent earth science lesson plans. Adapt them for cooperative learning by adding one or more of the strategies described in this chapter.

Rock classification activity

http://ericir.syr.edu/Virtual/Lessons/Science/Earth/EAR0019.html

Making metamorphic rock pancakes

http://ericir.syr.edu/Virtual/Lessons/Science/Earth/EAR0014.html

Assessment: Compare the Internet version of the activity with your adaptation. Which lesson plan places more of the responsibility for completing work with the student?   ■

Constructing Your Knowledge of Science and Science Teaching

After completing this chapter, begin to reflect on your new knowledge. This chapter presents cooperative learning theory and research, as well as many practical strategies that you can implement in your classroom. Think about the benefits of using cooperative learning in the classroom. Make a list. How will you group students for cooperative learning? Will you use homogeneous teams, heterogeneous teams, or interest groups? When is it appropriate to use each one? Think about the elements of cooperative learning. When you incorporate them into your lessons, will you have a more equitable classroom? Finally, think about the different cooperative structures you can use. In which of your lessons can you use them?

Key Terms

cooperative learning (p. 263)
positive interdependence
    (p. 266)
mineral (p. 267)
rock (p. 267)

Mohs scale (p. 268)
individual accountability
    (p. 269)
luster (p. 270)
simultaneous interaction (p. 271)

streak test (p. 272)
equal participation (p. 272)
timed pair discussion (p. 272)
acid test (p. 273)

Reviewing Chapter 10: Questions, Extensions, Applications, and Explorations

1. You want to know if your students know what the numbers on a thermometer mean. Design a lesson using cooperative learning so that you can find out.

2. Your students know that when they tap a glass, a sound results. If there is water in the glass, the sound changes. Design a lesson using cooperative learning so that your students can discover how changing the amount of water in the glass changes the sound produced when they tap the glass.

3. Your second-graders are studying about magnetism. You tell them that magnets attract items made of iron. You gather a number of objects, and you want your students to decide whether or not they are magnetic. Design a lesson using cooperative learning so that your students can discover which objects are attracted to the magnet and which are not.

4. You are introducing a unit on environmental science. You want to motivate and include all students. You begin by discussing how organisms affect the environment. Design a lesson that uses cooperative learning so that your students share their ideas about this topic.

5. You will give a quiz on lightning and thunder. Your students know that light travels at 186,000 miles per second and sound travels 1 mile in about 5 seconds. You teach them how to calculate how far they are from the center of a storm. (Note when the lightning flashes, then count the seconds until you hear the thunder, then divide by 5.) You make a sheet of problems for them to answer so that they can practice calculating. How would you use cooperative learning to help your students prepare for the quiz?

Print Resources

Armstrong, H., Barna, C., Brook, R., O'Neill, M., & Tisdale, M. (1997). Set in stone. *Science and Children, 35* (3), 33–40.

Baloche, L. (1998). *The cooperative classroom: Empowering learning.* Englewood Cliffs, NJ: Prentice-Hall.

Booth, J. (1988). *The big beast book: Dinosaurs and how they got that way.* Boston: Little, Brown.

Brandenburg, A. (1981). *Digging up dinosaurs.* New York: Harper and Row.

Brandenburg, A. (1990). *Fossils tell of long ago.* New York: Scholastic.

Candler, L. (1995). *Cooperative learning and wee science.* San Clemente, CA: Kagan Cooperative Learning.

Candler, L. (1995). *Cooperative learning and hands-on science.* San Clemente, CA: Kagan Cooperative Learning.

Cohen, E. (1994). *Designing groupwork.* New York: Teachers College Press.

Cohen, E. (1994). Restructuring the classroom: Conditions for constructive small groups. *Review of Educational Research, 64* (1), 1–35.

Kagan, S. (1994). *Cooperative learning.* San Clemente, CA: Kagan Cooperative Learning.

Lasky, K. (1990). *Dinosaur dig.* New York: Morrow Junior Books.

Mastny, A., Kahn, S., & Sherman, S. (1992). *Science TEAMS: An approach to cooperative learning and science.* New Brunswick, NJ: Rutgers University Consortium for Educational Equity.

Sharan, Y., & Sharan, S. (1992) *Expanding cooperative learning through group investigation.* New York: Teachers College Press.

Sherman, S. (1994). Cooperative learning in science. In S. Sharan (Ed.), *Handbook of cooperative learning methods* (pp. 226–244). Westport, CT: Greenwood Press.

Sylvan, P. K. (1999). Primary paleontologists. *Science and Children, 36* (4), 16–20.

Electronic Resources

Frank Potter's Earth Science Gems
http://www-sci.lib.uci.edu/SEP/earth.html
This site links to 2,000 science education resources.

 Tennessee Science Curriculum Framework
http://www.utm.edu/departments/ed/cece/SAMK8.shtml
This is an excellent source of standards-based earth science lesson plans.

Pro Teachers Expect the Best from a Girl
http://www.proteacher.com/110021.shtml
This is another excellent resource for earth science lesson plans.

Ask Eric Lesson Plans
http://ericir.syr.edu/Virtual/Lessons/Science/Earth/index.html
You are probably familiar with this excellent site by now. It contains hundreds of lesson plans.

Athena Curriculum Earth Resources
http://www.athena.ivv.nasa.gov/curric/land/index.html
This NASA site contains earth science lesson plans.

Earth Science Lesson Plans
http://www.eecs.umich.edu/~coalitn/sciedoutreach/funexperiments/agesubject/earthsciences.html
This site contains excellent lesson plans on earth science and more.

Kagan Cooperative Learning
http://www.kagancooplearn.com/
If you have questions about cooperative learning, contact this site.

Children's Literature

Mahy, Margaret
The Greatest Show Off Earth
(Scholastic Trade, 1996)
ISBN: 0-14-037926-6
Grades 3–7

Kerrod, Robin
Matter and Materials
(Marshall Co., 1995)
ISBN: 0-7614-0031-1
Grades 5 and up

Time-Life Book Editors
Structure of Matter
(Time-Life, Incorporated, 1992)
ISBN: 0-8094-9662-3
Grades 4 and up

Heller, Robert
Earth Science
(The McGraw-Hill Companies, 1978)
ISBN: 0-07-028037-1
Young adult

Stacy, Tom
Earth, Sea, and Sky
(Random House, 1991)
ISBN: 0-679-80861-2
Grades 2–5

Zike, Dinah
Earth Science Book: Activities for Kids
(John Wiley & Sons, 1993)
ISBN: 0-471-57166-0
Grades 3–7

Parker, Steve
The Earth and How It Works
(DK Publishing, Inc., 1993)
ISBN: 1-56458-235-3
Grades 3 and up

CHAPTER 11

Integrating Educational Technology with Science Instruction

Robert began using computers when he was a young child. His parents bought the family's first personal computer just about the time he began kindergarten. To Robert, communicating via a computer was a part of everyday life, just as his parents used the telephone to communicate.

Even more important, Robert discovered a method of thinking that was much different from what he was used to in school. He learned about logic. Here's how: in second grade, Robert began programming in LOGO, a very basic computer language (you will read more about LOGO later in this chapter). He realized that by typing a series of simple commands, he could create a complex picture. Robert began looking at things differently now. He began to understand that by piecing together parts of an object, he could create a whole. The computer was the tool that made this possible.

Robert's teachers recognized that he responded to computer learning better than to any other method, so they continued to challenge him. Interestingly, many of his teachers had never used a computer before, but realized this could be their opportunity to learn. Robert and his teachers learned side by side, and they

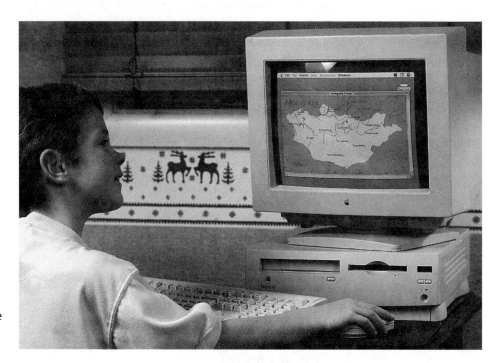

Young children can use the computer to learn how to think.

gradually moved from simple programming in LOGO to the slightly more intricate language known as BASIC. Robert would often spend hours working through the logic of a complicated computer program. In fact, by the time he reached middle school, he was designing educational computer games that his friends would play in school.

Years later, the challenges that Robert's elementary school teachers presented him paid off. He works in a job that requires him to think through complicated processes—to use the same basic logic that he learned from using a computer when he was in kindergarten. Today Robert continues to use the tools that his teachers provided for him more than two decades ago.

This chapter introduces you to the ways you can use computers in the elementary science classroom. As you read through the chapter, think about the answers to these questions:

1. **How can I use word processing, databases, and spreadsheets in my classes?**

2. **What is the Internet, and how do I use it in my classes?**

3. **Where do I find lesson plans on the Internet?**

4. **What types of instructional software are appropriate for my students?**

5. **How can I teach my students about weather using technology as a tool?**

Using Educational Technology in Your Classroom

Ways to use technology in the classroom

Advancements in the field of technology bring you limitless possibilities for teaching with computers and technology. There are the Internet, the World Wide Web, all types of instructional software, opportunities for computer programming in LOGO and other languages appropriate for your students, word processing, presentation software, publication on the Internet, multimedia, hypermedia, paint and draw programs, and the list goes on. Where do you start? How do you find out what's available to you and the best ways to use technology in your science classroom? This chapter will help you answer these questions and more. Before you begin to explore the world of computers and technology, you will meet an elementary school teacher who specializes in teaching with technology.

Meet Carol Olson, an Elementary Technology Specialist

Carol Olson taught elementary school for several years before taking time off to raise a family. When she was ready to return to work, she accepted a position with Apple Computer Company in Minnesota as a teacher/researcher. She started with little experience with technology but learned quickly through on-the-job training.

Her first research project involved finding out how technology affects children's writing. She started out with two groups of children, the control group and the experimental group. The experimental group had computers on their desks all day, every day, and used technology throughout the day in every activity that required writing; the control group worked without computers. At the end of the study, both groups were compared. What were the results? Ms. Olson says that children who used computers as a tool wrote significantly better than those who did not use computers. By the end of the study, Ms. Olson was convinced that using technology was the way to go, and she went on to specialize in teaching with technology.

Select the form of technology that matches a child's learning style

Today Ms. Olson works with elementary science teachers and their students. She helps them bring technology into their classrooms through use of the Internet, by providing a variety of software programs for different purposes, and through the use of simple programming, word processing, presentation software, and multimedia applications. She is particularly interested in learning styles and technology and explains that within the realm of technology, teachers must provide opportunities for students to work with tools that match their learning styles: "There are visual learners; auditory learners, students who prefer to write; those who like to do research, engage in problem solving, or drill and practice." She believes that schools must provide opportunities that best match the learning preferences of students with different needs.

Using technology and science process: Science process

What should new teachers know about teaching with technology? In addition to familiarity with what is currently available, Ms. Olson explains that teachers must have knowledge about ways to use technology for collaborative work. "Classes can communicate with each other over the Internet and by using email. Students can see each other if at least one computer per class is equipped with an inexpensive camera and software program. Students can share findings on a web page. They can send email to scientists if they have questions. They can create graphs and compile databases." These are some of the ways in which Ms. Olson helps teachers bring technology into their classrooms. You will now read about these methods and more.

Using the Computer as a Tool

Perhaps the best way to think of a computer is as a tool. However, unlike a screwdriver or a hammer, which lets you do only one thing, a computer lets you do many different things. You will now explore some of the things you can use a computer to do and learn how you can integrate them into your elementary science classroom.

What Is Word Processing?

Almost everything you read is a product of a word processor. This book, for example, was written on a word processor. The flyer hanging in the hallway was created on a word processor. And when you are looking for a job and need to create a résumé, you will want to use a word processor.

A word processor is a program known in the computer world as an **application** that runs on a computer. A **word processor** allows you to type in words, put in pictures, change what you write, and move words around. When you finish, you have created something called a **document**.

What makes a word processor so useful is that you can change what you have done and fix it, all with just a few quick keystrokes or clicks of the mouse. If you make a mistake, you can fix it in just a few seconds. On a typewriter, it could take you 10 or more minutes to correct a mistake that takes just 10 seconds to fix on your word processor.

Uses of word processing

Today's more complex word processors let you do even more, such as create tables and graphs, check your grammar and spelling, use a thesaurus to look for the best words to fit your meaning, or create mailing lists. You could use a word processor, for example, to create a list of all your students' names and addresses, make a mailing list from the data, and create labels to send home progress reports. The most popular word processors are Microsoft Word and WordPerfect.

What Is a Database?

A **database** is like a very big, very powerful file cabinet. You organize data in a database program just as you would organize data in a file cabinet. But unlike with a file cabinet, you can use a database program to create lists that contain only the data you want to use. And you can sort that data just about any way you want to so you have the information you need right at your fingertips. In a database, you put information in areas called **fields** and arrange the fields into a **form**.

Using a database increases your efficiency

Let's say you want a way to keep track of your students' progress throughout the year. They may have 15 different goals to reach before they complete the whole year's curriculum. If you have 25 students to keep track of, that's 375 items. That's a lot of information! Plus, if you wanted to write notes next to each item using a manual filing system, you would need a lot of paper and a very good organizing system to analyze a particular student's progress.

Here's where a database comes into play. You can create a simple form with just a few fields. The first field is the student's name. The second field contains check-off boxes for each of the 15 goals. The third field is a comment box. Now, whenever a student completes one of his or her goals, you simply click a check-off box and you're done! And with a few clicks of your mouse, you can easily go back and track a student's progress. Such a database is very useful if you are using alternative assessment. Popular databases are Claris FileMaker Pro and Microsoft Access.

What Is a Spreadsheet?

Using a spreadsheet to keep track of grades

A **spreadsheet** is a program that can be thought of as a huge electronic grid. You put information in the boxes of the grid, called **cells**, then program other boxes to "do something" with that data, called **calculation**. Suppose you want to keep track of your students' progress throughout the semester. First, you set up a column with the students' first names and another with their last names. (You do this so you can sort the list alphabetically by last name, a commonly used sort procedure.) Then you set up a column that lists the name of the first assessment (for example, "Mammals"). You continue creating columns for each of the assessments you want to keep track of. Finally, you create a column titled "Average" that calculates the average score. Now, in seconds, you can find out how a student is performing by checking your spreadsheet (see Table 11.1). The most popular spreadsheet programs are Microsoft Excel and Lotus 1-2-3.

Table 11.1
Example of a Spreadsheet

First Name	Last Name	Mammals	Reptiles	Insects	Average	
Johnny	Laine	90	95	92	92	
Maritza	Alicea	85	100	93	93	
Meizu	Lui	80	83	97	87	

Using These Tools in the Elementary Science Classroom

Using a database to track weather data: Earth and space science

All of the preceding examples show ways you can use a word processor, database, or spreadsheet for your tasks as a teacher. But you can also use these tools with your students in the elementary science classroom.

Consider a lesson on clouds. You could work with your students to develop a database that keeps track of all the different kinds of clouds you observe in a month. You could set up fields for size, shape, and color. The next part of the activity might have students observe weather associated with each type of cloud. A spreadsheet would allow the students to keep track of the clouds and the frequency with which a certain type of cloud precedes a particular type of weather system. Then, after the observations are completed, the students could use the word processor to type up a report of the entire experimental process. Figure 11.1 shows a database for recording observations about clouds.

The Internet

Let's say your students now want to find out about weather in other parts of the world. This is the perfect project for the Internet, perhaps the newest and most exciting "technology tool" for science teachers!

The Basics of the Internet: What Is It and What Does It Do?

It is difficult to describe the Internet in a single sentence, because it is so many different things at once. The Internet is a post office, a library, a shopping mall, a newspaper, and more—all at the same time! You can use the Internet to send

	Monday	Tuesday	Wednesday	Thursday	Friday	Saturday	Sunday
Size of cloud (Look at cloud. Cover the cloud with your fist. How many fists big is it?)							
Shape of cloud							
Color of cloud							
Type of cloud							
Today's weather							

Figure 11.1
Using a Database to Study Clouds. Remember not to look directly at the sun when looking at the sky

messages to friends or fellow teachers, to find out which libraries have that book you're looking for, or even to help you prepare the perfect meal for dinner tonight. You can use the Internet to track a storm as it travels across the country, view an outline of your professor's lecture, or order your groceries.

The Internet is a tool that allows you to do just about anything—all with a few clicks of your mouse. And in most cases, you will not have to buy any new or expensive hardware or software to use the Internet. All you need is a computer with a modem and access to a telephone line. You will now look at some different parts of the Internet and some terms you will likely hear in our discussion of ways to use the Internet in your classroom.

Activity 11.1 Online: A Tour of the Internet

Touring the Internet

Overview: In this activity, you will visit several sites as you tour the Internet.

Procedure: Log onto these sites and take your tour:

Discovery Channel: **http//discoveryschool. com/schrockguide/yp/iypabout.html**

Roadmap 96: **http//netsquirrel.com/roadmap96/syllabus.html**

Assessment: What did you learn from your Internet tour? ■

What Is the World Wide Web?

The **World Wide Web** is the part of the Internet that has web pages, which are graphics-oriented documents. The Web can be thought of as a library without walls, as it contains an ever-growing number of web pages with data on just about any topic you could imagine.

What Is Email?

Learning to use email: Technology

Email, or **electronic mail**, is the part of the Internet that functions as a post office. Messages are sent from one user to another, just as postal mail is sent from one person to another. If you have an email account, your class can communicate with classes anywhere in the world.(*Web 66* is a site that lists schools you can contact all over the world. You can access Web 66 at http://web66.coled.umn.edu/.)

Activity 11.2 Online: Learning to Use Email

Overview: This activity teaches you about email.

Procedure: Log onto http://w3.one.net/~alward/ and follow the guide.

Assessment: What did you learn about sending email? ■

Some Nicknames for the Internet

Perhaps the most common nickname for the Internet is the **information super-highway**. People use this description because information travels between computers on the Internet just as automobiles travel between cities on a highway. Another often used nickname for the Internet is **cyberspace**, a word that relates to the fact that the Internet is not a tangible object.

Internet Service Provider (ISP)

Internet Service Provider, or *ISP,* is a fancy name for the company that helps you gain access to the Internet. Gaining access to the Internet works just like gaining access to the telephone in your house. To get access to phone service, you subscribe to a telephone company. To get access to the Internet, you subscribe to an ISP. America Online, GTE, Prodigy, and CompuServe are popular ISPs.

Activity 11.3 Online: Links to Internet Service Providers

Learning about Internet Service Providers: Technology

Overview: In this activity, you will log onto a site that informs you about Internet Service Providers.

Procedure: Log onto *Barker's Online Connection* and explore. The address is http://www.barkers.org/online/. Then log onto http://k12science.stevens-tech.edu/connect/connect.html for more information on ISPs. For a list of all ISPs, log onto http://thelist.internet.com/.

Assessment: What have you learned about ISPs? ▪

Web Browsers

Learning to use web browsers: Technology

Once your computer connects to an ISP, you need a program that allows you to locate and view web pages. This program is called a **web browser.** The most commonly used browsers are Netscape's Navigator and Communicator and Microsoft's Internet Explorer.

Activity 11.4 Online: Learning About Browsers

Overview: In this activity, you will view a list of browsers and learn more about one of them.

Procedure: Log onto this site for a complete list of browsers:

http://www.jumbo.com/pages/internet/sections.asp?x_sectionid=2763

Assessment: Are you prepared to discuss browsers with your colleagues and students? ▪

Addresses on the Internet

Learning about addresses on the Internet: Technology

Everyone is familiar with mailing addresses. If someone asks you where you live, you may say, "I live at 5 Main Street in Centerville, Massachusetts. The ZIP code is 12345." Addresses on the Internet work very similarly. An Internet address is called a *domain name* and is broken up into several segments. Let's work with the following example: beast.tcnj.edu.

The final part of the address, *edu,* tells us what kind of place owns that address—in this instance, an EDUcational institution. In the United States, other options are *gov* for GOVernment institutions, *com* for COMmercial businesses, *mil* for MILitary sites, *org* for nonprofit ORGanizations, and *net* for administrative organizations of the InterNET. Other countries use similar suffixes, but they supplement the address with a two-letter country code. Thus, a site in Finland might be mystore.com.fi.

Working to the left, the next part of the Internet address indicates where the site is located. In this case, *tcnj* tells us that we are looking at The College of New Jersey. So together with the final part of the addresses, we now have a pretty good idea of the location of our Internet site: The College of New Jersey, an educational institution. Going back to our analogy of a mailing address, *tcnj.edu* is similar to saying you live in Centerville, Massachusetts.

But where in Centerville, Massachusetts, do you live? Or, on the Internet, where exactly at tcnj.edu do I find what I'm looking for? The next part of the address tells us the computer name. In our example, the name of the computer that holds the data we are searching for is "beast." Going back to our analogy of a mailing address, *beast* is similar to saying you live on Main Street.

A bit more goes on "behind the scenes" when you use a web address, but it shouldn't affect you very much. Just as the post office converts *Centerville, Massachusetts* into a ZIP code, the Internet converts domain names such as *tcnj.edu* into something called *IP*, or *Internet Protocol* addresses. An IP address consists of four numbers, each separated by dots. In most cases, though, you will not have to worry about IP addresses.

Username

When sending a letter, if you just wrote "Main Street" on the envelope, the letter probably would have a hard time getting to the recipient. A lot of people live on Main Street! On the Internet, you might have the same problem if usernames didn't exist. *Usernames* are specific addresses for specific people; only one person can have a particular username at a domain, just as only one house on Main Street in Centerville, Massachusetts, can be number 5. So to send mail to the user with the name *shermans* whose account is on the computer we talked about earlier, you would send email to shermans@beast.tcnj.edu. We put the @ ("at") symbol in the address to separate the username from the domain name.

HTML

Learning about HTML: Technology

Web pages are written in a special language called *HyperText Markup Language,* or *HTML.* This is apparent in the names of web page files, which normally end with the suffix *.html* or *.htm.* Other, new languages are being developed that will allow web pages to be more powerful and more flexible. So soon you may see pages with the suffix *.xml* or *.asp.*

HTTP

When you use a web browser, you need to tell it to look for a web page. (Web browsers can look at other kinds of data too, but we won't get into that much detail here.) The prefix *http* (an abbreviation for *HyperText Transfer Protocol*) tells your browser that you will be searching for a web page.

Uniform Resource Locator (URL)

Uniform Resource Locator, or *URL,* is the fancy name for the specific location of a web page. It begins with a standard Internet domain address, then adds the directories and folders in which the page is stored. Keep in mind that web pages are stored on web servers in the same way you store your files on your desktop computer. For example, if your term paper called *final.doc* is stored on your hard drive in a directory called *myfiles,* then in a subdirectory called *sci101,* you write that out as *c:/myfiles/sci101/final.doc.* A web page URL is written very similarly. If you are looking for the file named beast.tcnj.edu, you write it out as *http://beast.tcnj.edu/myfiles/sci101/final.doc.* As you can see, this process is very similar to finding a document.

What Is a Listserv?

A listserv is another tool of the Internet, but it functions differently than most others. A **listserv** is used for discussion on the Internet. Someone posts a question on a listserv, and that message is sent to everyone who subscribes, or joins, the listserv. Any time someone responds to the original question, everyone on the listserv receives that response. Often a listserv message can generate dozens of responses each day! Many people enjoy being members of listservs because they can learn about issues that they otherwise may not have exposure to.

Locating science listservs: Technology

A complete list of science listservs is available at
http://www.catalog.com/cgibin/find/vivian/tmplist or try
http://catalog.com/vivian/interest-group-search.html

Searching the Internet, or What Do I Do If a Student Asks Me a Question and I Don't Know the Answer?

In a library, you go to the card catalog to find a book. But how do you find something on the Internet, especially since it is expanding so quickly? This question was pondered by a number of people in the early 1990s, but perhaps the most successful answer was developed by some students at Stanford University.

Jerry Yang and a few of his friends decided to start a web site that was a huge database of web pages. They would allow people to add their web site listings to the catalog. A simple search page would allow others to type in key words that they wanted to search for; then the site would return a list of pages that contained those key words.

Yang's idea has made him worth over a billion dollars (personally!) and started an industry that produces tools called *search engines.* Yang's relatively simple idea is now known as Yahoo! (http://www.yahoo.com), perhaps the world's largest catalog of web pages. (A little bit of Internet trivia: http://www.yahoo.com is the most often visited site on the Internet.)

By accessing a search engine, you can search for virtually any piece of information. If you want to know about Chinese restaurants in Boston, you can type in "Chinese food and Boston" and Yahoo! will give you a list of web sites that contain information about where to find Chinese food in Boston. Yahoo! is also arranged into categories that make it easier to search for often requested information. For example, you can click on "Education", then "K–12" to find all sorts of sites that are of interest to an educator in elementary, middle, or high school. For a more specific search, you could type in "elementary and science" to find elementary science web sites.

Yahoo! has even developed a search engine just for children, called Yahooligans!. It can be found at http://www.yahooligans.com and contains a special section on science.

Most popular search engines

Table 11.2 lists several other popular search engines.

Activity 11.5 Online: What Are the Major Search Engines?

Overview: In this activity, you will identify the major search engines and learn more about them.

Procedure: Log onto the following web site and explore a thorough list of search engines:

http://discoveryschool.com/schrockguide/yp/iypsrch.html

Visit the following site for a review of major search engines, created by Marilyn Pedram, reference specialist at the Kansas City Public Library:

http://www.kcpl.lib.mo.us/search/srchengines.htm

Assessment: Which search engine would you select to search for elementary science lesson plans? ■

Class Projects on the Internet

Finding class projects on the Internet

Now that you know about search engines, you can find just about anything you want. You can try looking for class projects by using key words that relate to the subject you are trying to teach. For a lesson on astronomy, you might use the keywords "astronomy," or "stars," or "planets" to begin your search. Since it takes only a few seconds to get a response from most search engines, keep trying different key words and narrowing down the search until you find just what you want.

Table 11.2
Major Search Engines

Alta Vista: This search engine works very quickly and searches a wide range of sites.

Excite: Plug in "concept" and "keyword," and this search engine can narrow down a search quickly.

HotBot: Sorts results by date and media type.

Infoseek: Accesses 50 million web pages. Many libraries use Infoseek.

Lycos: Accesses 1.5 million web sites.

Northern Light: Accesses 1,800 periodicals, newspapers, and other publications.

Web Crawler: Accesses 200,000 major web sites.

Stevens Technical Institute Projects

If you want to use a tried-and-true class project, you can find a listing of such projects at the Stevens Technical Institute web site at

> http://k12science.stevens-tech.edu/curriculum/curichome.html

Projects on this page are grouped by grade level and include projects for elementary-, middle-, and higher-level students. National curriculum projects are located at

> http://k12science.stevens-tech.edu/curriculum/national.html

Ask an Expert

Finding a science expert on the Internet

A special feature on the Stevens page is a link to the Ask an Expert page. This link takes advantage of one of the best features of the Internet: the broad range of experts that are easily accessible. The Ask an Expert page offers a quick, one-step process for finding experts in any field.

The Stevens web site also provides a link that allows you to find out how your students can take part in the Stowaway Adventure, a project that uses live, remote sensing data from cargo ships at sea to take you on a virtual adventure. You can use this project in conjunction with a lesson on weather, for example, using satellite and radar images to identify upcoming storms on the ship's course.

The Stevens site is probably the best source of real-time data on the Internet. This is because the Stevens staff has written activities for students that require accessing real sites and gathering real-time data. You can't take a live field trip to the middle of the ocean to locate and track a ship, but this site allows you to gain access to this information with a few clicks of the mouse.

Virtual Frog Dissection Kit

Dissecting a frog on the Internet: Life science

Dissecting frogs has been a part of science curricula for decades. In recent years, however, many elementary schools have ended this project because of its complexity and because some people object. But Internet lets you bring this project back to your class.

Researchers at the Lawrence Berkeley National Laboratory have developed the Virtual Frog Dissection Kit, available online at

> http://www-itg.lbl.gov/ITG.hm.pg.docs/dissect/info.html

The program allows interactive dissection of a frog, and includes the capability to make movies. You can test your students' knowledge of frog anatomy with the Virtual Frog Builder Game, or even hear sounds of North American frogs on this page!

Eyes Eyes Eyes

Dissecting an eye on the Internet: Life science

A more graphic dissection takes place at

> http://www.internz.com/walton/Room2/Eyes/eye2.html

This is definitely a site to be seen! This web site, which is very easy to navigate, shows you the different stages of an eye dissection. Students learn the names of the various parts of the eyes and how they function.

Creating a Web Page

Creating a web page

Making your own web page is becoming easier every day. Teachers often create web pages so that their students can display their work. Remember what you read about alternative assessment techniques in Chapters 7 and 8? One way for students to show what they know is to create a web page. This is a form of authentic assessment. Once you learn how to make a web page, you can teach this process to your students.

Netscape's Communicator software includes a program called Composer that lets you design a web page, very much as you would design a flyer on a word processor. You highlight text and click a button to make text bold or underlined, and in just two simple steps you can create a link to another web site. Many commercial sites also have programs that guide you through the process in a step-by-step tutorial. Or, if you are daring, you can experiment with programming in HTML!

Once the web page is finished, you need a way to display it on the Internet. Most schools have ways to make that happen. Check with your school's technology specialist to find out the procedure. If your school doesn't have a technology specialist, check with your local ISP to find out how you can display your page on your own.

Blocking Software for Schools

Locating blocking software

A major concern for many educators is that students will access information on the Internet that is intended primarily for adults. There are a number of ways that schools can prevent this from occurring. A description of Internet safety can be found at http://k12science.stevens-tech.edu/safety/safety.html. The page contains links to articles that discuss Internet safety for children, as well as links to sites with Internet safety software.

Internet safety software is perhaps the best way that a school can prevent students from accessing sites that are not geared for children. You or your school's technology coordinator could install the software on each computer or on a server, then tell the program what you want it to do. For example, you could tell the filter to look for certain objectionable words on a web page and prevent students from accessing pages that contain those words. Some programs come with a built-in list of sites that children should stay away from. One such program, Cyberpatrol, keeps students away from sites that contain violence, profanity, nudity, or sexually explicit text or graphics. The software updates itself every seven days so that even new sites are kept on the "off-limits" list. Other programs monitor usage so you can see what sites your students have visited.

Finding Lesson Plans on the Internet

Locating lesson plans on the Internet

Search engines provide the easiest way to find lesson plans on the Internet. A good place to start is at http://www.yahoo.com/Education. Many professors and schools of education also have links to lesson plans on their web sites. For example, my own web page has links to hundreds of lesson plans. You can find my page at http://www.tcnj.edu/~shermans/home.html. The following box lists some of the most comprehensive sites for lesson plans. There are also sites where your students can find help with homework questions.

Where to Find Lesson Plans on the Internet

http://discoveryschool.com/lessonplans/subjects/k-12.html

http://discoveryschool.com/schoolhome.html

http://www.lessonplanspage.com

http://www.homeworkcentraljr.com/indexjr.html

http://ericir.syr.edu/Projects/Newton/

Homework Help

Here is a good site for students who need help with homework. For students who need enrichment, the site offers questions for them to think about. If students finish a lesson early, they can go to the computer and visit a site such as this one. This site also contains lesson plans for teachers.

http://www.homeworkcentraljr.com/indexjr.html

Instructional Software

Software includes all the things your computer can do, as well as the instructions to make it run

In addition to all the Internet resources available, there is software that you can use in your classroom. **Software** includes all the things your computer can do, as well as the instructions that make it run. Software includes "media stored as computer files, recorded music, videotaped programs containing the information presented with hardware" (Grabe & Grabe, 1998). What should you know about elementary science software? Stephen Wulfson, who writes a column called "Software Reviews" for *Science and Children,* explains that new teachers don't have to know much about this software to begin using it: "Be quite familiar with a computer, learn how to load software, be unafraid of trying things on a computer, and read the various reviews of software on the market." He recommends that teachers read such journals as *Electronic Education, T.H.E. Journal, Science and Children*, and *The Science Teacher* for soft-

Make friends with your local computer store

ware reviews and general information about what is available. He also advises, "Make friends with your local computer store and ask if you can try out software there, or communicate with the company and see if you can examine the software on a trial basis." Some companies will send teachers demo (demonstration) disks so that they can examine the software and see how it fits into the curriculum.

Journals for Teachers

▶ *Science and Children,* National Science Teachers Association, 1840 Wilson Blvd., Arlington, VA 22201-3000. Phone: 703-243-7100; fax: 703-243-7177.

▶ *The Science Teacher,* National Science Teachers Association, 1840 Wilson Blvd., Arlington, VA 22201-3000. Phone: 703-243-7100; fax: 703-243-7177.

▶ *Electronic Learning,* 902 Sylvan Avenue, Englewood Cliffs, NJ 07632.

▶ *T.H.E. Journal,* Technological Horizons in Education, 150 El Camino Real, Suite 112, Tustin, CA 92780-3670.

Categories of elementary science software

There are four categories of elementary science software: (1) productivity software, which enhances a student's ability to learn; (2) experimental or data-gathering software, which allows students to collect and analyze data; (3) content-based software, which contains the information found in a textbook or an encyclopedia; and (4) career software, which brings real people to the classroom in electronic form so that students can learn about careers and fields of study. In addition, a fifth category, teacher software, makes teaching more efficient. The thrill of technology is that it brings resources to all schools at a low cost. No longer must a school purchase an expensive encyclopedia or constantly update books now that technology is so affordable (Wulfson, 1998). You will now read about each type of software.

For a compilation of the different types of software available, log onto
http://k12science.stevens-tech.edu/tools/windows95.html

Productivity Software

Productivity software enhances a child's ability to learn

The first category of software, **productivity software,** enhances a child's ability to learn. The word processor is the most essential piece of productivity software for your classroom. Students should know the computer and use the word processor as early as possible. They should use the Internet (on a computer equipped with blocking software) to do research. Spreadsheets are also important productivity tools for elementary students. Paint and draw programs allow students to create drawings. Productivity software allows students to write stories and even create crossword puzzles. They can create newsletters, web pages, posters, banners, and charts. Special software is available for students with a variety of disabilities. Adaptive technology brings to classrooms programs for students who are visually impaired, hearing impaired, or have other needs.

Experimental and Data-Gathering Software

The next category, experimental and data-gathering software, allows students to collect and analyze data. They can attach sensors and probes to the computer and

Experimenting and data-gathering software enhances science process: Science process, technology

collect real-time data. This means that as the experiment takes place—in real time, in the real world—your students collect the actual data. Then they analyze the data, as with any science experiment. There are temperature sensors, which are like electronic thermometers, and probes that measure acidity, speed, light, and motion. The following example illustrates the use of this type of software.

Teaching with Experimental and Data-Gathering Software

PASCO computer-based software allows students to see sound: Physical science, technology

Several years ago, two of my student teachers, Tom Terzano and Kristen Hellmers, were teaching a unit on sound to their sixth-graders. They wanted to make this abstract concept more concrete. At that time we didn't have access to experimental and data-gathering software at our college, so we visited the Princeton Plasma Physics Laboratory, a national laboratory located nearby, which had access to the equipment that Tom and Kristen needed. Kristen and Tom learned to use a PASCO computer-based system that allowed their sixth-grade students to "see" sound. PASCO software and its associated hardware interface allow a general-purpose personal computer (Macintosh or PC based) to serve as a variety of scientific instruments.

A journal excerpt documents Tom's initial challenges:

When I first picked up the manual for the science software, it seemed to disregard the fact that I possess little physics knowledge. It was intimidating; filled with charts, formulas, and foreign scientific notations. I felt as though it would be a

These students are using PASCO science software with sensors and probes to collect scientific data.

struggle, at the very least, to learn how to operate this software. My task was to research its uses for implementation in a sixth grade general science class, and whatever I learned in my introduction to this program, I had to teach not only to my elementary school students, but to my student teaching partner, and to my twenty three college classmates. (Personal journal of Tom Terzano, 1997. Used with permission.)

To gain expertise in using the software, Tom worked with Dr. Hulse, a scientist, and Mike, a talented high school student who was studying with the scientist. He writes:

Experimenting with insulating properties of cups: Physical science, technology, science process

When I visited the laboratory I met Mike, a very bright high school student with experience in using the software. He was working on an experiment testing the insulating properties of various cups. At the time he was using hot water and a foam cup. He was also using the PASCO software system to chart each cup's progress.

"How are you doing that?" I asked.

The computer collects data: Science process, technology

"Easy. This is the electronic thermometer I can leave in the cup, and the computer does all the work for me." I understood, but I must have had a confused look on my face, so he further explained. "The computer does all of the data collection, and I interpret it. I don't have to sit next to the cup and read a mercury thermometer every minute and then plot the results. I can walk out of the room and the computer can do it for me. See?"

I went over to the computer to look at the graph. The computer had created a graph plotting temperature over time, and I could very easily see the cooling curve of the water. I asked, "What else can you do with it?"

What I learned in the next few minutes was that there existed a variety of functions for the PASCO system. There were thermometers, microphones, and all sorts of tools to use with the computer. There was an oscilloscope, which was essential to the unit on sound that my partner and I were creating. (Personal journal of Tom Terzano, 1997.)

Together Tom and Kristen created a series of experiments to teach about sound, developing three experiments to use in class with the sixth-graders. They needed a computer and a video projection system to display the computer screen to the class, the PASCO Science Workshop, a sound sensor (microphone), musical instruments, and tuning forks. They asked their sixth-graders to bring a variety of musical instruments to class that day.

All three experiments went well. After reading student journals describing students' understanding of concepts before and after using the technology, and after analyzing the results of pre- and posttests on sound given to their students, Tom and Kristen concluded that their lessons were a success. Tom writes:

The only real difficulty I found in using the PASCO system was in having confidence in myself using the technology; in essence, not to be intimidated by the manual. I had little difficulty explaining what I learned to my teaching partner or to my fellow classmates. When we brought the system to the elementary school class, we found that the kids were able to better understand the lessons on sound than we had previously taught without technology. (Sherman & Hulse, 1999.)

Content-Based Software

Suppose your students are learning about snakes. They could go to the library to find books on snakes. They could also use content-base software, which would allow them to insert a CD into a computer and see movies and pictures of snakes, and read about them as well. They could also hear interviews with scientists who study about snakes, a major advantage of using such software. There are encyclopedias available, as well as journals, with audio and video, on just about every topic that elementary science students study. About 99 percent of the software on the market is content-based software, and the cost is relatively low.

Career Software

What about science-related careers? Your students can learn about available careers and find out about female scientists and scientists of every ethnic and racial group by using career software. This is an excellent addition to the science curriculum that you should bring into your classroom.

Teacher Productivity Software

Do you like to make certificates for your students? Would you like to keep an electronic grade book? What about lesson plans or science curricula? Would you like help with these jobs? There is software on the market that will allow you to do all of these things. One program will even help you write lesson plans and correlate them with national science standards and some state science standards! Other software will help you create newsletters, banners, and posters for your classroom (Wulfson, 1998).

Introducing Your Students to Programming

Programming refers to writing the instructions that tell a computer how to perform an operation: Technology

Programming refers to writing the instructions that tell a computer how to perform an operation. You can use programming to show your students how to work through a project from beginning to end. Programming encourages your students to think about what they are doing every step of the way and allows them to determine how changing one piece of a project affects all of the others.

Programming is very useful because it can be adapted to fit the level of learners who will be programming. Recall what you read about Robert at the beginning of this chapter. He learned to write programs when he was in second grade! Elementary students can create simple programs that make a turtle move or start or stop a motor. Experienced programmers can create complex programs that do such things as calculate the location of the space shuttle as it travels through space. Programming can be accomplished through text commands or through visual interfaces that actually let students see what is happening every step of the way.

LOGO is a programming language appropriate for children: Technology

The LOGO language has been used in elementary schools for many years. LOGO is used to develop programming skill and possible content knowledge and general problem-solving ability (Grabe & Grabe, 1998). Students learn to use sets of instructions to make the computer perform complex tasks. LEGO-LOGO, an extension of LOGO, allows students to build simple machines and use the computer to control those machines by using an interface box. With LEGO-LOGO, students can explore concepts in physics, mathematics, and engineering. It is not difficult to use; after a three-hour session, all of the students in my class were able to program the computer to perform simple tasks.

Elementary science students should use programming to explore a new way of thinking, and also to see how they can affect the world around them. Most students find it amazing that a few simple commands can create something incredibly complex. As a science teacher, you can relate this to other aspects of your curriculum. For example, you could explore how simple changes in the environment have wide-ranging effects on our lives.

Teaching with Technology

You will now put your knowledge of technology into practice by teaching with technology. You will study about the weather using the Internet as a source of lesson plans and a way to bring the real world into the classroom.

These students are using design and technology to solve a problem.

Activity 11.6 Online: A Video Tour of Weather Around the World

A video tour of weather events on the Internet: Technology, earth and space science

Overview: In this lesson activity, you and your students will take a video tour of the world and find out about current weather conditions.

Materials: You will need at least one computer connected to the Internet if you are going to do this (and the activities that follow) on your own. If you will present the lessons to your students, you will need a classroom computer laboratory with Internet hookups or a single computer connected to the Internet and a video projection system that magnifies the computer screen.

Procedure: Log onto WeatherNet at

http://cirrus.sprl.umich.edu/wxnet/

Scroll down to *WeatherCams,* and click. You will see a list of more than 100 live videos located in more than 100 locations throughout the world. Select as many sites as you have time for, and take your tour!

Assessment: Where did you go on your video tour of the world? What was the weather like? ■

Activity 11.7 Online: Weather Forecasts for Cities in the United States

Weather forecasting on the Internet: Technology, earth and space science

Overview: In this activity, you will locate a map of the United States and find the weather forecasts, conditions, warnings, and weather graphics for each state.

Procedure: Log onto http://cirrus.sprl.umich.edu/wxnet/. Scroll down to *USA Weather,* and click. Select the locations of interest to you, and learn as much as you can. If there is a printer hooked to your computer, print the data for a particular city. Study it and save it for the next activity.

Assessment: Select some of the cities that you visited with the live WeatherCam. Do the maps and the weather data match the video you saw? ■

Activity 11.8 Online: Viewing Radar and Satellite Maps

Viewing radar and satellite maps on the Internet: Technology, earth and space science

Overview: In this activity, you will view radar and satellite maps of the cities you visited in Activity 11.7 (see Figure 11.2).

Procedure: Log onto http://cirrus.sprl.umich.edu/wxnet/. Scroll down to *Radar and Satellite,* and click. Print a radar (Nexrad) and satellite map of the city you are studying. You can find radar maps at www.intellicast.com/weather/usa/radsum/. Have students study the maps. Locate north, south, east, and west. What symbols do they find on the map? What do the symbols mean?

Assessment: How do the live videos, the weather data, and the radar and satellite maps of your location compare? Repeat this activity over a series of days. Have students create data charts. How do the weather maps change? Discuss the causes of weather change with your students. From their observations of the weather maps, what do they think causes some of the weather changes? What do they think carries weather changes from place to place? Based on their study of weather maps, have students predict what they think the weather will be like the next day in a particular location. ■

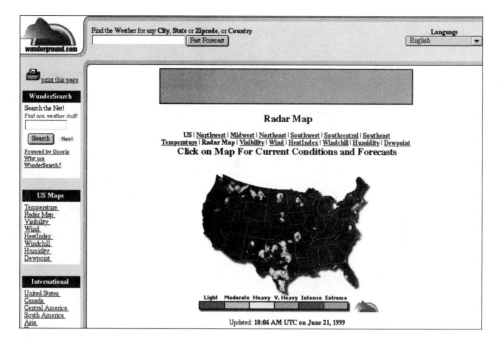

**Figure 11.2
A Radar Map**

Used with permission of
The Weather Underground.

Activity 11.9 Online: Visiting the Weather Underground

*Reading maps with
information on
temperature, wind
chill, heat index, humidity,
precipitation, and wind
speed on the Internet:
Technology, earth
and space science*

Overview: In this activity, you will visit a site that has maps of countries around the world. You can learn about temperature, wind chill, heat index, humidity, precipitation, air pressure, and wind speed (see Figure 11.3 on page 308).

Procedure: Log onto http://www.wunderground.com/. Select a city and click on it. You will see a data chart that gives the weather conditions. Check the weather in the tropics (see Figure 11.4 on page 309).

Assessment: Visit several cities and find out about the cloud formations. The next activity addresses types of clouds and weather prediction. ■

Activity 11.10 Hands-on Science: Making Popcorn Clouds

*Integrating science and
literature*

Overview: In this activity, you will read the book *Cloudy with a Chance of Meatballs* by Judi Barrett. This is the story of the town of Chewandswallow, where everything that everyone ate came from the sky. Discuss what we find in the sky, including clouds. Then discuss the different types of clouds. To integrate art and science, make popcorn clouds.

Materials: For a class of 25, you will need a pound of butter or margarine, two 16-ounce bags of mini-marshmallows, a 2-pound bag of popcorn, a roll of waxed paper, a pot, and a hot plate or burner. Your students should not make this mixture, as they could burn themselves easily.

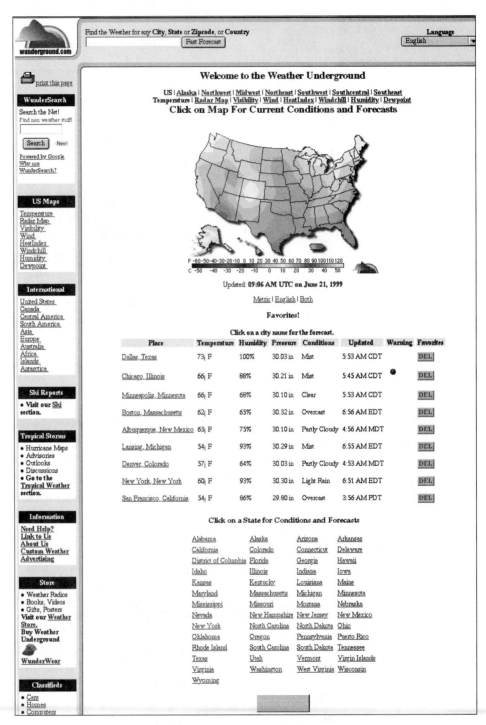

**Figure 11.3
Map of Current
Conditions, Forecasts,
and Accompanying
Data Table**
Used with permission of The
Weather Underground.

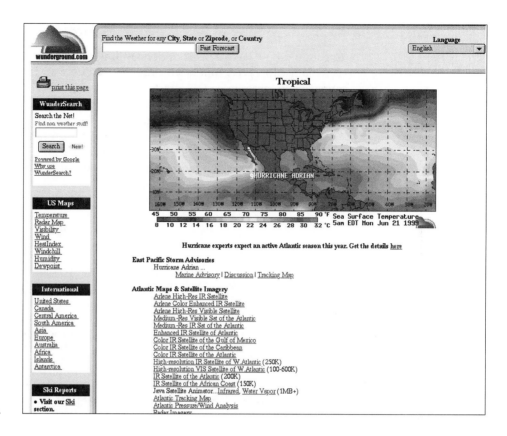

Figure 11.4
Map of the Tropics
Used with permission of
The Weather Underground.

**Learning about clouds:
Earth and space science**

Procedure: Read the book and discuss things that are found in the sky. Focus on the different types of clouds. Log onto http://seaborg.nmu.edu/clouds/types.html. You will find descriptions of nine different kinds of clouds, their appearance, and altitude. Click on *Clouds Photo Page* and view photos of the clouds. Have each student select one cloud and study its shape.

*Integrating science
and art*

In the pan, melt the butter and marshmallows. This takes about 5 minutes. Then add the popcorn. You will have a gooey mixture. Give each student a piece of waxed paper and a lump of the mixture. Instruct students to make a sculpture of one of the clouds. When they are done with their sculptures, use a cooperative learning technique called *roam the room:* have them move from table to table figuring out what type of cloud each student created. This activity is lots of fun. I've done it several times in my college classroom and with elementary science students. They usually guess correctly and remember the different types of clouds they have created.

Assessment: Have your students associate each type of cloud with a particular type of weather. (In the next chapter, you will learn more about weather as you and your students use design and technology to create instruments to gather weather data.)

Constructing Your Knowledge of Science and Science Teaching

You should now have a basic understanding of what technology can bring to your classroom. However, unless you find a computer and get to work using it, you cannot truly experience the effects of technology on your students. Think about what you read in this chapter. What is the Internet? How can you use it in your classroom? What software programs have you used? How do they fit into the curriculum? Do you have any experience with programming? If not, try to find the LOGO program and get started. As you can see, it is difficult to construct your knowledge of computers and technology by simply reading this chapter. This is a case where hands-on experience is essential.

Key Terms

application (p. 290)
word processor (p. 290)
document (p. 290)
database (p. 290)
field (p. 290)
form (p. 290)
spreadsheet (p. 291)

cell (p. 291)
calculation (p. 291)
World Wide Web (p. 293)
email (electronic mail)
 (p. 293)
information superhighway
 (p. 293)

cyberspace (p. 293)
web browser (p. 294)
listserv (p. 296)
software (p. 300)
productivity software (p. 301)
programming (p. 304)

Reviewing Chapter 11: Questions, Extensions, Applications, and Explorations

1. Three of the major software companies offering elementary science products are Tom Snyder, Sunburst Communications, and Broderbund. Use one of the search engines to find these sites. Send for catalogs to keep in your classroom.

2. The Annenberg/CPB Math and Science Collection contains many high-quality videos. Log onto their site at www.learner.org, and explore. Make a list of products that you can use in your classroom.

3. To learn more about experimental and data-gathering software, explore the PASCO site. Use a search engine to find the site. Send for a free catalog.

4. Find an elementary science lesson plan on the Internet. Evaluate the quality of the lesson plan.

5. Check this site: www2.childrenssoftware.com. Here you will find reviews of software for children. Select ten products that could accompany your lessons.

6. Log onto http://www.homeworkcentral.com/navjr/science.html. Examine the *Ask an Expert* page. Contact one of the experts and ask a question.

7. Log onto the Houghton Mifflin Education Place at http://www.hmco.com. Visit the College Division's Education Web site. Enjoy your journey! There's a great deal to explore.

Print Resources

Books

Classroom Connect Staff (1996). *Educator's Internet companion.* Lancaster, PA: Wentworth.

Frazier, D. (1995). *Internet for kids*. Alameda, CA: Sybex.

Grabe, M., & Grabe, C. (1998). *Integrating technology for meaningful learning.* Boston: Houghton Mifflin.

Papert, S. (1980). *Mindstorms: Children, computers, and powerful ideas.* New York: Basic Books.

Papert, S. (1993). *The children's machine: Rethinking school in the age of the computer.* New York: Basic Books.

Journals

CD-ROM Today, 1350 Old Bayshore Highway, Suite 210, Burlingame, CA 94010

Computers in the School, 75 Griswold Street, Binghamton, NY 13904

Electronic Learning, 902 Sylvan Avenue, Englewood Cliffs, NJ 07632

Journal of Computers in Mathematics and Science Teaching, P.O. Box 2966, Charlotsville, VA 22902

NewMedia Magazine, 901 Mariner's Island Blvd. Suite 365, San Mateo, CA 94404

Science and Children, National Science Teachers Association, 1840 Wilson Blvd., Arlington, VA 22201-3000

Technology and Learning, P.O. Box 49727, Dayton, OH 45449-0727

The Science Teacher, National Science Teachers Association, 1840 Wilson Blvd., Arlington, VA 22201-3000

T.H.E. Journal (Technological Horizons in Education), 150 El Camino Real Suite 112, Tustin, CA 92780-3670

Electronic Resources

Everything Weather: The Essential Guide to the Whys and Wonders of Weather

Learn about weather events and investigate all aspects of weather.
Sunburst Software (1-800-321-7511)

Earth Explorer: Multimedia Encyclopedia of the Environment

This CD provides an interactive tour of our planet.
Sunburst Software (1-800-321-7511)

Interactive Earth

This multimedia resource teaches students about global trends, world maps, and patterns and relationships.
Sunburst (1-800-321-7511)

Dr. Science Weather Systems Video

This video shows experiments involving weather. Appropriate for grades 5 through 10.
Teacher's Discovery (1-888-97-SCIENCE)

Logo Products and Control Systems

The Adventures of Hilary and other explorations in science and technology.
Valiant Products (1-888-366-6628)

Children's Literature

Jacobs, Marian
Why Does It Rain? (Rosen Group, 1998)
ISBN: 0-8239-5273-8
Preschool and Grades K–2

Humphrey, Paul
The Weather (Children's Press, 1997)
ISBN: 0-516-20238-3
Preschool and Grades K–3

Christian, Spencer
Can It Really Rain Frogs? The World's Strangest Weather Events
(John Wiley & Sons, 1997)
ISBN: 0-471-15290-0
Grades 3 and up

Cutts, David
I Can Read About Thunder and Lightning
(Troll Associates, 1997)
ISBN: 0-89375-217-7
Preschool and Grades K–2

Thompson, Kim and Paskiet, Mark
I'd Like to Be a Meteorologist
(Twin Sisters Productions, 1996)
ISBN: 1-57583-021-3
Preschool and Grades K–4

Gillis, Jennifer
Puddle Jumpers: Fun Weather Projects for Kids
(Story Books, 1996)
ISBN: 0-88266-938-9
Preschool and Grades K–2

Cole, Joanna
The Magic School Bus Inside a Hurricane
(Scholastic Trade, 1995)
ISBN: 0-590-44686
Preschool and Grades K–4

Robinson, Fay
Where Do Puddles Go? (Children's Press, 1995)
ISBN: 0-516-06036-8
Preschool and Grades K–2

CHAPTER 12

Technology as Design Knowledge: Science and Technology Education United

In Chapter 11, you learned how to teach with technology. The focus of that chapter was learning ways to use the computer as a tool for teaching and learning. This chapter is also about teaching with technology, but, as you learned in Chapter 1, the word *technology* has more than one meaning. Besides computer technology, also called **educational technology** or instructional technology, there is technology education. In this sense, **technology** means changing the natural environment to satisfy perceived human needs and wants (International Technology Education Association, 1998). Technology does this by identifying and solving problems that people face. **Technology education** involves teaching people to solve problems and satisfy human needs and wants in a practical way. To determine just what these needs and wants are, a wide range of factors must be considered simultaneously. Thus, technology brings together, or integrates, many different subject areas.

Teaching with technology means presenting students with important, interesting problems to solve

Since technology involves satisfying human needs and wants, teaching with technology is a powerful tool for enhancing science instruction. By presenting students with meaningful, important, interesting problems to solve, you help them to learn science content for a purpose. Learning science and applying what they learn helps students to solve their problems. The motivation to learn comes from within. The process is active, purposeful, and engaging.

Presenting students with interesting problems

Kathy Dullea is a middle school teacher who specializes in teaching with educational technology and writing curriculum materials that integrate science, mathematics, and technology. She created a unit called "Dinotopia," which is about people and dinosaurs living together on an island. As the unit begins, she presents students with four problems. They are to select and solve one of them. The problems are:

1. Create an environmental game to teach the children of Dinotopia about the environment.
2. Make playground apparatus for the children and the dinosaurs.
3. Create a small town on the island where pilots and flying dinosaurs are trained.
4. Use 100 straws to build a water tower on the island that stands as high as possible. The water tower must be able to support the weight of a baseball.

Before you read on, think about these questions. Where is the technology in these activities? Where is the science? Where is the mathematics?

Students learn relevant science concepts to solve technological problems

Working in groups of four or five, students select one of the problems and get started. They have four days to work on the problem from start to finish. Their time is limited, so they plan carefully. Most of the materials they use are recycled products. In the process of solving the problem, they will learn relevant science concepts. Their knowledge of math skills is just as important as their science understandings. The solutions to the problem are diverse, and they do research and learn on their own.

Students learn about ecology, ecosystems, biomes, and habitats to design an environmental game: Technology

One group decides to create an environmental game. Students must first learn about the environment. They search the Web, visit the school library, read magazines, journals, and their science text, and view short videos. They design a game that teaches the children of Dinotopia about ecology, ecosystems, biomes, and habitats. They study these concepts because this information provides a way to solve a problem: creating an environmental game. The science concepts they learn are applied immediately.

Learning about children and dinosaurs to design playground equipment: Technology and life science

Another group makes playground equipment for children and dinosaurs. They learn about children, how they play, and what equipment would be appropriate for them. They study about different types of dinosaurs: their sizes, their shapes, ways in which they move, and what they eat. They compare this knowledge with what they know about children. They design playground equipment of many different sizes and shapes.

Learning about primary wind direction to design an airport: Technology and earth and space science

The next group designs a town for training pilots and flying dinosaurs. They design an airport, and in the process learn about primary wind direction and how it affects the locations of the runways. The houses in the town have hangars instead of garages, and all of the streets are wide enough to accommodate small planes and flying dinosaurs.

Designing an irrigation system: Technology

Still another group researches irrigation and designs an irrigation system. They locate a source of water, find out what building an irrigation system involves, and design a network of pipes to bring the water to the soil. They also learn about pumping water through the pipes. The students who build the tower out of straws learn about structures. They try many different designs before identifying the best one.

All of the students have a reason for learning. They are solving problems that are meaningful to them and are enjoying their work.

When assessing student work, Ms. Dullea looks at how students use science, mathematics, and technology. Using alternative assessment techniques, she assesses the content and process knowledge they gain. She looks for evidence of problem solving. She finds that when students solve one problem, another one comes up. They want to solve these new problems because they are interesting. If Ms. Dullea had directed her students to learn the very same things they learned in doing these activities, they would have said they were learning at her request. But using technology, they learned for the purpose of solving an interesting problem. They generated personal knowledge and accumulated their own experience. The motivation came from within.

Technology is about finding practical solutions to practical problems: Technology

Solving a technological problem often helps students gain insight into science and math

Technology is about finding practical solutions to practical problems. It allows students to put their thinking into a context that is meaningful to them. Many students need to start with a relevant problem before they can understand a science idea. Sometimes solving a practical problem helps them to gain insight into science or math (Catlin & Douglas, 1998, p. 2).

As you read this chapter, think about the answers to these questions:

1. **What is technology as design and problem solving?**

2. **How do technology education and educational technology differ?**

3. **How does technology as design and problem solving bring together, or integrate, many different subject areas?**

4. **What is the design loop?**

5. **How does technology strengthen math and science instruction?**

6. **How can I create design challenges and bring technology education to my students?**

7. **What happens when students learn with a purpose? How does this differ from learning without a purpose? How does technology provide the purpose for learning?**

8. **How is knowledge of simple machines useful for design and problem solving?**

The Nature of Technology

Benchmarks for Science Literacy: Project 2061 (American Association for the Advancement of Science [AAAS], 1993) contains two chapters that focus on technology education. Chapter 3, "The Nature of Technology," discusses what knowledge about the nature of technology students need to develop scientific literacy, includes ways of thinking about technology, and examines relationships between science and technology. Chapter 8, a companion to Chapter 3, focuses on "technological systems, such as agriculture and manufacturing, and describes what scientific, social, and historical understandings students should gain" (AAAS, 1993, p. 181).

The standards remind us that "as long as there have been people, there has been technology." What evidence do we have? As we look back at the beginning

Technology shapes and reflects the value of our social enterprise: Technology

Carrying out a design challenge.

of human culture, we find evidence of people shaping tools to foster the development of civilization. Technology both shapes and reflects the values of our social enterprise.

STANDARDS

According to *Benchmarks for Science Literacy:*

> In the broadest sense, technology extends our abilities to change the world: to cut, shape, or put together materials; to move things from one place to another; to reach farther with our hands, voices, and senses. We use technology to try to change the world to suit us better. The changes may relate to survival needs such as food, shelter, or defense, or they may relate to human aspirations such as knowledge, art, or control. But the results of changing the world are often complicated and unpredictable. They can include unexpected benefits, unexpected costs, and unexpected risks—any of which may fall on different social groups at different times. Anticipating the effects of technology is therefore as important as advancing its capabilities. (AAAS, 1993, p. 41)

A Look Back at History

History abounds with inventions that resulted from identifying problems and needs and developing ways to satisfy them (Clayfield & Hyatt, 1994). Think about early civilizations. People survived by hunting and gathering, rearing livestock, and farming. Successful farming allowed more food to grow. That caused populations to increase and created a need for housing. Soon there were villages, towns, and empires (Catlin & Livingstone, 1995).

As civilizations developed, problems arose and were solved with technological solutions: Technology

As civilizations developed, new problems arose. For example, some towns were located near rivers. There was plenty of water, but sometimes the rivers overflowed their banks and caused flooding. Another problem arose in towns located away from the rivers, where there was wilderness and desert. In the first case there was too much water, which resulted in the need to divert it away because it would ruin crops, destroy buildings, and kill people. In the second case there wasn't enough water, which resulted in an inability to grow crops and a shortage of drinking water. These problems needed to be solved for civilizations to survive.

After studying the problem, a way to control flood water was needed. When the river swelled too high, water had to be diverted. At the same time, dry land needed water. Someone had to design a water control system (Catlin & Livingstone, 1995). Consider the following activity.

Activity 12.1 Problem Solving: Technology and History

Overview: Suppose it is 4000 BC and you live in the region of Mesopotamia near the Tigris River, where the soil is fertile. Your home is near the river, which often overflows its banks. You and your neighbors need a way to control the water level of the river so it won't cause harm to your homes, crops, or families.

Materials: The choice is yours.

Designing a water control system: Technology

Procedure: Design a system to control flood water and prevent massive destruction to your village when the water level becomes too high. (Did you make a working model?)

Assessment: If you made a working model, test it to see if it works. ■

Sluice gate, noria, and shadoof are water control systems: Technology

Here is how early civilizations solved this problem. People invented systems such as the sluice gate, noria, and shadoof to control water level (see Figure 12.1). When the *sluice gate* is down all the way, it dams the water in the river. When it is lifted, water flows through the river. A *noria* is like a ferris wheel. Instead of seats there are buckets attached to the wheel, which rotate with it. Unlike a ferris wheel, the lower portion of the wheel is submerged in the water. When the wheel reaches the water level, the buckets are submerged, and they fill up. When they reach the top of the wheel, they tip over and empty into something that looks like a playground slide with high sides, sending the water into a primitive irrigation system that brings it to dry land. A noria can be built with foot pedals so that people turn the large wheel. If it is placed in water that flows, the water power can turn the wheel, and pedals aren't needed. The *shadoof* is a simple bucket connected to a lever. When the bucket is lowered into the water, it fills up. Then it is raised and swung around so that it turns upside down and empties onto the surrounding land (Catlin & Livingstone, 1995).

**Figure 12.1
Early Technological
Solutions**

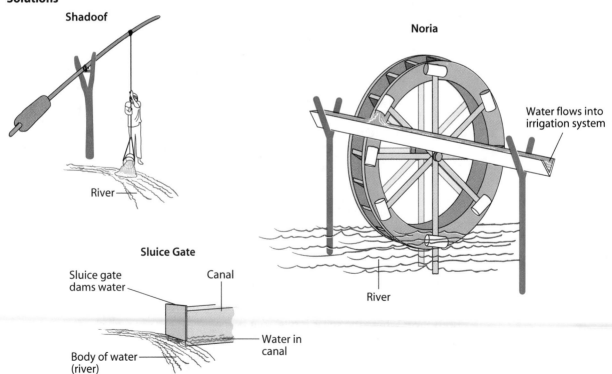

Activity 12.2 Online: Technological Advances in Communication

Using the Internet to learn about technology

Overview: In this activity, you will log onto a web site and examine a series of lesson plans exploring technology and communication.

Materials: A computer hooked up to the Internet

Procedure: Log onto

http://www.ncrtec.org/tools/camp/techno/techno1.htm

Check out the lessons called *Technological Advances in Communication: The Pony Express Rides the Information Highway.* The lessons, written by teacher Linda S. Hallenbeck, engage students in exploring the technological advances made in the field of communication. Students learn about various forms of communication, the human needs they satisfy, and the benefits and trade-offs associated with each invention.

Assessment: Do your students have a better understanding of how technology has shaped our lives? ▪

People use tools to make things and accomplish tasks: Technology

Engaging in design and problem solving using scientific knowledge to solve practical problems

When you present your students with problems such as these, they can learn many different things. Young children see that people can use tools to make things. If tools weren't available, some tasks could not be done as well, and sometimes they could not be done at all. For example, it would be difficult to lower the level of the river without tools to accomplish the task more effectively. Children in the upper elementary grades can learn that throughout history, people have invented and used tools. Today's tools are different from those of the past. By using tools and technology, people have changed the world. They have been able to attend to human needs such as food, shelter, and defense. Middle school children can learn that people who engage in design and problem solving use scientific knowledge to solve practical problems. When doing so, they have to consider human limitations and society's values (AAAS, 1993).

The Design Loop

Design is the process of planned change: Technology

Technology is a tool developed to accomplish a purpose. Design and technology go hand in hand. **Design** is the planned process of change. Designing helps you to plan change so that you end up with the desired results, minimizing trade-offs and controlling risk (Hutchinson & Karsnitz, 1994; Hutchinson & Sellwood, 1996). Minimizing trade-offs means that sometimes you have to sacrifice some features to get others, or you may need to emphasize some aspects of a design and downplay others.

The design loop is a problem-solving strategy: Technology

Design enables you to develop solutions to problems in a careful, planned way. Is there a particular way to do this? Technologists use the **design loop** to make problem solving effective. It is an active process that enables you to define a problem and specify in detail the requirements of the solution. You then do research and investigate the information you need to help solve the problem. Once that is done, you generate a number of possible solutions. After careful thought and discussion, you choose what you determine to be the best solution.

Steps of the design loop: Technology

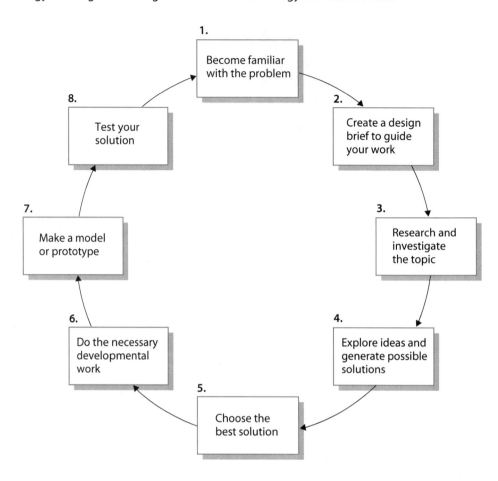

**Figure 12.2
The Design Loop**

Then you do the developmental work needed to build a model. You construct, test, and evaluate the model. Figure 12.2 shows the design loop.

When your students use the design loop, they learn that there is no perfect design. A design that is excellent in one respect, such as appearance or ability to do the job, may cost too much to produce. Even the best designs can fail. You can work hard to reduce the likelihood of failure, but you can't prevent it entirely. Sometimes the solution to one problem causes another (AAAS, 1993). Motor vehicles have made transportation quite easy, but think of the pollution they have caused. It's not as easy to get around using a horse and buggy, but it certainly causes much less pollution.

Take constraints and limitations into account while designing

Students in the middle grades should learn that they must take constraints and limitations into account when designing. Constraints include the properties of the materials they are using, gravity and other forces of nature, and economic, political, social, ethical, and aesthetic constraints (AAAS, 1993, p. 51).

Sometimes an idea needs more research and testing before a system is designed

Here are some examples of limitations and constraints. Antibiotics are important for controlling disease, but they often they have harmful side effects. Spray cans are useful in dispensing aerosols such as hair spray, cooking oil, or paint, but in the past they damaged the ozone layer. Today we have spray cans that don't harm the environment. Students should know that sometimes an idea needs more research and testing before a system is designed. The limitations and constraints need careful consideration. You should discuss these issues with your students when engaging in design and problem solving.

Identifying the Problem

Identify the problem and think about it carefully

You will now learn about the design loop by solving a design challenge. A **design challenge** is a meaningful problem that you solve by using the design loop. Design challenges often require a technological solution. The National Science Education Standards (1996) says that suitable design tasks for students at the elementary and middle school levels should be "well defined, so that the purposes of the task are not confusing. Tasks should be based on contexts that are immediately familiar in the homes, school, and immediate community of the students" (p. 161).

The first step in the design loop is to identify the problem and think about it carefully. Here is a simple design challenge that results from the need for children to eat healthy foods. It is one that you can try in your college classroom or with your students.

> Children should eat nourishing meals, but they often don't. They often skip meals or eat junk food. List five ways in which eating habits of children could be improved.

Creating a Design Brief

The design brief clarifies the problem and describes the task

After you identify possible problems by listing five ways to improve the eating habits of children, you clarify and specify one that you will solve. The next step is to create a design brief. The **design brief** clarifies the problem and describes the task. Here is an example.

> Create a new type of sandwich that includes foods that are nutritious. Make the sandwich colorful and appealing to elementary school–age children.

A design brief is similar to a performance task. It is a statement of the problem to solve and the criteria to meet. Notice how the design brief is structured. Students must create a new type of sandwich and include foods that are nutritious. You don't tell them to study about foods that are nutritious; they figure this out for themselves and then learn on their own. According to the NSES (1996), the "criteria for success and the constraints for design should be limited" for students in the elementary and middle grades. "Only one or two science ideas should be involved in any particular task" (p. 161).

Gathering Information

Children engage in research to gather information about the problem

Now the problem is specified. The next step is for students to do their research. They will learn about the food groups, about taste, and about color. They have a reason for learning, because they will apply that knowledge in the design process.

Generating Aternative Solutions

Generating alternative solutions is part of the design loop

In this step, students apply their research as they design many different sandwiches (solutions). They brainstorm different ideas. They decide which ones are unworkable and which ones make sense. They decide on criteria for selecting the best design. Criteria might be number of foods in the sandwich, chewability, visual appeal, and nutritional value. Notice that although certain criteria were specified in the original design brief, in this step students refine and expand the criteria. As they gain more knowledge about the problem and consider constraints and limitations, they assign their own criteria to the solution. Once again, students generate their own knowledge as they engage in problem solving.

Choosing the Best Solution

Consider benefits and trade-offs when choosing the best solution

In this step, students apply the criteria to the designs and decide which ones meet them and which ones do not. Some sandwiches may contain too many different foods, some may be difficult to chew, some may not be visually appealing, and some may not be nutritious. Students consider benefits and trade-offs as they work.

Doing the Developmental Work to Plan for Construction

Designing a solution requires developmental work and planning

Now your students are ready to do the technical planning before they construct the sandwich. They sketch the sandwich and decide what needs to be done to make it work. In the case of the sandwich, there is little developmental work to be done. More complicated designs require developmental work and planning. Think about the problems associated with the river overflowing its banks. Much more developmental work is required in planning for construction of the devices that will control the water level.

Making a Model

Making a model to see if your solution works

Your students are finally ready to make a model of the sandwich. They can do this in many ways. Using the computer, with a program such as Kid Pix, they can draw a model of the sandwich. They can use different-color play dough or colored clay to build an appearance model to show what the sandwich will look like. Then they can make the actual sandwich.

Testing and Evaluating the Model

Test a solution to see if it meets specifications set forth in the design brief

Now that the sandwich exists, your students can test and evaluate it. Does it meet the specifications set forth in the design brief? Does it include foods that are nutritious? Is the sandwich colorful and appealing to elementary school–age children? After evaluating the model, your students might like to go back and test another solution.

Activity 12.3 Online: Solving the Rain Forest Challenge

Solving a design challenge about the rain forest

Overview: In this activity, you will visit an elementary school web site and solve a design challenge involving the rain forest.

Materials: A computer with an Internet connection

Procedure: Log onto http://visi.net/~wcooper/Design_Tech.html and explore the web site. Then log onto http://visi.net/~wcooper/design_brief.html to read the design brief.

Assessment: Examine the science log at http://visi.net/~wcooper/technology_log.html. Notice the careful design and use of alternative assessment strategies. ▪

Activity 12.4 Problem Solving: Creating a Technology Design Challenge for Your Students

Overview: In this activity, you will create a technology design challenge for your students. You can do the activity with your students or try it in your college classroom.

Materials: The choice is yours.

Procedure: Begin by selecting a topic and brainstorming possible solutions. From there, determine a need and brainstorm ideas generated from that need. Then write a design brief, clearly stating the task. Make decisions about what materials to use and ways in which to construct, test, and modify the model. Use the design loop to guide the work.

Assessment: Observe your students as they work. Make an informal assessment of what happens during the lesson. Do any problems arise? What types of discussions are taking place in the groups? ▪

Implementing the Design Loop

Using the design loop, your students can tackle challenges they encounter every day, working together to come up with solutions. They study a problem, learn everything they can about it, and formulate a variety of possible solutions. They stick with a problem until it is solved.

Designing a solution to a problem is not a linear process

Using the design loop gives your students another way to solve problems that they can use throughout their lives. In earlier chapters, you learned to use scientific thinking. Now the design loop gives you an additional problem-solving strategy to teach your students. The design loop is a guide that makes problem solving more effective, providing a structure for thinking and doing. Designing a solution to a problem is not a linear process that unfolds in sequential steps. Instead it is a creative process in which students work in an "acting-doing" mode (Hutchinson & Karsnitz, 1994; Hutchinson & Sellwood, 1996). Recall what you just read about the design loop. It causes students to think, question, evaluate solutions, create design briefs, make models, and revisit their models and make changes as necessary. They come up with solutions to problems, test them, then come up with alternative solutions.

Solving Social Problems with the Design Loop

Before introducing a problem that requires a technological solution, you can start a lesson or unit by presenting your students with a real-life social problem. They brainstorm solutions and possible consequences. Here is an example that Ms. Dullea uses with her class:

> You have made arrangements to meet your friends at the mall. Your parents tell you that you have to clean your room before you can go to the mall. It's getting late. What will you do?

Using the design loop to solve social problems

Students discuss the problem. They use the design loop to become familiar with the problem, explore ideas, plan and develop solutions, test their ideas, and present their solutions. They find that there are many ways to solve the problem. They can disobey their parents and go to the mall without cleaning the room. That, they say, is not such a good solution. They can clean the room and keep their friends waiting. Not a good idea, either. They can approach their parents and negotiate a later time for cleaning. A good possibility. They can call their friends and set a later meeting time. Another good possibility.

Can you think of another real-life problem to present to your students?

Presenting Design Challenges

You can move from social problems to simple science problems by presenting design challenges. Begin with open-ended questions to make students think and draw from their experience. Have them use the design loop to solve these challenges. Here are some examples you can try.

The Oil Spill Challenge

Studying the effects of an oil spill on the environment: Technology and earth and space science

Ask students, "What problems does an oil spill cause?" This question will stimulate many different answers. Then give students hands-on experience with the situation as they encounter an oil spill firsthand in the classroom.

Built into the challenge are science and technology. Here is the technology. Using an aluminum foil pan, playground sand, and water, students make a "beach" in a pan. By adding a tablespoonful of cooking oil, they have an "oil spill." Then they make a model of a bird. Using 2-inch diameter foam (Styrofoam) balls, feathers from a craft store (or a feather duster), pipe cleaners for legs, and movable eyes from a craft store, they create the bird. The "bird" finds its way to the "beach" and swims in the oil-contaminated water, coating its feathers with oil.

Then you identify the problem. Ask, "What does the oil spill do to the environment? What does it do to wildlife?" Students do research to answer these questions. You ask them to develop a way to clean up the bird and the beach. Using the design loop, they work together to come up with ways to clean up the oil spill. They try different materials. Some students use soap and water to clean up the bird. Others use mineral oil. Suddenly it occurs to them that this bird isn't even alive; this oil spill was caused by cooking oil, and it's not an easy job to clean up the bird. Imagine what it would be like if this were a real bird and crude oil, not cooking oil!

Integrating literature and technology

Cleaning up the beach is not easy either. Students use sponges and paper towels. Some students use squares cut from old pantyhose to skim off the oil, which they find works the best. They learn about the properties of different materials. Others invent a creature that eats oil. As they feed it, the creature gets bigger. It eats all of the oil spills in the world. You can use literature to bring across the message, with books such as *Sign of the Seahorse* by Graham Base and *The Lorax* by Dr. Seuss. (Note: If you try this activity, be sure to use cooking oil, not motor oil. Motor oil is considered a hazardous waste in some states.)

I presented this activity to several sixth-grade classes and was impressed with the positive results. Students worked diligently to formulate solutions and had fun trying different ideas. Quite a mess was created in the classroom, and I watched as students organized the clean-up effort. When they were finished, every desk was spotless, the floor was clean, and all of the materials were where they belonged. My students enjoyed the activity very much. They wanted to do more activities of this nature, and knew this wouldn't happen if they didn't clean up the mess.

Activity 12.5 Problem Solving: Johnny Appleseed's Birthday Challenge

Overview: On Johnny Appleseed's birthday, you can present this design challenge, which was created by Ms. Dullea.

Materials: An apple, Legos, an empty milk container, popsicle sticks, other materials of students' choice

Using the design loop to solve a problem.

Designing an apple mover: Technology

Procedure: The challenge is to use the design loop to build an apple mover that can move an apple. It must be able to move up and down, as well as from side to side. Students can use Legos with gears, empty milk containers, popsicle sticks, or whatever else they like. They usually learn about simple machines as they solve the problem.

Assessment: How did the activity go? Have students describe the experience in their journals. ▪

Activity 12.6 Problem Solving: The Bridge Challenge

Overview: This activity involves construction and uses the design loop.

Materials: A sheet of paper, a stack of books, scissors, a ruler, 10 pennies

Designing a paper bridge that holds pennies: Technology

Procedure: Present your students with this problem: You have a sheet of 8.5" x 11" paper, a scissors, a ruler, 10 pennies, and two stacks of books. Using only these materials, design a paper bridge that will support pennies placed in the middle of the span. You may cut or fold the paper, but you can't use glue or tape.

Assessment: Once students are satisfied with their designs, have them test their models by stacking pennies on the bridge (American Institute of Physics, 1997). (Did they use a strip of paper to make an arch as a support?) ▪

This challenge is similar to the one you read about in Chapter 7 when you studied density. In that chapter, you designed an aluminum foil boat that could remain afloat while holding as many pennies as possible. Try repeating that activity, this time using the design loop.

Activity 12.7 Problem Solving: The Timer Challenge

Overview: Here is an interesting challenge that your students will enjoy. The task is to invent a 15-second timer.

Materials: Two clear, plastic cups, a straw, scissors, pencil and paper

Designing a 15-second timer: Technology

Procedure: Here is how some students have done this task. One group took two plastic cups, one taller than the other (see Figure 12.3). They lined them up side by side. They

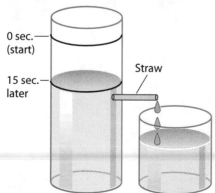

0 sec.— (start)

15 sec.— later

Straw

made a hole in the taller cup and placed a small length of straw in the hole. They filled the taller cup with water and let it drip into the shorter cup through the straw, marking off the starting level and the level of the water 15 seconds later. They calculated how much water dripped into the cup in 15 seconds—and that's how they measured time!

Figure 12.3 Designing an Instrument to Measure Time

Assessment: Have students describe their designs. How do they work? Did students build a working model? ▪

Developing Integrated Thematic Units

You can present your students with design challenges that last a day or two, or you can develop long-term units of study centered around a topic or theme. You will now read about two integrated thematic units: the litter critter and the board game about plants.

The Litter Critter

Designing a Litter Critter: Technology and environmental science

Ms. Dullea and her colleagues created a unit of study with insects as the theme. This thematic learning unit, designed for students in grades 6 through 8, integrates mathematics, science, and technology. Students create a Litter Critter, an insect body consisting of three parts and no appendages, using pieces of recycled trash. The insect has three pairs of jointed legs to help it move on land or water or climb vertically. It has two external structures to increase its awareness of its environment. After creating the insect, students report to the class, describing the insect's structure and identifying its habitat, or environment (Cundari et al., 1996).

When machines increase force, they give a mechanical advantage: Technology and physical science

In the math portion of the unit, students study levers and linkage systems and use math to determine the mechanical advantage of their systems. A **mechanical advantage** results when machines increase force. (You will learn about simple machines such as levers and inclined planes later in this chapter.) In the science class, students investigate insect structure and characteristics.

Using design to integrate math, science, and technology

Students then build the insect, which is where the technology comes in. Using a homosote board or stiff cardboard, oaktag, and pushpins, they design a two-dimensional linkage system that performs a function. They defend the model mathematically.

Next, using the design loop, students create a three-dimensional model of a linkage system from wood, Legos, or other, similar materials. Again, they defend the model mathematically. They learn vocabulary words such as *abdomen, anatomical, antennae, compound eye, environment, exoskeleton, facets, femur, habitat, head, jointed appendage, linear, ovipositor, proboscis, simple eyes, spiracles, thorax,* and *tympanum.*

The assessment is outstanding. Students write stories about insects using all of the vocabulary words in context. They write the stories in book form using graphics. Including at least one lever, one linkage system, and one pop-up, they create a pop-up book. The design brief appears in Figure 12.4.

Creating a Game That Shows Knowledge of Plants

Designing a game demonstrates knowledge of plants: Technology and life science

A group of first- and second-grade teachers created a unit on plants, which is an exploration of plant life on our planet. Students participate in a design challenge that has them create and construct a game that demonstrates their knowledge of plants. Students are told that Aliens have landed on the roof of their school and they make friends with them. The Aliens have a fascination with plant life on earth, since there are no plants on their planet. The challenge is to create a game that the Aliens can take home to teach those on their planet about plants, their components, and their needs and uses (Caliendo et al., 1997).

Scenario: People have consistently learned from their environment and frequently modeled their inventions after nature. Insect appendages and mouth parts have been used to model robot structures. You are on Planet X, a sister planet to earth. Planet X has all of the characteristics of earth.

Problem Statement: Your challenge is to build a robot arm that models an insect appendage and that performs at least two non-aggressive functions that will assist you as you live on Planet X.

Suggested Materials: oak tag strips, stapler, rubber bands, nails, balsa wood, brads, homosote, wood scraps, foam core, packaging tape, dowels, straws, craft sticks, wooden coffee stirrers, tongue depressors, brass paper fasteners, pipe cleaners, paper clips, egg cartons, pushpins, twist ties, hand drill, glue gun, glue sticks

Specifications

- Divide into groups of 3 or 4 (suggestions for task assignments: equipment manager, data manager, recorder, quality control officer).

- Use only the materials provided.

- Define your habitat and create a mind map (concept map) describing briefly as many ideas as you can generate in 5 minutes. In other words, BRAINSTORM. Your robot must be modeled after appendages and linkage systems.

- Robots should perform at least two special functions.

- Draw sketches of at least three of your group's robot ideas (one for each member of your group).

- Produce a final scale drawing of your robot arm on paper.

- Design and build a two-dimensional model of your robot arm and mount it on homosote board.

- Defend this model mathematically by creating a database.

- Using the two-dimensional model as a guide, build a three-dimensional model that is student powered.

- Make your model no larger than 1 meter in total.

Assessment:

- The model must meet the specifications listed above and perform its specified function,

- The design portfolio must contain evidence of planning, designing, and redesigning.
- There should be:
  1. A mind map for brainstorming
  2. Sketches of three ideas
  3. A scale drawing of the final product
  4. Written daily logs
  5. An explanation of the linkage system from both a technological and mathematical standpoint
  6. A description of your habitat and robot operation that enables you to live on Planet X

Created by Frances Cundari, Kathleen Dullea, and Deborah Stapenski of the Applegarth Middle School in Monroe Township, New Jersey; Irene Gavin, Roger Jinks, and Jane Joseph of the Clinton Public Schools in Clinton, New Jersey; and Kathy Granquist, Mary Ann Puglia, Billy Wheeler of the Indian Mills Memorial School in Shamong, New Jersey. Edited by Kathleen Dullea.

Permission granted by Kathleen Dullea.

**Figure 12.4
Design Brief for
"Insects, Rulers of
the World"**

This student is observing how a butterfly moves before building a model butterfly with movable parts.

Good directions are essential for engaging in design and technology

In doing their research for the game, students learn about plants, their needs and parts, and places in which they grow on earth. They also learn how people use plants. Their new vocabulary words include *blade, botanist, bulb, cereals, chlorophyll, cutting, evergreen, flower, fruit, grain, needles, petals, pistils, plant, pollen, root, seed, sepals, spore, stalks, stamens, stem, trunk,* and *veins*. This gives you an idea of what they learn on their own in the research process. Teachers assess the students' science logs, their preliminary drawings of the game, how they construct the game, observations of group work, field testing and revising of the game, and student descriptions of the experience. Students complete a daily feedback log to summarize each day's activities, tell about the new things they learned that day, and describe how they helped others in the group. They also give suggestions for how to make the group work more effectively.

Managing the Classroom

Teaching with technology can create a great deal of excitement in the classroom, and you want to be certain that students don't get out of hand. You can first get control by engaging students in short activities to gain their interest. Let them know that when they step out of line, the activity stops. Set limits, and teach them to accept limits. Sometimes you have to say, "We have to stop if you can't control your behavior." They will stop. Be serious, and be consistent. Don't wait for them to get out of control; stop them quickly.

Because you will be engaging in design and technology, expect the noise level to be high. Tell your principal what you are going to do before you do it. Invite him or her in to watch your class in action. Work with your colleagues so they, too, can learn to teach with technology. Write letters to parents telling them about your work. Support from all members of the school community is important for your efforts.

Good communication and ability to follow directions are essential when teaching with technology. Begin each year by having students learn to follow directions. Here is how Ms. Dullea does this. At the beginning of the year, she asks a student to give her directions for making a simple peanut butter and jelly sandwich. Even when she follows every direction the student gives, the sandwich doesn't turn out as expected. Everyone has a good laugh, and students learn that directions are important.

Learning About Simple Machines

Machines make work easier to do by changing the kind of work that we do: Physical science

A force is a push or a pull: Physical science

Machines allow a small force to overcome a larger force: Physical science

Simple machines have only one or two parts: Physical science

Machines change the size and direction of the force: Physical science

A crowbar changes the amount of force needed to open a crate: Physical science

Many of the technological tools you develop when you solve design challenges are machines. **Machines** make our work easier for us by changing the kind of work that we do. **Work** is done when a force moves an object over a distance. A **force** is a push or a pull. Machines change the size or the direction of the force needed. When you do work, you put in effort. In scientific terms, **effort** is the force—the push or pull—that produces an action. Machines make it easier for us to work because they can allow a small force, the effort, to overcome a larger force, called the **load**.

Here is an example. Suppose you try to open the lid of a crate with your hands and no tools. Depending on how strong you are, this might be an impossible task. If you had a simple tool such as a crowbar, the task would become much simpler. A crowbar is an example of a simple machine. **Simple machines** are technological tools that make work easier to do. They are called *simple* machines because they have only one or two parts. There are six simple machines: the lever, the wedge, the inclined plane, the wheel and axle (including the gear), the screw, and the pulley.

Machines change the size or the direction of the force needed. How does this happen? If you open the lid of a crate with a crowbar, the end of the crowbar that opens the lid (with great force) travels only a short distance. The other end of the crowbar travels a much longer distance, but receives a substantially smaller force. The crowbar changes the amount of force needed to open the crate. Think about climbing from the bottom to the top of a steep mountain. That takes a great deal of work. Can you get to the top without having to work so hard? If you walk along the side of the mountain as the road curves gently, the distance you walk will be greater, but your effort will decrease. If you climb straight up to the top of the mountain, the distance you walk will be shorter, but the effort you expend will be greater. When you are doing work, the more effort you expend, the shorter the distance you travel; the less effort you expend, the greater the distance you travel.

To learn more about simple machines, you will engage in activities in which you build and use them. You can try these activities in your college classroom or with your students. Be sure to supervise students carefully as they carry out these activities. Use your judgment and consult with your professor and host teacher when trying these activities in an elementary school classroom. Students in grades 4 and above can carry them out with greater success than younger children who may not be ready to understand the concepts.

Activity 12.8 Online: Learning About Simple Machines

Overview: In this activity, you will visit two web sites and review the basic concepts of simple machines.

Materials: A computer with access to the Internet

Procedure: Log onto the following sites, and read about and engage in activities that will broaden your knowledge of simple machines.

> **Activities involving simple machines:**
>
> **http://www-sci.lib.uci.edu/SEP/CTS/Machine.html**
>
> **Background information for students and teachers:**
>
> **http://www.mos.org/sln/Leonardo/InventorsWorkshop.html**
>
> **Background information for teachers:**
>
> **http://youth.net/cec/cecsci/cecsci.09.txt**

Assessment: Have these sites been helpful in expanding your knowledge of simple machines? ■

Activity 12.9 Hands-on Science: Using an Inclined Plane

A ramp is an inclined plane: Physical science

Overview: In this activity you will build an **inclined plane**, or ramp. Then you will make a rough comparison between the amount of force needed to lift an object straight up and the amount of force needed to pull the same object up the inclined plane. You will also build a measuring device (a crude scale) to make the comparison

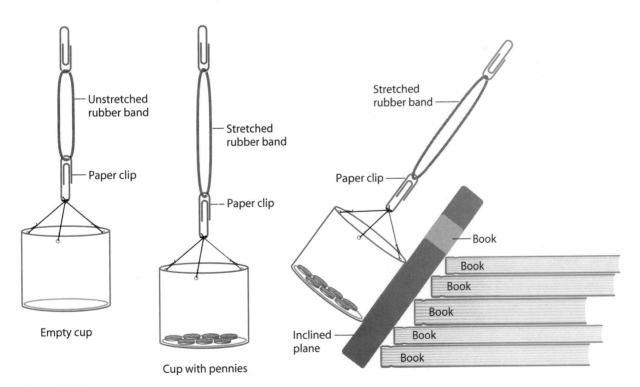

Figure 12.5
The Inclined Plane Reduces the Effort

more quantitative. If you have access to a spring scale, you won't have to construct the crude measuring device.

Materials: 1 medium-size rubber band, 2 paper clips, 50 cm of string (kite string is good), 1 paper cup, a stack of books, 50 pennies. If you have a spring scale, don't make the measuring device; use the scale instead.

Procedure: You will make a crude measuring device that will allow you to measure the force needed to move an object. The device is made of a rubber band, string, two paper clips, and a cup. We will call it a crude scale and use the amount of stretching that the rubber band does to measure force expended (see Figure 12.5).

Hold the rubber band vertically. Attach a paper clip through the bottom loop of the rubber band and another through the top loop. Set the device on the table. Carefully poke three holes in the top of the cup (they should be equidistant from each other), tie a piece of string through each hole, and join the strings by tying them together at the bottom of the paper clip. This is your crude scale. Your measure is the amount of stretching the rubber band does.

Stack your books so that they make a ramp, or an inclined plane. (You will come back to the inclined plane in a minute.) Next, put the pennies in the cup. Hold the rubber band/cup apparatus vertically by the top paper clip. Move the apparatus straight up so the cup doesn't rest on the table. Record how much the rubber band stretches. Now pull the cup up the inclined plane, holding it by the same paper clip. Again, record how much it stretches. Compare how much the rubber band stretches when it holds the cup and when it pulls the cup up the inclined plane.

Assessment: The inclined plane should have made it easier to lift the pennies. The rubber band should have stretched less when being moved up the inclined plane than when being held straight up. The inclined plane should reduce the effort. Did this happen? Can you design a better spring scale? Experiment with inclined planes set at different angles. What happens to the effort expended as the angle becomes steeper? Compare this with the amount of energy a person expends when first walking straight up a mountain and then walking up the gently sloping sides of the mountain. How are these two activities similar? ■

Activity 12.10 Hands-on Science: Using a Screw

A screw is an inclined plane wrapped around a cylinder, shaft, or pole: Physical science

Overview: In this activity, you will make a screw. A **screw** is an inclined plane that is wrapped or curved around a cylinder, shaft, or pole. Screws fasten objects together.

Materials: Pencil, paper, and scissors

Procedure: Place the pencil on top of a sheet of paper. Cut the paper into a rectangle that is the length of the pencil. Now cut the rectangle into a triangle so that it looks like an inclined plane. Be sure that one end of the triangle is the length of the pencil (see Figure 12.6 on page 333). Wrap the paper (the inclined plane) around the pencil. You now have a paper screw.

Assessment: To see what a screw does, you will need a metal screw, a screwdriver, and a piece of wood. Carefully turn the screw into the wood. If you would like to try this with your class, first check with your professor and host teacher to be sure it's appropriate and safe for your students. ■

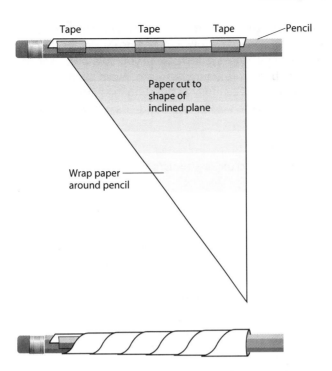

Figure 12.6
The Screw

Screws apply a great deal of force with very little effort. Think about a car jack, which uses a screw. It does a tremendous amount of work for a small amount of effort: it lifts a car!

Activity 12.11 Hands-on Science: Using a Wedge

A wedge is an inclined plane that pushes objects apart: Physical science

Overview: A **wedge** is an inclined plane that pushes objects apart. In this activity, you will use a wedge to make a sculpture.

Materials: Pictures of an axe, saw, razor, chisel, nail, pushpin, and knife; a bar of soap and a plastic knife for each student

Procedure: Have students look at the pictures and observe the different wedges. How is each an inclined plane? (Each one is an object that tapers to a thin edge.) Students use their knives to make a sculpture out of the bar of soap. They should wear safety goggles. (Check with your professor and host teacher to be sure this activity is appropriate and safe for your students to perform.)

Integrating design and art

Assessment: Did the wedge allow students to make a sculpture from the bar of soap? What did they sculpt? Could they have done this without the wedge? ■

Activity 12.12 Hands-on Science: Learning About Levers

A lever is a bar that turns on a fixed point: Physical science

Overview: In this activity, you will learn what Archimedes meant when he said, "Give me a lever, and I'll move the earth." A **lever** is a bar that turns on a fixed point called the *fulcrum*. Like the other simple machines, it makes work easier to do.

Materials: Pictures of a crowbar, seesaw, broom, screwdriver, tweezers, hammer, salad tongs, shovels, oars on a rowboat, balance scale, shears, pliers, hinged nutcrackers. Use real objects if they are available and if you, your professor, and host teacher believe they are safe to bring into your classroom. Avoid sharp, potentially dangerous items, and supervise students carefully as they engage in this activity.

Log onto these sites to find hundreds of excellent pictures. You can find examples of levers among them.

Photo sites:

http://www.ncrtec.org/tools/picture/goodsite.htm

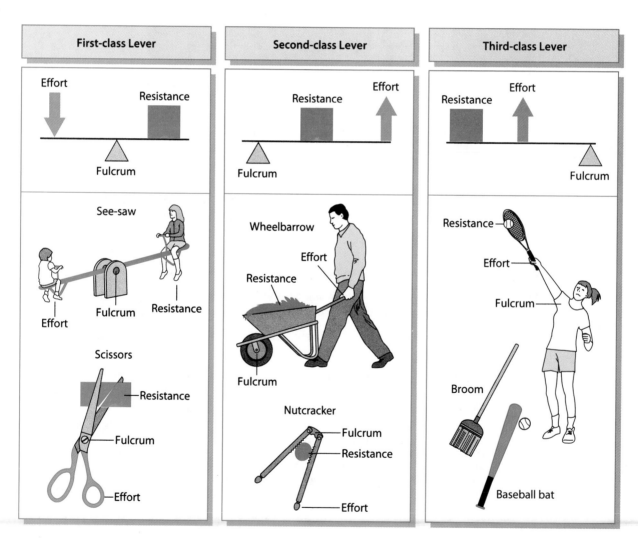

**Figure 12.7
Levers**

The Amazing Picture Machine:

http://www.ncrtec.org/picture.htm

The fulcrum, effort arm, and resistance arm are parts of a lever: Physical science

There are three classes of levers: Physical science

Procedure: A lever has three parts. The **fulcrum** is the pivot point. The **effort arm** (effort) is the end of the lever that you push on, and the **resistance arm** (resistance) is the end that pushes on the object you want to move. Levers are divided into three categories depending on the locations of the fulcrum, effort arm, and resistance arm. A **first-class lever** has the fulcrum located between the effort and the resistance. A **second-class lever** has the resistance located between the effort and the fulcrum. A **third-class lever** has the effort located between the resistance and the fulcrum (see Figure 12.7). Look at the pictures of the different levers and classify them as first-class, second-class, or third-class. What is the relationship between how far you are from the fulcrum and how far your force is multiplied?

Assessment: Were you able to classify the levers? As you increase the length of the effort arm, the work becomes easier. Show that this is true by going on a seesaw with a friend and moving farther from and closer to the fulcrum. ■

Activity 12.13 Hands-on Science: Searching for a Wheel and Axle

A wheel and axle is a lever connected to a shaft: Physical science

The pedal of a bicycle is an example of a wheel and axle.

Overview: A **wheel and axle** is a lever connected to a shaft. A doorknob and the knob on your car radio are examples of a wheel and axle: the knob is the wheel, and the shaft is the axle. For a simple machine to be a wheel and axle, the wheel and axle must rotate to-gether. In this activity, you will identify examples of the wheel and axle.

Materials: None

Procedure: Look around your school, home, and neighborhood. List examples of machines that are made of a wheel and axle. Check the Internet sites that contain photos.

Assessment: Some examples are the steering wheel of a car, the pedal mechanism of a bicycle, and knobs that spin. How many did you find? ■

Activity 12.14 Hands-on Science: Uses for Pulleys

A pulley is a wheel that spins freely on an axis: Physical science

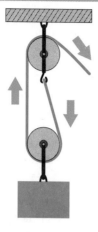

**Figure 12.8
A Pulley**

Overview: A **pulley** is a wheel that spins freely on its axis. The pulley system allows force to be transferred from one location to another. A block and tackle and a crane are examples of a pulley (see Figure 12.8)

Materials: None

Procedure: Students work in groups to brainstorm uses for pulleys. When are pulleys commonly used? Use at least one cooperative learning technique (see Chapter 10) to equalize participation in the group.

Assessment: How did the groups function? What uses for the pulley did they brainstorm? Have students design and build a simple pulley. ■

Activity 12.15 Problem Solving: Using Simple Machines to Design the Machine of the Future

Overview: In this activity, you will use your knowledge of simple machines to design the machine of the future.

Materials: Your choice

Procedure: Here is the design brief: Using your knowledge of simple machines, design the machine of the future. Use the design loop throughout this project. Use a science notebook to document your progress.

Assessment: What did you create? What human need does your machine satisfy? What simple machines did you use? ■

Activity 12.16 Hands-on Science: Taking Apart a Toy

Overview: In this activity, you will take apart a simple toy to look for simple machines.

Materials: A toy that you can take apart

Procedure: Using simple tools, disassemble the toy. What simple machines did you find? Be sure to wear safety goggles when you work. If a toy has sharp parts, it is not safe to work with; select another toy.

Assessment: If you were to do this activity with your students, how would you ensure their safety? (Select an appropriate toy and first disassemble it yourself to be sure it's safe for your students. Check with your professor and host teacher before trying this activity with students. I know of a kindergarten teacher who disassembles toys with his students, but he selects the toy carefully. Caution students not to try this without adult supervision.) ■

Designing Weather Instruments Using Simple Machines

Recall that in Chapter 11, you used the Internet to study weather maps and learn about clouds. Meteorologists use many different instruments to gather data about the weather. You are probably familiar with some of these. The thermometer measures air temperature, the barometer measures air pressure, the hygrometer measures moisture in the air, rain and snow gauges measure precipitation, the anemometer measures wind speed, and the wind vane measures wind direction.

In this section, you will use your knowledge of simple machines to design and build weather instruments to use in your classroom. Your students should know that professional meteorologists use much more advanced technology to predict weather events. Weather satellites provide information on air movement, cloud movements, and weather disturbances. Computer-generated maps assist with weather forecasting.

Activity 12.17 Online: Expanding Your Knowledge of Weather

Overview: In this activity, you will visit a web site to learn more about weather.

Materials: A computer with access to the Internet

Procedure: Log onto

http://www-sci.lib.uci.edu/SEP/CTS/Weather.html

Familiarize yourself with the lessons on weather, weather forecasting, and tools for measuring weather as you visit this site, which contains lessons and links. The site was prepared by Monica Grim, Capistrano Unified School District, San Juan Capistrano, California.

Assessment: Examine the rubric that follows the lesson plans. What criteria does the rubric assess? ■

Activity 12.18 Online: Learning About Weather Instruments

Overview: In this lesson, you will learn about sophisticated instruments such as doppler radar and high-altitude balloons used by the National Weather Service to gather weather data. In the activities that follow this one, you will design your own weather instruments using design and technology.

Materials: A computer with access to the Internet

Procedure: Log onto

http://www.scottforesman.com/sfaw/resources/ya/wetool.htm

Learn about the tools used for weather forecasting.

Assessment: Create a concept with the term *weather tools* as the main topic and *weather instruments* as subtopics. ■

Activity 12.19 Problem Solving: Designing a Thermometer

Designing a thermometer: Technology

Overview: In this activity, you will design a thermometer. If you have the materials, you can build it.

Materials: Your choice

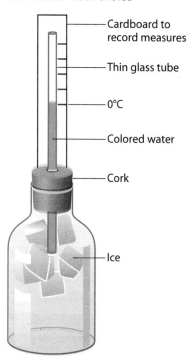

Cardboard to record measures

Thin glass tube

0°C

Colored water

Cork

Ice

**Figure 12.9
A Homemade
Thermometer**

Procedure: Most thermometers are composed of a thin tube containing a liquid such as mercury or alcohol. When the temperature rises the liquid expands, and when the temperature drops the liquid contracts. Using paper, pencil, and the design loop, create a design for a thermometer that uses colored water.

Assessment: If you have the materials, build the thermometer. Does it work? ▪

Here is how one teacher did this activity. She gathered a thin glass tube, colored water, a bottle with a cork, and a piece of cardboard a little longer than the glass tube (see Figure 12.9). She drilled a hole in the cork, smeared petroleum jelly around it, and very carefully slipped the glass tube into the hole. (If you push too hard, the glass tube is likely to crack in your hand.) She filled the bottle with colored ice water and corked it. The water rose into the thin tube. She placed the cardboard behind the glass tube and marked the water level as 0 degrees Celsius. As the water warmed up, the liquid rose in the tube. How do you think she could find out the temperature of the colored water as it moved up the tube? How could she calibrate the homemade thermometer? (Use a real thermometer to tell you the temperature of the liquid.)

Activity 12.20 Problem Solving: Designing a Hair Hygrometer

Designing a hair hygrometer: Technology

Overview: Air is able to hold water vapor. On humid days air holds a great deal of moisture, and on dry days it holds little moisture. On rainy days, the air holds as much water vapor as possible. The amount of water vapor air can hold varies with temperature. The warmer the air, the more water vapor it can hold. **Relative humidity** is the amount of water vapor the air holds in relation to the greatest amount of water vapor it could hold at that particular temperature. On rainy days, the relative humidity is 100 percent.

Hair is affected by humidity. On dry days hair is very tight, and on humid days it stretches a bit. Humidity can affect a person's hairstyle (causing a "bad hair day!"). You can use the stretching and tightening properties of hair to create a hygrometer that measures humidity. In this activity, you will design a homemade hair hygrometer.

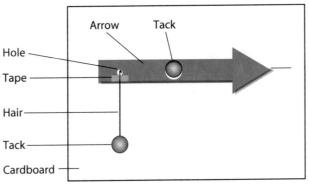

Materials: Paper, pencil, and the design loop

Procedure: Using a piece of paper, pencil, and the design loop, design a hair hygrometer.

Assessment: If you have the materials, construct a working model. What simple machines did you use in the design? ■

**Figure 12.10
A Homemade Hair
Hygrometer**

Here is how one group of seventh-graders did this activity. They took a thick sheet of cardboard and cut it into a 12-inch square. They cut a sheet of thin cardboard into the shape of an arrow. Using a thumbtack, they tacked the arrow to the cardboard square so that it could rotate. They found a 6-inch strand of someone's hair, and washed and dried it. They poked a hole shaped like an arrow in the cardboard. The hole was on the nonpointy end of the arrow (see Figure 12.10). They threaded the hair through the hole and taped it to the arrow. The other end of the hair was wrapped around another thumbtack and tacked to the thick cardboard. The hair was fixed in place between the arrow and the second thumbtack. When the air is moist, the hair stretches and the arrow moves down. When the hair tightens, the arrow moves up. This is how their hygrometer works (Albert, 1995).

Activity 12.21 Problem Solving: Designing an Anemometer

Designing an
anemometer: Technology

Overview: An *anemometer* is a weather instrument that tells you how fast the wind is blowing. In this activity, you will build a model of a wind speed indicator. It won't be able to accurately measure how fast the wind is blowing, which a real one would do. Your instrument will give you only approximate readings of wind speed.

Materials: Your choice

Procedure: Using a paper, pencil, and the design loop, design a wind speed indicator. Gather the materials and build it.

Assessment: How well does your instrument work? Does it tell you how fast the wind is blowing? What simple machines did you use in the design? ■

Here is how two groups of students did this activity. One group gathered cardboard, a stapler, four light plastic cups, a pencil with an eraser, a pushpin, and a lump of clay. They cut the cardboard into two strips of equal length and width and stapled them together, forming four cardboard blades. A plastic cup was stapled to each blade. They stuck the pushpin through the center of the blades and into a pencil eraser. The pointy end of the pencil was pushed into a lump of clay. When the wind blew, the blades turned. The faster the wind blew, the faster the blades spun.

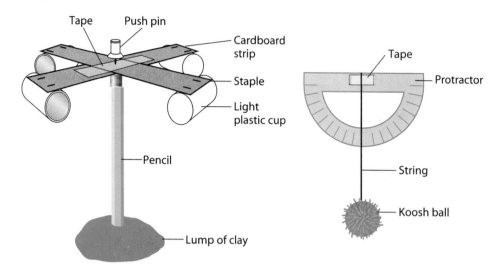

**Figure 12.11
Homemade
Anemometers**

The second group made a completely different design. They started with a protractor, a string, a koosh ball, and tape. They taped one end of the string to the protractor and the other end to the koosh ball. As the wind blew, the string and the ball moved. They used the protractor to measure the speed of the wind (Delta Education, 1988).

Figure 12.11 shows both designs.

Activity 12.22 Problem Solving: Designing a Wind Vane

Designing a wind vane:
Technology

Overview: In this activity, you will design an instrument to indicate wind direction.

Materials: Your choice

Procedure: Using paper, pencil, and the design loop, design an instrument to indicate wind direction. Gather the materials and build the instrument.

Assessment: Does the instrument work? Could you refine your design? Were there limitations and constraints? What simple machines did you use in the design? ■

One group of students took a sheet of light fabric and sewed it into the shape of a 12-inch sock. They connected it to a wooden dowel with two pieces of string. When they held it in the wind, it indicated wind direction. Another group cut an arrow out of thick cardboard. They cut the arrow in half and fastened each end to a drinking straw. They connected the wooden dowel to the straw with a pushpin. When taken outside, the instrument indicated wind direction. The students used a compass to locate the direction of the wind. Figure 12.12 shows both designs.

By now you should have a basic understanding of how to bring design and technology into your classroom. Think about how you can bring this way of "thinking and doing" to your students.

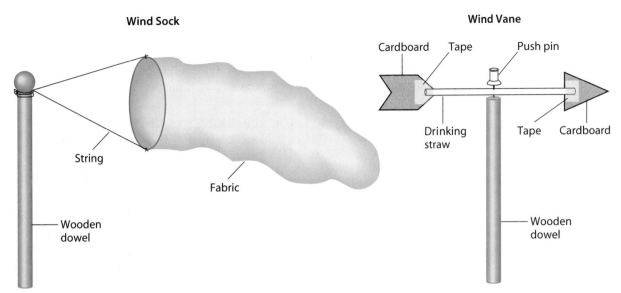

**Figure 12.12
Homemade Wind
Direction Indicators**

Constructing Your Knowledge of Science and Science Teaching

After completing this chapter, begin to reflect on your new knowledge. This chapter presents information about technology as design and problem solving, as well as many practical strategies that you can implement in your classroom. What is technology education? How does it differ from educational technology? Think about the meaning of design and problem solving. Can you think of any inventions that are a result of solutions to technological problems? What is the design loop? How does it compare with the type of scientific thinking scientists use? Why does the design loop foster active learning? How does technology strengthen science and math teaching?

Key Terms

educational technology (p. 313)
technology (p. 313)
technology education (p. 313)
design (p. 319)
design loop (p. 319)
design challenge (p. 321)
design brief (p. 321)
mechanical advantage (p. 327)
machine (p. 330)

work (p. 330)
force (p. 330)
effort (p. 330)
load (p. 330)
simple machine (p. 330)
inclined plane (p. 331)
screw (p. 332)
wedge (p. 333)
lever (p. 333)

fulcrum (p. 335)
effort arm (p. 335)
resistance arm (p. 335)
first-class lever (p. 335)
second-class lever (p. 335)
third-class lever (p. 335)
wheel and axle (p. 335)
pulley (p. 336)
relative humidity (p. 338)

Reviewing Chapter 12: Questions, Extensions, Applications, and Explorations

1. Create a machine that will be useful to students of the future. What problem does your machine solve?

2. Design a bird feeder. What do you have to know about birds to make a bird feeder?

3. Design a lunchbox to keep a grilled cheese sandwich warm until lunchtime. What do you need to know before you can start this design challenge?

4. Design a game to teach about insects. What do you have to learn about insects to design the game?

5. Design a poster to teach about the design loop. Did you use the design loop to create the poster?

6. Take apart a simple toy. (Wear safety goggles while you work.) Did you discover that the toy was made of simple machines? If so, which ones?

Print Resources

Albert, T. (1995). *Weather and climate*. Greenbrook, NC: Carson-Dellosa Publishing Company.

Buckland, M. (1985, September). The fifty minute robot. *Science and Children*, 21–22.

Catlin, D., & Douglas, P. (1998). *How to use Inventa*. London: Valiant Technology Limited.

Catlin, D., & Livingstone, M. (1995). *Food and farming*. London: Inventa Topic Book.

Clayfield, H., & Hyatt, R. (1994). *Designing everyday things*. Portsmouth, NH: Heinemann.

Delta Education. (1988). *Weather instruments*. Hudson, New Hampshire: Delta Science Modules.

Dunn, S., & Larson, R. (1990). *Design and technology: Children's Engineering*. Bristol, PA: The Faliner Press.

Hiner, M. (1996). *Paper engineering for pop-up cards*. Wonderland Books: Cleveland Heights, Ohio.

Hutchinson, P., & Sellwood, P. (1996). *Design and problem solving*. Cincinnati: Thomson Learning Tools.

Hutchinson, J., & Karsnitz, J. (1994). *Design and problem solving in technology*. Albany, NY: Delmar Publishers.

Johnson, P. (1996). *Paper engineering*. Philadelphia: Falmer Press.

Pace, G., & Larson, E. (1992, February). On design and technology. *Science and Children*, 12–15.

Raizen, S., Sellwood, P., Todd, R., & Vickens, M. (1995). *Technology education in the classroom. Understanding the designed world*. San Francisco: Jossey-Bass Publishers.

Sherman, S., & Weber, R. (1999). Using technology to strengthen mathematics and science instruction in elementary and middle schools. *Journal of Women and Minorities in Science and Engineering, 5*(1), 67–78.

Todd, R., Todd, K., McCrory, D. (1996). *Introduction to design & technology*. Cincinnati, OH: Thomson Learning Tools.

Watt, F. (1996). *The Usborne book of paper engineering*. Tulsa, OK: EDC Publishing.

Electronic Resources

Roamer Robot
http://www.roamerworld.com
This site contains dozens of teacher-made lesson plans on robotics from the primary grades to middle school. For more information on the Roamer Robot, contact Dimensions in Learning, Forest Park, Illinois (phone: 1-888-366-6628; fax: 708-366-8348).

International Technology Association
http://www.itea.org
This site contains information about the organization and has resources for teachers.

Technology for All Americans Project
http://www.scholar.lib.vt.edu/TAA/TAA.html
At this site, you can learn about plans for bringing technology education to schools.

Toys of Tomorrow
http://www.media.mit.edu/toys/totweb/index.html
The MIT Media Lab is initiating a special, five-year research program to invent the Toys of Tomorrow. While you are logged on, check out the rest of the Massachusetts Institute of Technology Media lab site.

International Society for Technology in Education
http://www.iste.org
This site contains general information about the organization and resources for teachers.

Children's Technology Workshop
http://www.hands.on.ca
Find descriptions of the CTW projects at this site.

Photo Sites for Locating Simple Machines
http://www.ncrtec.org/tools/picture/goodsite.htm

The Amazing Picture Machine
http://www.ncrtec.org/picture.htm

Children's Literature

Zubrowski, Bernie
Structures (Cuisenaire Company, 1993)
ISBN: 0-93858-735-8
Grades 5–8

Hoskings, Wayne
Flights of Imagination (National Science Teachers Association, 1990)
ISBN: 0-87355-067-6
Grades 5–12

McCormack, Alan
Inventor's Workshop
(Lake Publishing Company, 1981)
ISBN: 0-82249-783-2
Grades 3–8

Sarquis, Mickey
Exploring Matter with Toys
(McGraw-Hill Companies, 1996)
ISBN: 0-07064-724-0
Grades 1–4

Sarquis, Mickey
Investigating Solids, Liquids, and Gases with Toys: States of Matter and Change of State
(The McGraw Hill Companies, 1997)
ISBN: 0-07048-235-7
Grades 4–6

Potter, Jean
Science in Seconds with Toys
(John Wiley & Sons, 1998)
ISBN: 0-47117-900-0
Grades 3–5

Potter, Jean
Science in Seconds for Kids (John Wiley & Sons, 1995)
ISBN: 0-47104-456-3
Grades 3–5

Curriculum and Its Integration in Science Teaching

Part Three takes the background knowledge for science teaching that you developed in Chapters 1–12 and applies it. In these chapters you'll learn to write integrated lesson plans, continue to use assessment techniques, and teach lessons to include special learners and students with diverse learning styles in your classroom. You'll write lessons that use multiple process skills and instructional strategies, and that focus on constructivist learning theory. You'll learn to write interdisciplinary thematic units and learn ways to manage the materials resources that you bring to your students. As in Parts One and Two, you'll continue to visit active, effective, inquiry-based elementary science classrooms and you'll continue to learn about life, physical, and earth and space science.

CHAPTER 13

Science Across the Curriculum

The ideas of teaching for meaning and connecting each lesson to your students' experience have been emphasized throughout this text. Integrating science across the curriculum is a practical tool you can use to help your students see meaningful connections between science and the other subjects they study in your classroom. It breaks the barriers between subjects, unifies disciplines, connects lessons to real-life experiences, and brings teachers together so they can collaborate in creating interdisciplinary units and lessons.

Benchmarks for Science Literacy: Project 2061 (American Association for the Advancement of Science [AAAS], 1993) tells us that there are "three senses in which *Project 2061* is solidly behind integration" (p. 320). The first is **integrated planning,** which occurs when teachers in all relevant subjects and grade levels plan collaboratively to develop curriculum in math, science, technology, and other subjects. Next is **interconnected knowledge,** which results when "students' experiences are designed to help them see the relationships among science, mathematics, and technology and between them and other human endeavors" (p. 320). Finally, there is **coherence,** which occurs when "students' experiences add up to more than a collection of miscellaneous topics, whether under themes (everything about, say, salmon), disciplinary subject headings (principles of chemistry), or activities ('neat things for kids to do')" (p. 320). According to the *National Science Education Standards,* integrating the curriculum often provides students with a "big picture of scientific ideas" (National Research Council, 1996, p. 104).

In Chapter 3 you met Linda Zalewitz, a Presidential Award Winner for Excellence in Mathematics and Science Teaching. One of her areas of specialty is integrating the curriculum. She believes that teachers should help students connect concepts, topics, skills, and themes across disciplines so that they link ideas from one subject to another (Fogarty, 1991). She also believes that teachers should help children think about and integrate the basic ideas that explain the world. She sees teaching as an integration of content and skills that starts with what students already know.

Using the Olympics to integrate disciplines

Applying the group investigation method of cooperative learning

A good example of one of Mrs. Zalewitz's projects is the Science Olympics, which she created to coincide with the Olympic games. Her fourth-graders are quite excited about the Olympics, so she plans classroom experiences that connect to this interest. At the start of this project, all students learn about the different events and sports that comprise the Olympic games. They learn about each sport individually, then select a sport of interest to them to study in depth. Mrs. Zalewitz studied Sharan and Sharan's group investigation method of cooperative learning (see Chapter 10), and she applies their principles in this project. She groups students by interest. If several students are interested in gymnastics, for example, that is the group they select.

Teachers can plan learning experiences that connect science and athletics.

The first task is to thoroughly research the sport. Mrs. Zalewitz provides students with guidelines for sources to use, which include the Internet, newspapers, magazines, books, and experts in the field. They are accountable for finding their own resources. Students research the history of the sport, the rules of the game, and how a person wins. Then they identify the math and science involved in the sport as they apply science concepts that they learn in class. For example, early in the year, they learn about the human body. Students apply this knowledge to understand how the bones and muscles work together in the athlete's body as they integrate biology and physics. They study about the importance of good nutrition and a healthy mind as they integrate nutritional science, biology, and psychology.

One group of students studying about figure skating became interested in doing ice-related experiments. They wanted to learn about the properties of ice, and they experimented with ways to prevent ice from melting quickly. They researched what happens when a skate blade moves

Studying about the inner ear and dizziness: Life science

across the ice. Another group became interested in how skaters prevent dizziness during spins. They studied about the inner ear and what happens to people when they become dizzy. They learned that by focusing on a stationary object, a skater can prevent dizziness.

Using science and mathematics together: Science and mathematics

Real-life application of mathematics: Science and mathematics

Mrs. Zalewitz's students learn and apply math as they participate in the Science Olympics. She asks them to identify what part math plays in the various sports. They learn that explanations are often clarified through measurement. They generate their own questions for study. Some groups study the size of the playing field and the weight of costumes and how those factors affect the athletes' performance. Others study the cost of equipment for a particular sport, calculating how much it costs to participate in that sport. Students become familiar with the different forms of currency around the world and learn how to use exchange rates. One group tackled the task of drawing the Olympic symbol, five interlocking rings, which is not an easy feat. They used geometry to draw equilateral triangles, which are the basis of the Olympic symbol.

Presenting research: Science process

Using community resources

On Science Olympics Day, students present their research to one another. Students learn about the math and science involved in each sport and compare their research with that of their classmates. It is an event that students enjoy and look forward to, and they do all of the work on their own. Mrs. Zalewitz provides some materials for them to use, and they are free to use what they choose. They may bring in materials from home. Sometimes they contact local businesses and companies if they need something that isn't available in the classroom. The Science Olympics makes an impression on students, and it's a project that they long remember.

As you read this chapter, think about the answers to these questions:

1. **What are some models of integrating the curriculum?**

2. **What are some practical examples of curriculum integration?**

3. **How do I write an interdisciplinary thematic unit?**

4. **How can I teach basic concepts of electricity in an interdisciplinary thematic unit?**

Models for Integrating Science Across the Curriculum

There are many different ways to integrate science across the curriculum. You will now look at the Berlin-White Integrated Science and Mathematics Model. Later you will explore the Hamm and Adams Model. Throughout the chapter, you will read many practical examples of integrated lessons and units created by science teachers.

Berlin-White Integrated Science and Mathematics Model

The Berlin-White Integrated Science and Mathematics Model (BWISM) was developed at Ohio State University by Donna Berlin and Arthur White (Berlin & White, 1994). Their model specifically looks at integration of math and science and focuses on viewing integration from many different perspectives.

Ways of Learning

Integrating subjects based on how students experience, organize, and think about those subjects

You can bring together, or integrate, science and mathematics based on how students experience, organize, and think about these subjects. "They must be involved in an active, exploratory learning process with opportunities for social discourse" (Berlin & White, 1994, p. 3). They need lots of time to investigate and make sense of their explorations, and their experience should be the foundation for the understanding of concepts and "big ideas." Think back on what you learned about constructivist learning theory in Chapters 1 and 5. *Ways of learning* means that your students can learn science, mathematics, and other subjects in an active, constructivist setting. Can you think of other ways of learning?

Ways of Knowing

Moving back and forth between inductive and deductive inquiry

Think back to Chapter 4, where you learned about inquiry teaching. What are the ways in which children can know? You provide questions and opportunities for exploration. Then you allow them to engage in hands-on activities, collect data, analyze the data, look for patterns, make sense of the data, and build understanding of a concept. This is inductive inquiry. Once children develop understanding of a concept, they apply that concept in a new situation to see if it works.

Here is another way of knowing. You can provide activities for children and lead them through those activities, helping them to gain understanding of a concept as they move through it. This is a deductive process. Students can "move back and forth between inductive and deductive ways of knowing" (Berlin & White, 1994, p. 3).

Process and Thinking Skills

Integrating subjects by using process skills

Berlin and White tell us that the science process skills, which are the same skills used for mathematical problem solving, are a basis for integration. Think about what you learned in Chapter 3. Classifying, collecting, and organizing data, communicating, controlling variables, developing models, estimating, experimenting, inferring, graphing, interpreting data, creating hypotheses, measuring, observing, recognizing patterns, and predicting are science process skills. They are also the skills we use for problem solving in mathematics. Science and math—and other subjects as well—can be integrated by using these skills.

Content Knowledge

Subjects, particularly science and mathematics, can overlap by content. Science and math have so much in common that it sometimes becomes more meaningful to look at them together. Several "big ideas" are common to both subjects. These include "balance, conservation, equilibrium, measurement, models, probability,

Integrating subjects by focusing on "big ideas"

Using the concept of scale to integrate math and science: Science and mathematics

principles of light, including reflection and refraction, scale (size, duration, and speed), symmetry, systems, variables, and vectors" (Berlin & White, 1994, p. 3).

Here is an example of how you can integrate subjects by identifying overlapping content. In Chapter 9, you learned about the concept of scale. The chapter opens with Jamie King's lesson on the "incredible shrinking fifth-graders." If you reflect on her lesson, you will see that she uses the concept of scale to integrate math and science. Students learn that "scale includes understanding that different characteristics, properties, or relationships within a system might change as its dimensions are increased or decreased" (National Research Council, 1996, p. 118). In this case, Ms. King uses math and science together to help her students understand the concept of scale.

Attitudes and Perceptions

Viewing science and mathematics in terms of student attitudes and perceptions of these subjects

You may view integration of science and math from the perspective of how children feel about their involvement in science and math experiences and how confident they are in their ability to work successfully in these subjects. Values, attitudes, and ways of thinking are common to science and mathematics. These include "accepting the changing nature of science and mathematics, basing decisions on data, a desire for knowledge, a healthy degree of skepticism, honesty and objectivity, relying on logical reasoning, willingness to consider other explanations, and working together cooperatively to achieve better understanding" (Berlin & White, 1994, pp. 3–4). Can you think of a way in which your students view math and science in terms of attitudes and perceptions?

Teaching Strategies

Using instructional strategies to integrate science and math

By integrating science and mathematics, students should be able to acquire scientific and mathematical knowledge of the world, as well as scientific and mathematical habits of mind (Berlin & White, 1994; Rutherford & Ahlgren, 1990). How can you do this in your classroom? Your instructional decisions should include time for students to work collaboratively and individually on inquiry-based problems; opportunities for communication; opportunities to use laboratory equipment and other tools, calculators, and computers; and many assessment strategies (Berlin & White, 1994).

Activity 13.1   Reflection: Berlin-White Integrated Science and Mathematics Model

Overview: In this activity, you will reflect on the BWISM.

Procedure: Think about the Berlin-White Integrated Science and Mathematics Model. Does it provide a framework that enables you to think about integrating science and mathematics? Does it provide a way to think about integrating other subjects as well?

Assessment: Does the BWISM provide a way to think about science and science teaching? ■

Integrating the Curriculum: A Natural Way to Learn

Integration helps to overcome a fragmented curriculum

In many schools, the curriculum is overloaded. Teachers have too many subjects to cover and too many topics to teach. In addition, the curriculum is often fragmented. Each subject——math, science, language arts, social studies, music, art, health, and physical education——has its own scheduled time slot (Chapman, 1993). Unfortunately, life doesn't work that way. Life is not compartmentalized; subjects overlap and integrate naturally and holistically. The brain too focuses on holistic learning. By providing students with the right type of stimuli, you get their brains to respond (Caine & Caine, 1990, 1991). Integrating the curriculum is a good way to make that happen. In this section, you will look at examples of integrated lessons created by teachers. In the next section, you will learn to write an interdisciplinary thematic unit of study.

George Washington Carver

As part of the social studies curriculum that Mrs. Zalewitz teaches, students learn about the contributions of George Washington Carver, a botanist and agricultural chemist who revitalized the agriculture of the American South in the early 1900s. Born of slave parents on a plantation near Diamond Grove, Missouri, Carver was unable to obtain a formal education, so he began to work as a farm hand on a farm in Kansas. Later, at age 25, he entered Simpson College in Iowa, eventually transferring to Iowa Agricultural College, which is now Iowa State University at Ames, Iowa. There he excelled as a botanist and agricultural chemist. He developed quite a good reputation for his work.

Depleting the soil of important minerals adversely affected the economy of the South: Earth science

Rotating plants enriches the soil and improves agriculture: Earth science

George Washington Carver developed 300 products from peanuts: Science and technology

In 1896, Booker T. Washington, head of the Tuskeegee Institute in Alabama, wrote to Carver, asking for his assistance. The agriculture of the South was in trouble, and Washington thought Carver could help. Two hundred years of planting cotton had depleted the soil of important minerals, and the economy of the region was adversely affected. Carver went to work at Tuskeegee as an agricultural scientist, convincing southern farmers that rotating plants would enrich the soil and improve agriculture. Carver suggested that farmers plant peanuts, clover, and peas, which would restore nitrogen to the soil. They heeded his advice. Through his research, he developed 300 products from peanuts, including milk and cheese products, shampoo, facial cream, soap, ink, and instant coffee (Green, 1996).

Mrs. Zalewitz asks her students what they think happened to the economy of the South as a result of George Washington Carver's work. They correctly predict that the economy improved dramatically. Then students participate in peanut activities, which you will engage in now.

Activity 13.2 Hands-on Science: Peanut Activities

Check for allergies to peanuts: Safety

Overview: In this activity, you will become a researcher as you work with peanuts. Some students can have allergic reactions to the odor of peanuts even if they don't eat

George Washington Carver at work in the laboratory.

them, so check with the school nurse and with parents before using peanuts in the classroom. Be certain that students with peanut allergies work with other nuts, such as almonds or chestnuts. You can also substitute peas in pods for nuts.

Materials: Peanuts, a balance, peas in pods, almonds, or chestnuts, a ruler, water in a cup

Procedure:

1. How many uses for a peanut can you think of? (To check your answer, carry out an Internet search on peanuts.)

Using estimation: Science process

2. Estimate the weight of the peanut.

3. Using a scale, weigh the peanut.

4. Open the peanut. What is the difference in its weight shelled and unshelled?

5. Do two peanuts weigh twice as much as one peanut?

6. Will any of the peanut parts float? Why or why not?

7. Estimate the length of something in the room.

Using a nonstandard unit of measurement: Science and mathematics

8. Measure something in the room using peanuts as a measuring device (1 peanut = 1 unit).

9. How does the peanut smell opened and unopened?

10. If you do not have a peanut allergy, eat a peanut. Describe its texture and taste.

Assessment:

1. If you were to describe a peanut to someone who has never seen one before, what characteristics would you use?
2. As a scientist, what skills do you use to perform the peanut activities?
3. As a mathematician, what skills do you use to perform the peanut activities?
4. What did you learn that surprised you?
5. In your group, think of and perform a song with the word *peanut* in it. ■

Activity 13.3 *Analyzing the Peanut Activities*

Overview: In this activity, you will relate a hands-on science activity to a model of integrating the curriculum.

Materials: Paper and pencil

Finding the math and science in an activity

Procedure: Look back on the peanut lesson (Activity 13.2). Think of all of the ways in which subjects were integrated. Are they reflected in the Berlin-White model? Think about the lesson again. How would you extend it? Can you think of another direction in which to move the lesson?

Researching why peanuts, clover, and peas restore nitrogen to the soil: Earth science, life science, physical science

As I look back on the lesson, an excellent topic for research emerges. Carver suggested that farmers plant peanuts, clover, and peas to restore nitrogen to the soil. Students in the upper elementary and middle grades could research the science that explains why this works. Can you think of a way to turn this series of lessons into a sustained inquiry? ■

A Lesson on the Rain Forest: Integrating Literature and Science

Integrating science and literature

As this lesson begins, you read aloud *The Great Kapok Tree* by Lynne Cherry (1990, Harcourt Brace). Then students read *Inside the Amazing Amazon* by Don Lessem (1995, Crown Publishing Co.). From these books, students learn about the layers of life in the Amazonian rain forest. They find out that more than half of all plant and animal species live in the earth's **tropical rain forest** systems. The warm, wet climate, with bright sunlight overhead, produces excellent conditions that encourage life. Different animals and plants live at different levels of the rain forests. Students learn about life in each layer. The tallest layer is the *emergent layer,* which is from 130 to 160 feet high. Next is the *canopy layer,* which is from 60 to 130 feet high. Here there is plenty of sunlight, warmth, and food. Beneath the canopy is the *understorey,* which goes from the ground to 60 feet high. Here it is darker and cooler, and the presence of wildlife is less varied. Climbing plants, such as vines, wrap themselves around trees and bushes.

The tallest rain forest layer is the emergent layer, followed by the canopy and under-storey: Earth science, life science

Graphing the layers of the rain forest and including vegetation and wildlife: Science process, life science, earth science

Now that they have this information, students think about what they want to do with it. They brainstorm ideas in small cooperative groups, then come up with a variety of interesting ideas. First, they decide to make a giant graph to map out the layers. They include information about the vegetation and wildlife present in each layer. Students create a very impressive graph.

Next, students learn about rain forest cycles. Nutrients, water, and oxygen cycle through the trees. The tropical rain forest is a warm place, and nutrients move quickly from the soil to the canopy layer by way of the trees. Students think about what effect this pattern might have on the soil. Some hypothesize correctly that the soil is nutrient poor and not good for farming. They also discuss the ways in which rain forests influence world climate. Students research the question and learn that rain forests take in significant amounts of carbon dioxide and release oxygen and water as a result of photosynthesis. While one group studies the water cycle, other groups research products from the rain forest, medicines from the rain forest, the effects of pollution on the rain forest, and what would happen to the earth if the rain forest were destroyed. As a culminating activity, one group makes a rain forest snack.

Students are involved in original research. They go through the process of research, produce a product, and along the way apply what they have learned in their subjects, make sense of things, and focus on anchoring conclusions to science concepts.

A Lesson on Viking Navigation

David "Freddy" Friedrich, one of my student teachers, wrote a two-week unit of study focusing on explorers that integrates science, technology, mathematics, and social studies. He uses ways of learning, ways of knowing, process and thinking skills, integration of content, and teaching strategies to construct learning experiences for his students.

In the unit is a lesson on how Vikings navigated. He explains that the Vikings did not have the complex navigational tools like the ones that benefit explorers today. Their technology was not the same as ours. They did, however, successfully utilize technology to solve the dilemma of determining their location at sea (see Chapter 12). Here is how Freddy's students solve the navigation problem like the Vikings did.

Freddy tells students that the Vikings collected four samples of water from the ocean that still remain today. Students will have the opportunity to sample them. Although you should never taste an unknown solution in a science class, Freddy explains that these are not *really* salt water solutions left over from the Vikings. He made them this morning for the activity, and they are safe to taste.

On the table in front of the room are four cups of salt water. The materials manager (see Chapter 10) in each group brings to the table a set of cups for each group member. The students sample each cup of salt water and describe the taste. After tasting the four different salt water solutions, they describe them in their journals. Freddy asks them to think about what they could say about the four solutions. The students explain that they can classify the solutions from least amount of salt to greatest amount of salt, because each one tastes different. Freddy tells them that the Vikings had to navigate without being hindered by darkness or fog. He asks them to think of a way the Vikings could have used salt water samples as a navigation tool.

Here is how Freddy's students solve the problem of navigating in fog or darkness. They assume the concentration of the salt water was not the same in every location in the ocean. This assumption follows from what they learned about the four cups of salt water, each with a different concentration. They explain this as follows. When a river containing fresh water flows into the ocean, the concentration of salt in the water decreases at that location. Less concentrated salt water would mean you are in a location where fresh water is diluting the salt water. You are probably nearing land. More concentrated salt water would mean you are heading out to sea. By tasting each salt water solution, the Vikings could determine their position in the ocean, even in fog or darkness, thereby creating a tool for navigation and a solution to the problem.

Activity 13.4 Reflection: Viking Navigation

Overview: In this activity, you will reflect on Freddy's lesson.

Procedure: Reflect on the lesson you just read. Think of all of the ways in which Freddy used integration.

Assessment: If you carried out this activity with your students, how would you assess student thinking? ■

Simulating Coal Mining: A Cookie Mining Activity

Integrating earth science and economics

The cookie mining activity is another creative way to integrate subjects. This is an inquiry-based lesson that centers around coal mining. When I presented this lesson in a fifth-grade classroom, we started by talking about coal mining and the importance of preserving the environment and finished by developing a basic economic system. The lesson fascinated students, and they came away with something even more valuable to them than basic knowledge about the environment.

Discussing the importance of coal as a fossil fuel: Earth science

As the lesson begins, talk about coal mining. After a brief discussion of the importance of coal as a fossil fuel, talk about the positive and negative effects of mining on the land. Focus on what can happen to land after it is mined. Explain that today students will experience "mining" firsthand. They will learn what can happen to land when it is mined. Instead of traveling out of the classroom or watching a video about mining, each student will be given a piece of a mine. A chocolate chip cookie will serve as the mine, and the chocolate chips will serve as the ore. This will be a bit of a stretch, so students will need to use their imaginations. The goal is to have students understand that mining can bring people useful products and much profit, but at the same time have a potential adverse effect on the land. You also want them to understand how people use technology (see Chapter 12) by making available some interesting tools. Remember: when you integrate subjects, you often focus on more than one concept at a time, tying ideas together and showing relationships.

Mining has positive and negative environmental impacts: Earth science

Miners routinely take loans from a bank, so you will need a banker and play money for this activity. It's easiest if you assume this role. At the start of the activity, each student receives $20 in play money from the bank. Walk around the room and distribute the money to your students. They will use it to purchase cookies, which will represent land rich in chocolate chips—the ore. The object of the activity is to mine the chips from the cookies and make a profit without destroying the land (the cookie).

When mining the chips, students are not allowed to use their fingers; they need tools (technology). They must purchase mining tools, which you will sell to them. They can use the $20 from the bank to buy them. Three types of mining tools are available at the following costs:

1. Flat toothpicks—$3 each
2. Round toothpicks—$5 each
3. Paper clips—$7 each

The other costs are:

1. Cookies—$5 each
2. Mining time—$1 per minute, with a maximum of five minutes allotted to mine the chips from the cookies

After you have given students $20.00 each in play money, give them time to think about which mining tools and how many cookies they will purchase. Then sell them the mining tools and the cookies. I usually start with four paper plates, one for each mining tool and one for the cookies. After students decide what they will purchase, I have them line up near the plates to actually make their purchases. As they come up with their money, have them figure out how much change they should get. Be sure they save money to purchase mining time. Then they return to their seats, draw a circle around the cookie, and wait for further directions.

Using a rubric to guide instruction

Once students have their tools, they are ready to mine. Remind them that the goal is to remove as many chips as possible without destroying the cookie. Share the rubric in Figure 13.1 with them. Have everyone start mining at the same time. Using a stopwatch, allow them to mine for one minute; then have everyone stop. Since some students break their tools (toothpicks), ask if anyone needs to buy a new tool. Find out if there are any problems. Then collect $1 from each student for the one minute of mining time. Once this is done, begin again. Allow students to mine for another minute, then call time. Again, check to see if anyone needs to buy more tools or another cookie. Collect another $1 for the second minute of mining time. Keep going until you reach five minutes of mining time.

After all of the miners have finished mining their chips, have them count them. The bank will purchase them for $2 per chip. The students use multiplication to figure out how much their chips are worth. Students usually make a profit as a result of mining.

Rubrics provide information about levels of performance

As the lesson proceeds, tie assessment to instruction, viewing assessment as a means of helping students to improve their work and enabling them to show their understanding. Students know from the rubric that the goal of the lesson is to make as much profit as possible without destroying the land—in this case, the cookie. The rubric provides information about levels of performance and makes it clear that to earn the most points possible, the student must make a profit of at least $20, but in the end the cookie must look like a cookie and not a heap of crumbs. This is analogous to saying that the land won't be destroyed. If the cookie turns into a mound of crumbs, which translates into destroying the land, the student earns fewer points. They fit the crumbs into the cookie template.

Levels of Performance	Criteria and Descriptors
4	Your cookie looks like the original cookie, **and** You have made a profit of at least $20, **and** You have followed all of the rules.
3	You have followed all of the rules, **and** You have made a profit of at least $20, **and** Cookie parts fit into the cookie template when you have finished mining.
2	You have followed all of the rules, **and** You have made a profit of at least $10, **and** Cookie parts fit into the cookie template when you have finished mining.
1	You did not follow all of the rules, **and** You have made a profit, **and** Cookie parts fit into the cookie template when you have finished mining.

Figure 13.1
Rubric for Cookie Mining

Here is what happened in one classroom. One student bought one cookie ($5) and one mining tool (a paper clip for $7), setting aside $5 for mining time, while another student bought two cookies ($10) and two round toothpicks ($10). The second student realized he had no money left to pay for mining time and returned one cookie. The purchases varied throughout the room, and all students appeared motivated and excited to begin mining.

I called time and mining began. Students chiseled away at their cookies with their mining tools. Some were very cautious and tried not to destroy the cookie, whereas others wanted to mine as many chips as possible and make a large profit without regard for the condition of the cookie. After five minutes, mining ended and students calculated their profits.

Reflecting on a lesson

After they completed the task, groups discussed a number of questions as they assessed their work (see Figure 13.2). They answered questions such as "What strategy did you use in this exercise? Would you change your strategy the next time? If so, what would you do differently?" There was also discussion about what happened to the cookies and what motivated people—the desire to preserve the land or the desire to make as much profit as possible. The discussion then moved to the real world, looking at examples of instances where the environment is preserved and restored after mining and of instances where it is harmed. The lesson took 55 minutes to complete, from start to finish. The students truly enjoyed the experience.

Activity 13.5 Reflection: Analyzing the Cookie Mining Activity

Overview: In this activity, you will reflect on the cookie mining activity.

Reflecting on a lesson

Procedure: Reflect on the lesson you just read. In what ways was integration carried out in this lesson? Do you think it is important for students to learn about economics in a science lesson? What is your opinion of the integration of math skills? Was the application of math important in this lesson? How useful were the tools in this activity? Did they bring across the point that technology helps people?

Assessment: How helpful was the rubric? How would the activity have been different if the rubric were not used? ■

Reflections on the Cookie Mining Lesson

No matter how much a teacher plans, unexpected things happen in a classroom. As I mentioned early in the book, each of the activities included was class tested by experienced teachers. A colleague and I tested the cookie mining activity several times in different schools. Our most interesting experience occurred in an inner-city third-grade classroom with about 30 students. Much to our surprise, we spent the entire morning on the activity. We started the activity by discussing mining. We usually spend five or ten minutes talking about mining, but the children were so fascinated by the concept that we stayed on the topic for nearly an hour. While we wanted to focus on the environmental aspect of cookie mining, our third-graders had a different idea. The economic aspect of mining captivated them.

Using mathematics in a practical way

We did the activity once, but they wanted to do it over again, so we did. They worked hard to decide how many cookies and which mining tools to buy. They wanted to figure out how to make as much profit as they could. They used their math skills and lots of decision making to do this. Their teacher believed that being able to use their mathematical knowledge in a practical way motivated

Questions to Assess the Cookie Mining Activity

1. How much money did you make?
2. How could you have made a greater profit?
3. Would you change your strategy next time? Explain.
4. What other strategy could you have used?
5. When you fit your cookie back in the circle at the end of the activity, did it still resemble the original cookie?
6. If you didn't know the rubric or how you would be assessed before doing the activity, how would that have changed your strategy?

**Figure 13.2
Questions to Assess the Cookie Mining Activity**

them. Our students convinced us to do a third trial. Then we had a long discussion about the effects of mining on the land and the importance of coal as a fossil fuel. We needed to put things in perspective.

As the morning ended, we realized that 30 third-graders were totally engaged in this activity, thinking mathematically and problem solving for several hours. Not one student asked to go to the bathroom all morning! The only question to us was "When are you coming back?"

Activity 13.6   Online: Teaching Integrated Math and Science with Bouncing Balls

Integrating science and mathematics with activities involving bouncing balls: Physical science

Overview: In this activity and the three that follow, you will examine a number of integrated lesson plans on the Internet. This will enable you to experience more lessons and gain new ideas. In this activity, you will carry out an integrated math and science lesson involving bouncing balls.

Materials: A computer hooked up to the Internet, materials suggested in the lesson plan

Procedure: Log onto

http://ericir.syr.edu/Virtual/Lessons/Science/Instruct_issues/ISS0002.html

Carry out the activity submitted by Bonnie Custer, St. Agatha School, Portland, Oregon. Adapt the activity to the grade level of your students.

Assessment: Review the Berlin-White Integrated Mathematics and Science Model described at the beginning of this chapter. In what ways does this lesson follow the guidelines for integration suggested by the model? ■

Activity 13.7   Online: Integrating Science, Art, and Reading

Integrating science, art, and reading: Physical science

Overview: In this activity, you will log onto the Internet to find a creative lesson called *Looking to the Sky for Color,* written for first-graders by Sandy Walker, a teacher at Anza Elementary School in Torrance, California. The lesson integrates video, literature, science, and art.

Materials: A computer hooked up to the Internet

Procedure: Log onto ArtsEdNet at http://www.artsednet.getty.edu/ and view this outstanding lesson.

Assessment: Refer to the Berlin-White model. In what ways does this lesson integrate disciplines? Think back on the kindergarten color-mixing activity described in Chapter 1. How could you bring together this lesson and the one described in that chapter? ■

Activity 13.8   Online: Teaching Science Using the Newspaper

Using the newspaper in science instruction

Overview: In this activity, you will log onto a web site and learn about 20 ways to use the newspaper in science instruction.

Materials: A computer hooked up to the Internet

Procedure: Log onto

http://ericir.syr.edu/Virtual/Lessons/Science/Instruct_issues/ISS0001.html

Read about different ways to use the newspaper in your classroom.

Assessment: Write a journal entry to record the ideas that are relevant for your teaching. ■

Activity 13.9 Online: Visiting Sites with Integrated Lesson Plans

Overview: In this activity, you will visit web sites with extensive lesson plan collections and search for integrated lessons.

Materials: A computer hooked up to the Internet

Procedure: Log onto these sites and explore the integrated lesson plans:

http://ericir.syr.edu/Virtual/Lessons/other.html

http://www.thegateway.org/collectionlist.html (the Gateway Collection)

Assessment: In an electronic journal (one that you keep on your computer), write about the sites you find. Keep this for future reference. ■

Creating Interdisciplinary Thematic Units

Using an integrated thematic approach to teaching is a good way to bring relevant, real-life situations to your students (Hamm & Adams, 1998). Organizing instruction in this way allows you to relate subjects, helps students to achieve higher levels of thinking, and makes learning more meaningful (Bybee & DeBoer, 1994; National Council of Teachers of English and International Reading Association, 1996). In the previous section, you examined integrated lesson plans. You will now learn to write an interdisciplinary thematic unit of study.

Hamm and Adams Thematic Approach to Teaching

A model for creating an integrated thematic unit

Mary Hamm and Dennis Adams (1998) explain that a thematic unit is "more than a collection of lesson plans. It should be viewed as a dynamic inquiry project" (pp. 48–49). They outline the following steps in creating an interdisciplinary thematic unit:

1. Select a theme that is challenging and related to real-world concerns. Have students solve a problem or ask an important question.
2. Decide on a desired outcome in advance. Outcomes may be related to skills and abilities that are important for your students.
3. Brainstorm key ideas for each subject area, and create a concept map or mind map.
4. Create a time line for each activity.

5. Determine the concepts and skills students should develop after working through the unit.

6. Decide what resources you will need to carry out the unit.

7. Create learning centers and bulletin boards to help your students meet the outcomes of the unit.

8. Create a cumulative activity to enable students to synthesize what they have gained from the "various disciplinary tools applied to the problem" (Hamm & Adams, 1998, p. 48).

9. Create an assessment plan that includes "performance assessment, portfolios, conferences, anecdotes, and exams" (Hamm & Adams, 1998, p. 48).

10. Write lesson plans that describe lesson objectives, concepts, materials, and procedures. You can update the lesson plans as needed.

Activity 13.10 Reflection: The Hamm and Adams Model

Overview: In this activity, you will reflect on the Hamm and Adams model.

Procedure: Think about this model of creating a thematic, interdisciplinary unit. Does having a series of steps to follow simplify the process for you?

Reading an article in Science and Children

Assessment: The article that suggests this model appeared in the September 1998 issue of *Science and Children*. If you have the time, find the journal and read the article. What is your opinion of the sample thematic activities presented in the article? ■

An Interdisciplinary Unit Focusing on Opera

An integrated thematic unit on opera

Here is an interdisciplinary unit based on the opera. You will read about how to develop and implement the unit in your classroom. It begins by having students brainstorm the elements of an opera: story, music, events, theme, climax, setting, and characterization. To help students learn more about opera, show a video such as *What's Opera, Doc?*, featuring Bugs Bunny and Elmer Fudd. After seeing the video, students revisit the elements of an opera and make adjustments to their lists based on the video. Once students have a basic understanding of opera, they study a particular one. They study the literature connected to the opera, view a video on it, and act out a version of the opera based on the literature. Then they view the video again, this time looking for the science-related information in the opera. Have students make a list and discuss their findings.

Now students are ready to create and produce an opera of their own. They write it first as a story and then as an opera. Then they look for the science, math, social studies, music, and art in their opera. Once again, they discuss their findings.

Activity 13.11 Online: Lesson Plans for Teachers of Theater

Overview: In this activity, you will familiarize yourself with web sites designed for teachers who bring theater into their classrooms.

Materials: A computer hooked up to the Internet

Procedure: Log onto these sites and locate relevant lesson plans.

Lesson Plan Exchange for Teachers of Theater:

http://artemis.austinc.edu/acad/educ/ATPWeb/lessons2.htm

Theater Unit Lesson Plans:

http://www.inet-edu.com/lessons/links/artslessons.html#music

Assessment: In an electronic journal, record notes about these sites. Save the notes for future reference. ◾

Designing lighting for the opera set: Physical science

It's time to plan for the performance. Students must first design a miniature set. It happens to be one that uses simple circuits for the lighting. They start by reading *Arthur's New Power* by Russell Hoban (1978, Crowell Publishers). Provide students with two D cell batteries, one flashlight bulb, several pieces of bell wire, and tape. Students experiment with ways to light the light bulbs. Then provide additional wire, more powerful batteries, bulbs, switches, and alligator clips, and let them explore series and parallel circuits. Have them create diagrams showing circuits that will work as they plan the lighting for the set. The following background information and activities will help you guide them.

What Is Electricity?

You probably know that all things are made of tiny particles called *atoms*. In the mid-1800s, scientists began to question whether atoms are indivisible. Could they be made of smaller particles? A series of experiments that took place in the decades that followed provided the answer to this question. Today we know that atoms are not indivisible; they are made of even smaller particles.

Atoms are divisible: Physical science

Some are positively charged, some are negatively charged, and some have no charge at all. The particles that are negatively charged are called *electrons*. *Protons* have a positive charge, and *neutrons* have no charge.

In Chapter 2 you read about an activity suggested by Jill Foley, a graduate student in plasma physics. In that activity, you rubbed a balloon against your hair and allowed it to pick up electrons, giving it a negative charge. Then you placed an empty soda can on the table so that it lay on its side. You held the balloon near the soda can and slowly moved it toward the can. Some of the electrons in the metal can were free to move.

Like charges repel, opposite charges attract: Physical science

Charges that are the same (like charges) repel, so the electrons went to the other side of the can, leaving a positive charge on the balloon side. Opposite charges (unlike charges) attract, so the can rolled toward the balloon, which picked up a negative charge when you rubbed it on your hair. This experiment works because of **static electricity**. When an object holds an electric charge, caused by either a gain or a loss of electrons, static electricity results. Here are some other examples of static electricity.

When an object holds an electric charge caused by either a gain or loss of electrons, static electricity results: Physical science

Did you ever move around on a rug and zap your friend with your finger? If you did, you released excess electrons from your finger that you picked up

Experimenting with ways to light the light bulb.

from the rug. Did your clothes ever stick to each other when you took them out of the dryer? This happens because clothes pick up a charge when they rub against each other as they dry. Did you ever hear a crackling noise when you pulled a sweater over your head? That's the sound of static electricity.

All these activities illustrate the presence of static charges. Static electricity is electricity that does not move or flow. When you want to power a machine or an appliance, static electricity is not very useful. In such cases you need **current electricity,** produced when electrons flow through a wire current. You can see examples of current electricity everywhere. Turn on a light switch, your computer, your stereo, or your hair dryer, and you will use current electricity. **Current,** the rate at which electrons flow, is measured in units called *amperes*.

Batteries use chemicals to produce electric currents. They store chemical energy and turn it into electrical energy. The path an electric current follows is an **electric circuit**. The parts of a circuit are the source of electricity, wires, and an electrical appliance such as a light, a motor, or a computer. Think about how a simple flashlight works. The current flows from the battery, through the switch, to the bulb, and back to the battery. For a simple circuit to work, all parts of the circuit must be able to conduct electricity and all parts of the circuit must connect to one another. That makes sense, for if one part of the circuit did not connect to another, or if one part was incapable of conducting electricity, the electrons could not flow from one point to another.

Conductors conduct electricity easily: Physical science

Insulators do not conduct electricity well: Physical science

Some materials conduct electricity easily; these are called **conductors**. Examples of good conductors are gold, silver, brass, copper, and aluminum. **Insulators** do not conduct electricity well. Examples of insulators are glass, rubber, and plastic. Insulators are important to us because they prevent electricity from reaching areas where it would be dangerous.

There are two types of circuits: series and parallel. Think of a class of children standing in a circle holding hands. That's how a series circuit is arranged. If two children in the circle stop holding hands, the circle breaks. If you set up a circuit

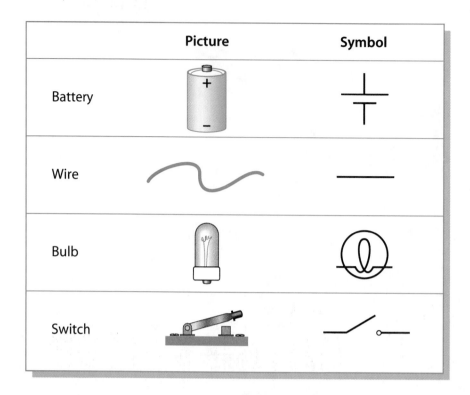

	Picture	Symbol
Battery		
Wire		
Bulb		
Switch		

**Figure 13.3
Symbols Used in
Electric Circuits**

There are two types of
circuits: series and parallel: Physical science

that contains many light bulbs connected to one another in *series,* if one light bulb
burns out, all of the others go out. In a *parallel* circuit, however, each bulb has its
own linkage to the battery. If one bulb goes out, the others still shine brightly.

Years ago, Christmas tree lights were arranged in a series circuit. If one bulb
burned out, the whole string of lights turned off. People had a difficult time figuring out which bulb was the faulty one. Today Christmas tree lights are
arranged in a parallel circuit, eliminating that problem.

When drawing series and parallel circuits, it's helpful to draw circuit diagrams. Figure 13.3 contains the symbols used in circuit diagrams. In the activities that follow, you will use these symbols to draw circuits.

Activity 13.12 Hands-on Science: Making Simple Circuits

Creating a simple circuit:
Physical science

Overview: In this activity, you will use a battery, a light bulb, and bare copper wire to
create a simple circuit.

Materials: Per student: one 1.5-volt D cell, one 1.5-volt light bulb, 2 pieces of 20- to 26-
gauge bare copper wire (20 cm). For the class: a wire cutter.

Procedure: Since using electricity found in the school or home is unsafe because of
high voltage, your students will experiment with batteries and bulbs. Before you
begin, check the batteries to be sure that none are leaky or corroded. After they have
the materials, have your students work together to come up with all the possible ways

**Figure 13.4
Circuits That Make a
Bulb Light**

to light the bulb using only the materials given them. Have them draw the simple circuits shown in Figure 13.4. Which ones work? Which ones do not? Have them identify the parts of a simple circuit.

Assessment: Have students draw the path the electricity takes to light the bulb. Then have them draw a circuit diagram (see Figure 13.5). ▧

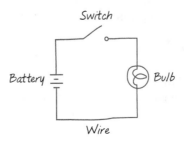

**Figure 13.5
A Simple Circuit
Diagram**

Activity 13.13 Hands-on Science: Making a Series Circuit

Creating a series circuit:
Physical science

Overview: In this activity, you will make a simple series circuit.

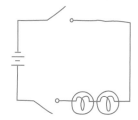

**Figure 13.6
Diagram for a Series
Circuit**

Materials: You will use the following materials for this activity and the next (you won't need every piece of equipment in each activity). Per group of four students: one 6-volt lantern battery, three 6-volt flashlight bulbs, three key switches or knife switches, either a battery holder and 3 pieces of 20- to 26-gauge bare copper wire (20 cm) or wire leads with alligator clips. For the class: a wire cutter, a buzzer.

Procedure: Using the diagram in Figure 13.6, construct a simple series circuit. Can you make the bulbs light? Switch the buzzer for the light. Can you make it buzz?

Assessment: Draw a diagram of the path the current takes. What happens if one bulb goes out? Use your equipment to make additional series circuits. ■

Activity 13.14 Hands-on Science: Making a Parallel Circuit

Creating a parallel circuit:
Physical science

Overview: In this activity, you will make a parallel circuit.

Materials: Same as for Activity 13.13.

Procedure: Using the diagram in Figure 13.7, construct a simple parallel circuit. Close both switches. Can you make the bulbs light? Close one switch and keep the other one open. What happens?

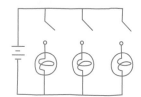

**Figure 13.7
Diagram for a Parallel
Circuit**

Assessment: Draw a diagram of the path the current takes. What happens if one bulb goes out? Use your equipment to make additional parallel circuits. Count the number of complete circuits. ■

Activity 13.15 Hands-on Science: Designing the Lighting for the Opera

Overview: In this activity, you will use your knowledge of simple circuits to design stage lighting for the opera.

Materials: Paper and pencil

Procedure: Working with teammates, design the stage lighting for the opera using series and parallel circuits. Draw circuit diagrams.

Assessment: Using batteries and bulbs you will assess your design by building a small-scale model of the lighting for the set. See Figure 13.8 for the assessment plan. ■

Learning About Sound

Vibrations of material
objects cause sound:
Physical science

Studying about sound comes next. When your students learn about sound, they learn that vibrations of material objects cause sounds. When the strings of a musical instrument such as a violin, viola, piano, cello, or guitar vibrate, they produce sound. Ask students what makes a human voice. After some thinking, they will probably decide that it is the vibration of the vocal cords. (Tell them that they are correct.)

Pitch accounts for the highness or lowness of sound: Physical science

Next, students learn about *pitch*, a characteristic of sound that accounts for its highness or lowness. Pitch is caused by the frequency of vibration of sound waves. Explain that high pitches sound shrill and low pitches sound bass. High-pitched sounds are produced by sources that vibrate at a high frequency, whereas low-pitched sounds come from low-frequency sources. Introduce students to different instruments such as the piano, the harp, and the bass; each has a different pitch. Bring in a pitch pipe, which is used to tune an instrument such as a violin or viola by producing the correct number of vibrations.

Then discuss the singers in an opera and the fact that each role calls for a singer with a specific voice range. Have students classify the roles women play from highest to lowest range (soprano, mezzo-soprano, and contralto) and the roles men play (tenor, baritone, and bass). Then students listen to operas and study the voices and the music.

Questions to Answer

1. Using the words atom, positive charge, negative charge, static electricity, current electricity, battery, bulb, wire, circuit, series, and parallel, write a paragraph or two about electricity. Your paragraph should be clear and informative.

2. You pop two slices of bread into the toaster, turn it on, and nothing happens. Using what you know about electricity and electrical circuits, explain how you would figure out what's wrong. Draw a circuit diagram to explain your reasoning. Your explanation should be concise and informative.

3. Use the words in question 1 to create a concept map about electricity.

Rubric for Assessing the Lighting Design

Criteria	Proficiency Level			
	4	3	2	1
1. Your circuit diagram is drawn correctly.				
2. You indicate whether it is a series or parallel circuit.				
3. You explain why you selected a series or parallel circuit.				
4. You describe the materials you used to construct the circuit.				

Figure 13.8 Performance Assessment for the Lighting Design
Adapted from Mitchell (1999).

Creating a musical instrument with a rubber band that vibrates: Physical Science

Give each group of students a paper cup, a pushpin, a paper clip, a long rubber band, and a ruler, and ask them to experiment and create a musical instrument that makes "music" when the rubber band vibrates. Many of the instruments will look like guitar strings stretched over the length of a ruler, anchored inside a paper cup at one end and anchored at the other end of the ruler by a paper clip and a piece of tape. Ask students to change the length of the part of the rubber band that vibrates and find out what happens to the sound. They will find that the longer the vibrating part of the string, the lower the pitch, and the shorter the vibrating part of the string, the higher the pitch.

Bring in a saxophone and a flute, and ask students to figure out how each instrument produces sound. In the saxophone, sound occurs when the reed vibrates; in the flute, sound is produced when the column of vibrating air leaves the mouthpiece. For homework, have students create a new musical instrument and explain how it produces sound. The next day will be very interesting as they share their creations with others.

Activity 13.16 Online: Musical Instruments on the Internet

Searching for musical instruments on the Internet

Overview: In this activity, you will search for musical instruments on the Internet.

Materials: A computer hooked up to the Internet

Procedure: Log onto the *Music Heritage Network Instrument Encyclopedia* at http://www.si.umich.edu/CHICO/MHN/enclpdia.html. Explore the diversity and creativity of musical traditions from countries around the world.

Assessment: In your electronic journal, write about what you found. Keep your notes for future reference. ■

Finding mathematics in the opera

Operas also involve mathematics Students design the set and make measurements of the stage area, props, and equipment. They calculate how much paint they need and determine how many square feet of carpet it takes to cover the floor. Since they work on a miniature set, they use proportion to determine how to plan for the actual set.

As you can see, the unit on opera is quite complex and requires a great deal of time. It is an excellent learning experience.

Activity 13.17 Reflection: Analyzing the Integrated Unit on Opera

Overview: In this activity, you will reflect on the interdisciplinary thematic unit on the opera.

Procedure: What do you think of the idea of teaching a variety of subjects through opera? Can you think of extensions and applications for the unit? Can you think of another topic—say, for the arts or social sciences—that can be used in the same way?

Assessment: How would you assess student performance in this unit? ■

Integrating science
with literature.

Preparing to Use an Integrated Approach to Science Teaching

Resources for locating integrated activities

When we discussed preparation for using an integrated approach to science teaching, Mrs. Zalewitz said, "There's lots of it!" She recommends that new teachers begin a collection of activities. "Always explore new resources," she says. Her favorite sources of activities include *AIMS (Activities That Integrate Mathematics and Science,* Fresno, California), *Science and Children* (National Science Teachers Association), *Teaching Children Mathematics* (National Council of Teachers of Mathematics), and *Newton's Apple* (National Science Foundation and 3M Corporation). It's worth a visit to the library to locate some of these materials.

Constructing Your Knowledge of Science and Science Teaching

After completing this chapter, begin to reflect on your new knowledge. This chapter presents information about integrating science across the curriculum, as well as many practical strategies that you can implement in your classroom. What is curriculum integration? How does it enrich your teaching? How does it make lessons more meaningful for your students? Think about your own experiences. How are subjects integrated in real life? Integrating subjects gives you an avenue for developing creativity as a teacher. Think about this as a means of continuing your development as a professional.

Key Terms

integrated planning (p. 346)
interconnected knowledge
(p. 346)
coherence (p. 346)

tropical rain forest (p. 353)
static electricity (p. 362)
current electricity (p. 363)
current (p. 363)

battery (p. 363)
electric circuit (p. 363)
conductor (p. 363)
insulator (p. 363)

Reviewing Chapter 13: Questions, Extensions, Applications, and Explorations

1. In addition to planning individual lessons that integrate subjects, you will plan units of study that provide students with a "big picture of scientific ideas" (National Research Council, 1996, p. 104). Organizing instruction in this way takes a much longer time period. Students study fewer ideas in greater depth. The *National Science Education Standards* guideline on unifying concepts and processes identifies five unifying concepts and processes that can serve as the basis for long-term units of study:

   • Systems, order, and organization

   • Evidence, models, and explanation

   • Constancy, change, and measurement

   • Evolution and equilibrium

   • Form and function (National Research Council, 1996, pp. 115–119)

   If you have access to this document, read about this standard. How can you organize instruction around unifying concepts and processes?

2. Ask your students to watch the Saturday morning cartoons. Have them classify the cartoon animals into categories. What categories do they develop? Design an activity that integrates science and the media. Use cooperative learning to do this activity.

3. Have your students engage in a shadow hunt, in which they list the places where they find shadows and determine what caused each shadow. Ask them if they think shadows change. Design an activity that integrates math and science as they select and study an object and its shadow. Have them measure the object and its shadow and compare their sizes. Then have them write about their findings. What else can you build into this activity? How will you assess student learning?

4. Ask your students if all magnets have the same strength. Have them find a way to measure how much stronger one magnet is than another. What subjects will they integrate in this activity? How will you assess this activity?

5. Locate the book *Egg to Chick* by Millicent Selsam (Random House, 1970), or find another, similar book. Use the book to design a lesson on the stages of the birth of a baby chick. What are your objectives for the lesson? Will this activity be a student-initiated investigation?

6. Read *The Little Red Hen* to your students. Change the ending of the story by pretending there are mealworms in the flour. Obtain a mealworm culture from a biological supply catalog or pet store. It will contain the stages of the mealworm: (1) egg, (2) larva (worm), (3) pupa, and (4) beetle. Have students use magnifiers to explore the culture and look for the stages of metamorphosis. Ask them to make up a song or poem to describe what they see. How can you turn this activity into a science investigation?

7. Obtain a copy of the wonderful resource *Using Children's Literature in Math and Science* (Columbus, OH: Eisenhower National Clearinghouse for Math and Science Education; email: mathsci@rbs.org).

Print Resources

Berlin, D., & White, A. (1994). The Berlin-White Integrated Science and Mathematics Model. *School Science and Mathematics, 94*(1), 2–4.

Chapman, C. (1993). *If the shoe fits . . .* Palatine, IL: IRI/Skylight Publishing Company.

Fogarty, R. (1991). *How to integrate the curriculum.* Palatine: IL: IRI/Skylight Publishing Company.

Harris, J. (1999). *Using children's literature in math and science.* Columbus, OH: Eisenhower National Clearinghouse for Math and Science Education.

Jacobs, H. (1990). *Interdisciplinary curriculum: Design and implementation.* Alexandria, VA: Association for Supervision and Curriculum Development.

Lang, H. (1995). *Teaching strategies and methods for student-centered instruction.* New York: Harcourt Brace.

Marzano, R., Pickering, D., & Brandt, R. (1990). Integrating instruction programs through dimensions of learning. *Educational Leadership, 47*(5) p. 45–51.

McDonald, J., & Czerniak, K. (1994). Developing interdisciplinary units: Strategies and examples. *School Science and Mathematics, 94*(1), 5–10.

Piaget, J. (1972). *The epistemology of interdisciplinary relationships.* Paris: Organization for Economic Cooperation and Development.

Vars, G. (1987). *Interdisciplinary teaching in the middle grades.* Columbus, OH: National Middle School Association.

Electronic Resources

Reading Rainbow
http://gpn.unl.edu/rainbow.htm
The Reading Rainbow catalog contains a long list of videos that integrate science across the curriculum. You can read about all of these videos at this web site.

Little Nino's Pizzeria
This integrated curriculum package includes a big book, video, curriculum guide, and pizza rounds. Students learn about food processing, chemical changes, cooking, experimentation with yeast, healthy lifestyles, kitchen safety, and foods from plants, along with social studies, the arts, language arts, and mathematics.

Hail to Mail
This integrated curriculum package contains a video, book, and curriculum guide. Students will learn about our natural world, scientists and their numerous discoveries, inventions and scientific achievments, along with map-reading skills, geography, language arts, mathematics, and multicultural art.

Seashore Surprises
This integrated curriculum package contains the book *Seashore Surprises* and focuses on erosion, animal adaptations, life cycles, simple food chains, ocean habitats, exosystems, tides and waves, and floating and sinking. It integrates social sciences, mathematics, the arts, and language arts.

Gregory, The Terrible Eater
This integrated package contains a video in which LaVar investigates the eating habits of people and animals. Science concepts include animals and their young, distinguishing animal characteristics, behavior of goats, recycling, healthy lifestyles, the five basic food groups, and cooking. It integrates language arts, mathematics, social sciences, and the arts.

The Salamander Room
This integrated curriculum package contains a book and video that take students to a treetop rain forest laboratory and to a zoo where a rain forest is being created. It integrates language arts, mathematics, the arts, and social sciences.

Children's Literature

Dipezio, Michael
Awesome Adventures in Electricity and Magnetism
(Sterling Publication, 1998)
ISBN: 0-8069-9819-9
Grades 2–5

Cooper, Jason
Electricity (fiction)
(The Rourke Book Company, 1992)
ISBN: 0-86593-327-8
Preschool and Grades K–3

Riley, Peter
Electricity (Franklin Watts, 1998)
ISBN: 0-531-11511-9
Preschool and Grades K–3

Lunis, Natalie
Discovering Electricity: (Newbridge
Communications, Inc., 1997)
ISBN: 1-56784-452-9
Grades 2–6

Richards, Elsie
Turned on by Electricity (Troll Associates, 1997)
ISBN: 0-8167-4254-5
Grades 3–6

Cole, Joanna
Magic School Bus and the Electric Field Trip (non-
fiction and fiction) (Scholastic Trade, 1997)
ISBN: 0-590-44682-7
Grades 1–4

Zabrocky, Natalie
Electricity: Big Book (Newbridge, 1997)
ISBN: 1-56784-324-7
Preschool and Grades K–2

Birch, Beverly
Benjamin Franklin's Adventures with Electricity
(Barron's Juveniles, 1996)
ISBN: 0-81209-790-4
Grades 2–6

Norman, Penny
I Can Become an Electro Wiz: Electricity
(Norman & Globus, 1995)
ISBN: 1-886978-00-x
Grades 4–6

Bennett, Paul
What Was It Like Before Electricity?
(Raintree/Steck Vaughn, 1995)
ISBN: 0-8114-5734-6
Preschool and Grades K–4

Brill, Ethel
Copper Country Adventure (fiction)
(Mid-Peninsula Literary Coop, 1988)
ISBN: 0-933249-05-5
Grades 4 and up

Wood, Robert
Electricity and Magnetism FUNdamentals:
FUNtastic Science Activities for Kids
(Learning Triangle Press, 1996)
ISBN: 0-07-071805-9
Grades 3–6

CHAPTER 14

Managing Materials and Resources in Classrooms: All Those Critters

Althea Amos and her teammate, Roger Jones, are new teachers. Their school has very limited science supplies, and they are in charge of compiling a list of materials and resources to order. They will present the list to their colleagues at the next faculty meeting. If everyone agrees that these items are essential, the principal will include them in her budget request. Ms. Amos and Mr. Jones know that budget cuts occur frequently in their district, but they hope that with the increased focus on science, they will have these supplies by next September.

A great deal of research goes into deciding what to order. In a corner of Ms. Amos's classroom is a small table filled with books and catalogs from publishing companies and science supply houses. Two essential guides that she and Mr. Jones often refer to are *Resources for Teaching Elementary School Science* (National Sciences Resource Center, 1996) and *Resources for Teaching Middle School Science* (National Sciences Resource Center, 1998), both written by the National Science Resources Center, the National Academy of Sciences, and the Smithsonian Institution. These comprehensive guides have chapters on curriculum materials, teachers' references, ancillary resources that include lists of museums and places to visit, and professional associations and governmental organizations. Another important reference is the *National Science Teachers Association Annual Supplement of Science Education Suppliers*. This guide is free to all NSTA members and provides a comprehensive list of companies that supply materials for science education, including contacts and product information.

Science equipment listed from most frequently to least frequently used

In searching through journals, Ms. Amos and Mr. Jones find a particularly useful "Problem Solver" column in *Science and Children* that addresses exactly what science resources an elementary school needs (Hardy & Tolman, 1998). The column reports the results of a survey conducted by the authors that asked teachers of kindergarten through grade 6 and science specialists to rank the pieces of science equipment, consumable science supplies, and reference materials most frequently used in elementary science classes. According to the study, the most frequently used science supplies are:

Hand lenses	Rocks and minerals	Beakers
Metric rulers	Graduated cylinders	Petri dishes
Magnets	Mirrors	Prisms
Balance scales	Hot plates	Wind-up toys
Thermometers	Gears and simple	
Microscopes	machines	
Eyedroppers		

Consumables listed from most frequently to least frequently used

Think back on the chapters you have read. By this point, you are familiar with just about every one of these resources.

According to Hardy and Tolman (1998), the most frequently used consumable science supplies are:

Paper and plastic cups	Balloons	Flour
Containers and trays	Vinegar	Cornstarch
Clear plastic bags	Craft sticks	Clear plastic wrap
Potting soil	Plastic spoons	Iron filings
Seeds	Baking soda	Matches
Paper towels	Aluminum foil	Small nails
Food coloring	Toothpicks	Alcohol
Drinking straws	Sand	Dry cells
Two-liter bottles	Salt	Insulated copper wire
String		

If you refer back to Chapters 1 through 13, you will find that you have used nearly all of these materials.

Teachers also need high-quality reference materials. The authors report that the most frequently used materials in this category are:

Trade books	Computer software	Basal readers
Periodicals	Newspapers	Government
Encyclopedias	Laboratory books	publications
Posters	Dictionaries	Networked computers

When asked to name the items most needed to improve elementary science instruction, K–6 teachers listed these:

Computer programs	Simple machines	Balance scales
Instructional space	Plant grow lamps	Video camera
Microscopes	Reference books	Rocks and minerals
Computer and modem	Aquarium	Hot plate
Models	Periodicals	Beakers and graduated
Storage space	Telescope	cylinder
Projecting microscopes	Chemicals	Tuning forks

Ms. Amos and Mr. Jones are off to a good start. They have a basic knowledge of what they need and will read the catalogs to decide what to order. In their presentation to their colleagues, they will discuss ways to manage resources in the classroom.

In Chapters 1 through 13, you learned about many of the resources you can bring into your classroom. In this chapter you will learn about more resources, and you will read specific information about managing animals and plants. As you read through this chapter, think of the answers to these questions:

1. **What resources are most useful to have in a science classroom?**

2. **What types of resources are available, and where do I get them?**

3. **What are science kits, and how do they fit into the curriculum?**

4. **What safety precautions should my students and I follow when working with animals, plants, and chemicals?**

5. **How do I handle critters in the classroom?**

6. **How do I teach about plants?**

Science Kits, Equipment, and Print Resources

Over the past several decades, a variety of agencies, such as the National Science Foundation, funded the development of major projects in elementary science. These projects have produced a variety of products, including textbooks, resource guides, and science kits. Science kits usually contain manuals for the teacher, sometimes workbooks or journals for students, and materials that enable teachers to carry out Hands-on activities. If Ms. Amos and Mr. Jones decide to order science kits, the equipment and materials they will need to carry out the Hands-on activities are included. They will have to replenish supplies that are used up, which are called **consumables**.

Experienced teachers pick and choose activities to fit into the curriculum

As you gain experience in teaching elementary science, you will likely encounter many of these materials. When visiting an elementary school, find out if kits are used. If they are, spend some time examining them. Most science kits on the market today are of high quality, and many are inquiry based. When teachers and supervisors develop a curriculum for a school, they often select at least one kit. Some districts purchase a variety of kits, and during the course of the year students may work with several kits as they focus on different aspects of life, physical, earth and space science and technology. Many experienced elementary teachers pick and choose activities from these sources to fit into the curriculum. They also select activities to suit the learning needs of their students.

You will now read about the most widely used curriculum projects on the market. Phone numbers and addresses are included for your reference. If you don't have access to them, I suggest that you call or write for information about these products and examine them on your own. If you attend a National Science Teachers Association conference or a regional or local science conference, you are likely to see these materials on display.

Full Option Science System (FOSS)

FOSS kits have K–6 modules in life, earth, and physical science

The FOSS program, marketed as the Brittanica Science System, was developed through funding from the National Science Foundation at the Lawrence Hall of Science at the University of California at Berkeley. The FOSS program consists of kits (modules) that comprise a K–6 curriculum. If you use the FOSS program, you use different kits throughout the year. There are modules in life, earth, and physical science. Students construct science concepts through hands-on activities. The kits contain the materials needed for the activities. Once the materials are consumed, you must replenish the kits. Some materials can be purchased in the supermarket or hardware store, or you can order replacements from Delta Education, which sells FOSS kits. Twenty-seven modules comprise the curriculum; 5 of them are for kindergarten (life and physical science), 6 are for grades 1 and 2 (life, physical, and earth science), and 16 are for grades 3 through 6 (life, physical, and earth science, scientific reasoning, technology). The topics are as follows:

Air and Weather	Landforms	Sand and Silt
Animals Two by Two	Levers and Pulleys	Physics of Sound
Balance and Motion	Magnetism and	Solar Energy
Earth Materials	Electricity	Solids and Liquids
Environments	Measurement	Structures of Life
Fabric, Food, and	Mixtures and Solutions	Trees
Nutrition	Models and Designs	Variables
Human Body	New Plants, Paper	Water
Ideas and Inventions	Pebbles	Wood
Insects		

You can get more information about the FOSS program from the Lawrence Hall of Science, University of California at Berkeley, Berkeley, CA 94720; phone: 510-642-8941 (National Sciences Resource Center [NSRC], 1996). Delta Education distributes FOSS materials; call 1-800-442-5444 or check the web site at www.delta-ed.com.

Science and Technology for Children

STC has inquiry-centered units for grades 1 through 6 in earth, life, and physical science

The John and Catherine MacArthur Foundation and the National Science Foundation provided funding for the development of the Science and Technology for Children (STC) curriculum. The curriculum consists of 24 inquiry-centered units for grades 1 through 6. There are four units per grade level, and the topics are life, earth, and physical science, with a focus on the technological applications of science and the interactions between science and technology. The titles available are as follows:

Animal Studies	Floating and Sinking	Organisms
Balancing and Weighing	Food Chemistry	Plant Growth and
Changes	Land and Water	Development
Chemical Tests	The Life Cycle of	Rocks and Minerals
Comparing and	Butterflies	Soils
Measuring	Magnets and Motors	Solids and Liquids
Ecosystems	Measuring Time	Sound
Electric Circuits	Microworlds	Technology of Paper
Experiments with Plants	Motion and Design	Weather

You can obtain information about the STC by contacting the National Sciences Resource Center, Arts and Industry Building, Room 1201, Smithsonian Institution, Washington, DC 20560, 202-357-2555, or by calling Carolina Biological at 1-800-227-1150.

Science Curriculum Improvement Study (SCIS/SCIS II/SCIIS/85/SCIS 3+)

SCIS kits promote the development of scientific literacy in children

Originally funded by the National Science Foundation in the late sixties and developed at the Lawrence Hall of Science at the University of California at Berkeley, the Science Curriculum Improvement Study (SCIS) promotes the development of scientific literacy in children. Over the years, a variety of modules were created under the original SCIS project, which evolved into SCIS II, then SCIIS 85, and now SCIS 3+. Students explore with materials, interpret information, and apply knowledge and skills to new situations. Each SCIS 3+ unit consists of a teacher guide with chapter summaries, lesson plans, assessment activities, student journals, and equipment kits with materials for 32 students.

The SCIS 3+ units include the following:

Material Objects	Relative Position and Motion
Organisms	Environments
Interaction and Systems	Energy Sources
Life Cycles	Communities
Subsystems and Variables	Scientific Theories
Populations	Ecosystems

You can obtain information about the SCIIS projects by contacting the Lawrence Hall of Science, University of California at Berkeley, Berkeley, CA 94720; phone: 510-642-8718. Materials can be purchased through Delta Education at 1-800-258-1302 (NSRC, 1996).

Activities Integrating Mathematics and Science (AIMS)

AIMS activities integrate math and science

AIMS activities are wonderful! They were initially developed as part of a National Science Foundation grant at Fresno Pacific College. The AIMS Education Foundation engages in research, provides workshops for teachers, and publishes integrated curriculum materials for elementary and middle schools. Its newsletters and books contain dozens of activities that you can use in your classroom to integrate science, math, and almost every other subject. They contain extensions and applications as well as background knowledge on the content. When you are teaching a particular topic, you can pick up a stack of AIMS newsletters, thumb through them, and select a suitable activity for your class.

AIMS activities do not come as a kit, but you can purchase the materials and supplies to accompany the activities from the AIMS Education Foundation. Some of my favorites are:

The Budding Botanist	Magnificent Microworld
Critters	Adventures
Down to Earth	Pieces and Patterns
Electrical Connections	A Patchwork in Math and Science
Fall into Math and Science	Soap Films and Bubbles
Hardhatting in a Geo-World	Water Precious Water

The AIMS Education Foundation is located at P.O. Box 8120, Fresno, CA 93747-8120; phone: 209-255-4094 (NSRC, 1996).

Great Explorations in Math and Science (GEMS)

GEMS activities integrate math and science using guided discovery

GEMS materials, also produced at the Lawrence Hall of Science at the University of California at Berkeley, consist of teachers' guides, presenters' guides, and exhibit guides. They help teachers integrate math and science using guided discovery. GEMS books contain activities that you can use with your students. You have to gather the materials on your own, since GEMS materials do not come as a kit. The topics covered in the guides are as follows:

Acid Rain	In All Probability
Animal Defenses	Investigating Artifacts
Animals in Action	Involving Dissolving
Bubble Festival	Ladybugs
Bubble-ology	Liquid Explorations
Build it! Festival	The Magic of Electricity
Buzzing a Hive	Mapping Animal Movements
Chemical Reactions	Mapping Fish Habitats
Color Analyzers	Moons of Jupiter
Convection: A Current Event	More than Magnifiers
Crime Lab Chemistry	Mystery Festival
Discovering Density	Of Cabbages and Chemistry
Earth, Moon, and Stars	Oobleck: What Scientists Do
Earthworms	Paper Towel Testing
Experimenting with Model Rockets	Penguins and Their Young
Fingerprinting	River Cutters
Frog Math: Predict, Ponder, Play	Shapes, Loops, and Images
Group Solutions: Cooperative	Solids, Liquids, and Gases
Logic Activities	Terrarium Habitats
Height-O-Meters	Tree Homes
Hide a Butterfly	Vitamin C Testing
Hot Water and Warm Homes	The Wizard's Lab
from Sunlight	

You can get more information about the GEMS program from the Lawrence Hall of Science, University of California at Berkeley, Berkeley, CA 94720; phone: 510-642-7771 (NSRC, 1996).

Improving Urban Elementary Science (Insights)

Insights modules integrate life, physical, and earth science across the curriculum

The National Science Foundation provided funding for Insights, which was developed by the Education Development Center in Newton, Massachusetts. The Insights curriculum consists of 17 modules, each requiring a month and a half to two months to complete. The topics covered are life science, physical science, and earth science, which are integrated across the curriculum, especially with math and language arts. The activities are intended to enhance critical thinking, communication, and problem solving (NSRC, 1996). The topics include:

Balls and Ramps	Circuits and Pathways	Human Body Systems
Bones and Skeletons	Growing Things	Lifting Heavy Things
Changes of State	Habitats	Liquids

Living Things	Reading the	Sound, Structures
Myself and Others	Environment	There Is No Away
The Mysterious Powder	The Senses	

You can contact the Education Development Center (Insights) at 55 Chapel Street, Newton, MA, 02160, 617-969-7100 or 1-800-225-4276 (NSRC, 1996).

National Geographic Kids Network

National Geographic Kids Network explores socially significant topics

The National Science Foundation provided funding for the development of the National Geographic Kids Network, a curriculum based on telecommunications. The curriculum, written for grades 4 through 6, consists of seven units that explore socially significant science topics. The product comes with software and classroom activities that allow students to design and perform experiments and discuss, share, and analyze their data with other students throughout the world using the Internet. The modules currently available are as follows:

Acid Rain	Too Much Trash?	What Are We Eating?
Hello!	Weather in Action	What's in Our Water?
The Solar System		

For information about the National Geographic Kids Network, contact TERC (Technical Education Research Centers) at 2067 Massachusetts Avenue, Cambridge, MA 02140, 617-547-0430 (NSRC, 1996).

Managing Classroom Resources

In this section, you will examine practical ways in which teachers manage many kinds of classroom resources. Darnel Brown, also a new teacher, is a colleague of Althea Amos and Roger Jones. Here is a practical example showing how he uses a variety of resources to enhance his teaching. As you read this section, pay particular attention to resource management.

As part of their environmental science unit, Mr. Brown's fifth-graders will learn about earthworms. He wants to make their study of earthworms active and meaningful, so he searches the Internet for activities involving earthworms. He finds one that fits into the curriculum on the National Wildlife Federation's web site. It is an investigation that centers around the role earthworms play in breaking down plant matter and creating fertile soil. He doesn't launch into this activity immediately, as his students must first develop a great deal of background knowledge about the environment.

Mr. Brown's students begin by learning about the *environment, environmental science, ecology,* and *ecosystems*. Then they will study an ecosystem that

Observing earthworms is interesting for children and they're usually easy to find.

Our Earth–The Human Environment

air

water

soil

rocks and minerals

plants

animals

bacteria

fungi

**Figure 14.1
Our Earth, the Human Environment**

includes earthworms. Their school is located in a rural region, so they will take a walk in the area surrounding the school, making a list of all the living and nonliving things they see. Students pair off for the walk, and Mr. Brown asks them to record any questions they have about their observations. When they return to class, they begin a discussion about what they saw. They talk about our earth, the human **environment** in which we live. Mr. Brown asks them to think about what makes up the earth. On the board they create a list of all of the physical parts of the earth (see Figure 14.1). They talk about **environmental science,** an approach that helps us to understand the human environment and the impact humans have on the environment. It also helps people find solutions to important environmental problems (Thompson & Turk, 1999).

The next day, they talk about what they saw on their walk. One student notes that grass grows in the park across from the school, but not under the trees. He wonders why. Someone turned over a log and noticed hundreds of live organisms wiggling around on the log. She wonders if the organisms live off of the log. Then there was a puddle of water. Students saw a bird drinking some water from the puddle. They wonder how the puddle and the bird affect each other. Mr. Brown asks his students to hold their questions for awhile; they will come back to them later. He thinks that all of these are good topics for investigation. He tells students that their questions are about **ecology,** the branch of biology that examines the interrelationships between plants and animals and the interactions between living organisms and their environment (Thompson & Turk, 1999). He explains that scientists study **ecosystems,** groups of plants and animals living together in their environment. The plants and animals affect each other, and they affect the environment as they live together. The students work in pairs to make a list of the ecosystems they found on their walk (see Figure 14.2). They note that both living and nonliving things make up an ecosystem.

Mr. Brown asks his students to do a quick Internet search. They must find out what types of organisms comprise an ecosystem. The students work together, and within minutes they find that producers, consumers, and decomposers compose an ecosystem. **Producers** use

Learning about producers, consumers, and decomposers: Life science, earth science

Figure 14.2 Ecosystems

> Ecosystems we found on our walk
>
> The small lake in the park
>
> The pond in the park
>
> The woods behind the park
>
> The park itself
>
> The field across from the school

energy from the sun and water and nutrients from the soil to make their own food. Examples of producers are green plants and algae. When sunlight is present, they take carbon dioxide from the air and water from the soil to produce oxygen and sugar. The sugar becomes their food, and the oxygen goes into the air.

Consumers are organisms that cannot produce their own food, so they depend on producers and other consumers for survival. Some consumers are animals that eat only other animals; they are called **carnivores**. Wolves, lions, tigers, owls, spiders, frogs, and snakes are carnivores. Consumers that eat only plants are called **herbivores**. Examples of herbivores are butterflies, cattle, deer, grasshoppers, mice, rabbits, and squirrels. Consumers that can eat both plants and animals are **omnivores**. Examples of omnivores are bears, chickens, some turtles, and people (Mastny, Kahn, & Sherman, 1992). **Decomposers,** such as bacteria and fungi, break down dead plants and animals (producers and consumers) and return nutrients to the soil and the air. Earthworms are animals that are decomposers. They find dead plant and animal matter in the soil, pass it through their bodies, and transform it into nutrient-rich compost, which is ready to supply nutrients for the next generation of plants. They also mix earth and compost, creating tunnels that permit air to flow in the soil. This allows water to seep into the soil and helps roots systems to develop.

Mr. Brown asks his students if they would like to investigate an ecosystem, and, as he predicted, they do. He takes out a jar filled with earthworms. They will work together to design an investigation that enables them to find out what effect earthworms have on an ecosystem. He has an investigation in mind, the one that he downloaded from the National Wildlife Federation web site. However, he wants his students to have their own input into the process. He allows pairs of students to work together, forming groups of four. They brainstorm ways to answer the question "What effect do earthworms have on an ecosystem?"

Activity 14.1 Lesson Design: Designing an Experiment to Determine the Role of Earthworms in an Ecosystem

Designing an investigation about the effects of earthworms on an ecosystem: Life science, earth science, science process

Overview: In this activity, you will design a lesson to answer the question "What effect do earthworms have on an ecosystem?"

Procedure: Before you read the activity suggested by the National Wildlife Federation, think about how you would design such an investigation. How would you organize the experiment? What materials would you use? What do you predict would happen as a result of your experiment?

Assessment: Design a performance assessment for your investigation. ■

In order to answer the question, Mr. Brown's students must set up an experiment. The National Wildlife Federation's activity suggests that students first collect earthworms by digging in moist soil in places where there are small, crusty lumps at the surface. If this isn't possible, you can order earthworms from a bait shop or biological supply house (see the following box). Students should begin by feeling the earthworm's body. They will notice that an earthworm's body has bristles, which help it to grip the sides of its tunnel.

Biological Supply Houses

Carolina Biological Supply Company
2700 York Road
Burlington, NC 27215
Phone: 1-800-334-5551; fax: 1-800-222-7112

Connecticut Valley Biological Supply House
P.O. Box 326
Southampton, MA 01073
1-800-628-7748

Delta Education
P.O. Box 915
Nashua, NH 03051
1-800-258-1302

Insect Lore Products
P.O. Box 1535
Shafter, CA 93263
1-800-548-3284

Wards
5100 West Henrietta Road
P.O. Box 92912
Rochester, NY 14692-9012
1-800-962-2600

Here is one way to set up the investigation. Take three clean jars, and add alternate layers (one inch thick) of soil and sand to each jar. Each time you fill in a layer, spray the top of the layer with water. The first jar is the control. It holds only sand and soil. (Why do you need a control?) The second jar contains soil and sand layers. You fill the top of that jar with nutrient-rich compost, such as vegetable waste and leaves. Avoid citrus peels and onions, as they are not healthy for earthworms. The third jar has the same contents as the second jar, but this time you add earthworms to the top layer.

Then cover the jars with cloth and place them in a cool, dark spot. Students should predict what will happen in each jar. Twice a week, students add more compost material to the second and third jars and lightly water the soil in each jar.

This is very important for the earthworms. What do *you* predict will happen in each jar?

Activity 14.2 **Hands-on Science: Determining the Effects of Earthworms in an "Ecosystem in a Jar"**

Overview: In this activity, you will examine ways to collect and analyze data for this lesson.

Determining the effects of earthworms on an ecosystem: Earth science, life science, science process

Procedure: How would you suggest that students in the primary grades collect data for this activity? How will students in the intermediate and middle grades determine the effect of the earthworms on this "ecosystem in a jar"? How should they analyze the data?

Assessment: How will you find out what students think and understand? ■

What Will Happen in the Jars?

You can expect nothing to happen in the first and second jars. In the jar with the earthworms, there will be a great deal of activity. The earthworms will mix and aerate the layers of soil-sand-compost mixture, making it easy for water and roots to penetrate the soil. Students should continue the activity for about a month. At that time, provide them with fast-growing seeds, such as marigolds. Have them plant the seeds in the three soil samples and move the jars from the shady spot to a sunny spot. What do you predict will happen? Why should you move the jars to a sunny spot?

Activity 14.3 **Lesson Design: Bringing the Activity to Closure**

Overview: In this activity, you will think about ways to bring this activity to closure.

Procedure: Consider how Mr. Brown might bring this activity to closure. What should his students learn from the activity?

Assessment: How should Mr. Brown assess students' understanding? Students still have unanswered questions from their initial observations made during the walk around the school. How should Mr. Brown handle these questions? ■

Activity 14.4 **Reflection: Managing Resources in the Classroom**

Overview: In this activity, you will reflect on Mr. Brown's lesson and think about how he managed classroom resources.

Materials: Paper and pencil

Reflecting on a lesson

Procedure: Think about Mr. Brown's lesson. Make a list of all the different resources he used. How many are there? How did he handle the classroom resources? What preparation was needed? What would have happened to his lesson if he had not prepared his resources ahead of time?

Assessment: What adaptations, if any, would you suggest if Mr. Brown had students with special needs in the class? Discuss the importance of planning and gathering resources before teaching a lesson. ■

Safety in the Classroom

Treat living things with respect

When working with animals, plants, and chemicals in the classroom, you must be concerned for the safety of your students. Your students should treat all living things with respect and show concern for their safety and well-being. They should be very careful when handling chemicals. If you feel they are not mature enough to handle such things, don't jeopardize the safety of your students or of the plants and animals. Sometimes it is better to give your students such experiences on a small scale in a very controlled setting. This might be a good way for you to start, especially if you are just beginning to gain expertise in classroom management. Deciding what to bring into the classroom requires good judgment, and you should make these decisions with your professor and host teacher.

Introduce living things on a small scale

Know your school's policy about animals in the classroom

Before bringing any living things to class, be sure you know your school's policy about animals in the classroom. Some schools encourage this, whereas others have policies that prohibit the presence of animals in classrooms. Also, be sure you are aware of state regulations regarding the presence of animals in the classroom. It might be necessary for you to receive written permission from parents or guardians if your students will investigate living organisms. Check with your principal to find out if such permission is necessary.

Report all accidents

Sometimes accidents happen even if you are careful. Be sure you are aware of your school's procedures in the event of an accident. Ask about these procedures when you start to teach. Report all accidents to the proper school authority, which is usually the principal or school nurse. Typically there are accident reports to complete. Be sure your students know they must report all accidents to you. Even small, seemingly insignificant events should be reported. You should keep a well-stocked first aid kit in your classroom for small incidents that you can handle. If you have any doubt about the need for medical attention and your school has a nurse, send the student to the nurse's office.

When working with animals or plants, be sure your students follow the rules to ensure their own safety. They must never touch their eyes, noses, ears, mouths, or faces after touching a plant or an animal. The same rule holds true for chemicals. They should wash thoroughly after handling these materials—and this includes fingernails as well as hands. The following story shows what can happen if students don't follow this procedure.

Mike's Story

Mike, age 11, returned home one Sunday afternoon after playing soccer. He complained of a headache. By morning he felt better, so he went to school. When he came home, he was coughing and running a low-grade fever. Two days later he was no better, so his mother took him to the pediatrician, who diagnosed a viral infection. Mike was sent home to rest.

After two days, Mike's condition worsened. He was coughing and running a high fever, and he now had a rash on his arms. He was put on antibiotics, but his condition continued to worsen. He was now coughing severely and having bronchial spasms.

His mother was quite concerned because he should have been getting better, not worse. She thought her son might not be suffering from a virus but was having an allergic reaction to something environmental, such as something in the park where he played each day. She decided to retrace Mike's schedule over the past two weeks to look for anything unusual that he might have been exposed to.

She checked his school for any unusual incidents. There were none. She checked the parks where he played. She called the township department of parks to see if anything had been sprayed on the field. Nothing had. She asked Mike if he had done anything unusual over the past two weeks. One event stood out slightly.

On the day his initial symptoms appeared, he was at a friend's house. He and his friend decided to build a tree house in the backyard, and they worked several hours cutting branches and constructing the tree house. Upon its completion, his friend's mother served pizza, which they devoured eagerly.

Mike's mother decided to learn more about the tree house and found that the boys used juniper branches to build it. She called the county health department to find out if junipers could cause allergic reactions. The health officer stated that the sticky sap from evergreens could cause allergic reactions in humans, and he recited a list of symptoms that were identical to Mike's. The puzzle was solved! Mike was allergic to juniper sap. When she discussed this with Mike, he recalled getting the sticky sap on his arms where the rash appeared. He may have also ingested some of it when he ate the pizza.

Mike's mother called the pediatrician and gave her the new information. She immediately placed Mike on Ventolin to relieve the bronchial spasms. He was given a nebulizer to help him breathe more easily. Two weeks from the start of the event, Mike's temperature was back to normal, the rash was gone, and his breathing returned to normal (Sherman & Sherman, 1999).

Sticky sap from evergreens can cause an allergic reaction: Safety

When your students work with plants, animals, or chemicals in the classroom, be sure you check for known allergies. Don't forget to have them wash thoroughly after handling potential allergens. You might even want to share Mike's story with them!

Managing Critters in the Classroom

There are many ways to make your science lessons come alive. I hope that by now your students have used a computer hooked up to the Internet if this resource is available in your school. Another way to make your lessons more meaningful is to bring critters of all sorts into the classroom. You probably have some questions about these classroom visitors. Where do I get them? What do I do with them once they are here? Is it safe for students to handle them? How can I ensure the safety of the critters? An excellent resource is *Animals in the Classroom: Selection, Care, and Observations* by David C. Kramer (1989, Crowell Publishers), which details the housing, handling, and feeding of 29 animals, ranging from worms and insects to birds and mammals, and includes information on how to obtain and care for them.

In this chapter, you will read about earthworms, mealworms, caterpillars, crickets, and hamsters. My purpose here is not to tell you absolutely everything about caring for animals but to trouble-shoot. I'll try to come to the point that I know beginning teachers worry about, in addition to giving you ideas for lessons and teaching tips.

Earthworms

You can do many activities with earthworms in the classroom. Your students can investigate earthworm behavior, the types of foods earthworms like to eat, how much they eat, how they affect soil, how they respond to different stimuli, and, for more advanced students, the types and amount of plant nutrients they release. If your students are interested in horticulture, they might like to study worm farming. Earthworm farms convert domestic organic waste into useful compost. Local governments around the world are creating worm farms to dispose of community waste, then selling the resulting fertilizer back to the communities for gardening. You might like to have your students research such operations.

Sources of earthworm activities

The box on page 388 contains a short list of books with earthworm activities that will help you plan for instruction. If you choose to purchase earthworms from a biological supply house, you will get a dozen large worms for about $7. They will probably be less expensive if purchased in a bait shop. And remember, you can also dig them up on your own.

> **Worm Books and Activity Kits**
>
> The following books and activity kits are available from *Let's Get Growing* (http://www.letsgetgrowing.com):
>
> *Wonder Worm Compost Kits*—Instructions, garden fork, and worms
>
> *Worms Eat My Garbage*—Starter book for learning about worms
>
> *Squirmy Wormy Composters*—Composting worms (ages 6 through 13)
>
> *Earthworm Model Activity Set*—Explore the inside of an earthworm
>
> *Wormania! The Video*—See live earthworms in their natural habitat
>
> *Worms Eat Our Garbage*—Classroom activities
>
> *Wonder Worm*™ Observation Hotel—Viewing chamber with instructions and a hand lens
>
> *The Wonderful World of Wigglers*—Cross-disciplinary activities and stories

In your classroom, you can keep worms in an aquarium or a similar container filled with rich humus and decaying plant leaves (http://www.aea10.k12.ia.us, 1999). Keep the environment moist, but not too wet. Earthworms can eat kitchen scraps—mainly fruit, vegetable, and cereal-based products—waste paper, used tea bags, and coffee grounds. Don't feed them silver paper, foil, colored paper, cardboard, glass, or plastic (http://www.cleangreen.com.au/wrmfrm.html, 1999). Cover the container with a cloth to eliminate a house fly infestation.

What If You Don't Like Worms?

Some people don't like to handle earthworms. If you or any of your students are squeamish about earthworms, try wearing rubber gloves, available in the supermarket, a pharmacy, or a science supply house. If the fear is just too great, find someone who doesn't mind working with worms. You might pair a squeamish student with a nonsqueamish one, letting the latter handle the worms. If you yourself can't bear touching earthworms, you can probably find several obliging students.

Arthropods

Arthropods have legs with joints and bodies with sections held together by joints: Life science

Arthropods represent more than three-quarters of all the different animals found on earth. The term *arthropod* means "having feet with joints," but arthropods actually have legs with joints, and their bodies have sections that are held together by joints. The most important groups of arthropods are listed in the box on p. 389.

These animals either swim or walk, so each body section has a pair of legs. Unlike most other arthropods, insects have only three pairs of legs, with one pair attached to each segment of the insect's chest. Just about all arthropods have a heart, blood vessels, and a nervous system; some have simple eyes, some have compound eyes, and some have both. They all have an **exoskeleton,** or an outside shell. Some shells, such as the lobster's, are very hard; other shells, such as the butterfly's and moth's, are weak.

Groups of Arthropods

Insects

▶ Bees
▶ Beetles
▶ Butterflies

Crustaceans

▶ Barnacles
▶ Crabs
▶ Lobsters
▶ Shrimp

Arachnids

▶ Mites
▶ Scorpions
▶ Spiders
▶ Ticks

Centipedes

Millipedes

Activity 14.5 Online: Learning About Insects

Overview: You can help your students learn about the life cycles of insects, their habitats, and their role in the ecosystem by forming an insect zoo in your classroom.

Materials: A computer hooked up to the Internet

Procedure: You will learn a great deal about collecting insects if you log onto the Internet and go to http://naturalpartners.org/InsectZoo/Curriculum/InsectZooKeeping/.

Assessment: Use a journal to make notes about what you find at this site. Much of the information contained in this section comes from this source. ■

Know your school's policy about bringing insects into the classroom

To begin, be sure that your principal and your school's policy allow students to bring insects into the classroom. If this is permitted, you can order insects from a science supply house. Don't leave them unattended for more than a weekend or you will endanger their lives. If you can't attend to them, free them. You can always collect or order more insects at a later date. Some of the most popular insects studied in elementary science classrooms are butterflies, praying mantids, lady beetles, Madagascan hissing roaches (they are slow moving, docile, wingless, and odorless, and, despite their name, they don't bite), ants, and certain spiders.

You can keep your insects in bug cages, glass aquariums, or 2-liter soda bottles. Bug cages are available from biological supply houses or even toy stores. They are usually small boxes with screened sides and a fitted top. A clear, plastic 2-liter soda bottle is also a good home for an insect. You should cut a rectangular hinged window in the side of the bottle and tape down the opening when not in use. A glass aquarium with a fitted, screened top is another possibility. It is easy to clean, is reusable, and makes viewing easy.

Keep insect cages clean

Insect cages must be kept very clean. The temperature in the cage should remain fairly constant, and there should be a proper amount of moisture and fresh food. If the food gets moldy, remove it; mold is unhealthy for the insects. If the heat is turned off in the school at night and the room gets cold, the school is not a good place to keep your insects.

After you feed the insects, look at the food. If it's gone after an hour, they need to be fed more. If some food remains after an hour, you don't need to add more right away. How do you know when the cage needs to be cleaned? When you see lots of *frass* (insect droppings), it's time to clean the cage. Now you will read about how to care for a variety of insects and other arthropods. To learn even more, log onto

http://naturalpartners.org/InsectZoo/Curriculum/ArthropodCareDirectory

Mealworms

Mealworms are easy to raise

For many years, I have kept mealworm colonies in my classrooms. They are easy to raise and provide a wonderful experience for children of all grades. Mealworms are not really worms; they are beetle larvae. There are yellow mealworms and dark mealworms. The scientific name for yellow mealworms is *Tenebrio molitor,* and the scientific name for dark mealworms is *Tenebrio obscurus.* You can keep mealworms in a container with smooth sides made of plastic, metal, or glass. I usually cover the container with a screen and place a rubber band around the screen to secure it. You can keep up to 1,000 mealworms in a gallon jar with a wide mouth.

Feeding mealworms

Mealworms like to eat wheat bran or cereal products such as uncooked oatmeal. You should fill half of their container with this food and add to it every few months. You will find the mealworms living in their food. Apple slices and fruit or vegetable matter, such as potato, carrot, or ripe banana, are good treats for mealworms; they also provide moisture for them. Place these foods on a clean, metal sheet or board so that they don't touch the cereal products. Remove the treats when they appear to have spoiled. If you allow the cereal products to get too moist, mold might form and mites might develop, ruining the mealworm culture. If you maintain the container well, you will have to clean it only about once a year. To clean the container, sort the mealworms and the food. Clean and dry the container, and put the mealworms back into the clean container with fresh food (Pope, 1997).

What if you want to start a new mealworm colony? Look at your existing colony. About once a month, the powdery residue called **frass,** made up of mealworm waste and eggs, builds up in the container. Using a strainer, sift this out, separating it from the food. If you put the frass in another container with some bran and vegetable slices, about a month later the eggs will hatch. Two weeks later, you will find the larvae, which you can put into a new container with food and vegetable slices. You will have a new colony. This procedure is described briefly at (http:www.cc.ndsu.nodak.edu)!

Mealworms do well at temperatures between 80 and 90 degrees Fahrenheit. If you want to keep the larvae in a dormant state, cover the container with a cloth and put it in the refrigerator, where the temperature is between 40 and 50 degrees Fahrenheit. If the temperature gets lower than that, the mealworms will die.

The mealworm in the larval stage looks like a little worm: Life science

Activities with Mealworms. A very simple mealworm activity is the mealworm observation. Give each student a mealworm that is in the larval stage, and have him or her place it in a plastic cup that contains bran or other cereal products. The mealworm in the larval stage looks like a little worm (see Figure 14.3). Once in awhile, the student will feed it an apple or a potato slice. Dark mealworms stay in the larval stage for three months and yellow mealworms up to nine months. Once they are full grown, the mealworms move from the larval stage to the pupal stage. The pupal stage lasts several weeks (it proceeds faster in heated buildings). Following pupation, the pupal skin is cast off, and the beetle emerges. This is very exciting for your students to observe. The female beetles lay eggs, with yellow mealworms laying about 275 eggs and dark mealworms about 475 eggs. The larvae and adults of both the yellow and dark mealworms are similar except that adult dark mealworms are dull black in color, and adult yellow mealworms are dark brown. For more information about mealworms log onto http://ctr.uvm.edu or http://entweb.clemson.edu.

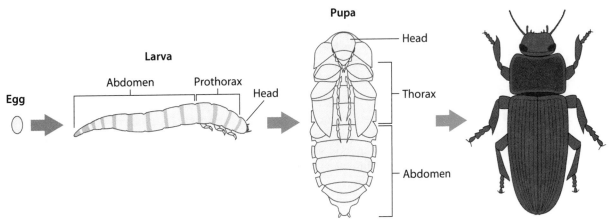

Figure 14.3
Mealworm

Activity 14.6 Hands-on Science: Observing Mealworms

Mealworm investigations

Overview: This activity provides some additional investigations to do with your mealworms.

Materials: Mealworms, a magnifying glass

Procedure: Use a magnifying glass to find out how many legs the mealworm has. Then count the number of segments in its body. Look for a head and a tail. Does it have one? How does it move? Can you locate its head by watching it move? Observe its movement. Does it move in a straight line? Does it move backwards? Does it roll over? How fast does it move? How will you measure the speed? Does it move at different speeds on different surfaces? What does it like to eat? Does it like light? Does it prefer a particular color?

Assessment: Draw a diagram of your mealworm. If you have access to the Internet, search the following site for more information about mealworms:

> http:www.minnetonka.k12.mn.us/groveland/insect/proj/describe.html ■

Caterpillars

You can find caterpillars on trees, shrubs, garden plants, and flowers, or you can purchase them from a biological supply house. Where do caterpillars come from? Female moths and butterflies lay their eggs on plants that serve as hosts for the caterpillars. When the eggs hatch, they are caterpillars. A moth caterpillar spins a cocoon and stays in the pupal stage until it emerges as a moth. A butterfly caterpillar spins a chrysalis before emerging from the pupal stage to form a butterfly (see Figure 14.4). When they emerge, both a moth and a butterfly look for food and a mate.

How should you keep a butterfly or a moth? If you buy it from a biological supply house, be sure to order the proper food. If you collect it from nature, you will need the right foliage for the specific species, so it's best to rely on the commercial source to ensure the safety of the butterfly or moth.

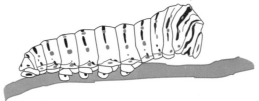

Figure 14.4 Caterpillar

The cage needs high humidity, so it's a good idea to keep a damp paper towel on the bottom of the cage. You should clean the cage every day to eliminate droppings and prevent mold formation. Caterpillars need a stick on which to pupate, so include a stick or a long twig. A piece of rotting fruit or a sponge soaked in sugar water or honey water provides nutrients. You can also purchase caterpillar food from a biological supply house. Your students will be able to study the life cycle of the caterpillar through this activity. They will also learn to care for them.

Crickets

You can probably find crickets around your house, or you can purchase them from a bait shop or biological supply house. You can keep them in a large container with glass or clear plastic sides so your students can see them. An aquarium tank or a see-through plastic container is a good cricket keeper. Crickets like to hide, so provide an empty cardboard egg container or a peat pot. They like to eat oatmeal, cornmeal, or dry dog food. Be sure to keep the food fresh and dry. They need moisture, so slices of apple or potato or lettuce leaves are important additions. Be sure the food is fresh and changed often. You will also need a plate of damp sand for the females to lay their eggs. As with other insects, be sure to keep the cage clean and dry to prevent disease.

Activity 14.7 Hands-on Science: Cricket Activities

Overview: This activity focuses on the many things your students can learn from crickets.

Materials: Crickets, a light source

Procedure: Have students observe how crickets respond to light. What do crickets look like in various stages of life? How do crickets behave in the presence of other crickets? How do crickets communicate?

Assessment: Have your students use their journals to write about what they learned about crickets.   ■

The higher the air temperature, the greater the number of cricket chirps per minute: Life science

Have your students draw a male and a female cricket wing. Students should notice that the pattern of veins in the male cricket wing is different from that of the female (see Figure 14.5). Since the male rubs its wings together to make the familiar cricket sound that attracts females, the male cricket has a much sturdier wing than the female does. People who study crickets have found that the higher

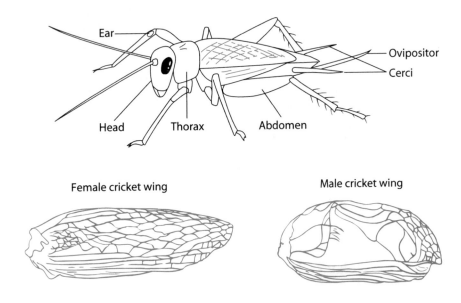

**Figure 14.5
Cricket**

the air temperature, the greater the number of cricket chirps per minute. Listen carefully to a cricket's chirp. Count the number of chirps per minute; then add 30 to that number and divide by 7. You will end up with a number that is very close to the temperature in degrees Celsius (Continuous Electron Beam Accelerator Facility Manual, 1992; Sherman, 1994).

Activity 14.8 Problem Solving: Insect Math

Integrating math and science

Overview: This activity presents some insect facts and math problems. Your students can use this information to create new problems that integrate math and science.

Materials: Paper and pencil

Procedure: Have your students write problems that bring together math and science. Here is the information they will use:

1. According to the National Museum of Natural History in Leiden, Netherlands, there are 1 million species of insects. All other animals fit into the remaining 25,000 species.

2. An ant weighs about 1/10,000 of an ounce. How many ants would it take to equal the weight of a 75-pound child? Log onto: http://naturalpartners.org/InsectZoo/Curriculum/Curriculum/Activities/math.html. You can learn more about insects at this site.

Assessment: Create an assessment instrument to score these problems. ◼

Hamsters

Adult hamsters are territorial and have a strong hoarding instinct: Life science

Hamsters are rodents that are commonly kept as pets. There are *Syrian hamsters,* also referred to as *golden hamsters* because of their original color (gold), and *teddy bear hamsters,* which have long hair. Hamsters are not social animals, and adult hamsters generally prefer to be alone. Juvenile hamsters, however, don't mind being with other hamsters. Adult hamsters have a strong hoarding instinct and are quite territorial. When placed with other hamsters, they generally fight and therefore should be separated, except during mating. After they mate, they should be separated or fighting will result.

Hamsters are fun to keep in the classroom. If you have just one hamster, little care is required. All you will need is a cage with a good locking system, bedding material, food, water, and an exercise wheel. Many different types of rodent cages are available. You can use an aquarium tank, a wire cage, or a cage specially made for hamsters, such as a habitrail or S.A.M. system. A glass aquarium makes a good home for a hamster. Just be sure to purchase one of at least 10- or 20-gallon capacity so the animal has enough room to run around. The benefit of such a home is that it contains the bedding quite well, and the glass is difficult to scratch when the animal gnaws at it. The disadvantage is limited air circulation, so be sure to buy a tank that is big enough. Also, make sure its lid is secure.

Wire cages are another possibility. They are good for keeping larger rodents. Make sure its grates won't allow the inhabitant to escape, as rodents are proficient

Thinking about having a hamster live in your classroom.

escape artists. Also, check the floor of the cage to ensure that it won't irritate or harm the animal's feet.

You can also purchase a hamster environment, such as a habitrail or S.A.M., at a pet store. They are colorful and popular with children, but they are made of plastic, which animals sometimes gnaw through. They come with a plastic wheel, which is generally safer for rodents than a wire wheel. Be certain that all parts of the cage are locked. Also, check frequently to see if the animal has gnawed away the plastic and can escape.

Over the years, we have kept several hamsters in cages. We find that the newer S.A.M. cages are easy to use and easy to clean. New models are more escape-proof than earlier models. If the hamster should journey away from the cage, place the cage on the floor with its door open and close the classroom doors and windows. You may find the animal back in the cage the next morning.

Rodent cages require bedding for warmth, insulation, and as a means to absorb waste. Wood chips and shavings make good bedding. Avoid cedar or pine bedding, which sometimes irritates rodents' skin and eyes because it contains volatile oils. You can purchase bedding in a pet store or biological supply house.

You will also need seeds for your hamster to eat; a biological supply house or pet store will carry the appropriate seeds. You will need a small bowl with water for the seeds. Water is best placed in a water bottle with a ball bearing at the end. (If you put a dish of water in the cage, the animal will almost surely tip it over, use it as a bathroom, or play with it, and the water will be gone in a short time.)

Rodents also need an exercise wheel, which usually comes with the cage. They love cardboard tubes from paper towel rolls to shred into shavings.

To care for your rodent, check it every day. Change the water every few days, and make sure there is enough food. Change the litter in the cage at least once a week. You will know when to do this because you will smell urine. If you leave too much waste in the cage for too long, the rodent can get sick. When you handle your pet, be sure your hands are clean. Handle it gently and avoid sudden moves, which will scare it. You can scoop it up and gently hold it in your hand. Holding and playing with your pet each day will help to tame it. There are no guarantees that your pet won't bite you occasionally, so beware of this behavior. Having a pet hamster in your classroom will give your students the responsibility of caring for an animal and will enable them to watch it grow and develop. For more information about pet rodents, log onto

http://www.webcom.com/lstead/rodents/hamsters.html

Plants in the Classroom

Plant investigations

Your students can learn a great deal when you bring plants into the classroom. They can study the needs of plants. They can examine seeds from plants, find out how they are alike and different, and then plant them in soil and see what happens. They can place the seeds in water and watch them sprout. They can study roots and learn that some plants, like carrots, store food in their roots. Students can also learn about leaves and flowers.

Students might like to investigate the life cycle of a plant, watching it grow from a seed to a plant. When the mature plant flowers, it produces seeds, which starts the life cycle again. This is a good lead into studying the life cycle of animals, comparing it with the life cycle of plants. You can also focus on what happens when living organisms die, which is a natural part of the life cycle. Following are some explorations involving plants that will give you ideas for your classroom.

Planting seeds and watching them grow is an important experience for children.

Activity 14.9 Hands-on Science: Observing Seeds from Fruits

Overview: A good start to a sustained investigation of plants is to look at plant seeds. From there your students can engage in inquiry that will lead in many different directions.

Materials: Ask your students to bring in different fruits such as tomatoes, oranges, lemons, tangerines, red peppers, green peppers, yellow peppers, honeydew, or squash. You will need a knife to cut the fruit and paper plates or trays to distribute them.

Classifying seeds from fruits: Life science, science process

Procedure: Have your students explore the fruits and their seeds. Let them come up with their own investigations. They might like to classify them by attribute—for example size, type, location, color of seed. They might like to plant them and see what happens.

Assessment: Develop an assessment instrument with your students. Once you know what they will investigate, have them write questions to assess their learning. ■

Activity 14.10 Hands-on Science: What Do Plants Need to Grow?

Overview: In this activity, your students make predictions and design and carry out experiments to find out what plants need to grow.

Materials: Seeds (fast-growing grass seeds work well), small flower pots, sterilized soil, water, a watering can, paper and pencil, a science journal or learning log

Determining what plants need to grow: Life science, science process

Procedure: Have your students work in groups to design an experiment that allows them to find out what a plant needs to grow. Monitor them as they work on their own. They should first predict what conditions they think are best. Then they design experiments. They might decide to set up experimental and control groups, varying the amount of sunlight and water each plant gets.

Assessment: Each day students should record changes in the plants in their journals. Have them begin by predicting what a plant needs to grow. They should analyze the data and make inferences about the conditions that foster growth of healthy plants. ■

Activity 14.11 Hands-on Science: Watching Pea Seeds Sprout in Water

Overview: In this activity, students find out what happens when pea seeds are placed in water.

Materials: Peas, plastic bags, paper towels

Watching seeds sprout in water: Life science, science process

Procedure: Have students predict what they think will happen when they place pea seeds in water for several days. (Focus on the emergence of the roots and stem.) Then have them find out what happens by experimenting. Soak the seeds in warm water overnight to make them sprout more quickly. Soak a paper towel in warm water and place it in a plastic bag. Place a few pea seeds on the paper towel. Place the bags in a location that is warm and not drafty. Add a small amount of water each day to keep the paper towel moist. Watch what happens.

Assessment: Have students use science journals to record changes in the seeds. Have them make drawings of what happens each day. ■

Activity 14.12 Hands-on Science: Watching Seeds Grow in Soil

Overview: In this activity, your students investigate what happens when they plant seeds in soil.

Materials: Pea seeds that have sprouted, sterilized soil, small pots for planting, other seeds (your choice)

Watching seeds grow in soil: Life science, science process

Procedure: Students plant the sprouted pea seeds. They also plant a variety of other seeds. Have them observe what happens. Students can formulate their own investigations. If they use different seeds, they might compare rates of growth. If they grow the same seeds (in different pots), they can compare conditions for growth.

Assessment: Have students use science journals to describe and draw what happens as the plants grow. What new plant parts emerge? What do the roots, stem, and leaves do for the plant? ■

Figure 14.6 Poisonous Leaves

The investigation can continue with a look at flowers and leaves. You can have your students collect and classify leaves. Be *very* sure they don't collect poisonous leaves such as poison ivy or poison oak (see Figure 14.6). Have them compare and contrast different leaves and identify the different parts of the leaves. They can also collect flowers. Lilies, tulips, and daisies are good flowers to study. Students can dissect them and learn about the parts of the flowers. You can find a unit about plants at

http://pan.tcnj.edu/

Follow the link to the unit on plants.

A Terrarium for Your Classroom

Constructing and maintaining a terrarium: Life science

You can grow a garden in your classroom if you construct and maintain a terrarium. A *terrarium* is a collection of small plants growing in a transparent container (Ruppert & Black, 1996). You can even use a fish bowl, a candy jar, an aquarium, a canning jar, or a large bottle for your terrarium.

Begin by lining the bottom of the container with pea-size gravel. The gravel should line the side walls of the bowl about one-fifth of the way up. This allows for proper drainage of water. Cover the gravel with a layer of charcoal, which will absorb unpleasant odors. Cover the layer of charcoal with a synthetic material such as discarded pantyhose or a sheet of an old fiberglass drape. This allows water to drain while preventing the soil from passing into the drainage system.

Next, you will need sterilized soil. You can buy sterilized, premixed terrarium soil in a garden shop or from a biological supply house. Some supermarkets sell this soil as well. You can also sterilize soil yourself by placing it in an oven roasting bag and baking it at 200 degrees Fahrenheit for a half-hour. If you start with plain soil and sterilize it on your own, you should add one part sterilized soil to one part sand and one part peat moss to get the right mixture. You will need to add enough soil mixture to go another one-fifth of the way up the side of the bowl. Be sure the soil does not touch the walls of the bowl. If you prefer, you can purchase a terrarium kit from a biological supply house, which contains everything you will need for the project.

Now you are ready for the plants. It's best to make a map of the types and arrangement of the plants you will choose before placing them in the terrarium. To make the terrarium aesthetically pleasing, tall plants should be in the center and shorter plants on the perimeter. This makes it easy to see the plants from all angles. Don't overwater the plants, as this may cause disease; water only when the soil is dry to the touch. Cover the terrarium, and place it in indirect sunlight. If you place it in direct sunlight, the interior may get too hot. If this happens and the terrarium becomes foggy inside, remove the lid and let some of the water evaporate.

Find out more about terrariums at these sites:

http://www.dlcwest.com/~createdforyou/gdinfo35.html

http://hammock.ifas.ufl.edu/txt/fairs/mg356

Activity 14.13 Problem Solving: Choosing Plants for Your Terrarium

Overview: In this activity, you will select plants for your terrarium.

Materials: A resource guide, paper and pencil

Procedure: Here are some plants that will grow well in your terrarium: African violets, wild violets, Chinese evergreens, zebra plants, dracaena, English ivy, baby's tears, cacti, wax plants, and Swedish ivy. Find out more about these plants, and create a terrarium for your classroom.

Assessment: What resource guide did you use? Describe the plants you will place in your terrarium. ■

Activity 14.14 Reflection: Thinking About Plant Activities

Overview: In this activity, you will reflect on the plant activities implemented in your classroom.

Materials: Your journal

Procedure: Think about the plant activities. What preparation do you need to successfully bring plants into your classroom? What safety issues are important to think about?

Assessment: Use your journal to record your thoughts about using plants as a classroom resource. Refer to it as you plan future lessons. ■

Constructing Your Knowledge of Science and Science Teaching

After completing this chapter, begin to reflect on your new knowledge. This chapter presents information about bringing a variety of resources into your science classroom. It also helps you learn to manage those resources, many of which are living things. Think about your vision of your own science classroom. What will it look like? Are there some resources you would like to have at the start? Do you have any favorites? If your school has limited resources, how do you think that will affect your ability to teach science? Does your community have any businesses or industries that can help provide funding if your school lacks resources?

Key Terms

consumables (p. 376)
environment (p. 381)
environmental science (p. 381)
ecology (p. 381)
ecosystem (p. 381)
producers (p. 381)

consumers (p. 382)
carnivores (p. 382)
herbivores (p. 382)
omnivores (p. 382)
decomposers (p. 382)
arthropods (p. 388)

exoskeleton (p. 388)
Tenebrio molitor (p. 390)
Tenebrio obscurus (p. 390)
frass (p. 390)

Reviewing Chapter 14: Questions, Extensions, Applications, and Explorations

1. *Brassica rapa,* a relative of turnip and mustard, is a plant with a short (35-day) life cycle. Developed at the University of Wisconsin, *Brassica rapa (Rbr)* are called "Wisconsin Fast Plants." You can study plant anatomy, growth and development, pollination (bees) and plant reproduction, physiology, genetics, tropism, and ecology in your elementary science classroom with Rbr. A mini trial kit is available from Carolina Science (1-880-334-5551) for about $7. If the cost isn't prohibitive, you and your colleagues can order a mini trial kit and begin to experiment with the plants. Using a search engine, search the Wisconsin Fast Plants web site for activities for your classroom.

2. Students in grades 2 and up can experiment with *Bottle Biology.* Developed at the University of Wisconsin by Dr. Paul Williams, a plant physiologist, *Bottle Biology* projects allow your students to model a rain forest, create a spider habitat, explore an ecosystem, or study composting. Using a search engine, find information about *Bottle Biology* on the Internet. *Bottle Biology* can be purchased through Carolina Biological Supply House.

3. Contact at least one biological supply house and ask for a free catalog. (It's a good idea to have several catalogs from different companies at your fingertips, so if you have the time, contact more than one company). Design your own elementary science classroom, making a scaled-down drawing complete with resources you would like to have.

4. Suppose you are on an interview for a teaching job, and someone asks you what resources you need to teach elementary science. How will you respond?

Print Resources

Hogan, K. (1994). *Eco-Inquiry,* Millbrook, NY: Institute of Ecosystem Studies.

Mastny, A., Kahn, S., & Sherman, S. (1992). *Science TEAMS: Environmental science and cooperative learning*. New Brunswick, NJ: Rutgers University Press.

National Sciences Resource Center. (1996). *Resources for teaching elementary school science*. Washington, DC: National Academy Press.

Pope, L. (1997). Mealworms. *The Wild Times Teacher Collection, 2*(3).

Thompson, G., & Turk, J. (1999). *Earth science and environmental science*. New York: Saunders.

VanCleave, J. (1997). *Play and find out about nature*. New York: John Wiley & Sons.

Electronic Resources

Insect Zoos
http://naturalpartners.org/InsectZoo/Curriculum/InsectZooKeeping/
http://naturalpartners.org/InsectZoo/Curriculum/ArthropodCareDirectory/
These sites provide instructions for keeping an insect zoo.

Keeping Rodents
http://www.webcom.com/lstead/rodents/hamsters.html
If you want to keep rodents in the classroom, check this site.

Building and Maintaining a Terrarium
http://hammock.ifas.ufl.edu/txt/fair/mg356.
http://www.dlcwest.com/~createdforyou/gdinfo.35html
These sites contain directions for building a terrarium from start to finish.

National Wildlife Federation
www.nwf.org/wlifweek/earthwks.html
This site contains wonderful activities for teachers and resources for students.

Children's Literature

Wosmek, Frances
The ABC of Ecology
(May Davenport Publishers, 1982)
ISBN: 0-943864-00-3
Preschool and Grades K–3

Wright, Alexandra
Can We Be Friends? Nature's Partners
(Charlesbridge Publishing, 1994)
ISBN: 0-88106-861-6
Preschool and Grades K–3

Schwartz, Linda
Earth Book for Kids: Activities to Help Heal the Environment (Learning Works, 1990)
ISBN: 0-88160-195-0
Grades 3–6

Hallinan, P. K. (author/illustrator)
For the Love of Our Earth
(Ideal's Children's Books, 1992)
ISBN: 1-878363-73-5
Grades K–3

Tresselt, Alvin
Gift of the Tree (Lothrop Lee & Shepard, 1992)
ISBN: 0-688-10684-6
Preschool and Grades K–3

Kallen, Stuart
If the Waters Could Talk (Abdo & Daughters, 1995)
ISBN: 1-56239-401-0
Preschool and Grades K–3

Linse, Barbara
Love the Earth: An Ecology Resource Book
   (Arts Publications, 1991)
ISBN: 1-878079-01-8
Grades 4–6

Sussman, Susan
Big Friend, Little Friend: A Book About Symbiosis
(Houghton Mifflin Company, 1989)
ISBN: 0-395-49701-9
Grades 2–6

Glossary

Achievement objectives   specific statements that set carefully thought-out learning outcomes, specify conditions for learning, and set expected standards for student performance.

Acid test   a test used to identify minerals that release carbon dioxide gas (fizz) when dipped in acetic acid (vinegar).

Adaptation   the tendency to adjust to the environment.

Affective domain   includes attitudes, beliefs, values, and feelings.

Alternate conceptions   misconceptions that students construct when their preconceived notions conflict with what they are learning.

Analytic rubric   a rubric that analyzes a performance and provides feedback on component parts of the performance.

Analyzing data   examining data methodically and separating the data into parts or basic principles to determine the nature of the whole.

Application   a program that runs on a computer.

Arthropods   organisms whose bodies have sections that are held together by joints.

Assessment   a term that describes all of the ways in which educators gather information about student learning.

Astronomy   the study of the objects in the sky and their motions.

Atom   the smallest part of an element that can enter into chemical combination.

Authentic performance assessment   assessment based on tasks that measure skills and behaviors that students need in the real world.

Barometer   a device used to measure air pressure.

Battery   a storage device that uses chemicals to produce electric currents.

Behavior analysis   a technique that involves analyzing academic tasks and breaking them into steps.

Biomedical engineering   the use of physics and engineering to build devices to help us study biology and medicine.

Buoyancy   the tendency of an object to float on water.

Calculation   a mathematical operation. Such operations can take place on a spreadsheet.

Carnivores   consumers that eat only other animals.

Cell   the boxes of the grid in a spreadsheet.

Cell physiology   the study of the structure and function of cells.

Chemical change   change that occurs when a substance reacts or changes to a new substance that has different properties.

Chemical properties   those properties that stem from the ability of a substance to react or change to a new substance that has different properties. Such change often occurs in the presence of another substance.

Chemistry   the study of matter and its changes.

Choosing and controlling variables   manipulating one factor while holding the others constant to determine the outcome of an event.

Classifying   arranging or organizing data according to category.

Cognition   the process of knowing, which includes perception, memory, and thinking.

Cognitive domain   includes intellectual abilities and skills.

Coherence   designing experiences for children that have a logical, orderly, consistent relationship.

Collecting data   collecting information organized for analysis or used as a basis for decision making.

Communicating   expressing oneself in a way that is readily and clearly understood.

Concrete operations   according to Piaget's theory, a developmental stage in which the child uses applied reasoning and logical thought structures to solve concrete problems; generally occurs between ages 7 and 12.

Conditions   the circumstances under which learning will occur.

Conductor   a material that allows easy passage of electricity.

Constructivism   a theory stating that the child actively uses information from the world, the lessons provided by parents and schools, the cultural legacy, and the species' biological inheritance as bases for constructing knowledge. Constructivist theory views the learner as a builder of knowledge.

Constructivist theory   a theory that encourages you to view your students as active learners and involve them in their own learning.

Consumables   supplies that are used up after a science activity.

Consumers   organisms that cannot produce their own food and depend on producers and other consumers for survival.

Cooperative learning   the use of small groups and teamwork to achieve a variety of academic and social gains in the classroom.

Creativity   the ability to generate unique, imaginative, creative, and original ideas.

Criteria   statements that tell students what they have to do to successfully meet the learning outcomes set forth in your objectives.

Criterion-referenced tests   tests that measure a student's ability with respect to some content-based standard or objective.

Current   the rate at which electrons flow; measured in amperes.

Current electricity   the flow of electrons through a wire.

Cyberspace   a nickname for the Internet.

Database   a program used to organize data electronically.

Decomposers   bacteria and fungi that break down dead plants and animals (producers and consumers) and return nutrients to the soil and the air.

Defining operationally   describing the nature of basic qualities of an object or a phenomenon based on information or experience with it.

Density   mass per unit volume.

Dependent variables   responding variables.

Design   the planned process of change.

Design brief   a part of the design loop in which the problem is clarified and needs and opportunities identified.

Design challenge   a meaningful problem that is solved using the design loop. The problem often requires a technological solution.

Design loop   an active process that enables one to define a problem and specify in detail the requirements of the solution.

Diagnostic assessment   an assessment technique used at the start of a unit or lesson to inform decisions about instruction; includes making decisions about pacing of lessons, selection of teaching strategies, and focus of instruction.

Discovery   *See* **inquiry.**

Discrepant event   something the child observes that puzzles him or her and stimulates thought.

Diversity   differences among individuals in terms of language, background, ability level, gender, learning style, and personality.

Document   something created by a word processing program.

Ecology   the branch of biology that examines the inter-relationships between plants and animals and the interactions between living organisms and their environment.

Ecosystem   groups of plants and animals living together in their environment and their effects on the environment and on one another.

Educational technology   the use of computers as instructional tools.

Effort   the force that produces an action.

Effort arm   the end of the lever that is pushed on.

Electric charges   particles with a positive or negative charge.

Electric circuit   the path that an electric current follows.

Electron   a particle with a relative negative charge of one unit.

Element   any of the basic building blocks of matter that cannot be broken down chemically or physically into simpler substances.

Email (electronic mail)   the part of the Internet that allows messages to be sent from one user to another.

Energy   the ability to perform work.

Engineering   application of mathematical and scientific principles to practical ends.

English system   the system of measurement used in the United States (foot, pound, fluid ounce, etc.).

Environment   the world around us.

Environmental science   an approach that helps us understand the human environment and the impact humans have on the environment.

Equal participation   a principle of cooperative learning requiring that students participate equally in their work groups.

Estimating   making an educated guess or approximate calculation about a quantity.

Estimation   involves finding an answer that is sufficiently close that decisions can be made, rather than an exact answer.

Evaluate   to interpret assessment data and use it to guide decisions and actions in education.

Exceptional learners   students who have special needs and have individualized educational plans (IEPs) to meet those needs.

Exoskeleton   an outside shell.

Field   an information area in a database.

First-class lever   a lever whose fulcrum is located between the effort and the resistance.

Force   a push or a pull.

Form   an arrangement of fields in a database.

Formal assessment   assessments that provide fair, unbiased information about student behavior and achievement. May include homework, systematic observation of students, tests of all sorts, oral reports, essays, performance appraisals, performance tasks, journals, learning logs, laboratory notebooks, class discussions, group discussions, self-assessments, interviews, portfolios of work, standardized tests, and report card grades.

Formal operations   according to Piaget's theory, a developmental stage in which the child uses systematic reasoning to solve problems; generally occurs from age 12 to early adulthood.

Formative assessment   an ongoing assessment that occurs throughout a lesson, task, or activity.

Forming and testing hypotheses   formulating explanations that account for a set of facts that can be tested by further investigation.

Formulating models   creating a tentative description of a system or theory that accounts for all of its known properties.

Frass   insect waste and eggs.

Fulcrum   the pivot point of the lever.

Gas   the least compact of the three physical states of matter. Gases have no definite shape or volume; they are easily compressible and will spread to fill the containers in which they are placed.

Genetics   the study of heredity and gene regulation.

Geology   the study of the solid earth, including rocks and minerals.

Goal   a statement of what you plan to accomplish in a lesson.

Herbivores   consumers that eat only plants.

Holistic rubric   a rubric that provides feedback on overall performance.

Hypothesis   something that is taken to be true for the purpose of argument or investigation.

Inclined plane   a ramp.

Inclusion model   an initiative that aims to place and teach all students in the regular education classroom for some of the time.

Independent variables   manipulated variables.

Indicators   statements that provide conditions or concrete examples that let you know when the criteria are met.

Individual accountability   a principle of cooperative learning stating that each group member is responsible for completing his or her own work.

Inferring   concluding from evidence or deriving a conclusion from facts.

Informal assessment   information obtained from such sources as observation of student characteristics, informal conversations, and interviews.

Information superhighway   a nickname for the Internet.

Information-processing model   traces the flow of information from the point of input, through the processing function, to the output.

Inquiry   the process of asking questions, seeking answers, and discovering new things.

Inquiry skills   *See* **process skills.**

Inquiry-based science   a new vision that includes the "processes of science" and requires that students combine processes and scientific knowledge as they use scientific reasoning and critical thinking to develop their understanding of science.

Insulator   a material that does not allow easy passage of electricity.

Integrated planning   collaborative planning among teachers in all relevant subjects and grade levels to develop curriculum in math, science, technology, and other subjects.

Intelligence   the capacity to acquire, process, and use information.

Interconnected knowledge   designing students' experiences to help them see the relationships among science, mathematics, and technology and between those areas and other human endeavors.

Interdisciplinary thematic unit   a unit that integrates several disciplines such as science, mathematics, social studies, music, or art.

Internalization   according to Vygotsky's theory, a process by which people transform social discussions into useful problem-solving strategies.

Interpreting data   to conclude from evidence.

Law of conservation of energy   states that in any chemical or physical change, energy is neither created nor destroyed; it is simply converted from one form to another.

Law of conservation of mass   the principle that mass is neither created nor destroyed in an ordinary chemical reaction.

Law of gravity   describes how objects behave when they fall.

Learning styles   the traits that learners exhibit in the classroom; include cognitive, affective, and psychological characteristics.

Lens   a transparent material that focuses light rays and forms an image.

Lev Vygotsky   a cognitive psychologist who extended Piaget's teachings to include the influence of language, interaction with adults, and the social and economic system.

Lever   a bar that pivots on a point called the fulcrum.

Liquid   the physical state of matter in which particles are held together but are free to move about. Liquids have a definite volume but take the shape of their containers.

Listserv   a tool used for discussion on the Internet.

Load   a larger force that is overcome by a smaller force (effort).

Luster   shine; can be metallic or nonmetallic.

Machine   a tool that makes work easier by changing the kind of work that is done.

Macroscopic   large enough to be detected by the unaided eye.

Magnification   the apparent enlargement of an object with the aid of an optical instrument.

Making charts and graphs   displaying data in a visual format.

Mass   a measure of the quantity of matter in an object.

Matter   anything that occupies space and has weight; may exist as a solid, a liquid, a gas, or plasma.

Measuring   making a comparison between an object and a standardized or unstandardized unit.

Mechanical advantage   the increase in force given by a machine.

Memory   the process by which we recall, or keep in mind, experiences that we have encountered.

Meteorology   the study of weather systems and the air or atmosphere.

Metric system   a system of measurement based on multiples of ten

Microbiology   the study of microbes such as bacteria and viruses.

Microscopic   too small to be detected by the unaided eye.

Mineral   a natural solid object with a definite chemical makeup and structure

Misconceptions   *See* **alternate conceptions.**

Model   a representation of an object, a system, or a mental idea that represents an object or process.

Mohs scale   a scale that determines hardness of minerals.

Molecular biology   the study of living things at the molecular level.

Molecule   the smallest particle of a compound that can enter in chemical reactions and retain the properties of the compound.

National science education standards   guidelines that provide an overall view of what needs to be done to achieve scientific literacy for all citizens.

Natural law   a principle that is developed when large numbers of related facts are combined.

Neutron   a particle with no electric charge.

Nominal scale   classifies objects into categories based on some defined characteristic, such as type of bubble bath.

Norm-referenced tests   tests in which performance is reported by comparing one student's performance to that of other students who have taken the same test and constitute a comparison or norm group.

Norms   records of the performances of groups that have previously taken a test; testmakers use the norms to determine how the score of an individual test taker compares with the scores of other test takers.

Observing   watching attentively and making a systematic scientific observation.

Omnivores   Consumers that eat both plants and animals.

Open-ended questions   Questions that make students think and synthesize what they already know.

Ordering abilities   ways in which students order new information.

Organization   the ability to systematize or combine processes into a coherent, logically related system.

Perception   the process by which we recognize patterns and begin to know objects, events, people, and processes.

Perceptual preferences   ways in which students prefer to gain information.

Performance assessment   assessment based on performance tasks such as developing demonstrations, creating products, or constructing responses to situations.

Performance task a statement that asks students to solve a problem. It gives them practice in applying concepts and thinking critically while allowing the teacher to gain insight into student thinking. It also gives students experience with real-life problems and situations.

Physical change (1) altering the physical state of matter (such as melting an ice cube), (2) mixing substances together (making hot cocoa), or (3) altering the size or shape of matter (grinding or chopping something).

Physical properties those properties that can be observed or measured without changing the chemical composition of the substance. Physical properties include state, color, odor, taste, hardness, boiling point, and melting point.

Physical science the study of the composition and properties of matter and energy.

Physics the study of the natural world at the most fundamental level. It requires analytical thinking, putting together an experiment, and focusing on what is important.

Jean Piaget a cognitive psychologist who emphasizes the child's personal construction of reality and actual developmental level.

Plasma a form of matter composed of electrically charged atomic particles. Many objects found in the earth's outer atmosphere, as well as many celestial bodies, consist of plasma.

Positive interdependence a principle of cooperative learning stating that for a team to be successful, all members must contribute.

Preconceptions Private understandings that students develop concerning the meanings and applications of science concepts.

Predict stating, telling about, or making known in advance on the basis of special knowledge.

Preoperational period according to Piaget's theory, a developmental stage in which the child forms concepts before the ability to use logic develops; generally occurs between ages 2 and 7 or 8.

Problem challenge *See* **design challenge.**

Process skills skills that help students learn about nature.

Producers organisms that use energy from the sun and water and nutrients from the soil to make their own food.

Product a substance produced in a chemical reaction.

Productivity software software that enhances the ability to learn or increases productivity, such as word processors, databases, and spreadsheets.

Programming writing the instructions that tell a computer how to perform an operation.

Proton a particle with a relative positive charge of one unit.

Psychomotor domain consists of basic bodily movements and performance, physical skills and abilities, perceptual abilities, and skilled movements.

Pulley a wheel and axle on which the wheel is free to spin on its axle.

Reactant any of the starting materials in a chemical reaction.

Reciprocal teaching a procedure that uses small groups and teamwork to improve reading comprehension and understanding of content in the reading materials.

Relative humidity the amount of water vapor the air holds in relation to the most vapor it could hold at that particular temperature.

Reliability the degree to which the results of a test are consistent, stable, predictable, and dependable.

Resistance arm the end that pushes on the object to be moved.

Rock a mass of one or more mineral substances found in the earth.

Rubric a set of guidelines that helps to evaluate a performance.

Salt a compound composed of the positive ion of a base and the negative ion of an acid.

Scaffolding a process by which a teacher supports students as they construct knowledge.

Schemes a child's concepts of reality.

Science an activity undertaken by people who are involved in the accumulation of knowledge about the universe. More than a collection of facts, it involves understanding, analyzing, and explaining facts, emphasizing physical cause and observed effect.

Science curriculum a work plan for science teachers.

Science process skills *See* **process skills.**

Scientific fact an established truth.

Scientific method a way of thinking and inquiring that allows people to investigate and explain nature and natural phenomena.

Screw an inclined plane that is wrapped or curved around a cylinder, shaft, or pole. Screws fasten objects together.

Second-class lever a lever in which the resistance is located between the effort and the fulcrum.

Sensorimotor period, according to Piaget's theory, a developmental stage in which children adapt to reality by sensing and moving; generally occurs between birth and 2 years of age.

Simple machine a machine with only one or two parts.

Simultaneous interaction a principle of cooperative learning requiring that there be opportunity for many students to participate at the same time.

Software all the things the computer can do, as well as the instructions that make it run.

Solid a substance with a definite shape and volume that it tends to maintain under normal conditions.

Spreadsheet a program used to organize and perform calculations on data.

Standardized tests tests that are administered, scored, and interpreted under test-taking conditions that are exactly the same for all students.

Standards standards that provide a vision of what it means to be scientifically literate, tell us what all students must know and do as a result of their cumulative learning experiences, and provide criteria for judgments regarding systems, programs, teaching, and assessment.

Static electricity an electric charge held by an object resulting from a gain or loss of electrons.

Streak test a way to classify minerals by the color of the streak powder formed when a mineral is rubbed against a streak plate.

Student-directed inquiry A method in which students decide what to study, ask questions, gather the materials for the investigation, set the research agenda, and freely explore the topic individually or in a small group.

Students and teacher as co-investigators A method in which the teacher chooses the topic and sets guidelines for inquiry, and students have a question to answer and materials to use.

Subproblems the smaller questions that come up in answering the broader question.

Summative assessment an assessment that includes written examinations, reports, portfolios, or productions that require application of many concepts into a final product; usually results in a final grade.

Sustained inquiry investigation of science topics over an extended period of time.

Systemic change change in the structure, operating procedures, ways in which people interact, and distribution of power of a school system.

Task commitment the ability to stay focused and remain with a project until its completion.

Teacher-centered methods of instruction methods in which students have less responsibility for their own learning than in the inquiry-based classroom. Teacher-dominated methods include lecture, recitation, teacher-directed small groups, sharing time, and seat work.

Teacher-directed inquiry A form of inquiry in which the teacher provides a set of guided experiences and expects students to make generalizations about these experiences. The teacher acts as a question answerer rather than question asker.

Technology the innovation or change of the natural environment to satisfy perceived human needs and wants.

Technology education education that involves solving problems based on satisfying a need in a practical way.

Tenebrio molitor yellow mealworm.

Tenebrio obscurus dark mealworm.

Thematic unit a series of lessons centered on a theme.

Theory systematically organized knowledge that is applicable in a relatively wide variety of circumstances; a system of assumptions, accepted principles, and rules of procedure devised to analyze, predict, or explain the nature of behavior of a specified set of phenomena.

Thinking the process of considering ideas and using such skills as comprehension, analysis, synthesis, and evaluation.

Third-class lever a lever in which the effort is located between the resistance and the fulcrum.

Timed pair discussion a technique in which each partner in a pair of students talks for a specified but equal amount of time.

Traditional paper-and-pencil tests assessments that ask students to do such things as fill in the blanks, match items in one column with items in the next column, or choose the correct answer from a series of answers in a multiple-choice exercise.

Traditional science classroom a classroom in which direct instruction is the predominant instructional strategy.

Tropical rain forest a dense evergreen forest in a tropical region of the world where it rains more than 2.5 meters per year.

Unit a series of lessons centered on a particular subject, concept, topic, or theme.

Validity the extent to which a test measures what it's supposed to measure.

Variable   a factor in an experiment that changes or varies.

Web browser   a program that allows the user to locate and view web pages on the Internet.

Wedge   an inclined plane that pushes objects apart.

Weight   the gravitational attraction of an object to the earth or any body.

Wheel and axle   a lever connected to a shaft.

Word processor   a program that allows the user to type in words, add graphics, and edit text.

Work   the result when a force moves an object over a distance.

World Wide Web   the part of the Internet that has web pages, or graphics-oriented documents.

Zone of proximal development   according to Vygotsky's theory, the difference between what a child can produce unaided and what he or she can produce with aid.

References

Abdi, S. W. (1997). Motivating students to enjoy questioning. *The Science Teacher*, 64(6), 10.

Akers, J. (1984). Not all math tests are created equal. *Learning*, 12, 34–35.

Albert, T. (1995). *Weather and climate*. Greenbrook, NC: Carson-Dellosa Publishing Company.

American Association for the Advancement of Science. (1990). *Science for All Americans*. New York: Oxford University Press.

American Association for the Advancement of Science. (1993). *Benchmarks for Science Literacy: Project 2061*. New York: Oxford University Press.

The American Heritage College Dictionary. 3rd ed. (1997). Boston: Houghton Mifflin.

American Institute of Physics. (1997). *Wonder Science*. New York: Delmar.

Anderson, L. (1995). *International encyclopedia of teaching and teacher education*. 2nd ed. Oxford, UK: Pergamon Press.

Aronson, E., Stephan, C., Sikes, J., Blaney, N., & Snapp, M. (1978). *The jigsaw classroom*. Beverly Hills, CA: Sage.

The Association for Students with Severe Handicaps. (1993). *TASH resolution policy statements*. Seattle, WA: Author.

Atkinson, R., & Shiffrin, K. (1968). Human memory: A proposed system and its control processes. In K. Spence & J. Spence (Eds.), *The psychology of learning and motivation: Advances in theory and research* (Vol. 2). New York: Academic Press.

Baker, D. R. (1987). Sex differences in classroom interactions in secondary science. *Journal of Classroom Interaction*, 22(2), 6–12.

Banks, J. A. (1990). *Preparing teachers and administrators in a multicultural society*. Austin, TX: Southwest Development Laboratory.

Beattie, C., Dowling, H., Martin, L., Patria, M., Pritchard, L., Wilson, J., & Wills, C. (1993). *Dorling Kindersley Science Encyclopedia*. London: Dorling Kindersley.

Becker, J. R. (1981). Differential treatment of females and males in mathematics classes. *Journal for Research in Mathematics Education*, 12(1), 40–53.

Berlin, D., & White, A. (1994). The Berlin-White Integrated Science and Mathematics Model. *School Science and Mathematics*, 94(1), 2–4.

Biehler, R., & Snowman, J. (1997). *Psychology applied to teaching*. Boston, MA: Houghton Mifflin.

Bloom, B., Englehart, M., Hill, W., Furst, E., & Krathwohl, D. (1956). *Taxonomy of educational objectives: The classification of educational goals. Handbook I. Cognitive domain*. New York: Longman Green.

Bloom, B., Madaus, G., & Hastings, J. (1981). *Evaluation to improve learning*. New York: McGraw-Hill.

Borich, G. (1996). *Effective teaching methods*. Englewood Cliffs: Prentice Hall and Merrill.

Brooks, J. G., and Brooks, M. G. (1993). *In search of understanding: The case for constructivist classrooms*. Alexandria, VA: Association for Supervision and Curriculum Development.

Bruner, J. (1960). *The process of education*. Cambridge, MA: Harvard University Press.

Burke, K. (1993). *How to assess thoughtful outcomes*. Palatine, IL: IRI Skylight Publishers.

Bybee, R., & DeBoer, G. (1994). Research on goals for the science curriculum. In D. Gabel. (Ed.), *Handbook of research in science teaching and learning*. New York: Macmillan.

Caine, R., & Caine, G. (1990). Understanding a brain-based approach to learning and teaching. *Educational Leadership*, 47(5), 66–70.

Caine, R., & Caine, G. (1991). *Making connections: Teaching and the human brain*. Alexandria, VA: Association for Supervision and Curriculum Development.

Caliendo, R., Wittreich, R., Gullo, D., Allen, C., Casey, A., Callos, E., Beckerrdite, L., Maimone, M., Simms, D., Hunter, G., & Kuti, R. (1997). *Knowing is growing: A unit on plants*. A thematic learning unit created by teachers enrolled in the New Jersey Statewide Systemic Initiative at The College of New Jersey.

Carbo, M., Dunn, R., & Dunn, K. (1986). *Teaching students to read through individual learning styles*. Reston, VA: Reston Publishing.

Catlin, D., & Douglas, P. (1998). *How to use Inventa*. London: Valiant Technology Limited.

Catlin, D., & Livingstone, M. (1995). *Food and farming*. London: Inventa Topic Book.

Chapman, C. (1993). *If the shoe fits . . .* Palatine, IL: IRI Skylight Publishing.

Chiapetta, E. (1997). Inquiry-based science. *The Science Teacher*, 64(5), 18–22.

Christian, S., & Felix, A. (1998). *What makes the Grand Canyon grand?* New York: John Wiley & Sons.

Clayfield, H., & Hyatt, R. (1994). *Designing everyday things.* Portsmouth, NH: Heinemann.

Cochran-Smith, M., & Lytle, S. (1993). *Inside/outside: Teacher research and knowledge.* New York: Teachers College Press.

Committee to Develop Standards for Educational and Psychological Testing (1985). *Standards for Educational and Psychological Testing.* Washington, D.C.: American Psychological Association.

Continuous Electron Beam Accelerator Facility Manual. (1992). *BEAMS Handbook.* Newport News, VA: U.S. Department of Energy.

Cundari, F., Dullea, K., Stapenski, D., Gavin, I., Jinks, R., Joseph, J., Granquist, K., Puglia, M., & Wheeler, B. (1996). *Insects: Rulers of the world.* A thematic learning unit created by teachers enrolled in the New Jersey Statewide Systemic Initiative at The College of New Jersey.

Delta Education. (1988). *Weather instruments.* Hudson, NH: Delta Science Modules.

Delta Education. (1989). *Pond life.* Hudson, NH: Delta Science Modules.

DeVries R., & Slavin, R. E. (1978). Teams-Games-Tournaments: A research review. *Journal of Research and Development in Education, 12,* 28–38.

Dewey, J. (1933). *How we think.* Boston: Houghton Mifflin.

Dewey, J. (1944). *Democracy and education.* Toronto: Collier-Macmillan.

Dixon, D. (1996). Rocks and minerals. London: A Quarto Children's Book.

Dodge, D., Jablon, J., & Bickart, T. (1994). *Constructing curriculum in the primary grades.* Washington, DC: Teaching Strategies.

Dorling Kindersley. (1993). *Science encyclopedia.* London: Dorling Kindersley Ltd.

Driver, R. (1990). Students' conceptions and the learning of science. *International Journal of Science Education, 82,* 119–128.

Driver, R., Guesne, E., & Tiberghien, A. (1985). *Children's ideas in science.* Philadelphia: Open University Press.

Duckworth, E. (1987). *"The having of wonderful ideas" and other essays on teaching and learning.* New York: Teachers College Press.

Dunn, R. (1996). *How to implement and supervise a learning style program.* Alexandria, VA: Association for Supervision and Curriculum Development.

Dunn, R., & Dunn, K. (1978). *Teaching students through their individual learning styles: A practical guide.* Reston: VA: Reston Publishing.

Eby, J., & Kujawa, E. (1994). *Reflective planning, teaching, and evaluation, K–12.* New York: Merrill.

Edwards, C. (1997). Promoting student inquiry. *The Science Teacher, 64* (5), 18–22.

English, F. *Deciding what to teach and test: Developing, aligning, and auditing the curriculum.* Newbury Park, CA: Sage.

Fogarty, R. (1991). *How to integrate the curricula.* Palatine, IL: IRI/Skylight Publishing.

Gage, N.L., & Berliner, D. (1998). *Educational psychology.* 6th ed. Boston, MA: Houghton Mifflin.

Gagne, R. (1984). *The conditions of learning.* New York: Holt, Rinehart, and Winston.

Gardner, H. (1983). *Frames of mind.* New York: Basic Books.

Ginsburg, H. (1977). *Entering the child's mind: The clinical interview in psychological research and practice.* New York: Cambridge University Press.

Gooding, K. (1994). *Teaching to the test: The influence of alternate modes of assessment on teachers' instructional strategies.* Paper presented at the meeting of the American Educational Research Association, New Orleans, LA.

Goodlad, J. (1984). *A place called school.* New York: McGraw Hill.

Grabe, M., & Grabe, C. (1998). *Integrating technology for meaningful learning.* 2nd ed. Boston: Houghton Mifflin.

Green, R. (1996). *A salute to black scientists and inventors.* Chicago: Empak Publishing Company.

Gregorc, A. (1998). *Gregorc Style Delineator.* Maynard, MA: Gabriel Systems.

Hamm, M., & Adams, D. (1998). Reaching across disciplines. *Science and Children, 36*(1), 45–49.

Hardy, G., & Tolman, M. (1998). Science supplies. *Science and Children, 36*(1), 10–13.

Hawkins, D. (1983, Spring). Nature closely observed. *Daedalus,* 65–89.

Hein, G., & Price, S. (1994). *Active assessment for active science.* Portsmouth, NH: Heinemann.

Hertz-Lazarowitz, R., & Sharan, S. (1984). Enhancing prosocial behavior through small group teaching. In E. Staub, D. Bar-Tal, J. Karylowski, & J. Reykowski (Eds.), *Development and maintenance of prosocial behavior: International perspectives* (pp. 423–443). New York: Plenum.

Hewitt, P. (1992). *Conceptual physics.* New York: Addison-Wesley.

Hibbard, K. M. (1996). *Performance-based assessment and learning.* Alexandria, VA: Association for Supervision and Curriculum Development.

Hirsch, E. D. (1996). *The schools we need and why we don't have them.* New York: Doubleday.

Hodkinson, H. (1992). *A demographic look at tomorrow.* Washington, DC: Institute for Educational Leadership/Center for Demographic Policy.

Hodkinson, H. (1993). American education: The good, the bad, and the task. *Phi Delta Kappan, 74*(8), 619–625.

Hughes, F., & Noppe, L. (1991). *Human development across the life span.* New York: Macmillan.

Hunt, N., & Marshall, K. (1999). *Exceptional children and youth.* Boston: Houghton Mifflin.

Hutchinson, J., & Karsnitz, J. (1994). *Design and problem solving in technology.* Albany, NY: Delmar Publishers.

Hutchinson, P., & Sellwood, P. (1996). *Design and problem solving.* Cincinnati: Thomson Learning Tools.

Inhelder, B., & Piaget, J. (1958). *The growth of logical thinking.* New York: Basic Books.

International Technology Education Association (1998). *Technology for all Americans: National technology education standards.* Reston, VA: Authors

Jaeger, R. M. (1992). World class standards, choice and privatization: Weak measurement serving presumptive policy. *Phi Delta Kappan, 74*(2), 118–128.

Johnson, B. (1993). *Teacher-as-researcher* (Report No. EDO-SP-92-7). Washington, DC: Office of Educational Research and Improvement. (ERIC Document Reproduction Service No. ED 355 205).

Johnson, D. W., Johnson, R. (1975). *Learning together and alone.* Englewood Cliffs, NJ: Prentice-Hall.

Johnson, D. W., Johnson, R., Tiffany, M., & Zaidman, B. (1984). Cross-ethnic relationships: The impact of intergroup cooperation and intergroup competition. *Journal of Educational Research, 72,* 75–79.

Jones, M. G., & Wheatley, J. (1990). Gender differences in teacher-student interactions in science classrooms. *Journal of Research in Science Teaching, 27,* 861–874.

Jung, K. (1976). *Psychological types.* Princeton, NJ: Princeton University Press.

Kagan, S. (1994). *Cooperative learning.* San Clemente, CA: Kagan Cooperative Learning.

Kamii, C. (1984). Autonomy: The aim of education envisioned by Piaget. *Phi Delta Kappan, 65,* 410–415.

Kendall, J., & Marzano, R. (1996). *Content knowledge: A compendium of standards and benchmarks for education.* Aurora, CO: Mid-continent Regional Educational Laboratory.

Kline, E. (1998a). *Assessment anthology guidelines.* Pennington, NJ: The Center on Learning, Assessment, and School Structure.

Kline, E. (1998b). *Assessment anthology slides.* Pennington, NJ: The Center on Learning, Assessment, and School Structure.

Kneller, G. F. (1978). *Science as a human endeavor.* New York: Columbia University Press.

Kolb, D. (1983). *Experiential learning: Experience as the source of learning and development.* Englewood Cliffs, NJ: Prentice-Hall.

Krathwohl, D., Bloom, B., & Masiz, B. (1964). *Taxonomy of educational objectives: The classification of educational goals. Handbook II. Affective Domain.* New York: David McKay.

Leadbeater, B. (1991). Relativistic thinking in adolescence. In R. M. Lerner, A. C. Peterson, & J. Brooks-Gunn (Eds.), *Encyclopedia of adolescence.* New York: Garland.

Lerner, J. (1997). *Learning disabilities: Theories, diagnosis, and teaching strategies.* Boston: Houghton Mifflin.

Lerner, P. (1997). *The forms of bias.* Bethesda: Interweave.

Liebman, B. (1997). Fraud or find. *Nutrition Action, 24*(7), 8–9.

Madden, N. A., & Slavin, R. E. (1983). Cooperative learning and social acceptance of mainstreamed academically handicapped students. *Journal of Special Education, 17,* 171–182.

Madden, N. A., Slavin, R. E., & Stevens, R. J. (1986). *Cooperative integrated reading and composition: Teacher's manual.* Baltimore: Center for Research on Elementary and Middle Schools, Johns Hopkins University.

Mastny, A., Kahn, S., & Sherman, S. (1992). *Science TEAMS: Environmental science and cooperative learning.* New Brunswick, NJ: Rutgers University Press.

Mayer, R. E., & Wittrock, M. C. (1996). Problem solving in transfer. In D. C. Berliner & R. C. Calfee (Eds.), *Handbook of educational psychology* (pp. 47–62). New York: Macmillan.

McCarthy, B. (1987). *The 4MAT System.* Barrington, IL: EXCEL, Inc.

McCarthy, B., & Keene, C. (1996). *About learning.* Barrington, IL: EXCEL.

McKenzie, G. R. (1979). Data charts: A crutch for helping students organize reports. *Language Arts, 56,* 784–788.

McKinnon, J., & Renner, J. W. (1971). Are colleges concerned with intellectual development? *American Journal of Physics, 39,* 1947–1952.

Meltzer, L., Roditi, B., Haynes, D., Biddle, K., Paster, M., & Taber, S. (1996). *Strategies for success: Classroom teaching techniques for students with learning problems.* Austin, TX: Pro-Ed.

Mestre, J. (1994). Cognitive aspects of teaching and learning science. In S. J. Fitzsimmons & L. C. Kerpelman (Eds.), *Teacher Enhancement for Elementary and Secondary Science and Mathematics: Status, Issues and Problems* (pp. 3.1–3.53). Arlington, VA: National Science Foundation (NSF 94-80).

Miller, G., & Gildea, P. (1987). How children learn words. *Scientific American, 257,* 94–99.

Mitchell, R. (1999). Real testing, real learning. *Science Scope, 22*(1), 4–5.

National Council of Teachers of English and International Reading Association (1996). *Standards for the English language arts.* Urbana, IL/Newark, DE: Authors.

National Research Council (1990). *Fulfilling the promise: Biology education in the nation's schools.* Washington, DC: National Academy Press.

National Research Council. (1996). *National Science Education Standards.* Washington, DC: National Academy Press.

National Sciences Resource Center. (1996). *Resources for teaching elementary school science.* Washington, DC: National Academy Press.

National Sciences Resource Center. (1998). *Resources for teaching middle school science*. Washington, DC: National Academy Press.

Novak, J. D. (1998). *Learning, creating, and using knowledge: Concept maps as facilitative tools in schools and corporations*. Hillsdale, NJ: Erlbaum.

Novak, J. D., & Gowin, B. (1984). *Learning how to learn*. New York: Cambridge University Press.

Nye, B. (1995). *Bill Nye the Science Guy's consider the following: A way cool set of science questions, answers, and ideas to ponder*. New York: Disney Press.

Orlich, D., Harder, R., Callahan, R., & Gibson, H. (1998). *Teaching strategies: A guide to better instruction*. Boston: Houghton Mifflin.

Palinscar, A. M., & Brown, A. L. (1984). Reciprocal teaching of comprehension-fostering and monitoring activities. *Cognition and Instruction, 1*, 117–175.

Piaget, J., & Inhelder, B. (1969). *The psychology of the child*. New York: Basic Books.

Pickford, T. (1992). Girls and science: The effects of some interventions. *Primary Science Review, 25*, 22–24.

Pope, L. (1997). Mealworms. *The Wild Times Teacher Collection, 2*(3), 1–4.

Powell, M. J. (1994). *Equity in the reform of science and mathematics education: A look at issues and solutions*. Austin, TX: Southwest Educational Development Laboratory.

Pressley, M., & McCormick, C. B. (1995). *Advanced educational psychology*. New York: HarperCollins.

Raizen, S. (1998). Standards for science education. *Teachers College Record, 100*(1), 66–121.

Raizen, S., Baron, J., Champagne, A., Haertel, E., Mullis, I., & Oakes, J. (1989). *Assessment in elementary school science education*. Colorado Springs, CO: The National Center for Improving Science Education.

Renzulli, J. (1978). What makes giftedness? *Phi Delta Kappan, 60*, 180–184.

Reynolds, M., Wang, M., & Walberg, H. (1987). The necessary restructuring of regular and special education. *Exceptional Children, 53*(5), 391–396.

Romberg, T. (1993). NCTM'S Standards: A rallying flag for mathematics teachers. *Educational Leadership, 50*(5), 10–13.

Rosenshine, B. V. (1979). Content, time, and direct instruction. In P. L. Peterson & H. J. Walberg (Eds.), *Research on teaching: Concepts, findings, and implications* (pp. 35–74). Berkeley, CA: McCutchan Publishing.

Rosenshine, B. V. (1986). Synthesis of research on explicit teaching. *Educational Leadership, 43*, 60–69.

Rosenshine, B. V., & Stevens, R. (1986). Teaching functions. In M. Wittrock (Ed.), *Handbook of research on teaching* (3rd ed., pp. 376–391). New York: Macmillan.

Rowe, M. B. (1974). Wait-time and rewards as instructional variables, their influence on language, logic, and fate control: Part one—wait-time. *Journal of Research in Science Teaching, 11*, 81–94.

Rowe, M. B. (1986). Wait-time: Slowing down may be a way of speeding up. *Journal of Teacher Education, 23*, 43–49.

Ruppert, K., & Black, R. (1996). *Plants and youth: Designing and building a terrarium*. http://hammock.ifas.ufl.edu/txt/fair/mg356.

Rutherford, E., & Ahlgren, A. (1990). *Science for all Americans*. New York: Oxford University Press.

Sadker, M., & Sadker, D. (1994). *Failing at fairness: How America's schools cheat girls*. New York: Scribner.

Sadker, M., Sadker, D., Fox, L., & Salata, M. (1994). Gender equity in the classroom: The unfinished agenda. *The College Board Review*, No. 170, 14–21.

Schwebel, M. (1972). *Logical thinking in college freshmen*. U.S. Department of Health, Education, and Welfare, Office of Education, Bureau of Research, Final Report Number 0-B-105, 22.

Schwebel, M. (1975). Formal operations in first year college students. *Journal of Psychology, 91*, 133–141.

Sharan, S. (1980). Cooperative learning in small groups: Recent methods and effects on achievement, attitudes, and ethnic relations. *Review of Educational Research, 50*, 241–271.

Sharan, S. (1990). Cooperative learning: A perspective on research and practice. In S. Sharan (Ed.), *Cooperative learning theory and research* (pp. 286–300). New York: Praeger.

Sharan, S., & Hertz-Lazarowitz, R. (1980). A group investigation method of cooperative learning in the classroom. In S. Sharan (Ed.), *Cooperation in education* (pp. 14–46). Provo, UT: Brigham Young University Press.

Sharan, S., & Hertz-Lazarowitz, R. (1982). The effect of an educational change project on teachers' perceptions, attitudes and behavior. *Journal of Applied Behavioral Science, 18*, 185–201.

Sharan, S., & Sharan, Y. (1976). *Small-group teaching*. Englewood Cliffs, NJ: Educational Technology Publications.

Sharan, Y., & Sharan, S. (1992) *Expanding cooperative learning through group investigation*. New York: Teachers College Press.

Shavelson, R., & Brown, J. (1996) *Assessing hands-on science: A teacher's guide to performance assessment*. Thousand Oaks, CA: Corwin Press.

Sherman, A. (1979). *The effect of a community college education on the cognitive development of students in liberal arts and laboratory technology curricula: An intervention study*. New Brunswick, NJ: Rutgers University Press.

Sherman, A., & Sherman, S. (1996). *How to run a non-competitive science fair*. San Francisco: Global Summit for Science and Science Education, National Science Teachers Association.

Sherman, S. (1994). Cooperative learning in science. In S. Sharan (Ed.), *Handbook of cooperative learning methods*. Westport, CT: Greenwood Press.

Sherman, S., & Hulse, R. (1999). *A collaborative model for involving scientists in preservice education.* Paper presented at the Holmes Partnership Annual Meeting, January 1999, Boston, MA.

Sherman, S., & Sherman, A. (1999). *Essential concepts of chemistry.* Boston, MA: Houghton Mifflin.

Shymansky, J., Hedges, L., & Woodworth, G. (1990). A reassessment of the effects of inquiry-based science curricula of the 60s on student performance. *Journal of Research in Science Teaching, 27*(2), 127–144.

Siegler, R. S. (1981). Development of sequences within and between concepts. *Monographs of the Society for Research in Child Development, 46,* No. 189.

Sigelman, C., & Shaffer, D. (1991). *Life-span human development.* Pacific Grove, CA: Brooks Cole.

Silverstein, S. (1981). *A light in the attic.* New York: HarperCollins.

Slavin, R. E. (1977). How student learning teams can integrate the desegregated classroom. *Integrated Education, 15*(6), 56–58.

Slavin, R. E. (1978). Student teams and achievement divisions. *Journal of Research and Development in Education, 12,* 39–49.

Slavin, R. E. (1979a). Student team learning: A manual for teachers. In S. Sharan, P. Hare, C. Webb, & R. Hertz-Lazarowitz (Eds.), *Cooperation in education* (pp. 82–136). Provo, UT: Brigham Young University Press.

Slavin, R. E. (1979b). Effects of biracial learning teams on cross-racial friendships. *Journal of Educational Psychology, 71,* 381–387.

Slavin, R. E. (1980). Cooperative learning. *Review of Educational Research, 50,* 315–342.

Slavin, R. E. (1983a). *Cooperative learning.* New York: Longman.

Slavin, R. E. (1983b). When does cooperative learning increase student achievement? *Psychological Bulletin, 94,* 429–445.

Slavin, R. E. (1984). Meta-analysis in education: How has it been used? *Educational Research, 15*(9), 5–11.

Slavin, R. E. (1985a). Introduction to cooperative learning research. In R. Slavin, S. Sharan, S. Kagan, C. Webb, R. Hertz-Lazarowitz, & R. Schmuck (Eds.), *Learning to cooperate, cooperating to learn* (pp. 5–15). New York: Plenum.

Slavin, R. E. (1985b). Cooperative learning: Applying contact theory in desegregated schools. *Journal of Social Issues, 41,* 45–62.

Slavin, R. E. (1988). Synthesis of research on grouping in elementary and secondary schools. *Educational Leadership, 46,* 67–76.

Slavin, R. E. (1989). Cooperative learning and student achievement. In R. E. Slavin (Ed.), *School and classroom organization* (pp. 129–158). Hillsdale, NJ: Erlbaum.

Slavin, R. E. (1991). Synthesis of research in cooperative learning. *Educational Leadership, 48,* 71–83.

Slavin, R. E., Leavey M., & Madden, N. (1983). *Combining student teams and individualized instruction in mathematics: An extended evaluation* (Technical Report No. 336). Baltimore: Center for the Social Organization of Schools, Johns Hopkins University.

Slavin, R. E., & Madden, N. A. (1979). School practices that improve race relations. *American Educational Research Journal, 16,* 169–180.

Slavin, R. E., & Oikle, E. (1981). Effects of cooperative learning teams on student achievement and race relations: Treatment by race interactions. *Sociology of Education, 54,* 174–180.

Solomon, D., Watson, M., Schaps, E., Battistich, V., & Solomon, J. (1990). Cooperative learning as part of a comprehensive program designed to promote prosocial development. In S. Sharan (Ed.) *Cooperative learning: Theory and research* (pp. 231–260). New York: Praeger.

Sternberg, R. J. (1991). Giftedness according to the triarchic theory of human education. In N. Colangelo & G.A. Davis (Eds.), *Handbook of gifted education* (pp. 45–54). Boston: Allyn and Bacon.

Sternberg, R. J. (1997). What does it mean to be smart? *Educational Leadership, 54*(6), 16–20.

Stevens, R., & Slavin, R. E. (1995). Effects of a cooperative learning approach in reading and writing on academically handicapped and non-handicapped students. *Elementary School Journal, 95*(3), 241–262.

Thompkins, G. (1998). *50 literacy strategies step by step.* Upper Saddle River, NJ: Prentice-Hall.

Thompson, G., & Turk, J. (1999). *Earth science and environmental science.* New York: Saunders.

Tobin, K., Capie, W., & Bettencourt, A. (1988). Active teaching for higher cognitive learning in science. *International Journal of Science Education, 10*(1), 17–27.

VanCleave, J. (1997). *Play and find out about nature.* New York: John Wiley & Sons.

von Glasersfeld, E. (1989). Cognition, construction of knowledge, and teaching. *Synthese, 80,* 121–140.

von Glasersfeld, E. (1992). A constructivist's view of learning and teaching. In R. Duit, F. Goldberg, & H. Niedderer (Eds.), *The proceedings of the International Workshop on Research in Physics Education: Theoretical issues and empirical studies.* Kiel, Germany: IPN.

Vygotsky, L. (1976). *Thought and language.* Cambridge, MA: MIT Press.

Vygotsky, L. (1978). *Mind in society.* Cambridge, MA: Harvard University Press.

Vygotsky, L. (1987). Thinking and speech. In R. W. Rieber & A.S. Carton (Eds.), *The collected works of L. S. Vygotsky (Vol. 1).* New York: Plenum.

Wakefield, J. (1996). *Educational psychology: Learning to be a problem solver.* Boston: Houghton Mifflin:

Wandt, E., & Brown, G. (1957). *Essentials of educational evaluation.* New York: Holt, Rinehart and Winston.

Wang, M., Haertel, G., & Walberg, H. (1994). What helps students learn. *Educational Leadership, 51*(4), 74–79.

Wang, M., Reynolds, M., & Walberg, H. (1986). Rethinking special education. *Educational Leadership, 44*(1), 26–31.

Weinstein, C. S. (1991). The classroom as a social context for learning. *Annual Review of Psychology, 42,* 493–525.

Wiggins, G. (1998). *Educative assessment.* San Francisco: Jossey-Bass.

Wiggins, G., & McTighe, J. (1998). *Understanding by design.* Reston, VA: The Association for Supervision and Curriculum Development.

Wittrock, M. C. (1989). Generative processes of comprehension. *Educational Psychologist, 24,* 325–344.

Wittrock, M. C. (1991). Generative teaching of comprehension. *Elementary School Journal, 92,* 169–184.

Witty, P. A. (1940). Some considerations in the education of gifted children. *Educational Administration and Supervision, 26,* 512–521.

Wulfson, S. (1998). A telephone interview with the editor of the "Software Reviews" column for *Science and Children.*

Index

Photo Credits